THE ECHOING GREEN

The Echoing Green

ROMANTICISM, MODERNISM, AND THE PHENOMENA OF TRANSFERENCE IN POETRY

Carlos Baker

PRINCETON UNIVERSITY PRESS

PRINCETON, NEW JERSEY

TO MY OLD AND REVERED FRIENDS

Datus C. Smith, Jr., and P. J. Conkwright

WITH WARMEST REGARDS

Sing louder around
To the bells' cheerful sound
While our sports shall be seen
On the echoing green.

—William Blake

Contents

Acknowledgments

THE AUTHOR'S thanks are due to the following for permission to reprint materials included in these essays: *Collected Poems* by W. B. Yeats: copyright 1916, 1918, 1928, 1933 by Macmillan Publishing Company, renewed 1944, 1946, 1956, 1961 by Bertha Georgie Yeats; copyright 1940 by Georgie Yeats, renewed 1968 by Bertha Georgie Yeats, Michael Butler Yeats, and Anne Yeats. *Essays and Introductions* by W. B. Yeats, copyright by Mrs. W. B. Yeats, 1961. *Autobiography* by W. B. Yeats, copyright 1916, 1936 by Macmillan Publishing Company, renewed 1944, 1964 by Bertha Georgie Yeats. British Commonwealth Rights to all the above from Macmillan London, Ltd. *The Poetry of Robert Frost*, edited by Edward Connery Lathem: copyright 1916, 1923, 1928, 1930, 1934, 1939 © by Holt, Rinehart & Winston; copyright 1936, 1940, 1942, 1944, 1951, © 1956, 1958, 1962 by Robert Frost; copyright © 1964, 1967, 1968, 1970 by Lesley Frost Ballantine. Reprinted by permission of Holt, Rinehart & Winston, publishers. *Robert Frost, Poetry and Prose*, edited by Edward Connery Lathem and Lawrance Thompson, copyright 1972 by Holt, Rinehart & Winston. *The Selected Letters of Robert Frost*, edited by Lawrance Thompson, copyright 1964 by Lawrance Thompson and Holt, Rinehart & Winston. Ezra Pound, *The Cantos of Ezra Pound*: copyright 1934, 1937, 1940, 1948, © 1956, 1959, 1962, 1963, 1968 by Ezra Pound. Reprinted by permission of New Directions Publishing Corporation. British Commonwealth Rights excluding Canada:

reprinted by permission of Faber and Faber Ltd. from *The Cantos of Ezra Pound*. Excerpts from *Collected Poems 1909-1962*, *The Family Reunion*, *Four Quartets*, and *The Cocktail Party*, all by T. S. Eliot, reprinted by permission of Harcourt Brace Jovanovich, Inc. Copyright 1936 by Harcourt Brace Jovanovich, Inc. Copyright 1939, 1943, 1950, © 1963, 1964 by T. S. Eliot. Copyright 1967, 1971, 1978 by Esme Valerie Eliot. British Commonwealth Rights and world rights excluding United States: *The Use of Poetry and the Use of Criticism* by T. S. Eliot, reprinted by permission of Faber and Faber Ltd. For nonexclusive rights in the English language throughout the world excluding the United States: *Collected Poems, 1909-1962*, Faber and Faber Ltd. Reprinted by permission of Farrar, Straus & Giroux, Inc.: excerpts from "Spleen" and "A Fable for Feasters" from *Poems Written in Early Youth* by T. S. Eliot, copyright © 1967 by Valerie Eliot. *The Collected Poems of Wallace Stevens*, published by Alfred A. Knopf, Inc., copyright 1923, 1931, 1935, 1936, 1937, 1942, 1943, 1944, 1945, 1946, 1947, 1948, 1949, 1950, 1951, 1952, 1954 by Wallace Stevens. *Opus Posthumous*, poetry and prose, published by Alfred A. Knopf, Inc., copyright 1957 by Elsie Stevens and Holly Stevens. *The Necessary Angel*, published by Alfred A. Knopf, Inc., copyright 1942, 1944, 1947, 1948, 1949, 1951 by Wallace Stevens. *The Letters of Wallace Stevens*, edited by Holly Stevens, published by Alfred A. Knopf, Inc., copyright 1966 by Holly Stevens. Nonexclusive rights in the English language throughout the British Commonwealth excluding Canada granted by Faber and Faber Ltd., London. W. H. Auden, *Collected Poems*, edited by Edward Mendelson, copyright 1976 by Edward Mendelson, William Meredith, and Monroe K. Spears, Executors of the Estate of W. H. Auden, published by Random House, Inc. *The Dyer's Hand*, copyright 1948, 1950, 1952, 1953, 1954; and © 1956, 1957, 1958, 1960, 1962, by W. H. Auden, published by Random House, Inc. *Letters from Iceland*, copyright 1937 by W. H. Auden. British Commonwealth Rights for seven poems, Faber and Faber Ltd. *Epistle to a Godson*, copyright 1969, 1970, 1971, 1972 by W. H. Auden. British Commonwealth Rights, Curtis Brown Ltd.

The author is indebted also to Modern Library, Rinehart Editions, the University of Georgia, and the University of Virginia for permission to reprint portions of his essays on Shelley, Wordsworth, Frost, and Pound. For welcome help of various kinds, warmest thanks go to George Bornstein, Reginald L. Cook, J. S. Finch, John Fleming, W. S. Howell, Samuel Hynes, A. W. Litz, Richard M. Ludwig, John R. Martin, Herbert Schneidau, Leonard Unger, Hugh Witemeyer, and the Rare Books staff, Firestone Library, Princeton University. The author also wishes to thank Jerry Sherwood, Tam Curry, and Sue Bishop of Princeton University Press, and Helen S. Wright, ace typist.

THE ECHOING GREEN

Introduction

THE PRESENCE OF THE PAST

 THE PURPOSE of this book is to examine and interpret the work of six modern poets against the background of English romanticism as represented by Wordsworth, Coleridge, Byron, Shelley, Keats, and to a lesser degree by Blake. Part One, "Ancestral Voices," offers critical assessments of these romantic poets. Part Two, "Modern Echoes," provides evidence of the numerous ways in which Yeats, Frost, Pound, Stevens, Eliot, and Auden responded to the poetry and prose of their predecessors. The intent here is to show which poems of that other epoch, including a few by Blake, most engaged the attention of these modern poets; to summarize their respective attitudes toward historical romanticism; to see what use they made of esthetic and ethical ideas derived from the critical prose of the period 1800-1825; and finally to take notice of when, where, and how they borrowed images and echoed phrases from romantic poetry for use in their own work. These poets were attracted to the romantics for reasons that are often of consuming interest, though frequently idiosyncratic, and commonly unpredictable. By providing at the outset a normative view of the romantic achievement as it looks to an objective but sympathetic observer in the late twentieth century, we establish a means of evaluating the responses to it that the modern poets made. Anyone interested in the overlay of the past upon the present should emerge

3

from a reading of these pages with useful information on the variant phenomena of literary transference from one generation to another.

No poet, as Northrop Frye once observed, "sits down with a pencil and some blank paper and eventually produces a new poem in a special act of creation *ex nihilo*. ... Poetry can only be made out of other poems." A corollary of Frye's remarks appears in a letter by Wallace Stevens: "We live in mental representations of the past."[1] Both generalizations are too exclusive. For every poet draws to some degree upon his personal experiences and direct observations from life as well as upon the background of his reading, and it is frequently the admixture of the two types of experience that gives to particular poems their uniqueness, the stamp of a special personality upon both traditional and more immediately empirical materials.

Such a reservation, however important, does not demolish the positions of Stevens and Frye: that no poet can afford to ignore the past, that essential substructure upon which he rears his own superstructures. Ben Jonson defined imitation as the ability to "convert the substance or riches of another poet" to fresh uses, as, for example, Eliot did in *The Waste Land* by appropriating and modifying Enobarbus's account of Cleopatra in Shakespeare's play. Goethe held that "only by making the riches of others our own do we bring anything great into being." Goethe's sometime disciple, Emerson, said that "the past is for us, but the sole terms on which it can become ours are its subordination to the present."[2] Emerson's disciple, Whitman, in the first preface to *Leaves of Grass*, insisted that "past and present and future are not disjoined but joined. The greatest poets form the consistence of what is to be from what has been and is." In our own time, Eliot expressed similar views: "The historical sense involves a perception not only of the pastness of the past, but of its presence." No poet, he added, "has his complete meaning alone. ... The most individual parts of his work may be those in which the dead poets, his ancestors, assert their immortality most vigorously."³ Yeats put the matter somewhat more succinctly: "The distant in time and place live only in the present." And again, "Works of art are always begotten by previous works of art, and every masterpiece becomes the Abraham of a chosen people."⁴

In *Romanticism and the Forms of Ruin*, Thomas McFarland advances the term *essentia* as representing "the most inescapable fact of human life." For we live always "in a 'now' looking to a past and future 'then,' " and we have therefore "a double nature: an existence 'now' which is palpable and concrete, and an existence in the past and future, which though spectral is none the less truly our own existence. . . . Poetic *essentia* is generated by the simultaneous awareness of our existence in these two forms." If we stand in a "now" and look at a "then," we may make the sense of "now" more vivid, treasuring it for what it is while recognizing its difference from "then." Or else, as in the phenomenon of romantic nostalgia, "we may devalue 'now' and treasure 'then.' "⁵ The palpable "now" and the spectral "then" are co-presences in the human consciousness. If, in Eliot's words, the presence of the past is a strong motivating force in all our lives, it is perhaps especially so in the lives of the poets. Wallace Stevens recognized as much in his demonstration of the way in which *la vie antérieure* assists in the development of *le bel aujourd'-hui*.

The present investigation shows that all six of our representative modern poets read the English romantics in their youth. The marks of their diverse enthusiasms are clear enough, both early and late. In the 1880s, for example, Yeats, at his father's urging, began reading Shelley and Blake, Byron and Keats, and afterwards called his reactions to these poets a sort of "violent imaginative puberty." In the 1890s, Frost read widely among the romantics, memorized Keats's poetry by the ream, chose something like Wordsworth's "real language of men" as a rough model for his own experiments in colloquial diction and rhythm, and even invoked Shelley's *Epi-*

psychidion as one ideological instrument in his courtship of Elinor White.

In the early twentieth century, Stevens repeatedly read Keats's *Endymion* with passion and enjoyment, and at intervals in his later career adapted ideas and images from Wordsworth, Coleridge, Keats, and Shelley both in his poetry and in his memorable essays on esthetics in *The Necessary Angel*. The adolescent Eliot gave himself a course of reading in the works of the English romantics, asserting that this experience markedly changed the colors and contours of the world around and within him. Although he later followed Irving Babbitt in disparaging several of these poets, he gradually rediscovered the virtues of some of them as his life wore on. Auden, the youngest of the present group, began by imitating Wordsworth, paid extensive tribute to Byron, admired the stateliness of Keats's odes and the critical acumen of some of his letters, borrowed ideas from Blake and Coleridge, and in spite of his professed abhorrence for the poetry of Shelley, seems to have read a good deal of it with sympathetic awareness, and to have followed the Shelleyan path toward the shrine of Agape.

As a young man, Pound evidently read the poets in question. During his years in London and Paris, he set himself to counteract the decadence of the romantic impulse in the late Victorian and Edwardian periods, crying out years later that "the common verse of Britain from 1890-1910" had been a "horrible agglomerate compost . . . a doughy mess of third-hand Keats, Wordsworth, heaven knows what, fourth-hand Elizabethan sonority blunted, half-melted, lumpy." Such withering blasts were designed to help rid contemporaneous poetry of "rhetorical din and luxurious riot" by emphasizing the need for austerity of utterance and images both hard and clear. Yet his own verse showed from the beginning a strong sense of the past, traceable to the Greek classics and the literatures and histories of medieval and Renaissance times, to say nothing of a genuinely romantic exoticism. It was as if, in striving "to resuscitate the dead art of poetry," he was eager to turn back to these primal periods as necessary correctives to the latter-day decadence he so fiercely impugned.[6]

All these poets functioned betimes as critics, as their spiritual ancestors had done before them. The bulk of what they had to say about the romantic poets can be found in their essays, public lectures, reviews, and personal letters. There they quoted, compared, judged, praised, appraised, and sometimes condemned. They offered commentaries on individual poems and adapted to their own purposes the critical pronouncements and terminologies of Wordsworth and Coleridge, Keats and Shelley, judging them by the culture of their own age. Above all, they showed that romanticism and some of its chief exponents in England of the period 1790-1850 continued to be a force in the formation of their own attitudes toward the poetical enterprise. Naturally enough, for most of them read fairly widely, it was not the sole operative force, nor did these moderns always follow its promptings. Still, as Denis Donoghue has said, "One has to imitate *something*. Even deliberately to write *against* something is to take one's bearings from it."[7]

Allied to the judgmental approach embodied in the poets' critical prose is another phenomenon, commonly called "influence," and meaning almost literally a flowing-in of materials—language, rhythms, images, ideas—from earlier sources. Robert Frost once distinguished "two kinds of peaks in poetry—the imaginative kind to the eye and to the ear"[8]—and it is true that the most readily discernible marks of influence are audial and visual. A good ear marks the best poets, and to have read widely in antecedent literatures, alert for memorable sequences of words and their sounds, is an essential desideratum for all whose business it is to bring poetic language up to the level of its greatest intensity. Verbal echoes, often of no great consequence in themselves, offer evidence of those times when the poets' auditory imaginations were awake and functioning. As Eliot remarked in 1932, "the mind of any poet would be magnetized in its own way, to select automatically . . . the material—an image, a phrase, a word—

which may be of use to him later."[9] With or without their original contexts, sounds do stick in the poet's memory and may come to the surface almost unbidden in the midst of creative action. This surfacing is usually unpredictable. Sometimes in Eliot's own verse it is willed into being, in full consciousness of its source as well as of its auditory relevance to a developing composition. More often, perhaps, in Eliot and the others, its arrival is adventitious, a flash in the brainpan in the light of which it is seen to belong where the poet chooses to place it. One instance of the latter kind appears at the end of Yeats's "The Lake Isle of Innisfree," where his phrase, "the deep heart's core," is made over from "the heart's deep core" in one of Blake's minor lyrics. The sound of the phrase, not the use Blake had put it to, was plainly the reason for Yeats's appropriation. Another example, probably more deliberate, is Stevens's use of the "Be thou" motif from Shelley's West Wind ode for his own poem, "Mozart, 1935."

In the paraphernalia of poets, the image is often the visual equivalent of the sound-print. "Why, for all of us," asked Eliot in 1933, "out of all we have seen, heard, felt [and he might have added, *read*] in a lifetime, do certain images recur, charged with emotion, rather than others?"[10] To such questions there can be no easy answers except to say that images, by their very nature, often take the form of pictures, arousing the emotional or intellective congruities originally associated with them in the poet's memory, and thus providing an impetus to recreative activity.

Among Wordsworth's criteria for the poet was his "disposition to be affected more than other men by absent things as if they were present." An image may be such an "absent thing," as present to the optics of the mind as an actual object or scene is to the physical eye. Of the daffodils that appeared to be dancing in the breeze off the lake, he wrote, "They flash upon that inward eye / Which is the bliss of solitude / And then my heart with pleasure fills." This "flash" in the eye of the mind is immediately followed by an emotive response. Looking back upon the poem from 1815, Wordsworth called his composite image "an ocular spectrum." His source, as it happened, was secondary, an entry in his sister Dorothy's journal for 15 April 1802. In this respect the passage resembled the portrait of the highland girl singing at her work in "The Solitary Reaper." She also was derived from a secondary source, Thomas Wilkinson's *Tour in Scotland*, where the tourist passed a field in which a "female . . . reaping alone . . . sung in Erse as she bended over her sickle . . . the sweetest human voice I ever heard." Wordsworth was sufficiently familiar with crowds of springtime flowers and solitary fieldworkers so that his readings from his sister's notebook and Wilkinson's travel book brought with them the final flashes of empirical recognition out of which the two lyrics developed.

Poems, or at any rate significant parts of them, "can only be made out of other poems," or, as in these examples from Wordsworth, from prose redactions powerful enough to evoke responses that fill the poet's heart with pleasure or some other emotion, and so to animate his creative impulses. All poems, thus considered, are living instances of a *then* that has become a *now*, arrayed in new carapaces of form, like bees in amber, for future contemplation. Wallace Stevens called them "the fluent mundos" that have "stopped revolving, except in crystal."[11]

Another aspect of the poetical relationships between the present and the past has been explored by Harold Bloom in *The Anxiety of Influence*. He admits that "the transference of ideas and images from earlier to later poets" happens all the time. Whether or not these borrowings cause "anxiety in the later poets is merely a matter of temperament and circumstances." But he thinks that when poetic influence involves "two strong authentic poets"—Shelley and Stevens, for example—it "always proceeds by a misreading of the prior poet," leading to a "deliberate, even perverse revisionism," so that "every poem is a misinterpretation of a parent poem." If strong poets do experience anxiety, they consciously or subconsciously "misread" their ancestral models, "so as to clear imaginative space for themselves."[12]

9

According to Bloom, much of literary history takes the form of a "battle between strong equals, father and son as mighty opposites." This notion leads him to a pair of key questions: (1) "Do strong poets gain or lose more, as poets, in the wrestling with their ghostly fathers," and (2) Do all "revisionary ratios that misinterpret or metamorphose precursors help poets to individuate themselves?" His answer appears to be that the "sons" do indeed gain power from the "fathers" even when their deliberate mutations in the inherited material stamp the new work with the unique thumbprints of their own temperaments. Poetic influence, he believes, "need not make poets less original; as often it makes them more original, though not therefore necessarily better."

It may be, as Bloom argues, that "the only guilt that matters to a poet" is "the guilt of indebtedness." Yet he seems also to think that it is only "through the quasi-willing mediumship of other strong poets" that "strong poets keep returning from the dead," though wearing "our colors, and speaking in our voices, at least in part, at least in moments."[13]

It is not difficult to agree with this conclusion. After all, Bloom is restating, in a vocabulary derived from Nietzsche and Freud among others, a position espoused by poets as various as Goethe and Emerson, Eliot and Stevens. His term *anxiety* easily translates into Auden's fear of unworthiness, as in the *New Year Letter* where the poet wonders who

> Is not perpetually afraid
> That he's unworthy of his trade
> As round his tiny homestead spread
> The grand constructions of the dead. . . .[14]

However this idea is expressed, the basic fact is that poets are always borrowing from their predecessors, sometimes with contradictory intent, and then refashioning what they borrow to make it fit new "constructions" of their own. The passage on sacrificial heifers in Auden's *The Shield of Achilles* is not less powerful when we recognize that its progenitor was Keats's garlanded heifer in the "Ode on a Grecian Urn." Nor is our

10

admiration for "Sailing to Byzantium" deintensified by Hugh
Kenner's suggestion that the Byzantine nightingale in Yeats is
"a transformation wrought on two odes of Keats, about a
bird not born for death and about a Grecian artifice of eter-
nity."[15]

🐦 IF THEY had ever assembled in such a literary Valhalla
as Auden brightly imagined in his *Letter to Lord Byron*, the
romantic poets would doubtless have been surprised to dis-
cover which of their poems, ideas, images, and forms were
most influential in stirring their twentieth-century heirs to
action or reflection. They might also have been disappointed.
Despite the many examples of influence put forward in the
present study, no massive infiltration of romanticism into
modernism actually took place. The real effect was far more
selective, depending upon the individual tastes and tempera-
ments of the receptor poets and upon those chance exposures
that often activate the alert and eager mind to what Robert
Frost called "counter-love, original response."[16]

They were accordingly able to pay tribute to the steadfast-
ness of the giant stars in the romantic constellation without
becoming wholehearted followers of the historical movement
itself. None of the moderns was a stronger exponent of ro-
manticism—at least as he defined it—than was Wallace Ste-
vens, not even W. B. Yeats, who proudly claimed a place
among the "last romantics." But Stevens, like the mature Yeats,
remained indubitably himself rather than a pale simulacrum
of any of his elders. The spoils he gathered from his quiet
raids into romantic territory became peculiarly his own and
stand as typical examples of that whole series of piecemeal
transferences and modifications, original responses to aborig-
inal provocations, which repeatedly took place when the mod-
erns confronted the work of their eminent forebears.

We turn now to an abbreviated account of what really
happened. A number of scholars have investigated limited
aspects of the phenomenon of transference, and their contri-

butions are thankfully acknowledged. What follows here is an attempt to map out the main lines of actual convergence between the romantic and the modernist generations.

Although a general consensus held that Wordsworth stood foremost among the English romantics, there were dissenters, including the irrepressible Pound. In 1913 he advised readers to look at "as much of Wordsworth as does not seem too unutterably dull." He co-opted an epigram of Ford Madox Ford's: "Wordsworth was so intent upon the ordinary or plain word that he never thought of hunting for *le mot juste.*" By 1917 he was saying that Wordsworth was "deemed so innocuous" that he had become, "if not the backbone, at least one of the ribs, of British kultur." In a sneering reference to "that drivelling imbecility about woodnotes so dear to the Wordsworthian epiglottis," he was probably recalling "one impulse from a vernal wood" from "The Tables Turned." Another comment mixed praise and ridicule: Wordsworth was "a silly old sheep with a genius, an unquestionable genius, for imagisme, for a presentation of natural detail, wild-fowl bathing in a hole in the ice, etc."[17] But the problem, said Pound, madly mixing his own images, was that this poet had "buried the fruits of talent" in a "desert of bleatings."*

Yeats never descended to such rant, but he had inherited from his father a belief that although Wordsworth was "undoubtedly a great poet," he had too often "condescended to moral maxims," mixing "the popular morality with his work," so that "his moral values were not often enough aesthetic values." His strong ethical sensibility unfortunately lacked "a theatrical element," a fault that gave some of his utterances a tone of "pedantic composure." Much of his verse, unlike that of Byron, was deficient in "natural momentum." In sum, Wordsworth struck Yeats, who nevertheless read him faith-

---

* Pound was probably echoing J. K. Stephen's parody-sonnet: "Two voices are there: one is of the deep . . . / And one is of an old half-witted sheep . . . / And, Wordsworth, both are thine."

fully, as "the one great poet who, after brief blossoms, was cut and sawn into planks of obvious utility."[18]

Eliot, on the contrary, saw Wordsworth as a true revolutionary, with "a very delicate sensibility to social life and social change" and a disposition to rebel "against a whole social order." This attitude extended to the revolution he proposed for poetic language, and Eliot believed that the critical insights of the 1800 preface were sufficient to raise Wordsworth to "the highest place." He found "exhilarating" Wordsworth's agreement with Aristotle that "poetry is the most philosophic of all writing." Although much of his verse, like much of Coleridge's, was "as turgid and artificial and elegant as any eighteenth-century die-hard could wish," his experiments with "common speech" proved once more that poetic language perennially requires revitalization from the grassroots. Of Wordsworth's poetry Eliot said little. Like Yeats and Auden and practically everyone else, he admired "The Solitary Reaper," and he called "Resolution and Independence" a great poem— as well he might, since it so effectively dramatized the incursions of that *mal du siècle* by which in his early thirties he was himself so heavily beset.[19]

Robert Frost's widowed mother had raised her children on Wordsworth's lyrics. This "influence" was afterward taken up by the poet's wife-to-be, Elinor White, one of whose favorite poems was the "Elegiac Stanzas" on Peele Castle. During a time of profound disillusionment in the 1890s, Frost found some philosophic consolation in the same poem, as well as in the "Ode: Intimations of Immortality." Some twenty years later, he told a professor / interviewer that Wordsworth was not only a "very great poet" but also one of the chief influences in his own development. Whatever Wordsworth may have done to stimulate his awareness of the natural world as a catalyst for the poet, Frost's usual *obiter dicta* centered rather on the listener than the seer. According to Frost, "the great fight of any poet is against the people who want him to write in a special language that has become gradually separated from the spoken language." Since "language really only exists in the mouths of men," said Frost, "Wordsworth was right in trying to reproduce in his poetry not only the words . . . actually used in common speech, but their sound." The poet ought accordingly to write with an ear for the speaking voice, and this in Frost's opinion was one great truth that Wordsworth had rediscovered and exploited. Frost confessed to having followed Wordsworth's lead in some of the "eclogues" in *North of Boston* where, as he later said, he had intentionally "dropped to an everyday level of diction that even Wordsworth kept above."[20]

As for Frost and indeed for all strong poets, words and their sounds lay close to Wallace Stevens's heart. He called one of his best essays "The Noble Rider and the Sound of Words" and in the midst of it quoted the 1800 preface to *Lyrical Ballads* on the great experiment of ascertaining "how far, by fitting to metrical arrangement a selection of the real language of men in a state of vivid sensation," a poet could impart to his readers the kind and quantity of pleasure that he felt within himself. This, said Stevens, was "a use of language favorable to reality," for we listen to words, "loving them and feeling them," and searching their sounds "for a finality, a perfection, an unalterable vibration, which it is only within the power of the acutest poet to give them." Again he wrote: "The poet must get rid of the hieratic in everything that concerns him and must move constantly in the direction of the credible." In another essay he agreed with Wordsworth that the "considered elaborations" with which eighteenth-century poets embellished their pages could no longer be expected to "click," whether in 1800 or in 1948. Although no one could possibly mistake a poem by Stevens for one by Wordsworth, the two poets were agreed in their championship of "a use of language favorable to reality." Indeed, Stevens might even have had Wordsworth in mind in one of his *Notes Toward A Supreme Fiction*, which speaks of compounding "the imagination's Latin with / The lingua franca et jocundissima."[21]

When Stevens declared in 1926, "Nature is my source of supply," the sentiment, if not the phrasing, was Wordsworthian. When he wrote that "a sense of reality keen enough to be in excess of the normal sense of reality creates a reality of its own," he came close to Wordsworth's theories on what the imagination is capable of accomplishing. The typical Gestalt patterning of Wordsworthian imagery is reflected in Stevens's view that "les plus belles pages are those in which things do not stand alone but are operative as the result of interaction." In support of his belief that the poet's role "is to help people live their lives," he turned for illustration to Wordsworth's magnificent sonnet on the view from the bridge on an early September morning in 1802. Apart from passing allusions to the immortality ode and the scattered stones of the unfinished sheepfold in "Michael," there is little additional overt evidence of fraternization between the two poets. On the other hand, Stevens's esthetic opinions frequently intersected and sometimes coincided with those of his predecessor.[22]

In 1938 Auden called Wordsworth "the greatest of the Romantic poets." His own early imitations of the master had ceased abruptly a decade earlier, but by that date he was already familiar with the most famous poems in the canon and had taken notice of the ways in which "Tintern Abbey" and the immortality ode had succeeded in giving "numinous significance" to natural objects and scenes. He thought of Wordsworth as the "great English poet of Nature" who had spent much of his career in seeking to describe a "Vision of Dame Kind," a dream in which Auden was unwilling to participate. Like many of his contemporaries, he speculated on the implications of Wordsworth's theories about the *lingua communis*, over which he felt there had been "too much fuss." What Wordsworth really needed was a language suitable to describe and explain his intense experiences with inanimate nature, and he probably did not really care where he found it so long as it sufficed for his purposes. Like Coleridge and many others, Auden thought that he wrote best when he ignored theory and followed his inner imaginative lights. If, as Auden suggested, every poet contains within himself both "an

15

Ariel who sings and a Prospero who comprehends," it was the Prosperonian that predominated in Wordsworth, who customarily showed "the least element of Ariel" that was compatible with being a poet at all, though Ariel broke through in parts of "Tintern Abbey" and most notably in that universal favorite, "The Solitary Reaper." The *New Year Letter* included a brief but brilliant political biography on Wordsworth's decline into orthodoxy long after those brave days when he had sat pensively amongst the ruins of the Bastille, convinced for the time being that a "benignant spirit was abroad / Which might not be withstood."[23]

Yeats once pointed out that all of Coleridge's best poetry, by which he meant "The Ancient Mariner," "Kubla Khan," the first part of "Christabel," and perhaps, though not certainly, "Frost at Midnight," had been written during an eighteen-month period in 1797-1798.[24] Eliot also stressed the brevity of Coleridge's *belle époque* as poet. "For a few years" he "had been visited by the Muse ... and thenceforth was a haunted man," subject to "a sudden, fitful, and terrifying kind" of inspiration, "with ghastly shadows at his back." One of the evidential poems, "Dejection: An Ode," so much impressed Eliot that he read from it at length in a Harvard lecture.[25] Yeats knew and quoted "Fears in Solitude." George Bornstein has suggested possible connections between "Frost at Midnight" and Yeats's "A Prayer for My Daughter" and believes also that the assertion in "Byzantium"—"I hail the superhuman; I call it death-in-life and life-in-death"—was borrowed from Coleridge's horrendous portrait of the spectre-woman in "The Ancient Mariner," for she is called "The Nightmare Life-in-death," and in both poems the other-worldly scenes are dimly illuminated by moonlight and starlight.[26] Coleridge's most famous poetic narrative led also to a verse-letter parody by Frost in 1907,[27] and to Auden's exploitation of its mythological aspects in *The Enchafèd Flood* of 1950.

Despite the labors of I. A. Richards, Coleridge as critic

received scant attention. Yeats's *Autobiography* contains indications of his occasional perusal of some of the prose works, and Pound very occasionally followed his example. Coleridge seemed to the young Eliot "perhaps the greatest of English critics,"[28] particularly because of his "subtlety of insight" and his understanding of the profound "philosophical problems into which the study of poetry may take us." Yet he believed that Coleridge's love of metaphysics had tragically eroded his poetical fervors, citing "Dejection" as his authority. He was content to quote without comment the passages on imagination in the *Biographia Literaria*, deriving his text from Richards's *Principles of Literary Criticism*.[29] The first time Stevens tackled Coleridge's prose, he found it "heavy going."[30] Years later, his reading in Richards's *Coleridge on Imagination* convinced him that S.T.C. was "one of the great figures" in the "approach to truth" by way of the imagination.[31] But he insisted that his own "reality-imagination complex" owed nothing to romantic antecedents.[32] Auden took over the terms of the famous distinction between the two degrees of imagination but defined them according to his own lights, which differed markedly from those of Coleridge.[33]

It was Auden who pointed out that "Kubla Khan" was the only legitimate trance-poem on record, though he later discovered that Coleridge's printed account of its origin was probably a "fib," invented to excuse the "failure" of the "fragment."[34] Failure or not, it was ironic that the poem elicited almost universal admiration among these modern poets. The lines on the River Alph as it plunged down to the sunless sea struck Robert Frost as one of the "top places" in English poetry.[35] Stevens, in a youthful mood of discontent, imagined himself wandering near the Alph's point of egress.[36] His "Academic Discourse in Havana" playfully changed Kubla's pleasure-dome into a Cuban casino where were "arrayed / The twilights of the mythy goober khan," and where "the indolent progressions of the swans / Made earth come right; a peanut parody / For peanut people."[37] Again, in "Man and Bottle," he altered Coleridge's "sunny pleasure dome with caves of ice" into his own "romantic tenements of rose and ice," with a hint that, like Kubla's, they were fated for destruction.[38]

Yeats was thinking of the same poem when he remarked that Coleridge may have needed opium "to recover a state which, some centuries earlier, was accessible to the fixed attention of normal man."[39] Of the poem itself, he said only that "every line, every word, can carry its unanalysable rich associations."[40] Like Auden, Eliot thought of the poem as a fragment. He was certain that its imagery, "whatever its origins in Coleridge's reading, sank to the depths" of his feelings, and "was saturated, transformed there—those are pearls that were his eyes'—and brought up into daylight again," an observation, incidentally, that reflected Eliot's familiarity with J. L. Lowes's approach in *The Road to Xanadu*.[41]

Both Yeats and Eliot testified to feelings of strong affinity with Coleridge. Eliot called him "rather a man of my own type, differing from myself chiefly in being immensely more learned, more industrious, and endowed with a more powerful and subtle mind." He described "Dejection" as a piece of "passionate self-revelation" that rose "almost to the height of great poetry."[42] Yeats confessed to more "delight" with the man than with the poet. After 1807, he believed, Coleridge was blessed with "some kind of illumination which was, as always, only in part communicable. The end attained in such a life" was "not a truth or even a symbol of Truth, but a oneness with some spiritual being or beings." Thus Yeats contrived to import the transcendentalist Coleridge into his own transcendental camp.[43]

Yeats and Auden emerge as the sole champions of William Blake. Yeats had a long head start, having been introduced to Blake's lyrics by his father in the 1880s, more than a quarter-century before Auden's birth. The elder Yeats told his son that a single line of Blake's poetry could enrich his vision, and William came to share his father's enthusiasm, calling Blake "the chanticleer of the new dawn" and "one of God's artificers uttering mysterious truths." He named Blake as the pioneer who had achieved the "first opening of the long-sealed well of romantic poetry."[44] For more than twenty years after 1888, he studied Blake sporadically, labored over a three-volume edition of the poetry and prose, chose a Blakean epigraph for his own first book of verse, *Crossways*, edited a book of Blake's lyrics in 1910, and revered him as a symbolist myth-maker able to express "invisible essences" and thus to aid in the enactment of "the revolt of the soul against the intellect." Blake's message, he said, was that Nature itself is a symbol, and that whoever discovers this great truth is ipso facto "redeemed from nature's death and destruction."[45]

Yeats paired Blake with his other early mentor, Shelley, because both men had developed cosmic "systems" of which their poems were the verbal projections and had independently convinced themselves that the true "fountain" of the universe was the "Holy Spirit." They were accordingly votaries of light, Blake's dominant image being the sun and Shelley's the star. He thought of Blake's Christ as the supreme symbol of the artistic imagination, "acting from impulse not from rules," and sending out his disciples to combat the legalisms of religious and civil governments.[46]

Certain of Yeats's ideas apparently owe their origin in part to his extensive experience with Blake. The remote ancestry of his own "system" as embodied in *A Vision* may be traced back to 1890, when he prepared a large chart of Blake's symbolic scheme. Although he specifically denied the influence of the Prophetic Books on his own "system," calling them "unfinished and confused," he indicated his feelings of spiritual consanguinity by placing Blake next door to his own Phase 17 in the Great Wheel and emphasizing the fiery power of Blake's individual images.[47] The notion that the universe was "falling into division," as set forth in "The Second Coming," appears to be distantly associated with a passage Yeats quoted from the *Four Zoas* in 1893, and he cited *Milton* and *Jerusalem* to support his own conviction that life in this world is an eternal conflict between Spectre and Emanation. Another idea, to which Yeats alluded in his essay, "The Bounty of

19

Sweden," after he had received the Nobel Prize, and repeatedly in the poetry of the last ten years of his life, perhaps had its origin in Blake's letter to George Cumberland (12 April 1827): "I have been very near the Gates of Death & have returned very weak and an Old Man feeble and tottering, but not in Spirit & Life, not in The Real Man The Imagination which Liveth for Ever. In that I am stronger and stronger as this Foolish Body decays."[48]

Yeats's final mention of Blake in "Under Ben Bulben" refers to his painting rather than his poetry. In this respect Yeats anticipated Robert Frost, whose only poetical allusion to Blake was to the striking picture of the "Ancient of Days," with the windblown beard and hair, striking with huge calipers the first circle of the as yet uncreated earth.[49] Ezra Pound impugned Blake as "dippy William," scorned his "Judaic" designs, and made him a madman in Canto 16.[50] In nearly sixty years of letter writing, Wallace Stevens mentioned Blake only twice, though once in the spring of 1904, during a hike along the Palisades, some contour of the landscape reminded him of Blake's band of angels crying, "Holy, Holy Holy." In a lecture on the relations between poetry and painting at the other end of his life, he praised Blake for having carried on in both métiers simultaneously, showing thus "the economy of genius."[51] One could almost believe Hugh Kenner's sly observation that "precisely because William Blake's contemporaries did not know what to make of him, we do not know either, though critic after critic appeases our sense of obligation to his genius by reinventing him."[52]

Eliot as critic made no such gesture. Both his essays on Blake began as book reviews, written by a busy editor with neither time nor sympathy for his subject. He rejected Blake as an "autodidact amateur" in philosophy and a "heretic" in theology who used his gift of "hallucinated vision" to describe "supernatural territories" in ways that illustrated the essential "meanness" of his cultural background as well as that "crankiness and eccentricity" which "frequently affects writers outside of the Latin tradition."[53]

It was Auden who came closest to matching Yeats's Blakean interests, though at a considerable distance in both time and degree. Attracted by the passage on Prolifics and Devourers in *The Marriage of Heaven and Hell*, he devoted a long essay to the subject in 1939, reinterpreting Blake's account to embody his own ethical ideas and beliefs and calling the result his own version of *The Marriage*.[54] Unlike Yeats, he gave little evidence of interest in the Prophetic Books, although, like Yeats, he echoed them with some frequency. On the whole, however, he cannot be said to have shown any profound engagement with Blake or his "system." The echoes and quotations are of the sort that could have been quickly gathered by leafing through the volume of Blake's poetry and prose that he owned, looking for arresting passages. He seems to have been most attracted by the apothegms, where Blake the rebel set down what Northrop Frye has called "parody proverbs," designed to overturn the customary proverbial counsels of "prudence and moderation." Finally, he had read enough about Blake to produce the brief and brilliant poetic "biography" that appears in *New Year Letter*.[55]

❧ BYRON's strongest advocate among our sextet was Auden, who admired *Beppo*, *The Vision of Judgment*, and most of all *Don Juan*, yet found little else in the canon worthy of present-day attention. Among his longest poems, the *Letter to Lord Byron*, though written in rhyme-royal rather than ottava rima, was a frank and funny imitation, sometimes almost a parody, of *Don Juan*. The verse-letter offers twentieth-century reflections of Byron's realistic social attitudes, as well as of his sturdy conviction that man's crimes, faults, and follies are ultimately incapable of permanent reformation. Apart from a handful of lyrics and a few stanzas of *Childe Harold*, Auden brushed aside the more "romantic" aspects of Byron's poetry, even though he singled out the apocalyptic "Darkness" as a memorable achievement.[56]

An early letter of Yeats's called Byron "one of the great

problems, the great mysteries—a first-rate man, who was somehow not first-rate when he wrote. And yet the very fascination of him grows from the same root with his faults. One feels that he is a man of action made writer by accident, and that, in an age when great style was the habit of his class, he might have been one of the greatest of all writers. His disaster was that he lived in an age when great style could only be bought by the giving up of everything else."[57] For all that, Byron's *Manfred* was one of Yeats's youthful favorites. He felt strongly drawn to this contemplative hero, particularly because of his nobility, his Faustian preoccupation with the acquisition of knowledge, his loneliness, his bereavement, his melancholia, and (important to Yeats) his ability to converse on terms of equality with the denizens of the spirit world. Like Shelley's Prince Athanase, Manfred the dreamer in his remote Gothic tower seemed to Yeats a supremely sympathetic figure, worthy of restoration or even reincarnation under various Celtic disguises.

If the printed records can be trusted, neither Frost nor Stevens paid Byron much attention. Pound's *Literary Essays* offer only the most superficial comments. His sole "Byronic" poem was "L'Homme Moyen Sensuel," written in 1915. It was meant as a satirical life-portrait of an American named Radway and used heroic couplets as Byron had done in some of his satires. But the model Pound had in mind was evidently *Don Juan*. The poem was not a success. No mention of Byron appears in Frost's letters, in the various accounts of his lectures and conversations, or in Lawrance Thompson's three-volume biography. Byron's absence seems odd when we remember Frost's high praise of Christopher Smart for his "cavalierliness with words" and his determination to "make free with the English language," qualities that both Eliot and Auden rightly associated with Byron.[58] If Frost, in Northrop Frye's generic distinction, was closer in his poetry to the low than to the high mimetic, his having chosen to ignore the Byron of *Manfred*, *Cain*, and *Childe Harold* is probably understandable. Yet one would have thought that the "low mimetic" Byron of *Beppo* and *Don Juan* might have found a listener in Frost. Wallace Stevens was yet another negative Byronian, though once, walking to Greenwich through a sultry August night in 1912, he gave himself breathing room by turning back his shirt collar, "precisely," as he said, "like that corsair of hearts, le grand Byron."[59]

It was not *The Corsair* but *The Giaour* that Eliot chose to analyze in his only essay on Byron. Eliot found him a verse narrator of "torrential fluency" who displayed the "cardinal virtue of never being dull." His real failure as a poet consisted in his having discovered "nothing in sounds . . . nothing in the meaning of individual words," so that in all his career he "added nothing to the language." Like Auden, Eliot reserved his strongest praise for *Don Juan*, of which he had once composed a boyish imitation. The form of the poem gave free rein to Byron's "genius for divagation," and his "continual banter and mockery" served as an "admirable antacid" to the "highfalutin" manner of the earlier metrical romances and *Childe Harold*. Eliot preferred the final cantos of *Don Juan* (the hero in England) over the other twelve on the grounds that Byron's "acute animosity" against English society in the Regency period had "sharpened his powers of observation" and enabled him to indulge to the utmost his hatred of hypocrisy.[60]

Keats left a congeries of memorials in the minds of his modern successors. Two wholly independent comments apropos of the "Ode to a Nightingale" prove that his skill with the exact epithet had earned him certain proprietary rights. Of Ruth standing "in tears amid the alien corn" Frost said that Keats had made *alien* so completely his own at that particular juncture that any other poet who used the adjective must do so at his own risk. At work on *Little Gidding*, Eliot rejected the adjective *easeful*, proposed to him by a friend, on the grounds that the line about being "half in love with easeful Death" had given Keats a virtual patent. " 'Easeful,' " wrote Eliot, "will never be any use until Keats's trademark has worn off."[61]

Eliot strongly admired Keats's letters for their revelations of "a charming personality," a "shrewd and penetrating intellect," and the kind of "philosophic mind" that a poet may lay claim to.[62] The latter statement reads like a partial reflection of Pound's view that "Keats had got so far as to see that [poetry] need not be the pack-mule of philosophy."[63] Auden said that the letters provided evidence of Keats's "witty and original intelligence" as well as his common sense and the strength of his dedication to poetry. He shared Eliot's conviction that Keats would have continued to develop if he had lived longer but went much farther than Eliot in suggesting that "he might well have learned to use all the psychological insight, wit, and irony which his letters show him to have possessed, in writing tales which would have made him the equal of and only successor to Chaucer." The letters, said Auden, proved beyond doubt that Keats was nothing like the lovable weakling and sensitive plant that Shelley had mistakenly depicted in *Adonais*.[64]

Eliot and Auden were drawn chiefly to the odes. Eliot called them "enough for his reputation," and Auden found them "calm and majestic in pace," as well as "skillfully and tightly organized."[65] Neither commentator was completely satisfied with the "Ode to a Nightingale." Eliot, who had used images of nightingales both in *The Waste Land* and in the best known of his Sweeney poems, was critical of Keats for having introduced into his ode "a number of feelings which have nothing particular to do with the nightingale, but which the nightingale, partly, perhaps, because of its attractive name, and partly because of its reputation, served to bring together."[66] Auden's objections centered on the problem of form: the ode contained too many structural variations in the roles and voices of the bird and the poet as over against such a steadily "syllogistic construction" as Andrew Marvell had accomplished in "To His Coy Mistress."[67] Of Eliot's favorite, the "Ode to Psyche," Auden had nothing to say. The two poets also parted company in their judgments of the "Ode on a Grecian Urn." Eliot called the "Beauty is truth" passage of stanza five "a serious blemish

24

on an otherwise beautiful poem."⁶⁸ Auden strongly disagreed, defending the assertion on the grounds that the words in question were uttered by the urn and not by Keats himself. He also saw, as Eliot evidently did not, that Keats had intentionally set out to portray "a certain kind of work of art . . . the kind from which the evils and problems of this life . . . are deliberately excluded." It was clearly no accident that this was the ode that Auden echoed in *The Shield of Achilles*, though he gave the language a twist of his own.⁶⁹

Yeats confessed to a boyish enthusiasm for Keats's early "Fragment of an Ode to Maia." During his experiments at speaking to the psaltery with Florence Farr in 1901, he tried out, not very successfully, some of Keats's most melodious lines. But his chief interest lay less in such sonorities than in Keats's pictorial powers: "He makes pictures one cannot forget." He took notice of Keats's debt to Spenser in "La Belle Dame" and the "Ode to a Nightingale" and was attracted to the intimations of nympholepsy in both poems. This ode struck him as a great work of art, as firmly "rooted in the early ages as the Mass, which goes back to savage folklore." We have already mentioned Hugh Kenner's suggestion that "Sailing to Byzantium" combines ideas and images from both the nightingale and the Grecian urn odes. Yeats traced Keats's love of "luxuriant song" to his attempt to forget his poverty and his illness. "Ego Dominus Tuus" gave Keats's "exaggerated sensuousness" the most memorable of poetic statements.⁷⁰

In "The Trembling of the Veil" Yeats quoted Keats's attack on the neoclassical poetasters who had "sway'd about upon a rocking-horse / And thought it Pegasus." They had taught "a school of dolts" to "smooth, inlay, and clip, and fit" until their verses tallied. Yeats picked up both the Pegasus image and Keats's word "dolt" for his sarcastic complaint against the "theatre-business" into which his labors for the Abbey Theatre had drawn him. In "The Fascination of What's Difficult," Pegasus appears as a colt unhappily reduced to dragging "road-metal." Yeats resents the loss of his own "spontaneous joy" because of each day's "war with every knave and dolt," and resolves in the end to free the colt of imagination from its lowly stable.[71]

He regarded Keats primarily as a visionary poet, able to achieve at will "an intense realization of a state of ecstatic emotion symbolized in a definite imagined region." Although this was also one of the qualities that had drawn him to Shelley, he saw the two as "distinct types" who could never have exchanged their respective approaches to poetry. Each "had to perpetuate his own method and neither lived long enough to do so." He thought that Keats "sang of a beauty so wholly preoccupied with itself that its contemplation" became "a kind of lingering trance." This tendency drew him steadily towards a "greater subjectivity of being and to the unity of that being," whereas Shelley's poetry gradually became so much more objective that "unity of being" was finally broken up.[72]

Frost and Stevens were both staunch admirers of Keats's poetry. Young Frost's favorite among the mythological narratives was *Hyperion*, and Stevens repeatedly returned to readings of *Endymion*. Frost echoed the sonnet, "Keen fitful gusts" at the close of "Stopping by Woods on a Snowy Evening." Clear evidence of his liking for "To Autumn" appears in such early lyrics as "Mowing" and "The Tuft of Flowers." The structural strategy of "Come In" seems to have evolved as a counterstatement to the "Ode to a Nightingale." Frost admired the lines on Chapman's Homer, and another of Keats's matchless achievements, the "Bright Star" sonnet, left its mark on "Something Like a Star." In short, Frost had much of Keats's poetry "by heart" in both senses of the word.

Stevens also gave evidence of familiarity with the "Bright Star" sonnet, which begins, "Bright star, would I were stedfast as thou art." His early lyric "Of Heaven Considered as a Tomb" celebrates "the light / Of the steadfast lanterns" that "creep across the dark."[73] In 1907 phrases from the Grecian urn ode and the sonnet "Keen fitful gusts" appeared in Stevens's letters, and one of his youthful poems contains clear echoes of "On Sitting Down to Read *King Lear* Once Again."

26

In 1910 he quoted from the "Epistle to John Hamilton Reynolds" with evident approval. Helen Vendler has proved conclusively that "To Autumn" left an indelible impress upon the closing stanza of "Sunday Morning." At other times, passim in the poetry, he seems to share Keats's love of the exotic and the luxurious, of harvests and the juicy fruits of harvest time. In one of his later poems, "Extraordinary References," we suddenly come upon the proper name Vertumnus: "In the inherited garden, a second-hand / Vertumnus creates an equilibrium." Whether or not Stevens knew that Vertumnus was a Roman god of fruits and orchards, a pruner of trees and vines, there is a strong likelihood that he was recollecting from his readings in *Endymion* the lines in book two, 444-46: "Taste these juicy pears / Sent me by sad Vertumnus, when his fears / Were high about Pomona." It may be that he called his own Vertumnus "second-hand" and the garden "inherited" because he knew very well that they had originated in *Endymion*.[74] Later in his life, he explained in a letter the ways in which the twenty-fifth stanza of "The Eve of St. Agnes" had directly influenced the final section of "Credences of Summer."[75] Such outcroppings from the deep stratum of memory seem to betoken, like those in Frost, a continuing debt to Keats.

After Keats, at least chronologically, Shelley was Stevens's favorite. A reading of *Prometheus Unbound* in 1906 established in his memory an idea of Shelley as "astral" poet, votary of stars and the other supernal lights, a worshipper, in Stevens's phrase, of those "celestial paramours" that "diffuse new day."[76] Almost forty years later, in his prose collection, *The Necessary Angel*, he quoted from *A Defence of Poetry* with evident admiration and partial agreement, almost as if Shelley, whom Arnold had demeaned as "a beautiful but ineffectual angel," stood out among the "necessary" angels in the history of poetry. He connected Shelley, rightly, with the Platonic tradition as well as with its tragic flaw, the failure of the Platonic imagination to "adhere to what is real." For

27

without the corrections that reality offers, the realm of imag-
ination is always in danger of becoming a merely mind-made
construct that cannot command our continuing interest. The
"fictive covering" that "weaves always glistening from the
heart and mind" of poets like Shelley may be deceptive in that
its fictitious aspects screen us away from needful association
with the realities below or beyond it.[77]

But in the 1930s and afterward, Stevens was ready enough
to take cues from the Shelley canon. The only time they ever
met, he surprised Harold Bloom by quoting from "The Witch
of Atlas"— evidently the lines in stanza twenty-seven: "Men
scarcely know how beautiful fire is — / Each flame of it is as
a precious stone," Bloom finds an echo of this simile in "The
Owl in the Sarcophagus," where Stevens referred to "a dia-
mond jubilance beyond the fire."[78] The "Ode to the West
Wind" and the sonnet "Ozymandias" were among his other
sources, echoed in "Mozart, 1935," *Owl's Clover*, and *Notes
Toward A Supreme Fiction*. Images suggestive of those aspects
of our nature that are "celestial"; of music that embodies
"lucid souvenirs of the past" and looks to "airy dreams of
the future"; of ruined statues lying amidst "the immense de-
tritus" of a worldwide wasteland, as well as ideas about the
perpetual need for change and about life asserting itself in the
midst of death are all associated with Stevens's readings in
Shelley. Like his "diamond jubilance," they are often im-
provements on the source. But they all bear out his belief in
keeping "pure" our sense of the romantic, meaning always
"the living . . . the imaginative . . . the potent," and bringing
into the present those ideas and images out of past poetry that
most deserve renewed expression. He was quite prepared to
believe with Shelley in "that great poem, which all poets, like
the cooperating thoughts of one great mind, have built up
since the beginning of the world." In "A Primitive Like an
Orb," Stevens's name for it is "the essential poem at the centre
of things. . . . It is something seen and known in lesser poems.
. . . / The essential poem begets the others." All this follows
Shelley's generalization and at the same time adds something

to it: "One poem," said Stevens, "proves another and the whole."[79]

Yeats's interest in Shelley was lifelong. In his youth he thought that *Prometheus Unbound* was "among the sacred books of the world," and in the 1880s he dreamed of creating "some new *Prometheus*, with Patrick and Columbkil, Oisin and Fion in Prometheus's stead."[80] In place of the mountains of the Caucasus where Shelley's hero had endured three thousand years of torture, he planned to substitute his native Ben Bulben. What eventuated was *The Wanderings of Oisin*, which included Patrick and Oisin, but no recognizable Promethean figure. In the following years Yeats's imagination reached out to embrace other Shelleyan heroes, the poet of *Alastor*, Prince Athanase and his aged preceptor Zonoras, and the enigmatic Ahasuerus, the legendary Wandering Jew, who had appeared in *Queen Mab* and *Hellas*, and was probably the ancestor of "Old Rocky Face" in Yeats's late poem, "The Gyres."[81]

At either end of an interval of thirty years, Yeats wrote two formal essays on Shelley. The first in 1900 showed his enviable grasp of the whole range of the poetry as well as the ethical and metaphysical doctrines that infused it, particularly the idea of Intellectual Beauty, which Yeats modified to suit his own purposes. The second section of the essay, called "His Ruling Symbols," analyzed them in detail. "There is hardly a poem of any length," wrote Yeats, "in which one does not find [the star] as a symbol of love, or liberty, or wisdom, or . . . that Intellectual Beauty which was to Shelley's mind the central power of the world." In 1906 he added that he had never been entirely content with Shelley's visionary poetry until he had massed in his own imagination those "recurring images of towers and rivers, and caves with fountains in them [as, for example, in *The Triumph of Life*], and that one Star of his." In the end, Shelley's "world had grown solid underfoot and consistent enough for the soul's habitation."[82]

His subsequent speculations on the *Anima Mundi* were strongly Neoplatonic, and about equally indebted to Edmund

Spenser's *Fowre Hymnes*, and to the account of the World Soul that pervades *Adonais*. In *A Vision* he placed himself, along with Dante, Shelley, and Landor, in Phase 17 of the Great Wheel, and in developing his doctrine of the Mask, he said that it could represent either intellectual or sexual passion, as in those "two images of solitude," Ahasuerus and Athanase, or in Dante's Beatrice as she appeared in the *Paradiso* and Shelley's Venus Urania of *Adonais*. Yet he was compelled to conclude that Shelley had "lacked the Vision of Evil" and that he could not "conceive of the world as a continual conflict," as Yeats himself had been doing under the guidance of William Blake. For this reason, great poet though Shelley was, "he was not of the greatest kind."[83]

These latter opinions adumbrated the essay of 1932, where Yeats disavowed many of his former convictions about Shelley. At first, looking back from the vantage point of middle age upon the Shelley who had aroused his youthful admiration, he had said that "unlike Blake, isolated by an arbitrary symbolism," Shelley had "seemed to sum up all that was metaphysical in English poetry" so that it was he rather than Blake who had been chiefly responsible for the shaping of Yeats's spiritual life. Now, at sixty-seven, Yeats was coming to think that the "justice" proposed in *Prometheus Unbound*, that once "sacred book," was probably little more than "a vague propagandist emotion" and that the heroic female figures who awaited in the drama the arrival of the new order were, after all, "nothing but clouds." Shelley's "system of thought" had been "constructed by his logical faculty to satisfy desire."[84] Yet in his late poem "Under Ben Bulben" he echoed Shelley's "Witch of Atlas" in his account of that "pale, long-visaged company" of immortals who ride the wintry dawn under the brow of the mountain within sight of which Yeats had spent so many of his formative years.

T. S. Eliot dated his first "intoxication" with Shelley from about 1903 but in the next twenty-five years turned radically against him under the double aegis of Matthew Arnold and Irving Babbitt. Although he never indulged in that polemical hyperbole that made Ezra Pound describe "The Sensitive Plant" as one of the "rottenest poems ever written," he was critical of Shelley's over-indulgence in adjectival modifiers, his occasional inaccuracies in the deployment of images, and the singsong rhythms of at least one passage in *Prometheus Unbound.* Some of Shelley's "shabby" ideas as set forth in *Epipsychidion* offended Eliot's moral sensibilities. He regretted that Shelley had not lived past thirty "to put his poetic gifts, which were certainly of the first order, at the service of more tenable beliefs." He seems to have been echoing Arnold in calling particular attention to Shelley's lack of humor and his tendency to self-delusion.[85]

Even though some of these animadversions were uttered as late as 1933, the first evidence of Eliot's change of heart had come in 1929 when he seems to have discovered for the first time that Shelley had been strongly influenced by Dante and called him the "one English poet of the nineteenth century who could even have begun" to follow in Dante's footsteps. The prime agent in Eliot's conversion was the terza rima passage relating to Rousseau in *The Triumph of Life.* Eliot returned to the subject in 1950, pointing out again that Shelley was the foremost Dantean among the English poets and praising his achievement in *The Triumph* as superior to his own experiments with the same verse form in the air raid sequence of *Little Gidding.* He added that the "Ode to the West Wind"— the poem, incidentally, that Stevens had variously imitated— also reflected Shelley's close knowledge of Dante. At the same time he performed a complete volte-face on *Epipsychidion,* which he had now come to recognize as a lineal descendant of Dante's *Vita Nuova.* His final gesture of approval came when he quoted in *The Cocktail Party* the passage on the Magus Zoroaster from the first act of *Prometheus Unbound.* Shelley's strange account of a meeting between doubles, one living and one dead, may also have given Eliot a nudge in Shelley's direction while he was at work on the air raid section of *Little Gidding.*[86]

Like Yeats before him, Robert Frost began his Shelleyan

readings with *Prometheus Unbound* and soon extended them to include the early *Queen Mab* and *The Revolt of Islam*, as well as most of the shorter poems and *Epipsychidion*, many of which he read aloud to his fiancée during their engagement. But Frost's primary loyalties were to Wordsworth and Keats, and the range of his work bears no visible sign of Shelleyan ideas or images. The wind he invoked as an agent of change ("Come with rain, O loud Southwester!") blew from another point of the compass than Shelley's, and the two witches he wrote about came from Coös and Grafton counties, New Hampshire, and were related to Shelley's Witch of Atlas only by profession.[87]

At age twenty-nine Auden remarked that the world view of Shelley's Prometheus was more to his taste than that of Shakespeare's Coriolanus but that, given a choice, he would "much rather read the latter." One of Shelley's chief faults was that he "never looked at or listened to anything except ideas." The very nature of his "intellectual interests demanded a far wider range of experiences than most poets require," yet he seemed to lack the ability "to have and record them." This failure caused Auden to regard the bulk of Shelley's work as "empty and unsympathetic." In his judgment, the closing sentence of *A Defence of Poetry* was "the silliest remark ever made about poets," for poets are not "the unacknowledged legislators of the world." The function of poetry, said Auden, was not to tell people what to do, but to extend "our knowledge of good and evil" so that "a rational and moral choice could be made."[88]

It was ironic that the most intellectual of modern poets should have condemned a literary ancestor for excessive preoccupation with ideas. But it was more likely Shelley's manner than his ideological matter that made Auden call him a "poet whose work I detest,"[89] for he had read widely in Shelley. Echoes of *Adonais, The Mask of Anarchy, Hellas,* and "To a Skylark" are perfectly audible in poems as various as "The Age of Anxiety," the *New Year Letter*, "Something is Bound to Happen," and "Epitaph on a Tyrant." The final hortatory section of "In Memory of W. B. Yeats" not only embodies the *Weltanschauung* of *Prometheus Unbound*, for which Auden had expressed admiration only three year earlier, but might also have served as a fitting memorial for Shelley himself. The real point of convergence between Auden and Shelley was their shared belief in the remedial power of love and in the possibility (it was no more than that for either of them) that from time to time the poet might assist in its rebirth in the minds of men.

It is true that Auden as moral realist felt obliged to emphasize the difficulties of such conversions. He wrote of "the lion's mouth whose hunger / No metaphors can fill" and repeatedly warned his listeners that "Art is not life and cannot be / A midwife to society." But such a poem as "Petition" sounds another note, hoping for "power and light" and asking the deity to "Harrow the house of the dead" and to "look shining at / New styles of architecture, a change of heart." The prayer that ends "September 1, 1939" is distinctly Shelleyan in matter if not in manner:

> Defenceless under the night
> Our world in stupor lies;
> Yet, dotted everywhere,
> Ironic points of light
> Flash out wherever the Just
> Exchange their messages:
> May I, composed like them
> Of Eros and of dust,
> Beleaguered by the same
> Negation and despair,
> Show an affirming flame.[90]

33

PART ONE

Ancestral Voices

William Wordsworth

🍂 FOR ALL those modern readers to whom poetry matters, the continual reexamination of the poetry of the past is quite as important an obligation as the encouragement of good poetry now. If we believe that there have been literary giants among the poets of our own age—and who would deny such stature to Yeats and Frost and Eliot and Stevens and Auden?— it is well to remember that these men were neither the first nor the last to have mastered the skill of uttering those true and lively words by which poetry imprints its wisdom and its melodies upon the innumerable pages of human experience. One of the giants whose ancestral voices still echo among us is William Wordsworth.

Like other giants before and since, Wordsworth had to earn his stature. As early as 1800 he warned prospective readers that they might "frequently have to struggle with feelings of strangeness and awkwardness" as they read the second edition of *Lyrical Ballads*. "They will look round for poetry and will be induced to inquire by what species of courtesy these attempts can be permitted to assume that title." In certain respects, readers have felt, looked, and inquired as the poet predicted, not only in 1800, but also in all the years between then and now.

Among the earliest of these were his peers. Coleridge idolized him, even leaned upon him at times as a sturdy moral monolith, yet devoted thousands of words in the *Biographia Literaria* to the errors of style, tone, and syntax into which he thought his friend had been lured by too great an absorption with an indefensible theory of poetry. These remarks set the sights for what has been a continuing, though sporadic, critical barrage. Coleridge's list of the ineptitudes in Wordsworth has not been improved upon, nor has it been appreciably added to: inconstancy of style producing inadvertent bathos; occasional mental bombast; linguistic incongruities; a certain solemn matter-of-factness suggesting an underdeveloped sense of humor; and an eddying rather than a progression of thought, like the muddy backwashes of a river rather than the clear, swift-running current of the main stream. Such errors of commission are scattered up and down the collected works.

A few others have been observed. Byron found him dull, mild, and flat, like a sauce into which the cook had forgotten to shake pepper. The bumptious young lord of *English Bards and Scotch Reviewers* called him a "dull disciple" of Robert Southey's and a "mild apostate" from the neoclassical rules. Homespun narratives like those of Martha Ray, the unwed mother of "The Thorn," or Betty Foy, "the idiot mother of an idiot boy" struck Byron as "Christmas stories tortured into rhyme." It was hardly to be expected, by anyone but Wordsworth, that they should "contain the essence of the true sublime." Keats approached the problem of sublimity from another angle. Having taken Shakespeare as his model for the poet's self-immolation in poetry, Keats was bothered by the recurrent "I" in Wordsworth. He wrote, not unkindly, of "the Wordsworthian, or egotistical sublime" and wondered whether Wordsworth's grandeur was not in some respects contaminated and rendered obtrusive by the poet's sonorous egotism. Shelley's latent satirical impulse was aroused by similar considerations. In his travesty, "Peter Bell the Third," he wrote of Wordsworth:

> He had a mind which was somehow
> At once circumference and centre
> Of all he might or feel or know;

Nothing went ever out, although
Something did ever enter.
He had as much imagination
As a pint-pot; he never could
Fancy another situation,
From which to dart his contemplation,
Than that wherein he stood.

Yet that same group could not help admiring Wordsworth;
as practicing poets they had the calipers to measure his stature.
Coleridge in his conversation poems and Byron from time to
time in *Childe Harold's Pilgrimage* paid him the compliment
of imitation. Keats's letters often launch into periods of praise
for the master. And Shelley, whose *Alastor* sometimes reads
as if Wordsworth had been guiding the pen, continues the
"Peter Bell" poem with this astute comment:

Yet his was individual mind,
And new-created all he saw
In a new manner, and refined
Those new creations, and combined
Them, by a master-spirit's law.
Thus, though unimaginative,
An apprehension clear, intense,
Of his mind's work, had made alive
The things it wrought on; I believe
Wakening a sort of thought in sense.

Whenever the giant nods, the caricaturists and parodists
can be counted upon to tiptoe out of the oven like mischievous,
small Jacks-off-the-beanstalk and to take up their stations
behind his chair. Admirers of "We Are Seven" can never quite
forget Max Beerbohm's portrait of a whey-faced old gentle-
man pontifically expostulating with the little wench in the
sunbonnet on the fact that seven less two leaves five. Laurence
Housman, himself a skilled parodist, was probably reflecting
the Beerbohm influence when he refused to reprint the poem

in his anthology of Wordsworth because, he said, it annoyed him from end to end.

The man the parodists call Wordswords or Worstworst is sometimes dull, homely, earth-bound, egotistical, humorless, obscure, and entangled in prosaisms. Some of his "incidents and agents from common life" seem trite, his ultrasimplified language silly—as if, say, we were being asked to genuflect before Mother Goose as the patron saint of the English Lake District. Yet such passages are infinitely less frequent than the parodists would have us think.

The Victorians were wise enough to see what must be done about it; they stressed the need of editing Wordsworth, cracking off the common blue clay that disguised and obscured the durable gems. When Arnold made his own selection of the poems in 1879, he said unequivocally that "the poetical performance of Wordsworth is, after that of Shakespeare and Milton . . . undoubtedly the most considerable in our language from the Elizabethan age to the present time." The impression made by one of his fine poems was, however, "too often dulled and spoiled by a very inferior piece coming after it." Wordsworth had allowed "a great deal of poetical baggage" to encumber the collected works. What Arnold called baggage, Walter Pater thought of as debris. Few artists work quite cleanly, said Pater. They do not always cast off all the rubble and leave us only "what the heat of their imagination has wholly fused" into diamond-hard crystalline forms. The critic, the editor, the anthologist must assume the obligation of carting away the refuse in order to reveal what was there all the time—strong, clear, firm, deep, and lasting—Wordsworth at his best. For behind the shale in the valley, beyond the common lower hills, like Skiddaw in the Lake District or Snowdon in Wales, the old giant still looms, a commanding presence.

❧ IF WE ASK what the particular power is that gives support to Wordsworth's giantism, Pater provides us with a starting point. To expunge the worst and to concentrate on the best

40

is, says he, to "trace the action of his unique incommunicable faculty, that strange, mystical sense of a life in natural things, and of man's life as a part of nature, drawing strength and color and character from local influences, from the hills and streams, and from natural sights and sounds. . . . That is the virtue, the active principle in Wordsworth's poetry." One notable example would be those parts of "Michael" where this sense of the beneficial interaction of man and nature is projected—not the fable itself, not the story of Luke's going bad in the great city, not even the memorable image of a father-son relationship in the unfinished sheepfold, but rather the portrait of old Michael himself, formed and strengthened by his mountainous environment and his enduring and durable will. *Levavi oculos meos in montes* runs the psalm; and this is part of Wordworth's testament.

Another instance, milder and less rugged, is the Lucy poem, which begins, "Three years she grew"—

> The stars of midnight shall be dear
> To her; and she shall lean her ear
> In many a secret place
> Where rivulets dance their wayward round,
> And beauty born of murmuring sound
> Shall pass into her face.

Housman rightly believed that the last two lines could not have been written by any of the other major English poets. They display the essential quality and character of his poetical mind at its best. Wordsworth himself knew that this was so. As early as 1800 he set himself to oppose the widespread and degrading "thirst after outrageous stimulation" that resulted from the atmosphere of war and genocide, "the increasing accumulation of men in cities," the sensationalism of newspapers, and the deluge of cheap fiction. "Reflecting," he said, "upon the magnitude of the general evil, I should be oppressed with no dishonorable melancholy, had I not a deep impression of certain inherent and indestructible qualities of the human mind, and likewise of certain powers in the great and permanent objects that act upon it, which are equally inherent and indestructible." Out of this profound interaction, long brooded over, arose the inherent and indestructible power of Wordsworth's poetry.

His dimensions were heightened also by his being what Coleridge called a philosophical poet. Reading the neo-humanist critics, one might conclude that Wordsworth was a latter-day blend of the hard-shelled naturalist Lucretius and the soft-shelled naturalist Rousseau. This view is open to question. It will never do to overstress the naturalistic element in his thought as over against the humanistic and theistic components. All three conspire to fructify in his belief in the motherhood of nature, the brotherhood of man, the fatherhood of God, and—it may be seriously added—the neighborhood of pain. If Wordsworth can write like a nature-mystic, a pantheist, or a panpsychist, he can never be said to have forgotten the human figures in the foreground or the supreme Intelligence in the background. The Wordsworthian equivalent of the Miltonic "great argument" becomes clear in the eloquent opening of his unfinished masterpiece, *The Recluse*. Turning aside from the ancient epic theme of arms and the man, he chose to write instead

> Of Truth, of Grandeur, Beauty, Love, and Hope,
> And melancholy Fear subdued by Faith;
> Of blessed consolations in distress;
> Of moral strength, and intellectual Power;
> Of joy in widest commonalty spread;
> Of the individual Mind that keeps her own
> Inviolate retirement, subject there
> To Conscience only, and the law supreme
> Of that Intelligence which governs all—
> I sing:—"Fit audience let me find though few!"

The individual mind of man, subject to the inner checks of conscience and of consciousness of the laws of God ("that Intelligence which governs all"), is clearly a problem vast enough

to preoccupy any poet. "Not Chaos," he wrote, still thinking
of Milton, not

> The darkest pit of lowest Erebus,
> Nor aught of blinder vacancy, scooped out
> By help of dreams—can breed such fear and awe
> As fall upon us often when we look
> Into our Minds, into the Mind of Man—
> My haunt, and the main region of my song. . . .

When Keats contrasted Milton and Wordsworth, he was
struck by the apparently lesser degree of Milton's "anxiety
for humanity." He wondered whether Wordsworth's epic pas-
sion had not been diverted in such a way that he had become
a martyr "to the human heart, the main region of his song."
As an explorer of the dark passages of Mind, Keats concluded,
"Wordsworth is deeper than Milton"—even though the depth
probably depended "more upon the general and gregarious
advance of intellect, than [upon] individual greatness of Mind."
The point is at least arguable. What is odd here is that the
stoical Keats does not go on to say what the stoical Words-
worth found at the end of the dark passages. Out of the
struggles, disappointments, and disillusionments of his youth,
Wordsworth slowly discovered how to blend "the still sad
music of humanity" into the larger harmony of his faith in
God and his belief in the dignity of man. If it was necessary
(and it was) for him to see "ill sights of madding passions
mutually inflamed"; if in country and town alike he

> Must hear Humanity in fields and groves
> Pipe solitary anguish; or must hang
> Brooding above the fierce confederate storm
> Of sorrow, barricadoed evermore
> Within the walls of cities . . .

he had found the means to subsume the sound of wailing into
a symphony whose overtones were not ultimately tragic.

One means to this end was through the timely "utterance
of numerous verse." Another, and anterior, possibility was to

fix his contemplation upon the inherent and indestructible powers visible alike in nature and human nature. From that vantage point, one could come to understand that moral evil ("what man has made of man") cannot finally cancel out universal good. Under "nature's holy plan," by observing the myriad ways in which the mind is "fitted" to the external world, as well as the world to the mind, one could discover a sufficient justification of God's ways to men. Dust though we are, the immortal spirit grows like harmony in music: this was a fundamental article of Wordsworth's faith, and he urged his listeners to share this conviction. The struggle of humanity, writes a modern novelist, is "to recruit others to your version of what is real." It was Wordsworth's struggle, too, precisely because of his "anxiety for humanity." All men must realize, so far as the capabilities of each would allow, the Vast Idea to whose exploration and illustration he had dedicated his poetic powers. "Nature is made to conspire with spirit to emancipate us." This was Emerson's cogent summary of the point Wordsworth made in a thousand ways throughout his poetical career. Followed through all its ramifications, it is the point that permits us to claim for him the title of philosophical poet.

Emerson, the prophet of democratic vistas, helps to make us aware of yet another source of Wordsworth's strength and stature. It is that, like another giant named Antaeus, he believes that the poet must keep his feet on the ground, deriving substance and sustenance from his mother, the earth. The politics of Antaeus are unknown, but no one can read Wordsworth for very long without the conviction that at the deeper levels his democratic faith stands like bedrock. In passages like those relating to Beaupuy in the ninth book of *The Prelude*, his political views come to the surface; later on, as we know, these opinions were subject to some adjustment in the direction of conservatism. Yet the readjustment does not affect the basic tenet of his democratic faith; few modern poets have embodied in their work, whether by statement or by implication, so firm a sense of the dignity or worth of the individual common man.

Whoever now reads the famous preface of 1800 afresh and without preliminary prejudice can scarcely do better than to see it as a declaration of the need for democracy in poetry. Essentially the defense of a theory of poetry, it has long been a battleground for critics because of Wordsworth's espousal of a special doctrine of poetic diction. There is more to it than that. The preface makes a whole series of distinctions and connections whose importance to esthetic theory are not so much modern as timeless. He distinguishes true elevation of style from the false methods employed by certain eighteenth-century poetasters, noting especially the frozen artifice of perception and expression and the "curious elaboration" that beset that cult. In a searching passage he distinguishes the task of the poet from that of the scientist. He indicates the triple necessity of thought, feeling, and good sense in all good poetry. He relates the language of poetry to that of prose. He tries to show the interaction between poetry and the primary psychological laws of human nature, including the pleasure-pain principle as enunciated by Jeremy Bentham. His outline of the creative process is astute and valuable; like Coleridge he is a good psychologist because he is able to contemplate objectively the operations of his own mind. He is also enough of a proponent of the "low" and the "common" to insist throughout his essay on the remarriage of poetry to *things*; for to him democracy is not an abstraction but a way of life empirically learned.

It is, however, in his conception of the poet and of poetry itself that his democratic leanings are most apparent. This is not to say that he treats the subject exhaustively, but only to suggest from what quarter his winds of doctrine blow. The poet, he asserts, is "a man speaking to men," not differing from them in kind but only in degree. Here is no vessel for the divine afflatus, set apart from his kind in lordly magnificence. Here is no frenzied enthusiast, no hierophant writing better than he knows, but rather one man, among men, speaking quietly to his fellows of what most moves his heart and what is most central to his profoundest thoughts on the interrelations of man, nature, and supernature, whether transcendental or immanent. The poet's sensibility is livelier than that of others. He is more imaginative, with greater enthusiasm, tenderness, and knowledge than the common man. He is more articulate, and takes a greater pleasure in all he sees and knows. But he is only the uncommon common man, risen naturally from the ranks of the natural *aristoi*, born of no diviner race than those to whom he speaks and writes.

To the question of what poetry is, Wordsworth answers: "the image of man and nature." It is also "the most philosophic" (that is, wisdom-loving, and the wisdom loved is that of the people) of all writing. "Its object is truth, not individual and local, but general and operative, not standing upon external testimony, but carried alive into the heart by passion." It is truth that "is its own testimony" because, having been proclaimed, it will immediately be recognized by other men as pertinent to the situations in which they find themselves. It is thus a direct revelation of reality, or of the poet's considered version of the actual. Therefore Wordsworth is able to say that "in spite of difference of soil and climate, of language and manners, of laws and customs; in spite of things silently gone out of mind, and things violently destroyed; the poet binds together by passion and knowledge the vast empire of human society, as it is spread over the whole earth, and over all time." To do so, poetry must keep the reader "in the company of flesh and blood." It is not involved with the tears of angels, but with "natural and human tears." No celestial ichor distinguishes its language from that of prose: "the same human blood circulates through the veins of them both." The poetry of earth is never dead; but we may be best assured of this, thinks Wordsworth, if we assert the ultimate democracy of poetic language: the words of a man speaking to men in the tongue all men know because they are human beings.

The revolution Wordsworth led was not primarily a back-to-nature movement. It was rather an assertion of the values to be found in a fresh and mutually fructifying reunion of reality and ideality. His special individual *virtue* as a poet comes from his preoccupation with the indestructibles in nature and in mind. His method is to combine the instruments and insights of the poet with the ideals of a philosopher whose bias is strongly humanistic. His continuing belief in the dignity and dependability of the common man brings his work into spiritual alignment with those democratic revolutions that in his time, both in Europe and America, were coming to the fore after centuries of the *ancien régime*.

❧ FINALLY, there is the artist. As befits a giant, Wordsworth's most persistent theme is growth. Because, in a special sense, the child is father to the man, he becomes absorbed in the growth of children. The subject may be Wordsworth himself passing through the three stages up the stairway toward maturity, as in "Tintern Abbey." It may be the child whose "progress" is detailed in the great ode. Gradually losing what Hazlitt called "the feeling of immortality in youth," he finds, somewhat reluctantly, that he must accept in its stead "the faith which looks through death" to the fair fields on the other side of the river, and the "philosophic mind" of the Christian stoic who has kept watch over man's mortality and learned, in the end, what it takes to be truly human. It may be his beloved sister Dorothy, or Coleridge, or the child called Lucy, or the small son of his friend Basil Montagu who appears charmingly in the "Anecdote for Fathers."

The theme of such early lyrics as "Expostulation and Reply," "The Tables Turned," "Lines Written in Early Spring," and "To My Sister" is once again growth. He wishes to show how the mind develops through sense experience and reflection upon it—John Locke's two great "fountains" of empirical knowledge. Or we may learn through the sudden leap of intuition, the unlooked-for epiphany by which one "impulse" (the word is a favorite of Locke's) from a springtime woodland *may* (Wordsworth does not say it necessarily *will*) teach the man of sensibility more about how men's minds work than a reading of all the sages could do. This is clearly an over-statement used for its shock value. Yet what is an epiphany but a visionary overstatement that one hopes time will prove to have been approximately right? A perceptive and reflective observer of nature and its laws is provided with all sorts of emblems, analogies, and implications by the simple expedient of taking a walk and keeping his eyes open. Wordsworth, the perambulatory poet, well knew that the growth of our minds is made possible both by what we perceive and by "what we half-create." If we have imagination, together with a consid-ered body of knowledge and conviction, we can "build up greatest things from least suggestions"—like the emblem writ-ers of the Renaissance, or the Fathers of the medieval Church, or like all the great practitioners of poetry down through the ages.

The subtitle of *The Prelude*, Wordsworth's most intricate exploration of the subject, is *Growth of a Poet's Mind*. He undertook the poem partly for practice, a way of learning to handle blank verse, but mainly as an exercise in understanding on the Socratic principle, "Know thyself." What were the formative forces that had been brought to bear upon that "stripling of the hills," that northern villager with whom, of all people, Wordsworth was most closely acquainted? His childhood luckily had been spent in Nature's lap. A nurse both stern and kindly, she had planted seeds of sympathy and understanding in that growing mind. "Fair seedtime had my soul," says Wordsworth. Its further growth was "fostered alike by beauty and by fear." The milder discipline of beauty informs such lines as those on the river Derwent, winding among its "grassy holms" with ceaseless calm music like a lullaby. The discipline of fear is embodied in the trap-robbing and boat-stealing episodes. The boy, troubled in conscience, seems to hear low breathings coming after him in the woods. From a thwart of the stolen rowboat, he watches in horror the huge looming of the black peak from beyond the sheltering grove by the lakeside—something like the incarnation of a

48

Mosaic commandment, which it was not, except as his conscience made it seem so. He is aware, of course, that Nature has no moral ideas. Natural scenes like the grassy Derwent river bank or the monstrous shape of the night-shrouded mountain played a "needful part" in the development of his mind simply by having been there on occasions afterward recognized as crucial. What gave them significance was the condition of mind with which they entered into permanent association.

There is a kind of "wise passiveness" (Keats called it "diligent indolence") by which Nature can become a veritable treasure house of suggestion. Natural scenes, taken in their intricate totality, often awakened in Wordsworth what he called "the visionary power." Once he tells of taking shelter from an approaching storm under a brow of rock, listening all awake and aware to "the ghostly language of the ancient earth."

> Thence did I drink the visionary power;
> And deem not profitless those fleeting moods
> Of shadowy exultation: not for this
> That they are kindred to our purer mind
> And intellectual life; but that the soul,
> Remembering how she felt, but what she felt
> Remembering not, retains an obscure sense
> Of possible sublimity, whereto
> With growing faculties she doth aspire,
> With faculties still growing, feeling still
> That whatsoever point they gain, they yet
> Have something to pursue.

He records dozens of these natural scenes, not so much for themselves as for what his mind could learn through the stimuli they offered. This one provided a long vista or distant prospect up the road he knew he must follow. Often, at such times, he seems to catch with his mind's eye "gleams like the flashing of a shield." The gleam is nearly always Merlin-like, magical, anticipating a time when apprehensions hitherto disparate will suddenly coalesce to form another level of understanding. From there he can presumably continue his ascent.

Because the structure of *The Prelude* is pyramidal, with a broad base in sense impressions and a capstone of semimystical insight into the ultimate unity of God's mighty plan, it is no accident, it is rather a triumph of the architectonic intellect that it should close with the Mount Snowdon episode. Once again the natural scene plays an emblematic part in what is essentially a religious intuition. Coming suddenly from the fog on the lower flanks of the mountain into bright clear moonlight; looking down on the cloud surface through which the backs of lesser peaks show like whales at sea; hearing, as from an abyss, the roar of mighty waters, the combined voices of innumerable streams, the poet has gained a symbol of such complexity as to be relatively inexhaustible to meditation. When he comes to recollect the scene's emotional impact in the tranquillity of a later time, he recognizes it, not for what it was, but for what, after rumination, it had become *for him*: a Gestalt pattern standing for the human mind at its highest stage of development, a mind sustained

> By recognitions of transcendent power,
> In sense conducting to ideal form.

Such minds are no longer the prisoners of sense impressions. Instead, the "quickening impulse" provided by sense stimuli prepares them all the better "to hold fit converse with the spiritual world" and to discover, as was never possible before, the true meanings of liberty and love. No wonder that Coleridge, having heard this immense poem read aloud, rose up at the end to find himself "in prayer."

Another way of watching the operation of the growth principle in Wordsworth is to see how and how often he uses it as an organizational device in the shorter poems. It may be called the double exposure technique. Because he is interested in the stages of growth, he often juxtaposes two widely separated periods of time in such a way that we are made dramatically conscious of the degree of growth that has taken place between the first and second stages. It resembles the effect that might be produced by our seeing a double exposure on photographic film, where the same person appears in the same setting, except that ten years have elapsed between exposures.

The device is not uniquely Wordsworth's, though he has given to it his own special stamp and hallmark, as one of his ways of seeing. Shakespeare, for instance, uses the technique for dramatic effect in the two balcony scenes of *Romeo and Juliet*. The first of these is an almost perfect embodiment of romantic young love, untested in the alembic of mature experience, surrounded by danger, overlain with moonlight, punctuated with extravagant vows, compliments, and conceits. Between this and the second and far quieter balcony scene a process of accelerated maturation has set in. Mercutio and Tybalt have been killed, Romeo has been banished, a forced marriage for Juliet is in the offing, the lovers have made their secret matrimony and spent their wedding night together. The effect of the second balcony scene is then to remind us of the first, and to underscore dramatically how far adverse circumstances and their own responses to them have matured the youthful lovers in the meantime.

Something very like this is constantly happening in the poetry of Wordsworth. We have the picture that has long been held in memory; over against it is laid the picture of things as they are in the historical now. Between the two exposures, subtle changes have always taken place. These may involve a simple translation of the protagonist from the conditions of the country to those of the city as in the early lyric, "The Reverie of Poor Susan." Here the song of the caged thrush at the corner of Wood Street in a poor part of London is the auditory image that, for a brief instant, opens the shutter in the *camera obscura* of Susan's mind. The film of memory still holds the impress of the rural scene, the "green pastures" where she happily spent the season of her childhood. Momentarily, and ironically, the drab present and the green past

51

are juxtaposed. Then the vision fades, and once more the prison house of the city closes round her.

The technique that gives "The Reverie" whatever distinction it possesses is used far more subtly in many of the better lyrics. In "Tintern Abbey," for example, the light in the eyes of his sister seems to reflect for Wordsworth the very set of mind with which, five years before, he had exulted over the beauties of this quiet rural panorama beside the river Wye. "I behold in thee what I was once." As he overlooks the scene once more, with the mental landscape of the past still in his purview, he is made doubly aware of a sense of loss (the past will not return) and a sense of compensation greater than the loss (the new maturity and insight that the advancing years have brought). Again, however, it is the collocation of two separate "spots of time" that dramatizes for him (and for us) the degree and kind of his growth in the intervening period. Again it is the technique of double exposure, this odd co-presence in the mind of the then and the now, which gives dramatic life to his reflective lyric.

The great ode "Intimations of Immortality" abounds in such a complexity of metaphorical activity as to differentiate it markedly from "Tintern Abbey." Yet its broad strategy of deployment strikingly resembles that of the earlier poem, for its vitality once more depends upon a dialectical interplay between ideas of innocence and ideas of experience. Here is the picture of the true innocent, trailing his clouds of glory, clothed with the sun. Yet here beside it is also the voice of experience, neither harsh nor grating though deeply informed with the knowledge of the possibilities of good and evil. The two voices make a sort of antiphonal chant that runs throughout this wonderful poem, accounting, perhaps, for the incantational quality it has for the ear when read aloud. The visual aspects, however, are more important than the auditory. Through the mind's eye we are made to see the two states of being in the sharpest contrast, but with the one overlying though not obscuring the other, as in a palimpsest. Thereby the interior drama of the poem—a parable, essentially, of experience and innocence—is made to transpire; and with what effect only the individual reader can decide for himself.

The same principle is at work in "The Two April Mornings," "She was a phantom of delight," and the "Ode to Duty." It gives special dramatic impact to a number of the best sonnets, including such triumphs as "Composed upon Westminster Bridge" and that moving sonnet of bereavement which begins, ironically, with the phrase, "Surprised by joy." A very clear manifestation appears in the "Elegiac Stanzas Suggested by a Picture of Peele Castle." Here one finds, still, the two pictures. One is in memory: a calm summer Wordsworth spent long ago by the seaside in the vicinity of the castle. The second is an actual canvas painted by the poet's friend and sometime patron, Sir George Beaumont. It shows the same castle in a season of storm and stress, ruggedly fronting the fierce onslaughts of waves and wind. Between these two moralized landscapes stretches the poem. The first eight stanzas set up the poet's dream of human life through the calm image of the castle "sleeping in a glassy sea." Recantation comes in the last seven stanzas with a farewell to the youthful dream and a willing acceptance of the actual as the passage of time has discovered it to be.

The examination of these poems leads at last to an explanation of the elegiac tone that overlies or penetrates so much of the work of this lyricist of human growth. Regret, a certain kind of lamentation, does battle with joy, a certain kind of paean for the blessings of this life, and the joy tends, on the whole, to win out. The regret is for things lost: a vision of immortality in youth, an absolute sense of nature's ultimate beneficence, an unchartered freedom, or (it may be) a daughter, or the "phantom of delight" one's future wife was when first she gleamed upon the sight. At the same time Wordsworth accepts, not only without complaint or sentimental self-pity but also with positive joy, those replacements that life eventually substitutes for the early raptures. These may be a faith that looks through death, a sense of the value of the "pageantry of fear" in natural scenes, a responsible pleasure in following the dictates of duty, a beautiful child to be admired though not owned, and (with all that means) a woman in place of a phantom loveliness that could never be real.

Maturity for Wordsworth is hardly a state in which peace or happiness are guaranteed. A number of the shorter poems—"Resolution and Independence" is a good example—offer "frequent sights of what is to be borne" by all men, everywhere, at some time or other. Ills of the spirit, like those of the body, must be endured and if possible overcome. The road the mature man travels may have its detours through the seasons of hell, unreasoning despairs, despondencies that will not be denied. This is mainly what *The Excursion* is about: an eloquent "morality" in the form of quasi-dramatic dialogue. The heart of its meaning is in the titles of books three and four—"Despondence" and "Despondency Corrected." Wordsworth knows what human life is, and what is required of us if we are to learn how to live in it. He is gigantic in the final sense that he is a moral realist.

Too much has probably been made of the alleged shrinkage of power in Wordsworth, as if, after forty, his stature had suddenly declined to that of a dwarf. We read of how his genius decays, of how "tragically" he is carried off the stage on the double shield of religious orthodoxy and political conservatism. This is a "despondency" about Wordsworth that needs to be corrected, and a number of modern critics have undertaken the task. "Some think," wrote the poet, "I have lost that poetic ardour and fire 'tis said I once had—the fact is perhaps I have: but instead of that I hope I shall substitute a more thoughtful and quiet power." The poet speaking here is not Wordsworth; the sentences come from a letter by John Keats. Yet it is a clear statement of what happened to Wordsworth. His powers ripened gradually, reached a peak in his middle and late thirties, and thereafter very gradually declined. In that development and decline, as in so many other respects, the giant Wordsworth is one of us: the epitome of the normal man.

S. T. Coleridge

❧ IF WHAT a man was may be partly summed up in what other men thought of him, Coleridge is the leading figure of the English Romantic Movement. Soon after his death in the summer of 1834, the social philosopher John Stuart Mill classed Coleridge with Jeremy Bentham as originator and promulgator of most of the major ideas on which early nineteenth-century England subsisted, and also as one who had effected nothing less than a revolution among the thinkers and investigators of the age. George Saintsbury regarded Coleridge as "one of the greatest critics of the world" and did not balk at grouping him with Aristotle and Longinus. In our time, René Wellek has called him "the intellectual center of the English romantic movement." Had Coleridge never existed, says Wellek, we would be likely to feel "that [English] Romanticism, glorious as its poetry and prose is in its artistic achievements, remained dumb in matters of intellect." We can discover "a point of view, a certain attitude" in the writings of Keats and Shelley. "We find the expression of a creed in Wordsworth." But it is only in the work of Coleridge that we "leave thought which is an integral part of poetry for thought which can be expressed in logical form, and can claim comparison with the systems of the great German philosophers" like Immanuel Kant.

The cumulative effect of the foregoing judgments is to raise Coleridge to a very high level indeed. To call him one of the world's greatest critics is remarkable enough. To praise him as one of two leading revolutionary thinkers in an age of revolutions and as the only major English romantic poet who knew how to use his head makes him something of a paragon. Even if the case has been somewhat overstated, too many voices have been raised in laudatory chorus to be ignored. The most cautious possible summary of the situation would be to say that in spite of certain ups and downs Coleridge's reputation as poet and critic, if not as formal philosopher, has been relatively secure since his death.

Yet to many of his contemporaries, himself included, this strange and harassed man seemed to be a failure. He left Cambridge University without having taken a degree; he projected a Utopian community on the Susquehanna in America only to abandon the plan. He married in haste but shortly discovered that his temperament was almost completely incompatible with that of his wife; he sired more children than he knew how to support. Two journals that he undertook to edit quickly expired. A combination of illness, self-doubt, laziness, and indecision constantly inhibited and often destroyed his plans for writing and lecturing. He moved restlessly across the English landscape, pursued by demons that he could not escape because they were inside him. He tried to forget his woes in Germany, Malta, Sicily, and Italy—without success. Through a large part of his adult life he fought vainly against the opium habit, more or less innocently contracted as a means of relief from pain, yet soon so boldly tyrannous that he might have died of it long before his earthly work was finished, and would doubtless have done so if it had not been for the frequent intercession of his friends.

Without success. Had he succumbed at forty, these two words could almost have served as his epitaph. He was already thinking of death and of the example of his own misspent life when he summarized his sense of failure in a letter to his friend Josiah Wade in the summer of 1814. "Conceive," he wrote, "a poor miserable wretch, who for many years has been attempting to beat off pain, by a constant recurrence to the vice that reproduces it. Conceive a spirit in hell, employed in tracing out for others the road to that heaven, from which his crimes exclude him! In short, conceive whatever is most wretched, helpless, and hopeless, and you will form as tolerable a notion of my state, as it is possible for a good man to have. . . . In the one crime of opium, what crime have I not made myself guilty of!— Ingratitude to my Maker! and to my benefactors—injustice! *and unnatural cruelty to my poor children*—self-contempt for my repeated promise—breach, nay, too often, actual falsehood! After my death, I earnestly entreat, that a full and unqualified narration of my wretchedness, and of its guilty cause, may be made public, that at least some little good may be effected by the direful example!"

This is but one passage drawn from the long train of self-recriminations where Coleridge tried to state, and thus perhaps to alleviate, the horror that assailed him whenever his conscience rose up to point an accusing finger. Restless, wretched, seemingly helpless, and often literally hopeless, he could have composed a "history" very nearly as "tragicall" as that of Marlowe's *Faustus*.

FAUSTUS: Where are you damned?
MEPHISTOPHELES: In hell.
FAUSTUS: How comes it then that thou art out of hell?
MEPHISTOPHELES: Why this is hell, nor am I out of it.

If not among us, at least among his contemporaries, the temptation was strong to condemn this man for his short-comings. So it was with William Hazlitt, despite his own foibles and failures, in a retrospective account of Coleridge preaching in the north of England. "His forehead was broad and high, light as if built of ivory, with large projecting eye-brows, and his eyes rolling beneath them, like a sea with

darkened lustre. His mouth gross, voluptuous, open, eloquent
. . . but his nose, the rudder of the face, index of the will, was
small, feeble, nothing—like what he has done." For Carlyle,
too, the contrast between Coleridge's promise and his actual
achievement carried the overtones of tragedy. "A ray of heav-
enly inspiration," he wrote, "struggled in Coleridge, in a trag-
ically ineffectual degree, with the weakness of flesh and blood.
. . . To the man himself, Nature had given in high measure
the seeds of a noble endowment . . . a subtle, lynx-eyed in-
tellect; . . . tremulous, pious sensibility to all good and all
beautiful . . . but imbedded in such weak laxity of character
. . . as made strange work with it." Once more, says Carlyle,
in the Scottish moralist's typical summing up, "once more,
the tragic story of a high endowment with an insufficient will."

It is all too easy to laugh over Coleridge, the cavalryman
who ran off and enlisted in the Light Dragoons only to dis-
cover that he was allergic to horses; or the impoverished Can-
tabrigian dandy disporting himself in swanskin waistcoat; or
the inexperienced lover, who dreamed of establishing a blissful
American abode with one of the nubile daughters of a bank-
rupt tinware manufacturer from the city of Bristol, only to
propose in haste and henceforth to find himself in holy dead-
lock for the long duration of his life. Or the endlessly inventive
projector whose everspringing hopes were almost invariably
quashed by his own ineptitudes and procrastinations. Or the
talker whose fascination with the musical murmur of his own
polysyllabic discourse denied to others the opportunity to in-
trude with so much as a monosyllable of their own.

All the male world is said to split between two camps:
father's boys and mother's boys. If the hypothesis has any
psychological validity, Coleridge must qualify as his father's
son, for he seems to have revered his philoprogenitive but
otherworldly sire, whom he lost when he was only nine, and
to have entertained emotions of mild scorn toward his mother.
Her determination that the children in her charge should amount
to something in the everyday society of her time drove Mrs.
Coleridge into a kind of practical dynamism to which her son,

like his father before him, was temperamentally indisposed. Coleridge remembered his father as the "perfect Parson Adams"—simple, learned, generously improvident, and (unlike Adams) "conscientiously indifferent to the good and evil of this world." In Coleridge's own paternal improvidence, in his voluminous and thronging fantasies, in his perpetual abhorrence of business arrangements and other forms of practical management, he is his father's ally and his mother's enemy.

Yet such are the vagaries of subtle and precariously balanced minds that he could not evade feelings of remorse and guilt whenever his own failure to fulfill his mother's (and later his wife's) desires for normal worldly respectability and success was borne in upon him. The love he was unable to develop toward his mother he tendered, rather sentimentally, to other women during adolescence and young manhood. His sense of bereavement upon the early death of his father led him to seek in male friendships a whole series of father substitutes, among whom Wordsworth for some years reigned uppermost, though he failed Coleridge in the end by outstripping him as poet if not as sage, and as paterfamilias if not as philosopher.

Among his masculine benefactors, none did more for him than Dr. Gillman, the surgeon of Highgate, into whose pleasant household he came, like a downtrodden *Übermensch*, just as the leaves were beginning to bud in the spring of 1816. He was nearly forty-four, too old to accept the doctor and his wife as spiritual foster parents yet so far gone in decrepitude and despair that his need for them was infinitely greater than theirs for him. They literally raised the roof to accommodate Coleridge. His cheerful attic room was reached by a flight of nine steep stairs. All one side of his chamber was lined with bookshelves from floor to ceiling. Centered in the opposite wall was a fireplace before which stood his writing table. A yard away was the large spool bed where, except for occasional outings at the seaside and one trip to the Rhineland with Wordsworth during his middle fifties, Coleridge spent nearly all the nights of his final eighteen years.

Beside the west window stood a dresser, ornamented by

Mrs. Gillman with potted geraniums and dark green myrtle, his favorite houseplants. On good days the view was fine, with the Nightingale Valley stretching away in the sunlight and the tree-covered vistas of Hampstead dotted with half-visible villas from whose chimneys, morning and evening, rose companionable evidence of human habitation. Here, said Carlyle, sat the sage, on the very brow of Highgate Hill, three hundred feet above the uttermost northern fringe of the vast city, "looking down on London and its smoke-tumult" as if he had escaped from "the inanity of life's battle"—a "heavy-laden, high-aspiring, and surely much-suffering man." And here, in his sixty-second year, his sufferings ended.

Behind the public Coleridge—Mill's epoch-making philosopher, Saintsbury's critical Colossus, De Quincey's eloquent discourser, Lamb's metaphysician and logician, Shelley's "subtle-souled psychologist"—stood another and far less confident creature: Coleridge the dreamer, or as one of his biographers called him, "the sublime somnambulist." This was the man of private dread, a curiously fragile victim of circumstances, whose "trembling, pious sensibility" discovered itself to the young Carlyle whenever he sat at the feet of the master in the tall old house at Highgate.

The forms of dread are among the keys to Coleridge's innermost personality. Like many another sedentary scholar he showed some degree of physical cowardice. Yet the impulse to fear took its origin far less from outward stimuli than from causes within his psyche. Throughout his life, though chiefly in his youth and young manhood, he seems to have been

> Like one, that on a lonesome road
> Doth walk in fear and dread,
> And having once turned round walks on,
> And turns no more his head;
> Because he knows, a frightful fiend
> Doth close behind him tread.

60

Although he protested that he did not believe in ghosts, having met too many of them personally, there were frequent occasions when his disbelief was unwillingly suspended while fiends of awful aspect stalked his footsteps. He well knew what he calls in "Limbo" the "horror of blank Naught-at-all." Far worse was the horror of what he might have denominated "Something-indeed." One notebook entry reads: "Friday Night, Nov. 28, 1800, or rather Saturday morning—a most frightful Dream of a Woman whose features were blended with darkness catching hold of my right eye and attempting to pull it out. . . . The Woman's name Ebon Ebon Thalud—When I awoke, my right eyelid swelled." Recurrent crowds of "shapes and thoughts" rose round him as he lay writhing on the borderlands of the subconscious. "The Pains of Sleep" records his shocked realization of his own innate capacity for sin; he recoiled at the discovery that he could desire hugely what he hugely loathed. Shame, terror, guilt, and remorse were goads in his flesh in that vast gulf that he once called "the unfathomable hell within."

Many of Coleridge's deepest fears intersected with the emotion of desolation—what D. G. James called "the desert island feeling." At bottom this was a dread, not so much of being alone as of being so profoundly alone that one was out of touch, perhaps irrevocably, with the whole range of the living universe. In *The Dungeon*, an extract from his tragedy *Osorio*, which he printed in the second edition of *Lyrical Ballads*, he mentioned with evident dismay the idea of *"friendless solitude."* The adjective here makes all the difference, for in a *friendless* as opposed to a *friendly* solitude, one is conscious of being encircled by stagnation and corruption, by all that rots and reeks, until the soul itself "unmoulds its essence" and becomes as "hopelessly deformed" as that of the prisoner in Coleridge's play. The bearing of all this on his figure of the ancient mariner is plain.

Even the dejection of which the poet complained in the memorable and moving ode of April 1802 owed its origin to his conviction of an essential disunity between his own orphaned sensibility and those multiple and potentially friendly forces that made up the natural and familial world around him. As with Satan after the wars in paradise, Coleridge felt himself damned while yet capable of "beholding good." In this condition, like his ancient mariner becalmed on the surface of an empty sea, he could evoke no harmonies, bring nothing into formal being. For the duration of the ode, at least, he inhabited "that inanimate cold world"—that spectral wasteland where the "poor loveless ever-anxious crowd" blindly gropes, as in Eliot's poem, having, as Coleridge said in another context, "eyes that see not, ears that hear not, and hearts that neither feel nor understand."

The antidote to all this was his recurrent dream of an earthly paradise. No one can be sure how it may have looked to him while his head was submerged under the glittering surfaces of his most golden visions. As it comes out in the reflective poems, however, it is nothing so grand as Kubla's pleasure-dome inside the walled domain of Xanadu. Humbly enough in these verses he asks no more than a place of peace where in times of spiritual agoraphobia he can take refuge and find solace. Such was the lime tree bower just over the wall from his cottage in Nether Stowey where he waited out a long June evening in 1797, gazing about at the sun-dappled foliage of the nearby walnuts and elms, hearing no other sounds than the twittering of swallows and the placid drone of a bumblebee. Like so many of the cosy bowers John Keats mentions, this was a friendly, not a friendless, solitude, made companionable both by the proximity of his own dwelling and by his thoughts of his friends Charles Lamb and William and Dorothy Wordsworth as they wandered over the low hills and meadows between the village and the sea. Such, too, was the interior of the same cottage one frosty midnight in the next winter when Coleridge sat dreaming of his own childhood and planning a happier and better one for his infant son, Hartley. On an April afternoon two months later he found "a green and silent spot" among the same hills his friends had explored—a "quiet spirit-healing nook" where he reclined on the golden coverlet of the "never-bloomless furze" to watch the descending sun and listen to the song of the ascending skylark. Here, as always, he permitted himself to dream of another world, one in which pure meditative joy in the flowering lap of nature might be prolonged rather than periodically interrupted and destroyed. In this situation, he anticipates both Shelley and Keats.

Interruption and destruction were in fact among his worst nightmares. Though his worship of nature was a good deal less intense than that of Wordsworth or Keats, he knew enough of meditative joy in the lap of nature to wish it could be made to last. It was the possibility of interruption and destruction that set him trembling even as he lay half-asleep "on fern or withered heath" in seeming content. He fittingly called one poem "Fears in Solitude." Its subtitle provided the date and cause of his fear: "Written in April, 1798, during the alarm of an invasion." Even in his vernal haven he could not forget the potential threat of what he knew so well—things changing for the worse. "My God!" he cries, "it is a melancholy thing" when a man who wishes only to "preserve his soul in calmness" must think of imminent war and its human consequences. Who could say that martial-minded France had not already set her men ashore? Even now strife might be stirring just beyond these silent hills—"invasion, and the thunder and the shout, and all the crash of onset."

The war he feared did not reach English soil. Neither then nor later did Coleridge's "divine and beauteous island" fall victim to a foreign conqueror. What arrests our attention in this reflective poem is rather the architectural image through which the poet summarizes his sense of what England has meant to him. It is, he says, a "most magnificent temple" where he has been able to "walk with awe" and sing his stately songs.

If this image is of no great consequence when taken alone, it assumes a striking pertinence when we think of it in connection with the pleasure-dome of Kubla Khan, another earthly temple whose owner dwelt in peace, though warned by "ancestral voices" that war and invasion might one day occur. It is this sense of possible destruction that gives dramatic force to Coleridge's autobiographical "Fears in Solitude." It is also of use in the interpretation of "Kubla Khan," that enigmatic parable which the author might have called "The Fall of the House of Kubla."

In this brief narrative lyric the pleasure-dome does not fall as did Poe's House of Usher, nor is Xanadu invaded and laid waste by barbarian hordes. Yet the poem hints clearly enough that both are distinct possibilities. The presiding concept in these fifty-four lines could be summed up in the word *precariousness*, which is exactly the emotion Coleridge felt as he lay in apparently blissful ease in the dell above Nether Stowey.

The most important feature of the poem's internal structure is the series of contrasts there developed. Coleridge, with whom the device of thesis-antithesis was a fetish, thought habitually in terms of polar oppositions. Part one of the poem shows four of these: light and darkness, civilization and savagery, heat and cold, peace and war. The descriptive imagery of the opening lines at once establishes a bright and sun-filled landscape, green, fertile, and orderly. Yet the poem is not five lines old before we are reminded of the sunless waste of water far below. Another contrast is made with similar economy: the well-tended gardens of the Khan as over against the deep, wild, cedar-shaded gorge where the River Alph bursts out of the earth like a Niagara in reverse. This region of Xanadu, which Coleridge calls "romantic" in the eighteenth-century sense of "wildly but pleasurably awesome," is as different from Kubla Khan's domesticated grounds as is an Alpine chasm from the clipped formality of an English manor house garden. "A savage place" is another of the poet's epithets. In Xanadu the rude and the civilized stand side by side.

The third contrast is not fully apparent until we have visualized the topographical features inside the protective wall. The pleasure-dome stands about halfway between the roaring fountain where the river springs up and the echoing caverns through which it dives out of sight. Between the appearance

64

and disappearance, the Alph meanders some five miles. As the Tartarean crow flies, the distance between the dome and either end of the river is not great, since Kubla Khan within his castle can hear the "mingled measure" of the torrent's rise and its fall. Lines 31 to 36 describe the miraculous situation of the pleasure-dome, which rests on a foundation of ice caves either beside or astride the River Alph.

> The shadow of the dome of pleasure
> Floated midway on the waves . . .
> It was a miracle of rare device,
> A sunny pleasure-dome with caves of ice.

Rare and miraculous indeed! The co-presence of heat and cold, of fire and ice, is enough to suggest the possibility that the dome's situation is precarious. Should the ice caves melt, or should the Alph wear them away, the whole structure would dissolve and vanish, never to reappear except as flotsam on the dark subterranean ocean.

One then asks whether the possible destruction of the pleasure-dome is elsewhere implied. The answer brings out the final contrast in part one: the opposition of peace and war. The dome is dedicated to peace, plenty, domesticated beauty, and the gentle arts of contemplation. The roar of the water as it dives below ground would not be oppressive if the Khan did not hear through the tumult the sinister sound of "ancestral voices prophesying war."

All four contrasts make us aware of the precariousness of the Khan's situation. During the second part of the poem, when the narrator-observer speaks for himself, his interests are plainly associated with order and creativity. Like Kubla Khan he wishes to be the builder of an earthly paradise. Unhappily, his inspiration—which is represented by the strains of music from the visionary maiden's dulcimer—has departed. Even if he could "build that dome in air," he would still be in Kubla Khan's predicament; he would have to take into account the always imminent forces of destruction. For the creation of castles in the air is involved with a long history of popular distrust and superstition. People are all too ready to suppose that such supernal pageants are the work of enchanters, possibly of demons. Does not this one show the flashing eyes of a man possessed? Clearly the wisest course among law-abiding citizens is to begin a ceremony of exorcism, weaving a circle three times round, closing their eyes in holy dread of his hypnotic stare. He has fed on honey-dew, the celestial ichor, and drunk the milk of paradise, a celestial liquor. So had Satan before he fell.

In the face of such opposition, the builder might well expect to see his cloud-capped towers dissolve into thin air before he could get them suitably mapped and blueprinted. By Coleridge's account this was what happened to his one vision of Xanadu when his reverie was interrupted and his privacy invaded by the arrival of a rank outsider—on *business*, too. Although he afterward retained "a vague and dim recollection of the general purport of the vision," all his "phantom world" had otherwise vanished.

Despite the brevity of the poem, its general purport is quite clear. It follows the normal lyrical mode of statement, application, and resolution. The statement hints four times that the earthly paradise is in jeopardy. If dissolution does not come from within—by crumbling foundations like those of the House of Usher—it may come from outside—by assault. The application and resolution combine to show that the visionary poet faces similar dangers. He has already lost his power to revive *within him* the music of inspiration. At the hands of a suspicious and antagonistic public he may likewise have to reckon with a "war" from outside.

❧ WE HAVE ALREADY noticed Coleridge's refusal to believe in ghosts on the grounds that he had seen too many of them. Enough of these experiences are on record in his writings to indicate that his mind was always playing him tricks. His generic term for this process was "somnial magic" by which he meant a range of effects broad enough to cover not only those times when he was actually asleep but also those varying degrees of wakefulness running from the simple daydream (when one is in full but relaxed command of his mind) all the way down to a kind of reverie where the "comparative powers" are suspended and images of mental origin seem as real as those of actual visible objects.

The *Biographia Literaria* asserts that psychology had long been one of Coleridge's hobbyhorses. If he had ever undertaken his proposed work on dreams, visions, ghosts, and witchcraft, he would have treated all such phenomena systematically and offered "scientific" explanations for them. Luther's encounter with the devil could, for example, be subjectively explained. It was nothing more supernatural than the result of a "deranged digestion" in a man of sedentary habits who had been intensively worrying about the problem of evil. Having himself passed through many similar adventures along the frontiers of sleep, Coleridge understood perfectly how Luther was able to see both his actual room, with all its furniture and appurtenances, and also a superimposed "brain-image of the devil, vivid enough to have acquired apparent outness." Coleridge would have found no difficulty in understanding the case of Ebenezer Scrooge and the three ghosts of Christmastide.

Illness and bodily pain stimulated the image making powers. Coleridge believed that "the optics and acoustics of the inner sense" helped to explain the "mode in which our thoughts, in states of morbid slumber, is delirium." When his friend Charles Lloyd, an epileptic, fell seriously ill in November 1796, Coleridge carefully observed and recorded Lloyd's state of mind. Most remarkable was the way in which actual events and sounds were assimilated and transformed into the substance of his imaginings. "All the Realities round him," said Coleridge, "mingle with, and form part of the strange dream. All his voluntary powers are suspended; but he perceives every thing and hears every thing, and whatever he perceives and hears he perverts into the substance of his delirious vision."

At the other extreme from Lloyd's delirium was the daydream of semicontrolled reverie like that recorded in "Frost at Midnight." Here the poet was perfectly aware of time and place, yet free to range at will over the past, into the future, and far outside the confines of the cottage where he ruminated at midnight beside a dying fire. His reveries were not always so pleasant. In the ode "Dejection" he recalls himself from a state of choking regret over the decay of his imaginative powers with an image suggestive of the Laocoön:

> Hence, viper thoughts, that coil around my mind,
> Reality's dark dream!
> I turn from you and listen to the wind,
> Which long has raved unnoticed.

He has sunk so deep into the buried life that he has forgotten to listen for the rising storm, a phenomenon earlier wished for in the hope that it might startle him out of his lethargy.

Two poems called "Day-dream" show, when they are compared, what a range of consciousness Coleridge meant his term to embrace. One says simply: "My eyes make pictures, when they are shut." The other states that "no deeper trance e'er wrapt a yearning spirit" than that from which the child Frederic awakened him. Whenever he dozed in his chair, regrets and nostalgias, hopes and fears, rose up in his mind as pictures. The various states and levels of reverie show what he once called "that *complexus* of visual images, cycles or customs of sensations, and fellow-traveling circumstances . . . which make up our empirical self."

Such phenomena sometimes occurred even when Coleridge was fully awake and actively engaged in writing. One of his letters to Southey mentions their old rooms in College Street. Then he interrupts himself to explain that even as he wrote the sentence about their former association in a particular house beside a familiar street, he was struck by an "ocular spectrum" of the room itself. He goes on to say that this ocular picture illustrates his own theory of association. When association occurs, it is often less a linkage between trains of ideas than of "resembling states of feeling." The *Notebooks* are full of his comments on cycles of sensations and fellow-traveling circumstances. "Renew the state of affection or bodily Feeling," says one entry, "same or similar—sometimes dimly similar, and instantly the trains of forgotten thought rise from their living catacombs."

Opium was not for Coleridge the "onlie begetter" of daydreams, but no one who has read his letters can doubt that it served him both as a narcotic and a stimulant. "Laudanum gave me repose, not sleep," he wrote in March 1798, and the distinction helps to explain the state in which after 1796 he often voluntarily placed himself. The repose (not sleep) that the dosage induced he once called "a spot of enchantment, a green spot of fountain and flowers and trees in the very heart of waste sands." The language here is plainly figurative, like Shelley's "green isle" in the "sea of misery." What it meant to Coleridge is what less dangerous anodynes mean to others: joyous relief from the gnawing edge of pain, a sense of euphoria in which the mind is set free from bodily misery (or even spiritual remorse), though always and only for the time being.

But opium was also a stimulant. If he did not enter the dope taker's nirvana of popular belief, he nevertheless found this "pernicious drug" oddly beneficial to him as a means of liberation. Sometimes it released "thoughts, hidden in him before," yet happily capable of producing the deepest emotional responses among "his best, greatest, and sanest contemporaries." For a "delusive time" this poison seemed to make the body a "fitter instrument for the all-powerful soul." Not only could it deaden the pain of such afflictions as toothache; it also opened inner doors to nobler traffic. In such a situation, he said, writing itself became a kind of "mental somnambulism, the somnial magic superinduced on, without suspending, the native powers of the mind." What ensued was a series of vivid and dramatic metaphors, closely accompanied by the lively words that would best express them. One need not wonder at his gradual addiction to such a drug as this. The catch, and well he knew it, lay in the paralysis of the willpower that accompanied this magical liberation and made him incapable of setting down more than the merest fraction of the wonders he had seen.

Great minds, said Coleridge in one of his aphoristic moments, are never wrong except as a consequence of being in the right, but imperfectly. In this, as in so much else that he wisely summarized, he was drawing on personal experience. Of his own imperfections he was the best expositor and the severest judge. Modern psychology and psychiatry, though they have attained to levels of achievement he could only dream of, yet confirm many of his opinions about the phenomena of the human mind under various forms of stress and stimulation. He was often wrong. But he was also often in the right, however imperfectly. One entry in the *Notebooks* refers to the "apostolic command of Try all things: hold fast that which is good." Whatever his shortcomings, and they were many, it was a command he always wished to obey.

🍎 THE FIRST two volumes of the modern edition of Coleridge's *Notebooks*, under the astute and patient editorship of Kathleen Coburn, appeared respectively in 1957 and 1961. One of Coleridge's entries of the fall of 1802 half-humorously confessed that he had laid too many intellectual eggs "with Ostrich Carelessness" in the "hot sands of this Wilderness, the World." Lesser scholars might have quailed before the immense task that confronted Miss Coburn when she began, for the ostrich eggs had not only to be unearthed but often unscrambled. Methods had to be devised for transcribing, dating, analyzing, annotating, tabulating, and indexing the most various and intransigent materials. In one of his letters Coleridge had made a typical pedantic coinage, "Lycophrontic tenebricosity," apparently meaning something like "the gloom of wolf-like thoughts." Such thoughts, wrote his editor, were "limpid daylight compared with some of the 'dark adyta' . . . of a [typical] notebook." Despite their frequent obscurities, the entries offer fascinating insights into the teeming mind of

Coleridge, and the darker passages often stand side by side with such straightforward statements as one he made in the Lake District in the fall of 1803: "I went to the window, to empty my Urine-pot, & wondered at the simple grandeur of the view."

It is no wonder that he was unable to be more systematic than he was. He wrote, says his editor, "under the influence of spirits and opium, in the dark, on fell-sides and mountain-tops, in bed, and probably in stage-coaches even when they were on the move." The glancing mercuriality of his mind, the variety of his interests, and his always recurrent tendency to sloth often combined to defeat his organizational efforts. As a result, the notebooks are filled with what Miss Coburn calls a "farrago of unrelated matters," even though many separate entries show him trying to organize and unify. He prepared an extensive alphabetical list of the common English flowers; made maps of the rugged terrain he walked over, recording with patriotic fervor the musical English place-names; kept account of prices paid for bed and breakfast, coachfare, and shoe repair; and in the domestic area set down sure-fire recipes for mutton stew, vermicides, ginger wine, purgatives, and stove blacking. Two of his favorite words, one of Latin and the other of Greek derivation, were "coaduna-tive" and "esemplastic"—both meaning to render multeity into unity. Many years later the poet Yeats listened seriously to a directive from one of his esoteric communicators: "Hammer your thoughts into unity."* Coleridge had tried it, too. Yet in the notebooks as in his life, the unifications he effected were often, if not nearly always, limited in scope, fragments that he used to shore up the grand ruins of his unrealized dreams.

The largest unity he achieved was that of being human. He loved an "O Altitudo!" as well as Sir Thomas Browne, and

---

* Yeats once wrote: "I am one of those unhappy people for whom between Thought and Deed lies ever the terrible gulf of dreams. I sit down to write and go off into a brown study instead, at least if circumstances offer me the slightest excuse." Coleridge repeatedly complained of similar problems.

yet next moment could talk as bawdily as Mercutio or Falstaff. We have met this up-and-down, patrician-plebeian Coleridge elsewhere, in letters and poems, in *Table Talk, Biographia Literaria,* and *The Statesman's Manual,* although he is more even-tempered in *Aids to Reflection,* the book that helped to provide so much of the philosophical underpinning for the American Transcendentalist movement. But the keeper of the journals is the exception to G. M. Harper's observation that Coleridge "could not even think without supposing a listener." Even in his familiar letters he is far more judicious, even in his tabletalk far more aware of his listening audience, of being on stage for the edification of his peers. The Coleridge of the notebooks shows a mind in *déshabille,* and he seems all the more human for that reason.

Most of his intellectual ostrich eggs, to paraphrase Christopher Morley, who was in turn parodying Thomas Gray's *Elegy,* are the rude forefathers of an omelet he never got round to making. The entries offer little that is really finished and polished. There are sharp literary judgments, metaphysical and psychological speculations, absorbing accounts of nightmares and dreams, and many pages on natural scenery and growing children, especially his sons Hartley and Derwent, one named for a philosopher, the other for a river.

We learn something of his unrequited love for Sara Hutchinson, the "Asra" of his poems, and find an example of his Greek letter cipher, devised (like that of Pepys) as a screen against prying eyes. Few entries are separately and intrinsically important, yet the multiple uses to which this admirable edition can be put remain to be discovered by qualified researchers for many years to come.

One important example of a discovery that owes its origin to this edition is that of Thomas McFarland. Coleridge ended chapter thirteen of the *Biographia Literaria* with a breakdown of the imaginative faculty into three component parts. He called them the Primary Imagination, the Secondary Imagination, and the Fancy. "It is probably fair to say," wrote McFarland, "that this is both one of the most famous passages

in all of English prose and one of the least satisfactorily under-
stood." For nearly a century and a half after the publication
of *Biographia Literaria* in 1817, the two hundred words that
Coleridge had devoted to his triple distinction were often quoted,
paraphrased, or interpreted. Yet they always seemed to hang,
like Mahomet's coffin, glistening but mysterious, somewhere
in the airy space between heaven and earth.

The clue—a single proper name that made it possible for
the passage to be grounded and examined—appeared in vol-
ume two of the Coburn edition. Coleridge wrote: "In the
Preface of my Metaphys. Works I should say—once & all
read Tetens, Kant, Fichte &c & there you will trace or . . .
track me." His connections with Kant and Fichte had long
been well known, but the name of Tetens was almost new to
the critical canon. When McFarland took up Coleridge's chal-
lenge to trace and track him, his subsequent research uncov-
ered a substantial two-volume tome, written by Johann Nic-
olas Tetens, "the most important German psychologist of
the *Aufklärung*," published at Leipzig in 1777 and carefully
read and annotated by Coleridge some twenty-five years later.
On examining Coleridge's copy of these volumes in the British
Museum, McFarland made the further (and epoch making)
discovery that "not only the formulation of the theory of the
secondary imagination, but also the entire threefold division
of the imaginative faculty" that Coleridge had set down in
the *Biographia* could be traced back to Tetens's pioneering
work, and that Tetens's exposition made it possible to illu-
minate most of the darker "adyta" in Coleridge's enigmatic
discriminations.

If Coleridge was heavily indebted to German thought for
much of his best work in the field of esthetics, it was to his
own capacity for introspection that he owed his greatest suc-
cesses in practical criticism. Apart from his critique of Words-
worth, which is the ancestor of many Victorian and modern
estimates, his powers as a "practical" critic emerge most ef-
fectively in his lectures on Shakespeare. By present-day stand-
ards, he had his limitations, with little knowledge of the thea-

ter and the actors of Shakespeare's time, and no visible interest in the dramatic background of the Elizabethan Age. His emphasis is upon Shakespeare as poet and as the genius capable of "darting himself forth" and passing "into all the forms of human character and passion, the one Proteus of the fire and the flood," an emphasis echoed in the letters of John Keats.

Two examples will serve. A report on one of Coleridge's public lectures shows him defending Lady Macbeth against the appellative of monster. She was not, he said,

> a being out of nature and without conscience: on the contrary, her constant effort throughout the play was . . . to bully conscience. She was a woman of a visionary and day-dreaming turn of mind; her eyes fixed on the shadows of her solitary ambition; and her feelings abstracted, through the deep musings of her absorbing passion, from the common-life sympathies of flesh and blood. But her conscience, so far from being seared, was continually smarting within her; and she endeavours to stifle its voice and keep down its struggles, by inflated and soaring fancies, and appeals to spiritual agency.

It is clear that Coleridge felt some spiritual kinship with Macbeth's incipient queen: for he, too, was a creature of visionary and daydreaming turn of mind, with a conscience continually smarting within him, though he was able temporarily to assuage it by soaring fancies and appeals to spiritual powers.

His views on the character of Hamlet again reflect his own personal predilections:

> In Hamlet . . . we see a great, an almost enormous, intellectual activity, and a proportionate aversion to real action. . . . The effect of this overbalance of imaginative power is beautifully illustrated in the everlasting broodings and superfluous activities of Hamlet's mind which, unseated from its healthy relation, is constantly occupied with a world within, and abstracted from the world without—giving substance to shadows, and throwing a mist

74

over all commonplace actualities. . . . [His] senses are in
a state of trance, and he looks upon external things as
hieroglyphics. . . .

The key phrases here—"enormous intellectual activity,"
"aversion to real action," "overbalance of imaginative power,"
"broodings," and looking "upon external things as hiero-
glyphics"—replicate some of those that Coleridge recorded in
his notebooks about himself. His ancestor-worship of the prince
of Denmark is reflected in one of his off-the-cuff remarks: "I
have a smack of Hamlet myself, if I may say so." His intro-
spective capabilities were strong enough to enable him to il-
luminate with his critical spotlight many dark corners in the
tragic characters of Hamlet, Othello, Lear, and Macbeth, among
others. Somewhere in his own attitudes he found a smack of
each.

🎔 WHAT A MAN was may be summed up not only in what
other men said of him but also in what he said of other men.
For he is likely to select for admiration and emulation those
qualities in his predecessors and contemporaries to which he
himself aspires. One of Coleridge's leading aspirations was to
excel in a whole spectrum of modes of expression, ranging
from soliloquies like those of Shakespeare to reflective poems
like those of Wordsworth and to blank verse that tried for
the high Miltonic rhetoric, to say nothing of the many avail-
able styles that lay between. If he was, in the end, neither the
greatest of poets nor the most systematic of philosophers,
neither the wisest of moralists nor the most learned of psy-
chologists, neither (certainly) the wittiest of playwrights nor
the cleverest of wits, he did manage on occasion to excel in
each of his chosen fields. Although the term *universal genius*
must probably be denied him, he came close enough to that
lofty station so that some examination of his views on the
subject of genius may now be germane.

He disagreed with Dr. Johnson's opinion that "the true

genius is a mind of large general powers, accidentally deter-
mined to some particular direction." He wished, in fact, to
distinguish sharply betwen the poetic power of genius and,
on the other hand, "a general talent determined to poetic
composition by accidental motives, by an act of will rather
than by the inspiration of a genial and productive nature."
Johnson's observation suggested that true geniuses appear more
frequently than they actually do. "Poetic genius," said Cole-
ridge, "is not only a very delicate but a very rare plant."

When genius occurred, he believed, one could always rec-
ognize it by the degree of its dominance over the materials it
worked with. Shakespeare, whose plays he never tired of ex-
ploring because each fresh reading disclosed new powers in
the dramatist, was assuredly no "mere child of nature; no
automaton of genius; no passive vehicle of inspiration pos-
sessed by the spirit, not possessing it." On the contrary (like
Wordsworth), he "studied patiently, meditated deeply, under-
stood minutely, till knowledge, become habitual and intuitive,
webbed itself to his habitual feelings." Inspiration, when it
came, had to be a positive act of the whole man, who must
possess wholly the knowledge he projected. Whatever he did
must be based on an empirical observation—first noticed, then
ruminated upon, and at last comprehended with the lordly
grasp of the master. Like that of any true genius, the kind of
poetry Shakespeare wrote required an activity of the will but
in a quite different connection from what one was likely to
find in the work of a merely talented man, for in genius, said
Coleridge, one discovers not so much a partnership as a union
of powers: "interpenetration of passion and will, of sponta-
neous impulse and of voluntary purpose."

"Idly talk they," cried Coleridge, "who speak of poets as
indulgers of fancy, imagination, superstition, etc. They are the
bridlers by delight, the purifiers; they that combine all these
with reason and order—the true protoplasts—Gods of love
who tame the chaos." Out of deference to reason and order,
Coleridge defined one side of genius as "originality in intel-
lectual construction." But the definition did not really satisfy

76

him. For it omitted one great activating principle, which consisted, as he often said, in the ability to carry on into the powers of manhood the freshness and feelings of childhood. The genius could so re-present familiar objects as to "awaken the minds of others to a like freshness of sensation concerning them."

The skeptic or idle talker may seek to depreciate the genius as a blind man offering to lead the blind, or at best as one "talking the language of sight to those who do not possess the sense of seeing"—a statement, incidentally, which exactly describes William Blake. Coleridge's response to such depreciation was to say that we are not all blind, though all of us from time to time may be subject to "distempers of the mental sight." We are all in error, though not all in the same error, or at the same time. It is the conceivable office of some great men to help heal others, to open their eyes to truths hitherto concealed. Such men are the true geniuses of any age.

The genius, therefore, is the bugler blowing reveille in the dormitory of the soul. He is the awakener, the freshener, the reactivator, and the discoverer or rediscoverer. "The character and privilege of genius," said Coleridge, is to "find no contradiction in the union of the old and new, to contemplate the Ancient of Days with feelings as fresh as if they then sprang forth at his own fiat." Like the poet in Keats's second *Hyperion* such men will "feel the riddle of the world, and may help to unravel it." But Coleridge insistently returns to the idea of an educated innocence as the *sine qua non* of true genius. So equipped, a man may somehow manage to "carry on the feelings of childhood into the powers of manhood" and to look with "the child's sense of wonder and novelty" upon those appearances that "every day for perhaps forty years have rendered familiar."

In this sense, Wordsworth was for Coleridge the *living* illustration of genius. When they began collaborating on *Lyrical Ballads*, Wordsworth's task was to "awaken the mind's attention from the lethargy of custom," directing it rather to "the loveliness and the wonders of the world before us." His performance, in Coleridge's judgment, proved the wisdom of the assignment, for Wordsworth had that kind of genius which "neither distorts nor false-colours its objects." Instead he brought out "many a vein and many a tint which escapes the eye of common observation, thus raising to the rank of gems what had been often kicked away by the hurrying foot of the traveller on the dusty high road of custom." He knew how to use the true and enlivening word.

How exactly Coleridge conforms to his own conception of greatness is a question for continuing debate. Whatever we may think of him as poet or philosopher, psychologist or moralist or metaphysician, he is literally a man to reckon with—if not (like Immanuel Kant) to tell time by. Compared with that industrious utilitarian Jeremy Bentham, the garrulous and often querulous Coleridge seems the very image of the *until*-itarian: a perpetual procrastinator, a John-a-dreams unpregnant of the means by which his best aspirations can be realized. Yet we may remind ourselves again that it was no less a person than John Stuart Mill who classed both men as the supreme "seminal thinkers" of the early nineteenth century. In the minds of all the thinking part of mankind, these two had managed to sow those ideological seeds which would sooner or later spring up and flourish. For both men, Mill's metaphor has proved to be just.

Lord Byron

"YOU WILL believe me, what I sometimes believe myself, mad," said Byron to Lady Blessington one day in 1823, "when I tell you that I seem to have *two* states of existence, *one* purely contemplative, during which the crimes, faults, and follies of mankind are laid open to my view (my own forming a prominent object in the picture), and the other *active*, when I play my part in the drama of life, as if impelled by some power over which I have no control, though the consciousness of doing wrong remains. It is as though I had the faculty of discovering error, without the power of avoiding it."

If Byron was mad, it was but north-northwest. He never drew a better self-portrait than this wryly romantic viva-voce sketch for his lady visitor. At thirty-five, he was able to look back over the perspective of what amounted to his whole career, lacking only its abortive conclusion at Missolonghi. His contemplative side had been responsible for the nine satires, wherein many of the usual human crimes and follies were laid open not only to his own but also to the public view. His active side, as he called it, was best displayed in the Byronic hero, that ultraromantic, swashbuckling paleface with the wildly wreathing dark hair, and the brain beneath it where sorrow and remorse were always contending for mastery. The hero's manifestations had ranged from Childe Harold through Lara and the Giaour and the Corsair to Manfred and Cain and Mazeppa. Byron must have recognized, even as he spoke to Lady Blessington, that many of the highlights of his self-portrait had also appeared more than two centuries earlier in Shakespeare's Hamlet, to whom at least two of his heroes, Harold and Manfred, were markedly indebted.

Even as he exposed the Doppelgänger in his soul, he had already nearly finished his masterpiece, *Don Juan*. Here, for the first time in his life, he had found a way of putting his two selves together so that the one supplemented and complemented the other, the cold laughing eye of the satirist often growing warm and moist with the powerful overflow of sentiment. It was a typical exaggeration when he said that in *Don Juan* he had meant to be "a little quietly facetious upon every thing," for the romantic strain in Byron frequently undermined the satirist's pose of cynicism. William Gifford, editor and chief critic of *The Quarterly Review*, having read canto two of *Don Juan*, said that he "lost all patience at seeing so much beauty so wantonly and perversely disfigured." Yet Byron held that he had written "the most moral of poems." If people failed to discover the moral, that was their fault, not his. To strip off "the tinsel of sentiment" might in itself become a moral act, while the alleged wantonness and perversity could be, and often were, effectively counterbalanced by the true voice of feeling.

Twenty years of growing, in and out of a dozen countries, had brought him to the state of mind and heart that made *Don Juan* possible. In every sense of the term he was now a man of the world, a true cosmopolite, scarcely comparable to the man of one-and-twenty who had launched his poetical career with the mediocre verse collection called *Hours of Idleness*. Fougeret de Monbron, author of *Le Cosmopolite, ou le Citoyen du Monde*, remarked in French that "the universe is a kind of book of which one has read only the first page if he has seen only his native land." Byron affixed the quotation to cantos one and two of *Childe Harold* when they appeared in 1812. He must have recognized that until his own grand tour, he had been stuck at page one of the book of the universe.

Although born in London, he had spent his childhood with his widowed mother in Aberdeen, where the local citizens knew him as Wee Geordie Byron, clad in a red jacket and nankeen trousers, speaking in broad Scots, and limping along on his congenital clubbed foot, encumbered but not defeated by tight bandages and visible braces. In 1798, just as Wordsworth and Coleridge were issuing the first edition of *Lyrical Ballads*, the ten-year-old stripling became the sixth Baron Byron of Rochdale and inherited the family estate at Newstead Abbey. By the age of thirteen he was cuffing his way through Harrow School, hating it at first, though coming finally to enjoy it, or at least the memories of it. At seventeen, "unsocial as a wolf," having discovered that there was no vacancy at Christchurch College, Oxford, he matriculated instead at Trinity College, Cambridge, where he became a notoriously indifferent student, dashing off verse to be published anonymously, skipping a term whenever he felt like it, and keeping a tame bear out of pique because a college rule forbade pet dogs. It was typical of him to tell his friends that the bear was to sit for a fellowship. There were romantic attachments both to boys and girls, shouting quarrels with his pitiable but insufferable mother, and a very gradual accession to a perilous balance of belief and social outlook. But in Fougeret de Monbron's terms, he was still a rank provincial.

His uncommonly adventurous grand tour of the Mediterranean Basin in 1809-1811 changed all that. When he set sail from Falmouth on 2 July 1809, he was only a few months past his twenty-first birthday and had but recently taken his seat in the House of Lords. His addiction to literature was already stronger than his vaguely Whiggish political opinions. Yet *Hours of Idleness*, deservedly enough, had fared poorly with the reviewers, and their animadversions had to be avenged. During the spring he had read proof on his witty and forthright rejoinder, *English Bards and Scotch Reviewers*, in which he did his best to wreak havoc among the elder members of the critical and literary establishment. Then he sailed away, out of the range of contumely.

"I am so convinced of the advantages of looking at mankind instead of reading about them," he later wrote, "that I think there should be a law amongst us, to set our young men abroad, for a term, among the few allies our wars have left us." Had he chosen, like his Cambridge crony and traveling companion, John Cam Hobhouse, to write a prose account of their excursion, he might have called it *Journeys Among Wars*. The itinerary included Portugal and Spain, where Napoleon was actively waging the Peninsular Campaign, and moved from Iberia by British warship to the fortress of Gibraltar, sailing thence to the well-defended island of Malta. When Byron and his retinue disembarked on the shores of Albania, they found that Ali Pasha, the shrewd and ruthless vizier of this province of European Turkey, was occupied with one of his innumerable border skirmishes farther north but would be delighted to receive them if they would accept his offer of an armed escort into the interior. Down among the Ionian islands and ashore on the Peloponnesus, the revolution of the Greeks against their Turkish masters was already beginning to fester. Although it would not burst out for another decade, the English travelers found a sullen enmity between the outnumbered natives and the "domiciliated military" who seemed to be in command of every phase of daily life. Byron was sadly struck by the squalid little Turkish provincial town of Athens, whose ragged population of ten thousand stood on the verge of starvation. Even when the travelers crossed to Smyrna and worked up the coast to the Troad, there was the ghost of another war and its ancient chronicler, the author of the *Iliad*.

Though he later cynically concluded that men were "equally despicable" in all countries and asserted that the only skill his trip had taught him was that of chewing tobacco, there can be no doubt that Byron's first pilgrimage was a powerful shaping force in his career as poet. By the time he returned to England in July 1811, he had passed through enough exploration and adventure, to say nothing of athletic and amatory exploits, to make him at least a surer if not a better man than he had been two years earlier. He owed to the tour not only the first two cantos of *Childe Harold* but also the atmospheric materials and scenery, as well as the predilection for violent action, that were shortly to appear in his metrical romances. More important, the journey was recollected in partial tranquillity when he came to write the inimitable first half of *Don Juan*.

❦ THE TWO LONG poems that bracketed Byron's grand tour show in high relief the opposing sides of his personality. In 1809, with *English Bards and Scotch Reviewers*, he had launched himself as a satirist in the great tradition of Alexander Pope, born exactly a century earlier than he. In the poetical epistles, the moral essays, and especially in *The Dunciad*, Pope had established a method, a theme, and a tone of voice that all his successors among verse-satirists could afford to ignore only at their peril. The tone was acerbic and crackling, and the voice was directed toward the throng of scribblers, whether critical or creative, who had polluted the literary air of Pope's time as their descendants were doing in the age of Byron. Pope had brought to perfection the whiplash couplet, an ideal instrument for the flaying of literary pretenders. Byron put as much of this as he could muster into *English Bards*.

Yet his superlatively romantic self was not to be denied. The poem that stood at the opposite end of his grand tour was *Childe Harold's Pilgrimage*. On his return to England he carried with him in his portmanteau the first two cantos of this semiautobiographical travelogue that first brought the Byronic hero into the public eye. Although it offered sufficient evidence of Byron's wit, *Childe Harold* was hardly intended to provoke laughter. In place of Popean couplets, he had taken up the stanza of Edmund Spenser, which had been used with considerable success in serious poems by such of his eighteenth-century forebears as Shenstone, Beattie, and James Thomson. Each stanza concluded with the dying fall of the alexandrine rather than the rude and ruthless pentameter bump that typically closed many of his satirical couplets.

Even in 1812, however, Byron was not yet fully committed

to serious narrative verse. In his traveler's luggage, along with *Childe Harold*, were two other satires, written in March 1811 during his temporary residence at the Capuchin Convent in Athens. The first was *Hints From Horace: Being an Allusion in English Verse to the epistle Ad Pisones, de Arte Poetica, and Intended as a Sequel to English Bards and Scotch Reviewers*. The other was *The Curse of Minerva*. The purpose of this poem was the severe castigation of Lord Elgin for having stolen from Athens the antique marble sculptures that ever since have borne his name. For some months Byron planned to include these satires as appendages to a projected fifth edition of *English Bards and Scotch Reviewers*. But in the end he was dissuaded by friends and publishers and suppressed his sequels in order to give all possible emphasis to *Childe Harold's Pilgrimage*. So the pro tempore satirist retired to the wings while the ultraromantic took the stage.

Since Byron as satirist was eventually to reappear at a considerably higher level of achievement, it is worthwhile to take the measure of his earliest experiments with this genre. *English Bards* was clearly intended to be a latter-day *Dunciad*, junior grade. Although it lacked Pope's elaborate machinery of presentation, and was nearly seven hundred lines shorter, it followed the track of the master in both theme and manner. "Prepare for rhyme, I'll publish right or wrong," he wrote. "Fools are my theme, let Satire be my song. . . . Laugh when I laugh, I seek no other fame. The cry is up, and scribblers are my game."

Whether as wit or as manipulator of pentameter couplets, Byron stood at a considerable distance behind his great Augustan predecessor. But both poets shared in one major historical blunder. This was the device of pillorying poetasters whose names soon disappeared like so many rusty needles in the haystacks of time. The result was that large sections of *English Bards* are as dull as comparable parts of *The Dunciad*, which, in satirizing dullness, lost much of its point when the dullards faded from memory and could be revived only by the mouth-to-mouth resuscitation of learned biographical footnotes. Yet where the victims remained reasonably famous, the satirical jibes of both Pope and Byron continued to evoke the laughter of succeeding generations. This is no doubt why, out of the thousand and some odd lines of Byron's poem, most of the commentators, in his day as in ours, have been chiefly drawn to the seventy couplets in which he aims his blunderbuss at Scott and Southey, Wordsworth and Coleridge, and Matthew Gregory Lewis, author of *The Monk* and other Gothic horror tales. Byron's method throughout was comparable to that of the caricaturist who seizes upon a few salient traits for exaggeration and ridicule, ignoring the undoubtedly grander totality. His first significant victim was Sir Walter, whose preeminence in the field of metrical romance Byron himself was soon to challenge and who was now jeered at for the supernatural excesses of *The Lay of the Last Minstrel* and the character of the hero of *Marmion*.

> Thus Lays of Minstrels—may they be the last!
> On half-strung harps whine mournful to the blast . . .
> And goblin brats, of Gilpin Horner's brood,
> Decoy young border-nobles through the wood,
> And skip at every step, Lord knows how high,
> And frighten foolish babes, the Lord knows why.

Even the "golden-crested haughty Marmion" was demeaned as "not quite a felon, yet but half a knight"—"a mighty mixture of the great and base." Byron's conclusion proved that he had already learned something about the art of sinking in poetry:

> These are the themes that claim our plaudits now;
> These are the bards to whom the muse must bow;
> While Milton, Dryden, Pope, alike forgot,
> Resign their hallow'd bays to Walter Scott.

Robert Southey, who would become Poet Laureate after Scott refused the appointment, was a favorite target of Byron's both early and late. The accusation was always the same:

Southey's work offered living proof of the adage that "a bard may chant too often and too long."

> But if, in spite of all the world can say,
> Thou still wilt verseward plod thy weary way . . .
> The babe unborn thy dread intent may rue:
> "God help thee," Southey, and thy readers too.

The Gothic fictions of Monk Lewis evoked a certain amount of Hallowe'en fun. His "Parnassus" was said to be a churchyard where he stood on ancient tombs, "by gibb'ring spectres hailed," while "thin-sheeted phantoms," "small gray men," and "wild yagers" praised him as Scott's prosaic alter ego.

Byron's trickery worked best with Wordsworth and Coleridge. Seizing on Wordsworth's preface to *Lyrical Ballads* (1800), the lyric called "The Tables Turned," and the catchpenny narrative, "The Idiot Boy," young Byron turned the tables on his elder contemporary:

> The simple Wordsworth, framer of a lay
> As soft as evening in his favourite May,
> Who warns his friend "to shake off toil and trouble,
> And quit his books, for fear of growing double;"
> Who, both by precept and example, shows
> That prose is verse, and verse is merely prose;
> Convincing all, by demonstration plain,
> Poetic souls delight in prose insane . . .
> Thus when he tells the tale of Betty Foy,
> The idiot mother of "an idiot boy;"
> A moon-struck, silly lad, who lost his way,
> And, like his bard, confounded night with day;
> So close on each pathetic part he dwells,
> And each adventure so sublimely tells,
> That all who view the "idiot in his glory"
> Conceive the bard the hero of the story.

Coleridge was disposed of in ten lines, which took off from one of his early newspaper effusions called "To A Young Ass: Its Mother Being Tethered Near It."

Shall gentle Coleridge pass unnoticed here,
To turgid ode and tumid stanza dear?
Though themes of innocence amuse him best,
Yet still obscurity's a welcome guest.
If Inspiration should her aid refuse
To him who takes a pixy for a muse,
Yet none in lofty numbers can surpass
The bard who soars to elegise an ass.
So well the subject suits his noble mind,
He brays the laureat of the long-ear'd kind.

The suppressed sequels to his first satire show that Byron, two years after the publication of *English Bards*, was still eager to exploit his "contemplative" side by offering further observations on the faults and follies of mankind. *Hints from Horace*, the milder of the two, is a free translation of some four hundred lines from Horace's *Art of Poetry*, modernizing the Latin original by interpolated allusions to English poets from Chaucer down—and Byron meant *down*—to Wordsworth, Scott, and Southey. Byron renders one of Horace's key sentences—*Denique sit quod vis, simplex duntaxat et unum*—as "In fine, to whatsoever you aspire, let it at least be simple and entire." For the time being, he was aspiring to the Horatian qualities of moderation, simplicity, and wholeness, none of which was native to his nature.

The Curse of Minerva, a serious rather than a laughing satire, was an evident offshoot of the attack on Lord Elgin in *Childe Harold*, canto two, composed a year earlier. The giant figure of the goddess appears to the narrator at sunset in a romantic Grecian setting and calls down a curse on Elgin's head. It was characteristic of Byron to convert his adventures and observations to immediate poetical use. Some of the stolen marbles from the Parthenon and the Erectheum were being crated up for shipment to England while he was in Athens in January 1810. Almost at once he condemned this egregious international thievery, "the last poor plunder from a bleeding land," and said that Caledonia ought to blush for having brought into the world the "dull spoiler" who was responsible. These angry sentiments reappeared in *The Curse of Minerva*.

The friends who urged him to hold back the lesser satires and move forward with the publication of *Childe Harold* were probably wiser than he. Regency London was ready to lionize the still youthful poet, and the romantic figure of Harold, widely recognized as a projection of Byron himself, was the prime agent in the lionization process. The poem opens as if it were going to be a Gothic romaunt, colored if not governed by medieval archaisms. But it is soon evident that the exotic rather than the Gothic will engage him, as Harold starts his journey through Portugal and Spain, moving ever toward the Middle East, known in Byron's time as the Levant. The magical place names, both classical and modern, chime through all the stanzas from Albion to Lisboa, from Cadiz to Zitza, Illyria, Calpe, Yanina, Lesbos, and Ithaca, Dodona and Tomerit, as if to remind the reader of the far away and the long ago, those inseparable constituents of romantic nostalgia, the emotion that predominates in Harold's restless passage from scene to scene and country to country.

Although Byron half-heartedly denied autobiographical intent in his portrayal of his hero, the resemblance was unmistakable.

> Whilome in Albion's isle there dwelt a youth
> Who ne in virtue's ways did take delight;
> But spent his days in riot most uncouth,
> And vex'd with mirth the drowsy ear of night . . .
> Few earthly things found favor in his sight
> Save concubines and carnal companie . . .
>
> Apart he stalk'd in joyless reverie,
> And from his native land resolved to go,
> And visit scorching climes beyond the sea;
> With pleasure drugg'd, he almost longed for woe,
> And e'en for change of scene would seek the shades
>   below.

This strong desire for change of scene is the major driving force in Harold's quest. There were plenty of other scorching climates besides that of Hell; each of them promised fresh experiences, antidotes to ennui, tacit invitations to philosophic reflection. Although Harold is said to have taken no special pleasure "in themes of bloody fray, or gallant fight," he sometimes lingers over "scenes of vanish'd war" like those of Actium, Lepanto, and Trafalgar, making ironic commentaries on the vanity of martial wishes. He surveys the vast and naked plain of Talavera, where three nations once came to combat, "as if at home they could not die," and left their dead to feed the crows and "fertilize the field that each pretends to gain." This is close to Hamlet's observation on the warriors of Fortinbras, "that for a fantasy and trick of fame go to their graves like beds, fight for a plot . . . which is not tomb enough and continent to hide the slain." Yet Harold clearly admires the heroic conduct of ancient men of action, "as on the morn to distant Glory dear, when Marathon became a magic word." Gallantry of a nonmilitary kind attracts him to the Spanish bullfight, eliciting a dozen lively stanzas on a typical *corrida* from the opening promenade of the toreros to the killing of the bull, an emotional climax to the first "fytte" of Harold's pilgrimage, like the tribute to the vanished splendors of Greece that rounds out the second.

Childe Harold, the incurable romantic, performs the customary genuflections before the shrine of nature in both its aspects, awesome and serene. "There is," he says, "a pleasure in the pathless woods," and he pauses wherever possible to hold "converse with Nature's charms" standing in sunlight amid rural scenery. Yet he has to confess that he has "loved her best in wrath," for she seems "fairest in her features wild"— like the cataract of Velino, a "hell of waters . . . horribly beautiful," or the threatening avalanche, "the thunderbolt of snow" among the higher Alps. His habitual gaze is upward— "where rose the mountains, there to him were friends," or beyond them to the stars, which he calls "the poetry of heaven." In his melancholy moods, which are legion, he consoles himself with the recognition that when Art or Glory or Freedom fail us, "Nature still is there"—*natura naturans* in perpetuity—and that his soul, however beleaguered, can always "mingle with the sky, the peak, the heaving plain of ocean," each of them an ultimate in natural grandeur.

In the final pair of cantos, composed respectively in 1816 and 1817, Harold's fast-moving odyssey carries him to Belgium, the Rhineland, Switzerland, and Italy. Byron was particularly proud of canto three which he called "a fine indistinct piece of practical desolation." He said that while putting it together in Switzerland he had been half-mad with "metaphysics, mountains, lakes, love unextinguishable, thoughts unutterable, and the nightmare of [his] own delinquencies." Out of this same congeries of thought and emotion came his lyrical drama, *Manfred*, a blank verse Gothic tragedy, partly Faustian and partly personal, with Byron and his half-sister Augusta as approximations of Manfred and his lost Astarte. Like Manfred, this later Harold is still the "outlaw of his own dark mind," his spirit "wrung with wounds that kill not but ne'er heal," and his ego inflexibly critical of superior power. Like Hamlet, he has "that within that passeth show," including a fierce hatred of murderous tyranny such as Napoleon had spread across the face of Europe.

Since the publication of the earlier cantos, a new Golgotha had come into being. As Byron himself had done less than a year after Napoleon's final defeat, Harold was made to stand upon that "place of skulls . . . the deadly Waterloo." The famous set piece narrative that begins, "There was a sound of revelry by night," establishes a dramatic opposition between the duchess of Richmond's ball in Brussels on the eve of the conflict and the nearby scene at the village of Waterloo after the battle, when the earth was "cover'd thick with other clay, which her own clay shall cover."

Over this bloody ground hung the spectre of the fallen emperor. Byron had once exclaimed that it was "impossible not to be dazzled and overwhelmed" by Bonaparte's "character and career." But in his "Ode to Napoleon," written soon after the abdication and exile of 1814, he had taunted "the Desolator desolate" whose "hero dust" was "vile as vulgar clay," and contrasted him with the great apostle of republican freedom, General George Washington, "the Cincinnatus of the West." In canto one of *Childe Harold* he attacked Napoleon as "Gaul's vulture," and in canto four would call him "a kind of bastard Caesar" overcome by personal vanity. In place of such epithets canto three attempted to anatomize the erstwhile emperor, calling him "neither the greatest nor the worst of men," but rather a spirit "antithetically mixt . . . extreme in all things," a leader who never learned that "tempted Fate will leave the loftiest star," or that any dictator "who surpasses and subdues mankind must look down on the hate of those below."

The chief literary heroes of canto three, with each of whom Byron could claim a brotherhood of sorts, were Rousseau, Voltaire, and Gibbon, the first for his celebration of romantic love, the second for his skill in destruction through ridicule, the third as the supreme "lord of irony" among eighteenth-century historians. Byron had long admired the *History of the Decline and Fall of the Roman Empire*, even recommending it to his wife before the break-up of their abortive marriage. It would appear that he was at least partly indebted to Gibbon for the *ubi sunt* motif, one of the strongest recurrent elements in *Childe Harold's Pilgrimage*. "Where have they gone?" was Harold's perennial question, to which he offered a series of dusty answers: "All, all forgotten . . . Swept into wrecks by Time's ungentle tide . . . Dim with the mist of years, gray flits the shade of power . . . Time hath reft whate'er my soul enjoy'd." One final echo of *ubi sunt* closed canto four on a note of rhetorical grandeur with Byron's paean to the ocean, which, like the mountains, the sky, and the stars, was a dependable constant in a world of perpetual change and decay:

Roll on, thou deep and dark blue Ocean—roll!
Ten thousand fleets sweep over thee in vain;
Man marks the earth with ruin—his control

Stops with the shore; upon the watery plain
The wrecks are all thy deed, nor doth remain
A shadow of man's ravage . . .
Thy shores are empires, changed in all save thee—
Assyria, Greece, Rome, Carthage, what are they?
Thy waters wash'd them power while they were free,
And many a tyrant since; their shores obey
The stranger, slave, or savage . . . not so thou,
Unchangeable, save to thy wild waves' play,
Time writes no wrinkle on thine azure brow:
Such as creation's dawn beheld, thou rollest now.

Having read canto three, the poet's estranged wife Anna-
bella made the astute observation that Byron was "the ab-
solute monarch of words," who used them, "as Bonaparte
did *lives*, for conquest, without more regard to their intrinsic
value." Despite the faults of *Childe Harold*—its architectonic
imperfections, its frequent divagations in which the hero drops
out of sight, its too great diversity of subject matter, its ex-
cessive dependence on the merely adventitious in each phase
of the hero's peregrinations, its failure to show any significant
development in the character of Harold himself—the poem
remains surprisingly forceful nearly two centuries after its first
appearance. That it does not hang together as well as it might
have is probably the result of Byron's habit of scribbling out
his stanzas on separate scraps of paper to be assembled at his
later leisure. If he was indeed the absolute monarch of words,
his rank as a strategist of form must fall considerably lower.

AFTER HIS long engagement with the Byronic hero, and
even as he was completing in Venice the fourth and fare-
well canto of *Childe Harold*, Byron's satirical impulses were
again coming to the fore. He had once called individual man
"a pendulum betwixt a smile and tear." Despite seven years'
immersion in the *lacrimae rerum* of Harold, he had never
forgotten the saving grace of laughter and its brace of jolly

henchmen, wit and humor. As the poetic pendulum swung back toward this extremity, the spirit of Rousseau was ready to give place to that of Voltaire, of whose works Byron had recently purchased a complete set in ninety-two volumes.

At about the same time he had discovered the virtues of the ottava rima stanza. Its rhyme scheme of ABABABCC enabled the skilled practitioner to build up the reader's expectations through half a dozen lines only to follow with a couplet that, as James Russell Lowell said, could put on the brakes with a jar that made one's teeth ache. The tactic was quite different from that of the Spenserian stanza with its down-cushion of the alexandrine, for the clever poet could begin the stanza with every appearance of serious intent and then practice what Pope had called *Peri Bathous*, or the art of sinking in poetry, tumbling the reader from presumptive grandeur into the bathetic. A latter-day Englishman and a fifteenth-century Italian inadvertently conspired to acquaint Byron with the ottava rima and its power for comic catharsis. John Hookham Frere had recently brought out a mock-epic narrative, *The Monks and the Giants*, an imitation of Luigi Pulci's *Morgante Maggiore*. Both poems, in the words of Byron's best modern biographer, Leslie A. Marchand, "rambled with colloquial ease over diverse subjects, incidents, and characters," which, as it happened, was exactly the planless plan that Byron wished to follow.

His first practice poem in the genre was slight enough, little more than an expansion of an anecdote he had heard from a Venetian draper, Pietro Segati, whose young wife Marianna was a frequent occupant of Byron's bed. He had little trouble devising ninety-nine octaves on the misadventures of Laura, an "Adriatic Ariadne" whose husband Giuseppe (called Beppo, as the poem was) vanished at sea only to return unexpectedly after she had taken up with a *cavalier servente*, a social term that Byron loosely and perhaps punningly translated as "vice-husband." The poet said that his new departure would at any rate prove to the public that he could write "cheerfully" and thus "repel the charge of monotony and mannerism" in his recent work. At play among his ingenious rhymes, and being often led by them well away from his main story line, Byron came close to making his spontaneous improvisations into a minor work of art. Less than half the poem related to the marital triangle of husband, wife, and lover. "Devil take it!" cries the narrator, "this story slips for ever through my fingers." Yet he managed, in the end, to make of it a gentle satire on the sexual hypocrisies of Venetian society as he knew them from actual experience, an approach to Venice quite different from that of the fourth canto of *Childe Harold* which opened with the hero—still Byron Agonistes—standing ruminant upon the Bridge of Sighs.

His self-imposed expatriation in Italy was a strong catalyst to his poetic productivity. Although he called Venice "the greenest island of my imagination," his notable fluency continued through his later residence in Ravenna, Pisa, and Genoa. From the time he leased the Palazzo Mocenigo on the Grand Canal in 1818 until his departure for Greece from Genoa five years later, his writing hand was rarely idle. This was the period during which the sixteen cantos of *Don Juan* and the 106 stanzas of *The Vision of Judgment* were composed. Yet Byron by no means devoted all his teeming energies to satire. Apart from such soufflés as *Beppo* and "The Blues," an amusing literary eclogue in playlet form on the tensions, hypertensions, and pretensions of learned women, he finished and brought to publication serious poems on Dante and Tasso, the Polish officer Ivan Mazeppa, whose heroic history he owed to Voltaire, and seven blank verse dramas, on subjects both philosophical and political. He returned to the heroic couplet and to the phenomenon of Napoleon's rise and fall in the late satire *The Age of Bronze*; and in *The Island* he told the story of mutiny on the *Bounty* more than a century before its modern retelling by Nordhoff and Hall and the subsequent dramatization which stamped Captain Bligh henceforth with the features of Charles Laughton.

Always excepting *Don Juan*, his best satire in the closing years was *The Vision of Judgment*, composed late in 1821, half a parody of Robert Southey's poem of the same title in which Byron's longtime enemy had commemorated the death and beatification of the mad old King George III. But the "spavin'd dactyls"—rather like Longfellow's Hiawatha on crutches—by which Southey had fulfilled his manifest duty as Poet Laureate, gave way in Byron's ottava rima stanzas to a side-splitting account of the consternation caused in heaven by the simultaneous arrival of the king and his laureate—one safely dead and the other at least moribund after much witty manhandling. "Ridicule," said Byron in another connection, was "the only weapon that the English climate cannot rust"— and he proved his point in what was probably the cleverest travesty in the English language.

He had already resumed his earlier attack on "the Lakers" in the dedication to the first canto of *Don Juan*, datelined from Venice, 16 September 1818, and calling Southey "my Epic Renegade," mocking Coleridge for the German metaphysics in the *Biographia Literaria*, and ridiculing Wordsworth for the length and impenetrability of *The Excursion*.*

If Wordsworth had not made this title his own, it might have served Byron for his own "renegade epic," whose hero was just then beginning an international excursion of far greater length and liveliness than that of the poet he called "Wordswords." He said that his aim was "to show things as they really are" by sending Juan "wandering with pedestrian muses" among the mazes of modern life. His adventures would eventually embrace both adultery and romantic love, shipwreck, a slave market, the interior of a Turkish seraglio, war between the Russians and the Turks, the court and boudoir of "Russia's royal harlot," Catherine the Great, and at last the country seats of British nobility, on which Byron gleefully (and wastefully) expended the final cantos. The whole was to extend to nearly 17,000 lines of verse, roughly twice the size of Words-

---

* Begun in July 1818, *Don Juan* was published piecemeal between 1819 and 1824, the year Byron died at Missolonghi. Before death intervened, he had completed fourteen stanzas of Canto 17. The "dedication" to Canto 1 was suppressed before publication, to be resurrected much later.

worth's *Excursion*, which Byron in canto three described as
"a drowsy, frowzy poem, writ in a manner that is my aver-
sion."

The "two states of existence" that Byron mentioned to Lady
Blessington were faithfully embodied in the poem, which was
filled with the faults and follies, and often the crimes, of un-
regenerate mankind, even as the young hero played his part
in the drama of real life, "discovering error without the power
of avoiding it," apparently impelled by forces, both social and
psychological, over which he exerted minimal control. In the
fashionable modern critical parlance, Juan has been called an
antihero. Byron did not think so. "If you must have an epic,"
he wrote Tom Medwin, "there's my *Don Juan* for you. It is
an epic as much in the spirit of our day as the *Iliad* was in
Homer's. There is no want of Parises and Menelauses. . . . In
the very first canto you have a Helen. Then, I shall make my
hero a perfect Achilles for fighting."

> My poem's epic, and is meant to be
> Divided in twelve books; each book containing,
> With love and war, a heavy gale at sea,
> A list of ships, and captains, and kings reigning . . .
> After the style of Virgil and of Homer,
> So that my name of Epic's no misnomer.

> There's only one slight difference between
> Me and my epic brethren gone before,
> And here the advantage is my own, I ween . . .
> They so embellish, that 'tis quite a bore
> Their labyrinth of fables to thread through,
> Whereas this story's actually true.

Don Juan somewhat resembles the classical epics, and es-
pecially the *Odyssey*, in its subject matter of love, war, and
adventure on the high seas, and the Haidée episode has some-
thing in common with Odysseus' encounter with Nausicaa.
In this modern narrative, however, religion has no vital part
to play, one finds no supernatural dimension, and we are

spared pagan fables about the intercession of jealous or protective gods into human affairs. "You have so many 'divine' poems," Byron told his publisher, "is it nothing to have written a *Human* one, without any of your worn-out machinery?"

Rather disingenuously, he complained in canto four that the wings of his imagination had gone flaccid and that "The sad truth which hovers o'er my desk / Turns what was once romantic to burlesque." Yet this statement, apparently so forthright, is neither exact nor trustworthy. Broad bands of burlesque appear at convenient intervals, but they are commonly and intentionally placed side by side with passages of sentimental romanticism in something close to the tone and spirit of *Childe Harold's Pilgrimage*. So, for example, the touching death of Haidée, along with that of the child she might have borne to Don Juan, is succeeded by the cynical account of the Turkish slave market, where Baba buys Juan to serve as bedmate to the imperious sultaness, Gulbeyaz.

The success of *Harold* had no doubt revealed to Byron the procedural virtues of the journey-as-plot. *Don Juan* emerges as a kind of picaresque novel-in-verse, as if the adventures of Don Quixote or Tom Jones or Peregrine Pickle had been jovially translated into ottava rimas. The poem is also, though less certainly, a sort of *Bildungsroman*, where each episode represents a step in the experiential education, if not the actual growth and development, of the hero. Like Voltaire's Candide, Juan is successively disillusioned, although he has never apparently believed that all is for the best in the best of all possible worlds. There is little in his pilgrimage to prove the wisdom of such an optimistic philosophy, although he does survive through sixteen cantos.

If he seems to be more acted upon than acting—a point that Wordsworth made about Coleridge's ancient mariner—he nevertheless stands out as an exponent of personal freedom in an uncertain world. Even though he is constantly being pushed around, he remains for the most part a stoical free agent, he is notably resilient and rarely baffled, and his character infuses the poem with a considerable vitality, a gusto at least equal to that of Keats, and a quality of indefatigability that from first to last carries him, though not without damage, over many of the paths that Byron himself had followed. "Almost all *Don Juan* is *real* life," was Byron's boast to John Murray, "either my own or from people I knew." He said that he detested "all fiction even in song," that even the most "airy fabric" must have "some foundation in fact" and that "pure invention" was "but the talent of a liar."

Sometimes Byron was obliged to invent, as when Juan's adventures carried him into realms like the sultan's seraglio in Constantinople, or the besieged city of Ismail at the mouth of the Danube, or the court of Catherine in Petersburg. Even in the rollicking midst of his grand tour of 1809-1811, Byron himself had never been unwise enough to penetrate Ali Pasha's harem, or any of its inhabitants. His frolicsome account of the night Juan spent, arrayed in women's clothes and "false long tresses," in the company of the girlish odalisques Lolah, Katinka, and Dudù, is accordingly "pure" invention, inimitably accomplished. Later on, in coming to portray the siege of Ismail in cantos seven and eight, having himself been only an infant at the time of the actual battle on All Hallows Eve 1790, he chose as his immediate source book a history of Russia by the Marquis de Castelnau. Juan's rescue of the child Leila from the smoking sabres of the Cossacks was based on a real-life incident in which the young duc de Richelieu, serving with the Russians, saved a small girl's life in a somewhat similar fashion. Byron's scene is very touching, like that of the fathers and their dead sons in the shipwreck episodes of canto two. But he was ready, as always, with a strong antidote to the lingering savors of sentiment. Only a few stanzas later, we find him sardonically expatiating on the curious asceticism of the Russian army after the fall of the city:

> The topic's tender, so shall be my phrase—
> Perhaps the season's chill, and their long station
> In winter's depth, or want of rest and victual,
> Had made them chaste;—they ravished very little . . .

[And] all the ladies, save some twenty score,
Were almost as much virgins as before . . .
Some voices of the buxom middle-aged
Were also heard to wonder in the din
(Widows of forty were those birds long caged)
"Wherefore the ravishing did not begin!"

In this way, beginning with Leila and the soft emotions attendant on her timely escape from what must have been certain death, Byron turns to hard satiric laughter over the connections and disconnections between Mars and Venus. As so often in the poem, Byron's Doppelgänger is operative in yet another reductive contrast.

As Yeats was to discover in using ottava rima for serious poetry, the closing couplet of the octave need not be used for satiric reversal. During his experimentation with upwards of two thousand stanzas, Byron found that many variations were possible. One notable example is the deathbed scene of Haidée:

Twelve days and nights she withered thus; at last
Without a groan, or sigh, or glance, to show
A parting pang, the spirit from her passed:
And they who watched her nearest could not know
The very instant, till the change that cast
Her sweet face into shadow, dull and slow,
Glazed o'er her eyes—the beautiful, the black—
Oh! to possess such lustre–and then lack!

The play on the word *lacklustre* in the final line could be interpreted as a defiant attempt on Byron's part to redeem the stanza from too abundant an expression of powerful emotion. Once it has been noticed, the pun produces a damming effect. For it is the office of all dams to say, in effect, "this far, no farther," and the final sharp monosyllable, ending the word play, induces just such a reaction in the reader.

A nearby stanza proves Byron's skill with the "romantic," nonsatirical use of the ottava rima. In this one he returns, following Haidée's death, to the *ubi sunt* motif that had appeared so often in *Childe Harold*. With some slight tinkering, the lines could easily be converted to the Spenserian form and assume a rightful place among the most memorable stanzas in the earlier poem. Its effect is in any case much the same, since it rings with what Shelley called the "sad autumnal tone" most suitable to its subject:

> That isle is now all desolate and bare,
> Its dwellings down, its tenants passed away;
> None but her own and Father's grave is there,
> And nothing outward tells of human clay;
> Ye could not know where lies a thing so fair,
> No stone is there to show, no tongue to say,
> What was; no dirge, except the hollow sea's,
> Mourns o'er the beauty of the Cyclades.

The device of satiric reversal is, however, far more nearly typical in *Don Juan*. Another seascape is a classic of its kind, building up the immense and rolling grandeur of the Black Sea and then accomplishing a sudden homely descent to the condition of the seafarer whom the turbulence compels to lean over the ship's rail:

> The wind swept down the Euxine, and the wave
> Broke foaming o'er the blue Symplegades;
> 'Tis a grand sight from off 'the Giant's Grave'
> To watch the progress of those rolling seas
> Between the Bosphorus, as they lash and lave
> Europe and Asia, you being quite at ease:
> There's not a sea the passenger e'er pukes in,
> Turns up more dangerous breakers than the Euxine.

Throughout *Don Juan*, as had happened also in *Childe Harold's Pilgrimage*, Byron's personal opinions and commentaries often intrude upon the straightforward march of his narrative, rising up to overshadow, at least temporarily, the toiling image of his young adventurer. One of Byron's terms for these digressions was "ponderings," a word capacious enough to accommodate half-serious philosophizing; instances of verbal sedition against the great enemy he called Cant; the purging away of shibboleths or factional watchwords; *ad hominem* attacks on pseudovillains like Southey or true villains like Robert Stewart, Viscount Castlereagh, who cut his throat in 1822 and elicited thereby the most scatalogical of Byron's epitaphs; comic exegeses of current events; brilliant esthetic observations thrown out along the way with seeming carelessness, and so on through a list of topics that has an end only because the poem does.

This digressive habit becomes especially noticeable once Byron has got his hero into England during the final cantos. Very little of any consequence happens to Juan in these sequences, and it may be that Byron's narrative imagination had begun, in his words, to droop its pinion. It is far too late to suggest that these "ponderings" might with profit be edited out. The poem without them would not be the poem it is, much as Melville's *Moby-Dick*, minus the metaphysical musings of Ishmael and Ahab, would be little more than a magnificent adventure story of the American whaling industry. Yet *Don Juan* does tend to unravel when Byron as Byron abandons his narrative obligations in the name of "ponderings" and fails for long stretches to carry his readers back to the zigzag track of Juan's "wanderings."

With this view of the poem, W. H. Auden did not agree. Since he was, among twentieth-century poets, the sturdiest admirer of Byron as comic writer and more than shared his predecessor's wit, his skill with rhyming, his capacity for verbal prestidigitation, and his virtual kingship over the domain of language, Auden's opinions are worth taking into account. He hails Byron's achievements in *Beppo, The Vision of Judgment,* and *Don Juan.* For the rest, he finds little to praise: "a few lyrics . . . two adequate satires . . . a few charming occasional pieces, half a dozen stanzas from *Childe Harold,* half a dozen lines from *Cain,* and that is all."

The centerpiece of Auden's essay is *Don Juan,* and to Auden, Juan himself seems "the least interesting figure" in the poem.

> His passivity is all the more surprising when one recalls the legendary monster of depravity after whom he is named. ... Far from being a defiant rebel against the laws of God and man, his most conspicuous trait is his gift for social conformity. ... Wherever chance takes him, to a pirate's lair, a harem in Mohammedan Constantinople, a court in Greek Orthodox Russia, a country house in Protestant England, he immediately adapts himself and is accepted as an agreeable fellow.

Now it is true that, unlike his legendary namesake, Byron's Juan is no monster of depravity, sexual or otherwise. It is also true that he proves his adaptability in a great variety of situations, many of them fraught with physical danger. If he is passive, where—one might ask—is a more active hero to be found? His "gift for social conformity" more often than not saves his neck, as in the Mohammedan harem. That he should be generally accepted as "an agreeable fellow"—though not by Donna Julia's fierce old husband, Don Alfonso, in canto one, not by the thirsty shipmates whom he stands off in canto two as they attempt to raid the grog room, not by Lambro, Haidée's piratical father in canto three—is something in his favor rather than the reverse. His character is well summarized by Byron himself, who says of Juan early on that "he did the best he could with things not very subject to control," including boyish lust, romantic love, tempestuous seas, and a hundred other temptations and tribulations.

Auden approvingly quotes Byron's boast: "It may be profligate, but is it not life, is it not the *thing*?" He goes on to say that "what Byron means by life ... is the motion of life, the passage of events and thoughts. ... At the description of things in motion or the way in which the mind wanders from one thought to another he is a great master." If this is true, then Don Juan, the hero, is perhaps the best embodiment of "things in motion," while Byron himself, as commentator and chorus, masterfully proves not only how the mind wanders from one thought to another but also how engaging a process it is to follow that mercurial spirit through its peregrinations— so long, that is, as they do not spoil the story.

Another of Auden's opinions is that Don Juan as a character seems to be "a daydream of what Byron would have liked to be himself." But he believes that such daydreams can be dull, except possibly to the dreamer, and that "if Byron had written *Don Juan* as a straightforward narrative in the style of *The Corsair* or *Lara*, it would probably have been unreadable. Fortunately, he had discovered a genre in poetry which allows the author to enter the story he is telling. Juan is only a convenience; the real hero of the poem is Byron himself."

This argument, while of great interest because of its source, is not without certain flaws. Much of *Don Juan* is a "straightforward narrative poem"—though happily not in the style of *The Corsair* or its sequel, as anyone can tell who reads those early metrical romances. Further, Byron did not really "enter the story he was telling." His voice was often audible, even insistently so, but he never participated as a character in the action. His role was that of commentator, a one-man Greek chorus, who observed the game from the grandstand and, like many another spectator, before and since, offered his views on its significance. It is finally doubtful that Juan was "a daydream of what Byron would have liked to be himself." If there is an overlap between the two, it is because the author placed his protagonist in locales and situations that he knew personally from having been there or invented freely on the basis of stories heard from others, whether by word of mouth or through books like de Castelnau's. The Byron of the poem is much like the Byron of the personal letters, talking, talking—with much worldly wisdom and lively wit and pungency of phrasing—but talking away like one possessed, as indeed he was, by the sound of his own voice.

The strong impact he exerted on the imagination of his age could not have been owing solely to his adventures at home and abroad, his social reputation, which in England was none of the best, or his ideology, which is of greater interest than is commonly understood. It was above all the force of his double-bladed personality, gleaming out through the inimitable language of his poetry and incarnated in his chief heroes, Harold and Juan, that made him a power to be reckoned with long after his death and even led Matthew Arnold to praise him in the very midst of a eulogy for Wordsworth. Through the dozen years that remained to him after the sudden and remarkable success of the first two cantos of *Childe Harold*, through his dizzy plunge into obloquy and his gradual ascension to almost universal fame, he continued to insist that his only muse was "the simple truth." In this respect he at least remotely resembles Sir Isaac Newton, who once said—and Byron quotes the words with wondering approval—that he felt "like a youth, picking up shells by the great ocean—Truth." His persistent desire was to explore, not the starry universe of Newton, but the whole texture of human life, his own included, and to tell the world about the world it had been given him to know. In this aim he evidently succeeded.

News of his death at Missolonghi "came upon London like an earthquake." People could not believe that death had so soon undone him. In 1816 he had left the metropolis under a cloud. Now in 1824 he returned to it in a cask of spirits, to lie in sunken state in Great George Street while the curious crowded round for a final glimpse of the poet whom Regency London had at first panegyrized and then driven into permanent exile. He had predicted this final moment in *Childe Harold's Pilgrimage*:

> My mind may lose its force, my blood its fire,
> And my frame perish even in conquering pain;
> But there is that within me which shall tire
> Torture and Time, and breathe when I expire.

Despite the addition of another century between Byron's age and ours, Torture and Time still show no signs of fatigue. But then, on the record, neither does Byron.

P. B. Shelley

❦ "HAD YOU never heard of Shelley?" said Mr. Bons to the boy in E. M. Forster's "Celestial Omnibus." Hanging his head, the boy said no. "But is there no Shelley in the house?" The boy's mother rose to the question. "Dear Mr. Bons, we aren't such Philistines as that. Two at the least. One a wedding present, and the other, smaller print, in one of the spare rooms." Mr. Bons smiled. "I believe," said he, "we have seven Shelleys."

Mr. Bons's figure was correct. The wedding present Shelley and the spare room Shelley may safely be ignored. But there are at least seven others who are worth paying some attention to: the radical reformer, the classical Hellenist, the romantic humanist, the lyricist, the philosophical poet, the tragedian of human corruption, and the unorthodox theist, as "god-intoxicated" as the German mystic Novalis, but even more firmly grounded in a hard-won idealistic system of thought.

With the possible exceptions of Blake and William Hazlitt, Shelley was the most consistent radical in the English romantic movement. His reforming zeal earned him the distrust of reactionary elements in the Regency period and the admiration of such Olympian revolutionaries of his own and later times as Byron and Bernard Shaw. *Queen Mab*, the earliest of his long poems, reflects his devotion to books like William Godwin's *Political Justice* and Holbach's atheistic and materialistic treatise, the *Système de la Nature*. With fierce youthful enthusiasm, Shelley embraced a majority of the religious and secular heresies which nineteenth-century Englishmen inherited from their "enlightened" forebears in England and France. The poem thunders ominously against the worship of Jehovah, who for Shelley is a figure comparable to Blake's Nobodaddy. The poet stridently opposes the Christian Church, its dogmas, its priesthood, and its historical record. On the secular side, his catalog of evils includes war, slavery, wealth, prostitution, commerce, and custom. Like much of his later poetry, *Queen Mab* cries out against the tyranny of all earthly kings whatsoever. But through the educated optimism of the prophetic fairy queen, Shelley also anticipates a future historic time when the lion will lie down with the lamb and the infant can safely undertake games beside the den of the cockatrice. Assuming man's possible perfectibility once he has overthrown his literally enthralling institutions, he sums up his program in Voltaire's directive: "Ecrasez l'infâme." The poet of *Queen Mab* would make the world safe for the millennium through the removal of all environmental infamies. After that, in another phrase of Voltaire's, "il faut cultiver notre jardin."

From 1814 onward, though Shelley's reforming purposes remained as strong as ever, his tone altered, and his didacticism became less oppressive. Although he still gladly assumed the moral duty of reminding men of what they might be, his hopes for the wholesale overturn of existing social institutions became less sanguine. *The Revolt of Islam*, his longest and least successful poem, is an idealized allegory of the French Revolution in which two rebel leaders named Laon and Cythna nearly succeed in converting Islam to a new order where the social law of love prevails. Their martyrdom, inevitable under the present political dispensation, shows that the world will not be ready to receive such saints until it can reform itself from the inside out.

To provide an outline of this process of internal revolution, for mankind's moral edification, is the central problem of Shelley's lyrical drama on the Titan. The point of *Prometheus Unbound*, like that of T. S. Eliot's latter-day *Waste Land*, is that when love fails all is lost unless love can be revived.

106

Chained to his lonely rock in the Caucasus, Prometheus is an image for man's mind enslaved to hatred and fear and tortured by all the ills that mentality is heir to. The furies that harass Prometheus are cousins-german to those in Eliot's *Family Reunion*, though they move across a lonely mountainside instead of hiding behind the drawing room curtains. Indeed it is a kind of family reunion—of the mind of man with the principle of divine love—toward which Shelley's heroic drama steadily moves. Only the elimination of Jupiter, the hate principle, can prepare the way for Prometheus' reunion with Asia, the love principle, and unbind the mind of man from the three-thousand-year thralldom that he has imposed upon himself. Blake had a phrase for the chains of Prometheus: in his angry lyric, "London," he called them "mind-forged manacles." But neither Blake nor Shelley supposed that so miraculous an about-face on the part of man was in immediate or even predictable prospect. Behind the insistent hopefulness of Shelley's drama, the conditional *IF* bulks large as life. He is not so much proclaiming that man is free as he is setting forth the only conditions under which genuine freedom is to be attained. "IF," in a word, is another name for the double-edged "law of Demogorgon." If the mind of man, now conditionally purged, should again allow hate to assume supremacy, Jupiter will reassert his dominion, and the chains will once again clamp Prometheus to his lonely rock.

Shelley's broadly ethical consideration of the problem of human welfare in *Prometheus Unbound* did not mean, of course, that he had abandoned his post as watchdog of European liberty. From popular hymns like his revisionist version of "God Save the King" to the carefully argued prose of his *Philosophical View of Reform*, Shelley's later political works were all occasional. The occasions were those on which he thought he saw liberty threatened, liberty destroyed, or liberty triumphant. He had early resolved to cry down oppression and to salute all positive acts of reform or revolution in the Europe of his time. *The Masque of Anarchy* is a popular allegory on the infamous Peterloo massacre, where mounted

dragoons bloodily broke up a workers' rally outside the manu-
facturing city of Manchester. *Swellfoot the Tyrant* amusingly
combines Sophocles and Aristophanes with Punch and Judy
in a satire on the marital misadventures of George IV and his
hapless Queen Caroline. On the positive side, one may count
the "Ode to Liberty," celebrating the Spanish popular revo-
lution of 1820, or the "Ode to Naples," Shelley's salute to
the Neapolitan uprising against Austrian rule. In *Hellas*, as
in these serious odes, the poet assumed the high style of *Pro-
metheus Unbound* and the generic form of the *Persae* of Aes-
chylus to praise the modern Greeks for their attempt to throw
off Turkish domination in that painfully misrun revolution
which claimed Byron's life in 1824. For Shelley the nineteenth-
century political outlook was dark but not hopeless. Whatever
poetry could do to enlarge the hope or dispel the darkness he
set himself to accomplish. He would never for more than a
moment have agreed with Auden's dictum that "poetry makes
nothing happen."

HIS TASK was not so hard as it might have been if he had
lacked a model. Luckily, he carried in his mind's eye, and used
as an instrument of measurement on all things modern, a
blueprint of earthly perfection as embodied in that ancient
City of Light, Athens in the age of Pericles. If Keats had
traveled widely in imaginary realms of gold where Homer
ruled, Shelley as classical Hellenist could have written a full-
length Baedeker on the intellectual life of Greece from Homer
to Aristotle. Incessant reading in the original language, cou-
pled with close study of classical models at school, at college,
and during his "Attic winter" with Hogg and Peacock, had
made him a respectable Hellenist even in a time when these
were far more numerous, on a per capita basis, than they are
today. He undertook extensive translations from the dialogues
of Plato. He "imitated" Aeschylus, Sophocles, and Aristoph-
anes. He took Socrates as one of his heroes. He set down
eloquent descriptive notes on the Greek sculptures in Florence,

grew ecstatic over the stonework of Phidias, and saw his earthly paradise enhanced with "Praxitelean shapes."

In the fresh classical revival that followed that of neoclassicism and is one of the distinguishing events of the romantic age, Shelley's role is therefore significant. Few of his contemporary poets knew the civilization of ancient Greece as well as he. Sometimes, as in the celebrated closing chorus of *Hellas*, he invests the rugged old peninsula and the waters round it with a dreamlike quality. But this is the result of excessive love rather than the idyllic ignorance of the amateur. "What the Greeks were," he cried, "was a reality, not a promise." He deeply believed that modern Europe owed all the best that it was or could hope to be to "the influence and inspiration of those glorious generations."

What the "holy city of Byzantium" was for William Butler Yeats, the Athenian city-state was for Shelley. Here, in defiance of the weathering of time, stood the "monuments of unageing intellect." Here lived in perpetuity the philosopher-kings of a nobler civilization. Yeats's image for the flux of things, "the dolphin-torn, the gong-tormented sea," is perhaps remotely comparable to Shelley's "tide of war" in one of the semichourses of *Hellas*. For like Byzantium,

> Greece and her foundations are
> Built below the tide of war,
> Based on the crystalline sea
> Of thought and its eternity;
> Her citizens, imperial spirits,
> Rule the present from the past;
> On all this world of men inherits
> Their seal is set.

Much of the esthetic behind Yeats's best and strongest poetry is summarized in the Byzantium lyrics; Shelley's own esthetic position is well illustrated in what he says of the literature of ancient Greece. "Homer embodied the ideal perfection of [infant Greece] in human character; nor can we doubt that those who read his verses were awakened to an

ambition of becoming like to Achilles, Hector, and Ulysses.
. . . The sentiments of the auditors must have been refined
and enlarged by a sympathy with such great and lovely im-
personations, until from admiring they imitated, and from
imitation they identified themselves with the objects of their
admiration." In the time of the great Greek tragedians, this
process was accelerated. The works of Aeschylus and Sopho-
cles are "as mirrors in which the spectator beholds himself
. . . stripped of all but that ideal perfection and energy which
everyone feels to be the internal type of all that he loves,
admires, and would become." This esthetic process—the
awakening and enlargement of sympathetic perception, the
growing desire (at once ethical and emotional) to imitate, and
the willed development of imitation to the stage of self-iden-
tification—lies at the foundation of all Shelley's visionary po-
etry. Yeats understood the matter perfectly, and counted him-
self among Shelley's followers.

Shelley's nearly absolute devotion to the Hellenic ideal for
man is an indication of the extent of his romantic humanism.
Though he was always the champion of the oppressed against
the oppressors and consistently supported the theoretical right
of the people to self-government, he had little faith in the
dependability of the common man. Such faith, indeed, was
rare in his country and his time. But uncommon man, man
as moral leader, man as philosopher-king, man as poet-thinker
claimed his veneration and his allegiance. Not men in general,
but deep-browed men like Socrates and Plato, Shakespeare
and Spenser, were worthy of being described, in the famous
phrase of Protagoras, as "the measure of all things."

He always revered true greatness; it was his conception of
what was great that changed subtly as he matured. As a youth
under the intellectual dominance of the Enlightenment, he was
seduced by the materialistic doctrine of necessitarianism, as
naturalistic a philosophy as any we know today. According
to this doctrine, mind is a function of matter, and man is
inexorably controlled, whether he knows it or not, by the
same laws that govern the material universe. In the early pam-

phlet, *A Refutation of Deism*, one of the disputants flatly asserts that "the laws of motion and the properties of matter suffice to account for every phenomenon, or combination of phenomena" in the knowable world. But Shelley could not long pay more than intellectual lip service to a position so thoroughly opposed to his native and temperamental idealism. By 1818, and probably before that, he had completely reversed his field of vision. Now he vigorously asserted the priority of mind over matter, urging his good friend Maria Gisborne to accept a kind of optimism "in which we are our own gods." In *Prometheus Unbound*, man is defined as "one harmonious soul of many a soul, whose nature is its own divine control."

With his reverence for greatness and his growing belief that man under proper moral guidance could be the master of his own destiny, Shelley combined a supreme faith in the sanative powers of poetry. For him poetry was always the outgrowth of some constructive ethical program usually supported by an idealistic metaphysic. His definition of the term was broad enough to include most of the great imaginative systems of thought from Plato to Spinoza. Had he anticipated Carlyle in writing a book on heroes, hero worship, and the heroic in history, he would have emphasized the hero as poet, whom he felt to be the strongest force for mental rehabilitation that human history knows.

A Defence of Poetry is perhaps his most extended contribution to the literature of hero worship. Its central idea is Shelley's explanation of the manner in which poetry acts to produce the moral improvement of man. "The great secret of morals," says the essayist,

> is love; or a going out of our own nature, and an iden-
> tification of ourselves with the beautiful which exists in
> thought, action, or person, not our own. A man, to be
> greatly good, must imagine intensely and comprehen-
> sively. ... The great instrument of moral good is the
> imagination; and poetry administers to the effect [moral
> good] by acting upon the cause [imagination]. Poetry

> enlarges the circumference of the imagination by replenishing it with thoughts of ever new delight, which have the power of attracting and assimilating to their own nature all other thoughts. . . . Poetry strengthens the faculty which is the organ of the moral nature of man [imagination] in the same manner as exercise strengthens a limb.

If the great secret of moral good is love, and the great instrument of moral good is the imagination, and the great strengthener of the imagination is poetry, we possess the theorem by which Shelley would prove the importance of poets in the development and stabilization of human morality. From Plato onward, says Shelley, a chorus of the greatest writers have successively celebrated "the dominion of love, planting as it were trophies in the human mind of that sublimest victory over sensuality and force." These writers are the true heroes of the western tradition, and the supreme *raison d'être* for Shelley's humanism.

DURING the nineteenth century Shelley's lyrics far outshone his longer poems in popularity. Generally speaking, if one had heard of Shelley at all, one knew "The Cloud" or the "Ode to the West Wind" or "To a Skylark"—that perennial triumvirate in whose name the more massive achievement of the symbolic thinker was ordinarily forgotten. The apparently innocuous beauty of these poems charmed the eye and pleased the ear. Taken together with some of the love poetry and the "Hymn to Intellectual Beauty," they helped to establish a stereotype of Shelley as Ariel, a fleet-footed, rosy-fingered messenger from another world who never stayed in one place long enough to invite or permit intellectual analysis or appraisal. Among the anthologists, Brooke and Palgrave thought nothing of extracting songs from the more extended works. In demonstrating the rhetorical skills of the poet, they felt safe in ignoring the context of philosophic poetry to which many of the lyrics owed their origin and their point. Arnold and Swinburne were agreed that Shelley was a lyricist; little else in the canon claimed serious attention. Near the end of the Victorian period, W. B. Yeats ironically said that the popularity of "The Cloud" was owing to the ease with which it could be understood. Shelley's more important poems, since they required of readers a real expenditure of imaginative energy, were frequently ignored.

This obvious imbalance between the known and the unknown Shelley has not been wholly redressed in the present century. The scholarly literature on Shelley is enormous, but much more of it has been devoted to literary source hunting and biographical fact hunting than to the attempt to see Shelley plain. Santayana, among the professional philosophers, has offered a perceptive essay, Croce a series of insights, and Whitehead an appreciation of the poet's scientific acumen. Among certain of the influential poet-critics of the past sixty years, however, it has been fashionable to use the worst of Shelley—"The Indian Serenade," for example—as a means of suggesting that his best is not much better.

If the imbalance is to be adjusted, the lyricist must give ground before that too little-known Shelley, the visionary philosophical poet. This side of his work, proportionately the most extensive by far, belongs in the line of descent from the myth-making Plato, through Dante and Milton, up to Blake and Coleridge, and on to the later Yeats. Shelley may well have descended from his great predecessors in other ways: in breadth of vision, in sustained quality of performance, in technical mastery of his various media. Wherever one ranks him, his most energetic and protracted effort as philosopher-poet lay in the ordering and projection of his vast cosmology, his serious and profound explanation of the way the world is put together. "The course of his philosophical growth," wrote Lionel Trilling, "is his claim to greatness and to the attention of our generation."

Shelley seems to have understood the difficulties of the problem in symbolic communication that he set for himself. He

113

knew from experience too much about the limitations of the public intellect, which has never shown a strong appetite for complex and erudite symbolism, to suppose that his system would be received with universal acclaim. If he resembled Blake in believing that he must create his own system or be enslaved by another man's, he went farther than Blake in his attempts to reach the public ear. He was finally obliged to admit that his success had not been noteworthy. "I can compare my experience in this respect," he glumly wrote, "to nothing but a series of wet blankets." Yet he persisted in his determination not to cheapen the quality of his most important work or to diminish, for public purposes, the magnitude of his vision. At the time of his death he was working on the best poem he ever did, but *The Triumph of Life* is also one of his most difficult works, embracing what is best in all seven Shelleys. If it is now possible to understand what he meant his poetry to be and to do, something like poetic justice has begun to operate in Shelley's posthumous career.

THE CONCEPTION of tragedy in Shelley's thought is worth restatement if only to counteract the widespread notion that sentimental optimism denied him the tragic view of human life. It is a mistake to suppose that his mature intellectual position was either unduly sentimental or immoderately optimistic. No one who has read through his poems and letters during the period from 1819 to 1822 could properly accuse him of optimism about the course of human affairs in Europe, in England, or in general. If his poetry of the same period exhibits something like optimism, it is because one of Shelley's theories about the higher kind of poetry was that it ought to hold up before the mind's eye certain "idealisms of moral excellence" in order to suggest to men what they might achieve if they dared. Always between the lines, and often in their very language, the perceptive reader will find evidence of Shelley's tragic sense of the gap between what is and what ought to be.

The tragic situation in Shelley arises from either of two sources: a corrupt and corrupting social environment ruled by custom and superstition; or the individual's failure, through spiritual obliquity or simple desperation, to keep to his moral ideals. According to Shelley, the proper response even to the worst injuries is kindness, forbearance, and "a resolution to convert the injurer . . . by peace and love." He seems never to have willingly condoned an act of violence. Any form of vengeance, any assertion of the *lex talionis*, seemed to him a pernicious error. Yet corrupt society was always forcing the individual's hand, with the result that he either forgot his ideals or sacrificed them to the exigencies of the moment. A degree of moral deformity inevitably resulted. An act of violence was never without a deleterious effect on the doer. Shelley defined as tragic any situation that produced moral deformity.

The case of Beatrice Cenci illustrates the point. In the old yellow book on the misfortunes of the Cenci family, Shelley found all the moral deformity he could use, as well as some that he felt obliged to delete in the hope of getting his play performed on the London stage. As Shelley presents her, Beatrice is at first a kind of saint, devoted to all the highest ideals of human conduct. Then the change is catalogued. Under the vindictive brutality of her psychotic father, and within the corrupt social environment of her native city, she is rapidly converted into an efficient murderess, destroying her father and defying the legal system that brings her to trial. Her moral duty was clear—to hold out for her ideals, to suffer the ordeals of incipient sainthood. Had she done so, said Shelley, she would not have been a tragic figure.

This conception of tragedy is neither Aristotelian nor Shakespearean, though it contains elements of both. It lays emphasis, however, on the English romantic's tendency to regard spiritual or moral corruption as the supreme error which flesh is heir to. Both Shelley and Blake took as their goal the fullest possible development of the human personality to a complete and rounded whole. If this goal were to be achieved, to par-

115

aphrase T. S. Eliot, it would cost not less than everything. Such an attitude is of course at odds with the spirit of acceptance or compromise that is the essence of a "realistic" ethic. Moral realism assumes a basic racalcitrance in the nature of things, a fundamental disability in all humankind. This is the doctrine of accepted imperfection; we make the best of the best bargain we are able to make. Unalterably opposed to such a conception of human destiny, Shelley and Blake would not willingly settle for anything less than perfection. The abrogation of personal integrity must therefore strike them both as a tragic loss to the individual potential.

🍎 SHELLEY's theistic thought was most notably embodied in two major poems belonging to the period 1818-1822, that crowning quadrennium in which his most mature work was accomplished. These are *Adonais*, the pastoral elegy for Keats and *The Triumph of Life*, a kind of narrative elegy for the human race. Nowhere else did this still young poet rise to such a majesty of utterance or to such a high level of imaginative "truth-telling." The metaphysical foundation of both poems is the faith that there is available to mankind an inexhaustible reservoir of spiritual energy, not unlike the power that Blake apotheosized in his Los-symbol. In two impassioned stanzas of *Adonais*, he defines his concept. First, it is the "plastic stress," where he is partly echoing Coleridge's coinage, *esemplastic*, meaning a force of unification, of the one supreme Spirit that sweeps through the dull, dense world in the continuing attempt to "torture" the unwilling dross up toward its own magnificent likeness. Second, it is that "sustaining Love" which burns brightly or dimly through the realm of being according to the imaginative capabilities of its various potential recipients. All creatures great and small are as mirrors reflecting this "fire for which all thirst" in Shelley's oddly Dantean synesthetic terminology. The state of grace in his theistic thought is the near approach to the Supreme Likeness, and the state of sin, as in early Hebraic belief, is a turning away from it. Cosmic Love is always there for those who earnestly seek it, and it ought universally to be sought as the only power that can give "grace and truth to life's unquiet dream."

Two legends inform the *Adonais*. One is the famous myth of Adonis from classical sources. The other is more or less adventitious, for Shelley appears to have been taken in by the widespread and long-lived fairy tale that Keats's death had been hastened if not caused by the malevolent attack on *Endymion* in the *Quarterly Review* for April 1818. The Adonis story was of course equally effective in modifying Shelley's poem away from historical actuality. Having chosen Adonis as the poetic prototype of Keats, he followed to a degree the limited characterization of Adonis as he found it in Bion's "Lament," while altering the original story whenever it best suited his pseudobiographical purpose.

It was characteristic of Shelley's mythopoetic approach to accept for his "ideal" poems only such situations as could be developed allegorically. Both by the use of a presumed variant of the name Adonis and by the application to the Venus figure of only one of her innumerable Greek surnames, Shelley partly concealed his source myth. But in modified form all the original elements are present: Venus's temporary absence from the side of her beloved, Adonis's daring of the boar, the beast's attack, the death of the hero, the arrival of mourners, the ministrations of various subdeities, Venus's attempt to revive her fallen lover, and finally, though this is merely suggested as one possible fate of Adonais, the victim's metamorphosis into a flower. The place of the boar in *Adonais* is occupied by the anonymous reviewer whom Shelley blamed for the death of Keats.

Urania herself is first of all what she is in the original fable, a goddess enamored of a mortal youth. But the epithet "Urania" immediately indicates that she is not to be confused with the lower or Cyprian Aphrodite of Bion and Moschus. She is rather a spiritual being at a much higher level, a goddess of heavenly love like Asia in *Prometheus Unbound*. The ob-

117

vious reason for showing her in love with Keats is that his poems had helped, as Shelley saw them, to spread the doctrine of divine love of which he himself was so ardent and consistent a champion. Urania, in fact, is both a symbol of heavenly love and, as her name would suggest to students of Milton, a muse who has in her charge the most sublime poetry. Among the nine muses of classical mythology, Urania is the overseer of astronomy. Shelley retained this conception in *Adonais* through the most precise development of a Lucifer-Hesper star image derived from Plato. But he was likewise aware that Milton, in the proem to the seventh book of *Paradise Lost*, had invoked her as guide to his highest poetic effort, the literally astronomical task of describing the Creation. In making Keats the "nursling" of the most noble muse, Shelley was paying him a very high compliment indeed.

Besides Urania, Adonais has several mortal mourners, among them Byron, Moore, Hunt, and Shelley himself. They appear in the thin disguise of mountain shepherds, and the conceit is that (like Keats) they watch over the sheep of their thoughts. Their mount of habitation might well be Helicon, domain of the muses, on one of whose peaks lies the "secret paradise" from which Urania-as-muse first descended in her attempt to reanimate Adonais. In deference to the memory of their fellow poet, their magic mantles (signifying imagination, as with the cloak of Prospero in Shakespeare's *Tempest*) are rent in mourning, and the leaves in their garlands are sere and yellow like those imaged by the bereaved Macbeth.

The first two-thirds of the elegy is developed with one eye on the Adonis myth, though Shelley has broadened and deepened the significance of Aphrodite, emphasized the importance of mourning shepherds, and charged the whole with angry vilification of the boorish reviewer whose attack precipitated the tragedy. But when one turns to the final third of the poem, a question of the unity of *Adonais* arises. As commonly analyzed, the poem is in two parts: thirty-seven stanzas of narrative, and eighteen more in which the narrative element is apparently dropped in favor of philosophic consolations. E. B.

Hungerford has argued, however, that the myth is not abandoned at all. It is rather carried along, at least by implication, to the time when Adonais enters the realm of the immortals to be permanently reunited with Urania, much as Shelley's Prometheus in the lyrical drama is enabled in the end to rejoin Asia, his long-lost bride. Meantime, Urania has been dissolved in light and transformed from an incarnated goddess into the mystic "One"—the Soul of the Universe. The muse of heavenly poetry is thus the goddess of heavenly love viewed in another aspect. It is fitting that Adonais, entering the immortal state, should be reunited with the divine light that infused his poetry during his earthly career.

According to this argument, then, *Adonais* is all of a piece. It is further unified by the use of star symbolism. Shelley is preoccupied with the notion of an astronomical hierarchy of dead poets. The clue to his intention here is provided by the Platonic epigram that he used as a headnote. In his translation:

> Thou wert a morning star among the living,
> Ere thy clear light had fled;
> Now, having died, thou art as Hesperus, giving
> New splendor to the dead.

The star alluded to is the planet Venus, which is both morning star (Lucifer: light-bearer) and evening star (Hesperus or Vesper). The conception is that when great poets die they become stars fixed in the firmament of time, stars whose light (the poets' works) continues to shine down on the benighted earth. Shelley imagines that the same wonderful transformation has occurred with Keats. As a "morning star among the living" he was a bringer-of-light through his poetry. When he entered the immortal realm, the light continued undiminished. He is now one of the "splendors" of Time's firmament, having climbed like a star to his preappointed height. Other dead poets assembled there greet him as "thou Vesper of our throng." And it is as Vesper, or the evening star, that he shines like a beacon light for Shelley's aspiring spirit in the last stanza of the poem. In some such manner as this, the star image of the Platonic epigram helps to unify the poem.

The last third of the elegy is filled with verbs ordinarily associated with fire and light: dazzling, burning, beaming, beneficently smiling, glowing, kindling, beaconing, and cold-consuming. Adonais's spirit has returned to the burning fountain of its origin. It has become a part, rather than only the earthly instrument, of that sublime fire, which continues forever to glow through time and change. Merged now with the divine fire, he can bear his part in the "plastic stress" that forces the unwilling dross of the temporal world toward, if never quite to, the condition and likeness of the eternal world. Yet immortality has a dual aspect. While functioning as agent, Adonais continues to serve as instrument through the powerful survival of his poetic works. All great poets, "the splendors of the firmament of time," may enter a temporary eclipse, but their light will never be extinguished. Their "transmitted effluence" cannot die out on earth, for it is a manifestation of the cosmic light whose smile unfailingly kindles the universe from within. The great poets are the "kings of thought" who strove against "their time's decay." They are the only parts of the past that will never pass away.

The substance of Shelley's informing vision is that the world as we know it is spiritually a Cimmerian desert, dark, storm-ridden, enveloped in mist. Far above it, arched beyond mortal sight, is the *primum mobile*, the divine light of the World-Soul, the "white radiance of Eternity"—a burning fountain like the sun. Its influences are felt throughout nature and in the mind of man. Its effectiveness corresponds exactly to the sensitiveness of that which receives it. As a vitalizing force, an *élan vital*, it impels all things in their degree to aspire toward the condition of immortality. In Shelley's precise phrasing, it "tortures the unwilling dross" toward "heaven's light." Idealistic poets are its most sensitive receivers, and in them the driving force, the *eros* or aspirational principle, is almost unendurably strong, for in a very real psychological sense, they are tortured by the wish to clarify and spread

120

among mankind the wonders of their vision of eternity. As "splendors of the firmament of time," they reign immortal in the memories of men. But their souls rejoin the World-Soul, thus carrying a joyous double burden in the enlightenment of this dark realm where we would otherwise be permanently imprisoned. This is the essential doctrine of Shelley's idealistic elegy on the death of John Keats.

The long poem on which Shelley was working when he died was called *The Triumph of Life*. Although he did not live to see it through, the lengthy fragment indicates that it might have been—indeed, it is—one of his greatest poems. It is filled with solemn music, charged with deep melancholy, mature in its inward control, and majestic in its quiet outward demeanor. The movement throughout is *andante*, as befits a poem that might be thought of as a return from the Paradiso of act four of *Prometheus Unbound* or the ineffable heights at the close of *Adonais*, to a kind of Purgatorio of life in this world. To many, on this account, it has seemed a palinode to Shelley's previous philosophic affirmations. Yet it is rather a reaffirmation than a palinode. In the course of his narrative Shelley looks again, from a different point of view, at the poet's relation to the life around him and his connections with the divine light that must always infuse the best work of the best poets.

The theme of the poem is well summarized in Wordsworth's lines about the light of heaven in the ode, "Intimations of Immortality" (lines 75 and 76):

> At length the Man perceives it die away,
> And fade into the light of common day.

The icy glare that emanates from the chariot of life in Shelley's "triumphal" procession is a more intensely felt and withering version of the older poet's "light of common day," which supersedes the "vision splendid" by which the youth in the "Ode" was once "on his way attended."

The dramatic method employed in the poem is analogous to that of Dante's *Inferno*, with Shelley and Rousseau in the place of Dante and Virgil. Instead of journeying, as in *The Divine Comedy*, Shelley and his companion stand in one place to watch the approach and departure of the car of the worldly life along a dusty highroad where millions of blind and aimless people hurry to and fro. In this bacchic rout, young and old are either crushed beneath or fall behind the moving chariot, like barbarian captives in a Roman *triumphus*. Only the "sacred few" of Athens and Jerusalem escape the malign influence of the worldly life to which the others have succumbed. They are those who established and never lost contact with the "living flame" of heavenly light. Evidently Jesus and Socrates are foremost among this small band of the truly elect.

Shelley's poem consists of a prologue, three unnumbered sections, and a final unanswered question. The opening forty lines provide a superb description of the physical setting, with the seer lying under a chestnut tree on a slope of the Apennines, facing westward toward the sea, with the sunrise behind him. Now comes the waking trance, which overspreads his mind as the sunlight of morning advances across the mountains. The first part (lines 41 to 175) is a detailed and graphic description of the visionary pageant of the worldly life. The second part (176 to 300) discovers the commentator Rousseau, who first identifies himself and then points to various famous victims as they drag past in the long procession. Part three (300 to 543) is Rousseau's "idealized history" of his "life and feelings" and occupies all the rest of the poem except the final question of line 544: "Then, what is life?"

In a series of personifications—Asia in *Prometheus Unbound* and Urania in *Adonais* are examples—Shelley had earlier incarnated in woman's shape his conception of the source of true poetic power. In *The Triumph* she appears as Iris, many-colored rainbow goddess, prismatic reflector of the rays of the supernal sun. Rousseau says that on an April morning long ago he was laid asleep under a mountain. Through its base ran a tunnel-like cavern, which caught the rays of the rising sun. Out of this cavern flowed a westward running brook along whose surface "a Shape all light" like Iris seemed to beckon him onward. But the fleeting tryst was interrupted by the chariot of the worldly life, the vision faded, and the "half-extinguished beam" of the "light of heaven" was at last reduced to a glimmer—"for ever sought, for ever lost."

The fragmentary state of *The Triumph* leaves uncertain the identity of the asker of the final question, "What is life?" But whether we conclude that the asker is Shelley or Rousseau, the answer is the same, for the "life" of the question is that which has been spoken of during the greater part of the poem: worldly life as a corrupting force, a slow stain, a cold light "whose airs too soon deform." In his *Defence of Poetry*, Shelley had recently argued that "the end of social corruption is to destroy all sensibility to pleasure." It spreads like a "paralysing venom" through imagination, intellect, affections, and even "into the very appetites"—until the whole complex is reduced to "a torpid mass in which hardly sense survives." On the other hand, the true poetic principle wages perpetual war against social corruption, and a poet is susceptible to decay only to the degree that he has cut himself off from his best source of power. The decadent shade of Jean Jacques Rousseau serves as an exemplum: one who turned his back on the splendor of his vision and followed the millions in the wake of the chariot of the worldly life.

The poet who would avoid "the contagion of the world's slow stain" (*Adonais*) must follow his vision to the last. It is probable that Shelley would have succeeded in doing so, given his adamant determination not to succumb to the blandishments of the corrupt and corrupting forces that spread abroad, as he thought, wherever human beings congregated in any numbers. If there were dangers on the other side, and there were, his death by drowning in a sailing accident in the Gulf of Spezzia preserved him from the fate of those who followed the chariot in his last great poem.

Less than a year before his death he had quoted the first two lines from the following passage of Goethe's *Faust*:

123

Over the noblest gift, the spirit's splendour,
There floods an alien, ever alien stream;
When this world's wealth is won, our souls surrender,
The larger hope we call a lying dream.
Our life of life, the visions grave and glorious,
Fade, and the earthly welter is victorious.
Imagination once, fire-winged with hope,
Filled all eternity, and flamed to heaven;
But now it dwindles to a petty scope,
While joy on joy falls round us, wrecked and riven.

The theme of this passage is germane to *The Triumph of Life* as Shelley set it forth, for again and again he had addressed himself to the recurrent problem: the impingement of the mundane and the meretricious upon the higher life of the visionary mind. From the perhaps inevitable stain upon the spirit's splendor Shelley was saved, if he needed saving, in the late afternoon of 8 July 1822, when the boat in which he was a passenger collided with another and foundered with all hands, including those that had set down what survives of *The Triumph of Life*.

It might have been Forster's Mr. Septimus Bons, but it seems rather to have been Alfred Stieglitz who once said that if there were two doors, one of them labeled "This Way to See God," and the other, "This Way to Hear a Lecture About God," everyone would choose the second door, fearing to face the implications of the first. But Shelley—like Dante, Milton, Blake, certain religious mystics, and the unnamed boy of "The Celestial Omnibus"—would have been willing to take his chances with door one. His most difficult and in many ways his best poetry is a serious attempt to relate in the truest and most lively possible words what his imagination discovered on the other side of that door.

John Keats

"HE IS A portion of that loveliness which once he made lovely." So wrote Shelley in *Adonais* as soon as he heard that Keats was dead. The proposed consolation was conventional enough, dating back to certain Greek elegists. Yet it was peculiarly applicable to Keats. His body now rested in the lap of nature, slowly dissolving into elemental forms, the common fate. What was uncommon was what Keats the artificer had contrived to do with his poetical forms during the brief quarter-century of his life and the five-year span when all his best work was done. Not only had he succeeded in making Nature seem lovelier and livelier than in actuality she was, but he had also seized upon a thousand natural truths, refashioning them through the singularity of his perception and the force of his imagination into poems that would survive him for centuries.

The physical dissolution, as everyone knows, began in Roman lodgings at the foot of the Spanish Steps, on the left-hand side going down, an hour before midnight on 23 February 1821. After the months of suffering, which are only credible because they really happened, the aftermath was normal enough. They made a plaster cast of Keats's lean face and performed an autopsy on the ruined body. Fearful of tubercular infection and avaricious of English pounds, the Italian owners of the house burnt the furnishings of the sickroom, scraped the walls, and scoured every corner, even replacing the doors and windows, the ceiling and the floor. Joseph Severn, who had so loyally watched over what Keats had called a "posthumous existence," saw the casket lowered into a corner of the Protestant Cemetery, noting with satisfaction that turfs filled with blooming daisies were afterwards fitted into place to conceal the raw earth. Back in England, where Keats ought to have remained for all the good his final journey had done, Charles Brown told friends about the anagram he had made from the letters of Keats's name: "Thanks, Joe." Then Joe Severn and all the others who had known this supremely gifted and gallant man took up their earthly business once more.

Yet now with a difference. For they were all changed from having known him, just as the course of English poetry was changed by what he had accomplished. In quantity it was not much as lives and works go—eight thousand days from birth to death, something like twice that many lines of finished verse. Qualitatively, however, Keats's impact was to be immense, as the fame of both his poetry and his letters has proved. In spite of many shortcomings, many failures in conception and execution, the best of his work displays a power as distinctive as his thumbprint. No other poet in the range of English literature could have achieved such sonnets as those on Chapman's Homer, the Elgin marbles, King Lear, the steadfast star, and sleep. Or such odes as he did for the nightingale, the urn, melancholy, and autumn. Or such narrative poems as "St. Agnes," "Lamia," and "La Belle Dame Sans Merci." Of such perfections the list can never be long. That of Keats runs to something like a dozen poems. Yet each is a triumph of its kind, an object unique in human history, a loveliness (to borrow Shelley's word) endowed with the power to last.

Loveliest and *last* happen to be the adjectives Keats applied to Psyche in his ode to the Olympian goddess who had not, in his view, been sufficiently celebrated during the heyday of classical paganism. However well it fits his poems, *loveliest* scarcely describes the manly Keats himself. With *last*, the case is altered, for among the major English romantic poets, he came last in chronology. It is curious to think that like Thomas Carlyle, who was also born in 1795, Keats might have gone

126

on to become an eminent Victorian if he had managed to survive another thirty years. It is also worth recalling that when he first drew breath, William Blake was already approaching forty, Wordsworth and Coleridge were in their middle twenties, Byron was a boy of seven, and Shelley a fair-haired child of three.

According to the British caste system, Keats was not only the last-born but also the least-born. Blake's father, it is true, was a tradesman, no high calling in the middle of the eighteenth century, but the others all sprang from more "respectable" levels of society. Wordsworth's father was a lawyer, Coleridge's (though improvident) a clergyman-schoolteacher, Shelley's a landowning squire, and Byron's at least nominally of noble lineage. Keats's father kept the Swan and Hoop Livery Stables at 24 Moorfields Pavement Row, some ten city blocks as the cock-sparrow flies to the north and east of Cheapside. There he sired four sons who were baptized John, George, Tom, and Edward, and later a daughter, Frances Mary, called Fanny. His eldest son was halfway through his ninth year when the father was killed in a fall from one of his horses.

Family circumstances contributed to making Keats the least well educated of the chief romantics, again excepting William Blake, another famous London-born poet who never went to college. Although none of them excelled as students, Wordsworth, Coleridge, Byron, and Shelley were all exposed for varying periods to university training. Keats studied for eight years, beginning in 1803, at Clarke's school in Enfield, but he was not yet sixteen when he entered upon premedical training as apprentice to a surgeon named Hammond in nearby Edmonton. This work ended and his crowning labors began in 1815, a month short of his twentieth birthday, when he was admitted to Guy's Hospital, across London Bridge in the borough of Southwark, as a full-fledged medical student. Ten months later he passed the examinations that gave him the legal right to practice as apothecary, physician, and surgeon. He seems never to have seen the inside of a university until his friend Bailey invited him to Oxford, where he spent most of September 1817 living in Bailey's rooms at Magdalen Hall, smoking "sagars," taking snuff, writing a little satire on the gluttony of parsons at the high table, and working on the third book of *Endymion*—hauling his hero, as he said, "through the Earth and Sea with unrelenting perseverance." But by this date he was well past the age at which he might have entered a university, even if he had possessed the means or felt the inclination. He thought Oxford "the finest city in the world ... full of old Gothic buildings—spires—towers—quadrangles—cloisters—groves ... and ... surrounded with more clear streams" than he had ever seen before. But he was only a visitor, not a scholar in cap and gown, and he was, moreover, already launched upon the only profession he would have time to follow—one in which he was to attain an eminence at least equal if not superior to that of his better educated coevals. Many of them recognized this fact. In 1821, when he and his friends all knew that he was dying, Leigh Hunt wrote Severn in Rome: "Tell him he is only before us on the road, as he was in everything else."

Next to poetry, Keats set the highest store by friendship. Among the friends he made in 1816-1817, many were afterward remembered chiefly because of their association with him. They were a rather mixed group. Besides Benjamin Bailey, who later became an archdeacon, Keats's closest associates included Leigh Hunt, who conducted the *Examiner* and became the poet's early mentor and first editor; Charles Cowden Clarke, whose father was headmaster of the school the Keats boys attended at Enfield; Charles Brown and John Hamilton Reynolds, prolific minor writers who shared many of Keats's literary and philosophical interests; and the painters Benjamin Robert Haydon and Joseph Severn, who between them contributed heavily to Keats's art education. There were likewise the publishers, John Taylor and James Hessey, as well as their legal adviser Richard Woodhouse, one of the earliest and most devoted collectors of Keatsiana, to say nothing of Keats's fast friendships with his brothers George and

Tom, his sister Fanny, and his sister-in-law Georgiana. Finally, one must mention Fanny Brawne, with whom Keats began a love affair in the fall of 1818. Although the incursions of tuberculosis ruined this, as it ruined so much else at the end of Keats's life, his ardor is apparent in his love letters, even while it is clear that a kind of intense warfare between devotion to the muse of poetry and devotion to Miss Brawne agitated the poet during the closing years of his life.

Poetry won, if only by physical default. Few English poets after Shakespeare have practiced their profession with such intensity. Although he died of more sinister causes, his neglect of self in application to his work can probably be said to have hastened his death. When he began *Endymion* late in April 1817, his first volume of poems had been out less than two months. Its contents represented two years' work and offered sufficient evidence of his poetical industry between the two Februaries of 1815 and 1817. There were twenty-one sonnets, the reflective poems "I stood tiptoe" and "Sleep and Poetry" (his first serious statements of esthetic purpose), three rambling verse epistles, and a handful of assorted lyrics—some thirty poems altogether. But by a year after the emergence of *Poems* (1817) the intensity of his ambition had become apparent: he had not only finished the four thousand lines of *Endymion* but also the long narrative of *Isabella* and another two dozen shorter poems—thus in a single year exceeding by far, both in quantity and quality, what he had taken two years to do at the outset of his writing career.

The final period of his writing life continued this astonishing productivity. Besides thirty shorter lyrics, he turned to the narrative mode in both versions of *Hyperion*, "The Eve of St. Agnes" and the fragmentary "Eve of St. Mark," "La Belle Dame," and "Lamia." As if this were not enough, he likewise wrote the great odes on which, as much as any of his poems, his continuing reputation depends, and the overly hasty plays "Otho" and "King Stephen." Even when one observes that many of these are incomplete, the record is hard to believe. There is little need to wonder why he had almost literally burnt himself out by the end of 1819. In the final thirteen months he wrote little. Along with all his bad fortune, it was his good fortune to see the "Lamia" volume of 1820 through the press, fencing off this further claim to immortality even as mortality closed in upon him. In July he was ordered to Italy, in September he followed instructions, in October he reached Naples, in November he arrived (more dead than alive) in Rome, and February was only three weeks old when this brief and brilliant life came to an end.

🍎 DURING the debate between Hic and Ille on the motivations of creativity in Yeats's "Ego Dominus Tuus," the name of Keats appears. According to Hic, "No one denies to Keats love of the world. Remember his deliberate happiness." To which Ille rejoins: "His art is happy, but who knows his mind?" Keats's letters provide the clearest of the several available avenues into the landscape of his thought, and one of them contradicts Yeats's phrase about "deliberate" happiness: "I scarcely remember counting upon any . . . I look not for it if it be not in the present hour." As a rule, his happiness was more adventitious than deliberate, acceptable when it came without having been consciously sought for.

The letters of 1818-1819 contain dozens of other insights into his essential character. This may be why Lionel Trilling believed that they "have an interest virtually equal to their writer's canon of creative work."* Our interest is so strong because Keats regularly leads his closest friends into his heart as well as into his mind. One of the letters to Fanny Brawne says, "I have two luxuries to brood on in my walks, your loveliness and the hour of my death." A reading of the complete correspondence brings us close enough to the author to understand that this was not mere romantic attitudinizing. It was Keats's way of facing and partly overcoming the eros-thanatos syndrome that circumstance had forced upon him.

* A similar opinion was advanced by T. S. Eliot in 1933, and echoed by W. H. Auden in 1954.

The passage also suggests what a number of the other letters seem to prove, that Keats was in love with tangibles and yet lived in perpetual dissatisfaction with the limitations of tangibility. The two poles of the loose dialectical scheme that informs many of them may be called a *living in gusto* and *an ending in speculation*. "I have been hovering," he once wrote, "between an exquisite sense of the luxurious and a love for Philosophy." Of this love of luxury, this preoccupation with gustatory sensibilities, Yeats's Ille said, "I see a schoolboy when I think of him, with face and nose pressed to a sweetshop window." Many years earlier, on reading Keats's poems, Carlyle sourly observed that they "could have been written by almost any young man with a sweet tooth." Byron, who once called Keats "a tadpole of the Lakes," rejected his more self-indulgent verses with a typical Regency vulgarism. Yet Matthew Arnold thought that Keats's skill with "natural magic" resembled that of the great Shakespearean actor, Edmund Kean, whose voice projected such an "indescribable gusto" for the words he uttered that, as Keats wrote in a review, he seemed "to have robbed 'the Hybla bees and left them honeyless.' " Unlike Byron and Carlyle, Arnold was not put off by such nectarean tendencies. Keats's frequent felicity of sensuous phrasing and his delight in hedonistic nomenclature were above all in Arnold's opinion the qualities that raised his poetry to the Shakespearean plane. What if he "was not ripe" for the "second great half of poetic interpretation, for that faculty of moral interpretation which is in Shakespeare, and is informed by him with the same power of beauty as his naturalistic interpretation," or for the highest "architectonics of poetry, the faculty which presides at the evolution of works like the *Agamemnon* or *Lear*?" Arnold was content with the first half and closed his essay with a passage from Keats's fragmentary "Ode to Maia" as if to call special attention to its final line: "Rich in the simple worship of a day."

Keats knew his power in this rich Hyblean mode and exploited it to the full. It is visible and audible in the hymn to Pan in *Endymion*, in the joyously appetitive enumeration of the items that make up Porphyro's feast for Madeline in "The Eve of St. Agnes," in "the wealth of globèd peonies" of the "Ode on Melancholy," and dozens of other contexts. It appears also in the letters, often mixed with humor, as in the justly celebrated disquisition on claret wine:

> Whenever I can have claret, I must drink it—'tis the only palate affair that I am at all sensual in. . . . If you could make some wine like claret to drink on summer evenings in an arbour! For really 'tis so fine—it fills the mouth . . . with a gushing freshness—then goes down cool and feverless—then you do not feel it quarreling with your liver—no, it is rather a peace maker and lies as quiet as it did in the grape—then it is as fragrant as the Queen Bee; and the more ethereal part of it mounts into the brain, not assaulting the cerebral apartments like a bully in a badhouse looking for his trull and hurrying from door to door bouncing against the waistcoat [wainscot?]; but rather walks like Aladdin about his own enchanted palace so gently that you do not feel his step— Other wines of a heavy and spirituous nature transform a Man to a Silenus; this makes him a Hermes—and gives a Woman the soul and immortality of Ariadne for whom Bacchus always kept a good cellar of claret—and even of that he could never persuade her to take above two cups. . . .

It seems likely that Buxton Forman was correct in supposing that the bubbles winking at the brim of the beaker in the "Ode to a Nightingale" must have belonged to some rare vintage of claret, cooled a long age in the earth, tasting of flowers and country greenery. Keats took delight in other "palate affairs"—breast of partridge, back of hare, wing and side of pheasant, and nearly all the fruits, among them the ripe nectarine he once engorged in the very act of composing a letter. At the climactic moment, he wrote, "all its delicious embonpoint melted down my throat like a large beatified strawberry." Examples of such "living in gusto" could be greatly multiplied from other letters and poems.

At the other end of his scale of values lay what he called "ending in speculation," by which he seems to have meant something like the free play of mind over a variety of esthetic and ethical ideas. These ideas commonly emerge as tentative hypotheses that he is content to *set down* in seemingly careless transit rather than to *pin down* with patient philosophical exactitude. In all his speculations he displays a considerable skill in what R. P. Blackmur used to call "saltatory heuristics"—roughly definable as discoveries made by means of sudden imaginative leaps, up and away from the fettering discipline of logic.

One memorable example is his distinction between Men of Genius and Men of Power, an idea to which he returned sporadically between the two autumns of 1817 and 1818. Shakespeare is his prime example of the first type, and Coleridge of the second. In one, the self or ego appears to be absent, in the other it is central. "Men of Genius are great as certain ethereal Chemicals operating on the Mass of neutral intellect—but they have not any individuality, any determined Character. I would call the top and head of those who have a proper self [*amour propre?*] Men of Power." A month later he wrote:

> Several things dovetailed in my mind, & at once it struck me, what quality went to form a Man of Achievement [i.e., Genius] especially in literature & which Shakespeare possessed so enormously—I mean *Negative Capability*, that is when man is capable of being in uncertainties, Mysteries, doubts, without any irritable reaching after fact & reason—Coleridge, for instance, would let go by a fine isolated verisimilitude caught from the Penetralium of mystery, from being incapable of remaining content with half knowledge. This pursued through Volumes would perhaps take us no further than this, that with a great poet the sense of Beauty overcomes every other consideration, or rather obliterates all consideration.

133

A poet of negative capability, as in the case of Shakespeare, "lives in gusto, be it foul or fair, high or low, rich or poor, mean or elevated— It has as much delight in conceiving an Iago as an Imogen. What shocks the virtuous philosopher, delights the camelion Poet. It does no harm from its relish of the dark side of things any more than from its taste for the bright one; because they both end in speculation." As to his own poetical character, Keats ranged himself on the side opposite Coleridge, who was allegedly "incapable of remaining content with half knowledge," and Wordsworth, exponent of the "egotistical sublime." He thought that he belonged among those who have "no Identity" but who are "continually in[forming] and filling some other body"—as Shakespeare had done in imagining the supremely virtuous Imogen and the supremely villainous Iago.

Arnold was quite willing to place Keats "with Shakespeare" in the realm of natural magic while denying him the "faculty of moral interpretation" that could eventuate in a tragedy like *King Lear*. But Keats, as if he could foresee in 1818 Arnold's mild strictures of 1880, advanced no claim to this second faculty. He was content to be "with Shakespeare" as a moral chameleon, taking on the color of his subject from the subject itself, undeterred by its moral darkness or its brightness, delighting in the "speculation" that any great poet, by total imaginative immersion in his subject, can subvert our moral considerations by the essential beauty of his presentation— the true and lively words he utters.

The most famous of his ethical speculations is probably the extended passage on the world as a "vale of soul-making." As Robert M. Ryan has shown in a revealing study of Keats's religious sensibility, this formulation grew out of the poet's attempt to imagine "a thought-system that might provide an alternative to revealed religion." Keats advances his idea quite seriously, and with a kind of tendentious enthusiasm, as a replacement for the more familiar—and in his view "misguided"—metaphor of the world as a "dim vast vale of tears," as Shelley had called it in the "Hymn to Intellectual Beauty."

134

The notion is essentially teleological, suggesting that there is actually a divine purposiveness in the means by which individual souls attain their fullest development while on earth.

The starting point is "intelligences or sparks of divinity." These are present "in millions" of minds, but their possessors "are not Souls till they acquire identities, till each one is personally itself." Such intelligences, says Keats, "are atoms of perception—they know and they see and they are pure, in short they are God." From this state of primal innocence, although the process may take many years, they are gradually schooled and organized through their growing knowledge of the human heart, for the heart is "the Mind's Bible, it is the Mind's experience, it is the teat from which the Mind or intelligence sucks its identity." Such a milieu as this world provides is necessary to fan a sparklike intelligence into the living flame of individuated identity. Keats used a Gestalt metaphor to describe the process.

> I can scarcely express what I but dimly perceive—and yet I think I perceive it. . . . I will put it in the most homely form possible—I will call the *world* a School instituted for the purpose of teaching little children to read—I will call the *human heart* the *horn Book* used in that School—and I will call the *Child able to read, the Soul* made from that *school* and its *hornbook*. Do you not see how necessary a World of Pains and troubles is to school an Intelligence and make it a soul?

Except in his indolent or escapist moods, which enveloped him from time to time as antidotes to the intensity with which he lived, he was evidently enough of a stoic to accept a human situation where pain and sorrow seemed often to prevail. The soul-making hypothesis, "a system of Spirit-creation," offered a rough rationale for any who asserted that human suffering might be a means to the important end of the fullest possible development of individual powers. This devoted lover of plenitude in all its forms thus hit upon something like the Aristotelian doctrine of entelechy, in which a dim potentiality grows and brightens into a completed actuality.

❦ IDEAS OF plenitude and entelechy meet and merge in "To Autumn," the last of the six great odes in time of composition and very likely the most fully realized production of them all. The technical triumph of the eleven-line stanzas, evolved from the ten-liners in the "Nightingale," the "Grecian Urn," "Indolence," and "Melancholy," which in turn grew out of Keats's extensive experience with the sonnet form, is nowhere matched in any of his earlier work. The philosophical triumph consists in the poet's selection of the one season that combines the cornucopia of plenty, the state of perfect ripeness, and the idea of harvesters loading bins and baskets with the produce of yet another year. He opens with a small myth of conspiracy, as if a strong-limbed, sun-browned peasant girl had silently agreed with Apollo, the sun god, to bless the tranquil scene with provender:

> Season of mists and mellow fruitfulness,
> Close bosom-friend of the maturing sun;
> Conspiring with him how to load and bless
> With fruit the vines that round the thatch-eves run.

The implicit personification is buttressed by images that suggest pregnancy approaching full term: the gourds are swollen, the hazel shells are plump, all fruits are filled with ripeness:

> To bend with apples the moss'd cottage-trees,
> And fill all fruit with ripeness to the core;
> To swell the gourd, and plump the hazel shells
> With a sweet kernel; to set budding more,
> And still more, later flowers for the bees,
> Until they think warm days will never cease,
> For Summer has o'erbrimmed their clammy cells.

"More, and still more" in superabundance, the autumnal foison seized at the very moment of perfection, the quiet work of nature at last fully accomplished—this is the joyous burden of the opening stanza.

In the second, he moves on to a kind of painterly polyptych where, in four tableaux, he depicts his peasant girl in poses appropriate to the season:

> Who has not seen thee oft amid thy store?
> Sometimes whoever seeks abroad may find
> Thee sitting careless on a granary floor,
> Thy hair soft-lifted by the winnowing wind;
> Or on a half-reap'd furrow sound asleep,
> Drows'd with the fume of poppies, while thy hook
> Spares the next swath and all its twinèd flowers;
> And sometimes like a gleaner thou dost keep
> Steady thy laden head across a brook;
> Or by a cyder-press, with patient look,
> Thou watchest the last oozings hours by hours.

The closing stanza turns from painting to the power of natural music:

> Where are the songs of Spring? Ay, where are they?
> Think not of them, thou hast thy music too—
> While barrèd clouds bloom the soft-dying day,
> And touch the stubble-plains with rosy hue;
> Then in a wailful choir the small gnats mourn
> Among the river sallows, borne aloft
> Or sinking as the light wind lives or dies;
> And full-grown lambs loud bleat from hilly bourn;
> Hedge-crickets sing; and now with treble soft
> The red-breast whistles from a garden croft;
> And gathering swallows twitter in the skies.

Despite the musical undertone—what Dorothy Wordsworth once called "the noiseless noise that lives in the summer air"—the wailful choir of the gnats among the willows along the River Itchen, the chirp of crickets, the whistling of the thrush, the twitter of the swallows, even the bleat of the full-grown lambs in their hillside pasture, this rural scene partakes

137

of that quietude to which Keats was perennially drawn. The early sonnet, "After dark vapours," contains the lines:

> The calmest thoughts come round us—as of leaves
> Budding—fruit ripening in stillness—autumn suns
> Smiling at eve upon the quiet sheaves. . . .

Now in the environs of Winchester nearly three years later, *natura naturans* was still serenely operative, and Keats's admiring response to it had not altered in the least.

Yet in other respects he was a far different poet from the apprentice versifier of January 1817, for he had now fully accepted the phenomenon of change as one of the laws of life. "Ode to a Nightingale" and "Ode on a Grecian Urn" are both built upon the dramatic contrast of flux and fixity, permutation and permanence. Looked at from one vantage point, nature is in a continuous state of flux. On the other hand, the seasons annually repeat themselves with minor variations, suns and moons rise and set, day and night succeed one another. In the midst of permutation there is an aspect of permanence.

The situation becomes more complex when Keats circumambulates his Grecian urn. The nameless sculptor who carved the frieze of "marble men and maidens" gave them a permanence impossible to their fleshly counterparts. They are caught and held in a state of arrested motion, and none of them will ever know the bathos which, in the world of the actual, commonly follows the completion of such activities as those that "now" engage them. They are therefore free of the laws that govern the phenomenal world, where any change, Keats seems to imply, is essentially reductive. This tree arrayed in springtime leaves would have to shed them in due course; the piper would grow weary of his incessant melodies; the lover, having succeeded in his amour, would suffer the letdown of its aftermath; and the priest, if he had brought his handsomely garlanded beast to the sacrificial altar, could only have butchered it in a welter of blood. The sculptor, however, eternized them all at the moment before the otherwise inevitable changes set in.

A century after Keats wrote this ode, Yeats undertook his imaginary voyage to Byzantium. There the noble citizens were surrounded by "monuments of unageing intellect," artifacts of eternity beyond the reach of time. So at least in his imagination, Yeats was able to evade the fate of those "caught in the sensual music" in the human realm of birth and death. Keats, too, by a similar empathy, projected himself into association with the marble men and maidens, the piper and the priest, and the leaf-fringed tree upon the well-wrought urn. "Thou, silent form, dost tease us out of thought as doth eternity." What thought could it be but our constant human awareness that change is the law of life? Shakespeare said it: "Golden lads and girls all must, like chimney sweepers, come to dust." Keats said it of a "peerless mistress" in his "Ode on Melancholy":

> She dwells with Beauty—Beauty that must die;
> And Joy, whose hand is ever at his lips
> Bidding adieu; and aching Pleasure nigh,
> Turning to poison while the bee-mouth sips. . . .

Having now for a moment lost himself in contemplation of those beauties that the sculptor engraved upon the urn, Keats has poetically actualized an experience beyond the reach of time. He has learned, in the words of Wallace Stevens, "how it would feel [to be] released from destruction." This is a "truth" learned through the interaction of his imagination with the silent marble forms. Because it is also undeniably involved with beauty, the urn, if it could speak, would affirm that in such experiences as this, truth and beauty are interchangeable.

The "Ode to a Nightingale" provides yet another memorable dramatic speculation upon the theme of flux and fixity. This time the stimulus is auditory rather than visual, a creature unseen, though recognizable by its song, moving like a dryad within a shadowy grove of beeches and "singing of summer in full-throated ease." The poem has opened with that spiritual

139

ache to which the easefulness of the nightingale's song provides so sharp a contrast:

> My heart aches, and a drowsy numbness pains
> My sense, as though of hemlock I had drunk
> Or emptied some dull opiate to the drains
> One minute past. . . .

The song is an antidote to the deadly hemlock or that other opiate that drags the mind toward Lethe, and the listener calls at once for a draught of a different kind, a brimming beaker "full of the warm South, / full of the true, the blushful Hippocrene / . . . that I might drink, and leave the world unseen," fading away into the shadowy forest with the easeful singer.

Stanza three returns to the images of pain by which the poem was launched, human woes that the nightingale has never known:

> The weariness, the fever, and the fret
> Here, where men sit and hear each other groan . . .
> Where but to think is to be full of sorrow
> And leaden-eyed despair,
> Where Beauty cannot keep her lustrous eyes
> Or new Love pine at them beyond tomorrow. . . .

So intense is the longing for imaginative escape from the realm of change and death that the listener mounts up "on the viewless [i.e., invisible] wings of poetry" to follow the singer "through verdurous glooms and winding mossy ways" into one of those sanctuaries of which Keats the claustrophile was always so fond. Here he pauses, standing in the "embalmèd darkness" for long enough to identify by their fragrances the flora of the season: white hawthorn, eglantine, "fast-fading violets," and "the coming musk-rose, full of dewy wine." Two words, *embalmèd* and *darkness*, are enough to move him to thoughts of death. Annihilation "with no pain" might well be as "easeful" as the nightingale's song at the end of the first stanza. Yet this nightingale, unlike its brethren in the phenomenal world, has nothing to do with mortality: if the listener were

140

to die now, death would only delete the music of its voice. Seven powerful monosyllables assert its presumptive divinity: "Thou wast not born for death, immortal bird." Its song, like the changeless figures on the urn, will go on ad infinitum. And yet—and yet— there follows another reversal, not in the nightingale's song, but rather in the consciousness of the listener, for now the bird's "plaintive anthem" begins to fade, softening away past meadow, stream, and hill into the farther valley. "Fled is that music" with its seeming promise of access to that other realm where nothing fades. Keats might have cried with Prospero, "Our revels now are ended." Yeats, meditating upon the swans of Coole Park, and knowing that he would "awake some day to find they have flown away," was writing, in his own admirable fashion, of a similar experience of evanescence.

IN SPITE OF marked differences from the others, Keats is a representative romantic poet. His fraternal membership in this distinguished entente appears, for example, from his eager participation in that whole series of revivals which gave English romanticism so much of its revolutionary effectiveness. Like the Elizabethan renaissance, it was a period devoted to the revivification of the past—the classical, the Biblical, the Gothic—for the benefit of the future. The influence of the Greek and Roman writers is everywhere apparent, most notably in the work of Byron and Shelley, but also in the prose of Coleridge, and sporadically in the poetry of Blake and Wordsworth. Keats's sonnets on Homer and on the Elgin marbles show something of what could happen when his imagination responded to the stimulus of Grecian sculpture and epic poetry, while *Endymion* and the two versions of *Hyperion*, which are replete with classical allusions and renovated classical mythologies, are obvious genuflections before the literary monuments of the distant past. Glowing in sylvan silence at the center of his great ode, the Greek funerary urn draws forth his most impassioned utterance on the values and durability of art forms.

Our own gradual loss of familiarity with Biblical literature should not blind us to its importance among the English romantics, where it was part of a revived interest in comparative religion and in the wisdom literature of the Middle and Far East. Blake and Byron owe most to the Bible. Its imagery and ideology gave Blake the foundation for his prophetic books. Byron based his lyrical dramas *Cain* and *Heaven and Earth* on passages from Genesis, while among his *Hebrew Melodies* are lyrics on Job, Saul, Belshazzar, and Jephtha's daughter, to name only a few. Shelley's anti-Christian sentiments, which Keats partly shared, made him more rather than less a student of the Bible. It is a memorable fact that both poets revered Jesus and Socrates as profound ethical teachers. Although Keats did not make extensive use of the Bible either in his poetry or his letters (his classical references are at least twenty times more numerous), his easy acquaintance with Esau, Jacob, Job, David the Psalmist, Ruth, Daniel, and Nebuchadnezzar is perfectly apparent.

Keats likewise shared in the revival of the Gothic strain in romantic poetry. That it was essentially derivative and pseudomedieval mattered as little to him as it did to most of his contemporaries. Blake's interest in King Arthur is typical of the time. The work of Chaucer was widely if ignorantly revered. Wordsworth held that all contemporary poets should be "proud to acknowledge" their obligations to Bishop Percy's *Reliques of Ancient Poetry*. Though known as imitations, Macpherson's *Ossian* and the poems of Chatterton were widely read. Coleridge's *Christabel* is a belated contribution to the literature of medieval witchcraft; Shelley's early prose and poetry are replete with Gothic horrors; Byron's *Childe Harold*, like his *Manfred*, opens in a carefully contrived atmosphere of the archaic—and so on through a list that could be almost indefinitely extended. Keats's response was completely unsystematic. Alfred the Great was one of his heroes. He wrote an early sonnet on a blank page of the supposedly Chaucerian "The Flowre and the Lefe." Much of his poetical epistle to Reynolds is "medieval" dreaming, and he told his friend that he was tired of most contemporaneous verse. "Let us have the old poets and Robin Hood," he cried, and wrote a poem on Sherwood Forest to prove that it could still be done. His medieval world is variously evident in "The Eve of St. Agnes" and "La Belle Dame Sans Merci," while both his blank verse dramas relate to medieval rulers.

Next to Wordsworth, Keats is the foremost representative of the romantic revival of interest in nature, which differs from many earlier views of the subject by proposing, and poetically documenting, a fresh conception of the multiple interrelations between matter and spirit. Blake advised particularization as the "alone distinction of merit" in art. Keats excels even so acute an observer as Wordsworth in attention to the minute discriminations of color and shape, texture and sheen. Where Blake showed little beyond a utilitarian interest in the "vegetable" universe, preferring to live in the visionary realms of the imagination, Wordsworth and Keats were far readier to dwell directly upon natural scenes and natural objects, recording what they felt in the actual or the recollected presence of what they had seen. In this difficult art of subjective nomenclature, none of his contemporaries is superior to Keats. But he is rarely content for very long even with the "fine surprise" of a well-chosen epithet. Although he may assert on occasion that he prefers a life of sensations to one of thoughts—the vital concretion over the abstract formulation—he continues to pursue the "vast idea" that lies expansed ("the shadow of a magnitude") at the farthest reaches of his inward vision. In *The Prelude*, Wordsworth speaks of the way in which sense impressions may ultimately "conduct" the free-ranging mind toward "ideal form." One of Keats's letters longs for the refinement of "one's sensual vision into a sort of north star which can never cease to be open-lidded and stedfast over the wonders of the Great Power." Both poets, in short, are votaries of the romantic process whereby natural facts, symbolically interpreted, are seen as emblems and indices of spiritual essences.

Keats is again a typical romantic in believing that the imagination is the chief agent in the foregoing process. He doubts that truth can be reached by "consequitive reasoning" and can never feel sure of any truth "but from a clear [imaginative] perception of its beauty." He believes that "whatever the imagination seizes as beauty must be truth" and says that he is "certain of nothing but the holiness of the Heart's affections and the truth of Imagination." One of his synonymous phrases for imagination is "acuteness of vision." A complex mind, he says, must be "imaginative and at the same time careful of its fruits"—must indeed exist "partly on sensation, partly on thought." Such affirmations simply imply that imagination functions as an intermediary between the phenomenal and the noumenal realms, a view that gains support from Keats's choice of a concrete illustration from the eighth book of Milton's *Paradise Lost*. God closes Adam's bodily eyes but not his "internal sight." In his trancelike state he has a prevision of the woman he will see upon awaking. "The imagination," says Keats, "may be compared to Adam's dream—he awoke and found it truth." English romanticism offers other definitions of imagination. Coleridge, for example, followed a somewhat different esthetic track in making his famous distinction between imagination and fancy. But the view that Keats shares is prevalent. Blake puts the matter with his usual bluntness. "One power alone makes a poet," says he "—Imagination, the Divine Vision."

A continuous concern with ethical problems is still another tendency that Keats shares with his great English contemporaries. Though he is neither so eccentric as Blake nor so insistently moralistic as Wordsworth or Shelley, he assisted in the romantic revival of interest in Spenser, Shakespeare, and Milton because they had given so much impetus to the exploration of the human psyche. Keats steadily admired the morally neutral strain in Shakespeare. He likewise thought that in a great poet the "Sense of Beauty" may overcome, perhaps even obliterate, all other considerations. Yet he does not permit such affirmations as these to hobble him in his "search after truth," whether moral or metaphysical, and the essential sturdiness of his moral outlook is impressive. He wished, as he said, to sharpen his own insight "into the heart and nature of man," as Milton had done and as Wordsworth was still doing. He wished also to convince his nerves of the fact that "the world is full of misery and heartbreak, pain, sickness, and oppression," no very difficult task in his own or any other age. Striving, as he put it, after "particles of light in the midst of a great darkness," he was increasingly agitated by the ambition "of doing the world some good," converting others to the religion of beauty, or, like the poet in *The Fall of Hyperion*, serving through his art as a "physician to all men." If Keats died too young to have attained Matthew Arnold's high concept of "the matured power of moral interpretation," it can never be held that he was unaware of its importance for great poetry.

One of Keats's early letters offers a preview of the program to which he afterward steadily adhered. It was, he said, to look upon "the sun, the moon, the stars, the earth and its contents as materials to form greater things . . . [than] our Creator himself made." Even as he set down the words, he half apologized for "talking like a madman." The thought may even have crossed his mind that such a plan partook of overweening pride, inviting the descent of Nemesis. Yet he never desisted from his high purpose nor surrendered his conviction that art could both enhance and indemnify the materials of this world, lifting them to a level of permanence above the flux of things, even enshrining them, like the heroic figures in the Elgin marbles, beyond the grasp of Time's "rude wasting," and in any case leaving them, to return to Shelley's phrase, "more lovely" than he had found them.

PART TWO

Modern Echoes

Living It All Again

W. B. YEATS AND ENGLISH
ROMANTICISM

Works of art are always begotten by previous works of art, and
every masterpiece becomes the Abraham of a chosen people.—Yeats,
Essays and Introductions

OF ALL THE greater modern poets, Yeats was the most
thoroughly grounded in the writings of the English romantics.
His talented, skeptical, and somewhat eccentric father was at
first his chief guide to the wonders of the earlier period. J. B.
Yeats's marginal sketches ornamented the first Shelley book
that young Yeats read, as if to attest to the transference of
the elder's literary enthusiasms to his son. The poet thought
of conversation as "an instrument of research" and was for-
ever talking and arguing with the painter about the virtues
and limitations of Byron and Shelley, Keats and Wordsworth
and Blake. "My father's influence upon my thoughts was at
its height," he wrote in his *Autobiography*.

> ... He would read out the first speeches of [Shelley's]
> *Prometheus Unbound*, but never the ecstatic lyricism of
> that famous fourth act. ... When the spirits sang their
> scorn of [Byron's] *Manfred*, and Manfred answered, "O
> sweet and melancholy voices," I was told that they could
> not, even in anger, put off their spiritual sweetness.* [My

* Manfred's actual words: "I hear / Your voices, sweet and melancholy sounds /
As music on the waters."

father] thought Keats a greater poet than Shelley, because
less abstract, but did not read him, caring little, I think,
for any of the most beautiful poetry which has come in
modern times from the influence of painting. All must be
an idealization of speech, and at some moment of pas-
sionate action or somnambulistic reverie. . . . He disliked
the Victorian poetry of ideas, and Wordsworth but for
certain passages and whole poems.[1]

For some years the elder Yeats continued to bombard his
son with critical opinions about the major romantics. In 1916
he wrote: "With a single line Blake and Shelley can fill my
vision with a wealth of fine things." He sided with Keats in
the belief that poetry must be great and unobtrusive and re-
called Keats's letter to Shelley of August 1820: "You I am
sure will forgive me for sincerely remarking that you might
curb your magnanimity and be more of an artist and 'load
every rift' of your subject with ore." Yeats's father explained
that by the word *magnanimity* Keats had meant "the new
philosophy of the abstract which even Shelley could not make
poetical," for it had come to him "second hand from the cold
brains of [William] Godwin." He also pointed out, apparently
with Shelley's *Queen Mab* or *The Revolt of Islam* in his mind,
that all attempts to "turn the intellectual awakening of the
French Revolution into poetry" had failed. "Let poets, by all
means, touch on ideas," he cried, "but let it be only a 'touch-
ing' and a tentative groping with the sensitive poetical fingers."

Like several others in his circle, J. B. Yeats "abhorred"
Wordsworth as "a sort of servile poet enforcing always will
power." He held that it was of no consequence whether or
not the author of "Ode: Intimations of Immortality" had
"actually believed Plato's doctrine of prenatal existence," be-
cause the idea itself was "not really an integral part of the
poetry." Here and elsewhere, Wordsworth might be filled with
ideas and beliefs, but in the end they were nothing but "long-
ings" for something he thought he had permanently lost.[2]

On this point and in some other respects W. B. Yeats shared in his father's disparagement of Wordsworth. As early as 1900 he had quoted with approval Goethe's opinion: "A poet needs all philosophy, but he must keep it out of his work." In 1913 he said that Wordsworth "condescended to moral maxims, or some received philosophy." Wordsworth thus differed from Keats and Shelley, who had "intermixed into their poetry no elements from the general thought, but wrote out of the impression made by the world upon their delicate senses," a clear echo of his father's opinion. Although Wordsworth undoubtedly "had not less genius than the others," one might be justified in regarding him as "a little disreputable."[3]

At the beginning of 1915 Yeats resolved to see for himself what Wordsworth had really amounted to. During a stay at Stone Cottage, Sussex, he tried to read through the whole seven volumes of Dowden's edition. By mid-January he had finished *The Excursion* and had begun *The Prelude*. "I want to get through all the heavy part that I may properly understand the famous things," he told his father.

> At the same time I am not finding the long poems really heavy. . . . He strikes me as always destroying his poetic experience, which was of course of incomparable value, by his reflective power. His intellect was commonplace, and unfortunately he had been taught to respect nothing else. He thinks of his poetical achievement not as incomparable in itself but as an engine that may be yoked to his intellect. He is full of a sort of utilitarianism and that is the reason why in later life he is continually looking back upon a lost vision, a lost happiness.

This was again an echo of the elder Yeats's position, but the son was evidently responsible for the allusion to the Benthamite philosophy. He repeated the charge in his *Autobiography*, calling Wordsworth "the one great poet who, after brief blossoms was cut and sawn into planks of obvious utility," and again in *A Vision*, where Wordsworth is said to have "filled his art in all but a few pages with common opinion, common sentiment."[4]

This judgment was little altered by the time of *Per Amica Silentia Lunae* (1917, published 1918). There Yeats held that though Wordsworth was undoubtedly a great poet, he was "flat and heavy," partly because his "moral sense" had lacked a "theatrical element." Already he had mentioned "the pedantic composure" of Wordsworth, and now he could not help thinking of him as he must have been in 1850, "withering into eighty years, honoured and empty-witted."[5]

When Yeats turned sixty in the middle 1920s, he had begun to find, "seemingly without any will of my own," that his verse was more and more following "the syntax and vocabulary of common personal speech." This was the very quality that Robert Frost had long since discovered in the poetry of Wordsworth. But Yeats believed that "the over childish or over pretty or feminine element in some good Wordsworth" could be attributed to "the lack of natural momentum in the syntax." This momentum was "far more important than simplicity of vocabulary," and it is of interest that Yeats now turned to Byron as a model.[6]

His immediate stimulus was evidently H.J.C. Grierson's *Background of English Literature*, which included two essays on Byron, one of them emphasizing the rhythms of personal speech in *Don Juan*. This was an effect that Byron was always trying for, said Yeats, even when he let it "die out in some mind-created construction." Although he told Grierson that Byron was probably not great "except in purpose and manhood," he was nevertheless the "one great English poet" who constantly sought out such rhythms.*

One passage that he and Grierson both admired occurred in the second canto of *Don Juan*. It described Juan's courtship

---

* In *A Vision* Yeats placed Byron among the "assertive men" of Phase 19, beside Gabriele d'Annunzio and Oscar Wilde—a curious trio.

of Haidée along the "wild and breaker-beaten coast" of Lambro's island among the Cyclades. Byron was here at his narrative best, with a syntactic momentum all his own, and presenting both the romantic scenery and the preoccupations of the lovers in a romantic stanza where the sentence order was perfectly straightforward and as down-to-earth as an account of young love could ever be.

> They look'd up to the sky, whose floating glow
> Spread like a rosy ocean, vast and bright;
> They gazed upon the glittering sea below,
> Whence the broad moon rose circling into sight;
> They heard the waves splash, and the wind so low,
> And saw each other's dark eyes darting light
> Into each other—and, beholding this,
> Their lips drew near, and clung into a kiss.[7]

It is worth noting that some of the greatest poems Yeats wrote in the period between the wars—roughly 1919 to 1938—were cast in ottava rimas. Although Byron was not the only begetter of this stanza form, he had left his stamp upon it in such narratives as *Beppo*, *The Vision of Judgment*, and *Don Juan*. Shelley had also used it in "The Witch of Atlas," one of Yeats's perennial favorites. Yeats took it up with immense success in ten major poems, beginning with the first part of "Nineteen Hundred and Nineteen" (1919-1922), moving on to the first and fourth parts of "Meditations in Time of Civil War" (1921-1922), establishing complete command in "Sailing to Byzantium," "Among School Children" (1926), and the two "Coole Park" poems (1929 and 1931); and concluding with "The Gyres" (1936), "The Municipal Gallery Revisited" (1937), and "The Circus Animals' Desertion" (1938). It is hard to escape the conviction that his syntactic momentum, his use of rhythms that suggested heightened personal speech, and even his vocabulary, may have in part arisen from the examples of Byron and Shelley. But he evidently cared nothing for the satiric use of the closing couplet, which Byron often employed, though by no means invariably, and Shelley not at all in his "visionary rhyme" about "The Witch of Atlas."[8]

Despite his father's limited admiration for Keats, Yeats in his boyhood had been greatly struck by the "Fragment of an Ode to Maia," where Keats had celebrated certain Grecian bards "who died content on pleasant sward, / Leaving great verse unto a little clan." This, said Yeats, had early seemed to him "the happiest fate that could come to a poet." By 1903 he had changed his mind, having come to think that such clannishness or sectarianism might well be too elitist. He told John Quinn that his own current work was probably "too full of a very personal comment on life, too full of the thoughts of the small sect you and I and all other cultivated people belong to, ever to have great popularity." Ten years later he said that instead of following his private visions, as Keats had done—defining vision as "the intense realization of a state of ecstatic emotion symbolized in a definite imagined region"— he was now trying for "more self-portraiture." His intention as of 1913 was to make his work convincing "with a speech so natural and dramatic that the hearer will feel the presence of a man thinking and feeling." François Villon was an example of a poet who had always managed to make "marvellous drama" from the circumstances of his own life. This was a skill that in Yeats's mistaken opinion John Keats had never really mastered.[9]

On the other hand, Keats excelled in pictorial power, far more so than the diaphanous Shelley. "He makes pictures one cannot forget," Yeats told his father in 1916, "and sees them as full of rhythm as a Chinese painting."[10] In this respect Keats was an obvious heir to Edmund Spenser, whose selected poetry Yeats had edited in a small volume published in 1906. Among his chosen passages from the second and third books of *The Faerie Queene* were those relating to what he called "the bad gardens of Phaedria and Acrasia" and "the good gardens of Adonis." The former, said Yeats, proved Spenser's power of describing bodily happiness and bodily beauty, which "gave to Keats his 'Belle Dame Sans Merci' and his 'perilous seas in Faerylands forlorn.' " Partly, no doubt, because they engaged both natural and preternatural magic, Yeats had long admired both the "Ode to a Nightingale" and "La Belle Dame." As George Bornstein has pointed out, "He Hears the Cry of the Sedge" in *The Wind Among the Reeds* volume of 1899 clearly echoes "La Belle Dame," and the same collection contains several nympholeptic poems like "The Song of the Wandering Aengus," using locales that resemble "Faerylands forlorn" with a strong overlay of Celtic mystery.[11]

Yeats's most extensive commentary upon the poetry of Keats appears in the slender volume called *Per Amica Silentia Lunae* (1918).* It opens with the poem, "Ego Dominus Tuus," dated December 1915, and continues with the essays, *Anima Hominis* (25 February 1917) and *Anima Mundi* (11 May 1917). The poem takes the form of a dialogue between Hic and Ille, and in the midst of their discussion Ille is made to ask:

> What portion of the world can the artist have
> Who has awakened from the common dream
> But dissipation and despair?

Hic answers: "No one denies to Keats love of the world; / Remember his deliberate happiness. . . ." And Ille replies:

> His art is happy, but who knows his mind?
> I see a schoolboy, when I think of him,
> With face and nose pressed to a sweet-shop window,
> For certainly he sank into his grave
> His senses and his heart unsatisfied,
> And made—being poor, ailing and ignorant,
> Shut out from all the luxury of the world,
> The coarse-bred son of a livery-stable keeper—
> Luxuriant song. . . .

---

* Yeats's title is from *Aeneid* II, 254ff. The passage tells of the Argive squadron sailing from Tenedos and seeking other shores "in the favouring stillness of the quiet moon," the prepositional phrase that Yeats adopts.

The essay *Anima Hominis* offers a prose redaction:

I imagine Keats to have been born with that thirst for luxury common to many at the outsetting of the Romantic Movement, and not able, like wealthy Beckford, to slake it with beautiful and strange objects. It drove him to imaginary delights; ignorant, poor, and in poor health, and not perfectly well-bred, he knew himself driven for tangible luxury; meeting Shelley, he was resentful and suspicious because he, as Leigh Hunt recalls, "being a little too sensitive on the score of his origin, felt inclined to see in every man of birth his natural enemy."[12]

Whether or not one agrees with this explanation for the love of luxury in Keats, and even if one suspects a degree of class consciousness in Yeats himself, who seems, both in the poem and the prose redaction, to look down a little upon the "coarse-bred son of a livery-stable keeper"; or further, if one recognizes that Keats's suspicion of Shelley had little or nothing to do with class warfare and everything to do with Shelley's sometimes extravagant humanitarianism, which, in Keats's opinion, undermined his artistry, there can be no doubt that Yeats has given the appetitive aspect of Keats's character a most memorable poetical statement. He adds one more reference to it in *A Vision*, when he places Keats as well as Wordsworth in Phase 14 of the Great Wheel and says, "In the poetry of Keats there is, though little sexual passion, an exaggerated sensuousness that compels us to remember the pepper on the tongue as though that were his symbol.* Thought is disappearing into image; and in Keats . . . intellectual curiosity is at its weakest."[13]

Horace's *ut pictura poesis* provided the rubric under which Yeats had grouped Spenser and Keats in 1906. "Spenser's genius was pictorial," he wrote, "and these pictures of happiness were more natural to it than any personal pride, or joy,

---

* Yeats had read Benjamin Haydon's story that Keats had once covered his tongue with cayenne pepper in order to appreciate the "delicious coldness of claret."

or sorrow."* The genius of Keats was much the same, though he "sang of a beauty so wholly preoccupied with itself that its contemplation is a kind of lingering trance." Much as he admired both, he was unwilling to regard either as a poet of the first magnitude. In his *Autobiography* he ranked Keats among the "great lesser writers." The chief problem with Spenser was the allegory. Yeats loved symbolism but was "for the most part bored with allegory, which is made, as Blake says, 'by the daughters of memory' and coldly, with no wizard frenzy."[14]

☙ THE DAUGHTERS of memory were not to be scorned if they could become the daughters of inspiration and thus evoke a wizard frenzy. Yeats was forty-five when he wrote introspectively about his "excitement at the first reading of the great poets which should be [and indeed was for him] a sort of violent imaginative puberty." Three years afterward he said that "the old images, the old emotions, awakened again to overwhelming life ... by the belief and passion of some new soul, are the only masterpieces." His own passions and beliefs are clearly evident in his responses to Shelley and Keats, Blake and Byron, Spenser and Shakespeare and Milton—to say nothing of such older giants as Plato and Porphyry, or Dante and Villon. He was preeminently the "new soul" awakened to "overwhelming life" by the images, emotions, and eidolons

* It was Keats's power in the pictorial mode that stayed longest with Yeats. In the midst of his grand climacteric during the winter of 1928, he settled in Rapallo, Italy, which he called "an indescribably lovely place—some little Greek town one imagines—there is a passage in Keats describing just such a town." He was distantly recalling the lines from "Ode on a Grecian Urn": "What little town by river or sea shore / Or mountain-built with peaceful citadel / Is emptied of its folk this pious morn?" Eight years later in Palma de Mallorca, looking out over miles of coast and sea, he rememberd a picture from Wordsworth's "Solitary Reaper," where the voice of the cuckoo breaks "the silence of the seas / Among the farthest Hebrides." (WBY, *LTRS*, 738, 850. See also *Vision*, 3; and *EI* 177.)

he had found in his incessant readings among his chosen literary ancestors.[15]

"I had many idols," he wrote in his *Autobiography*. At about the age of seventeen he had begun "to play at being a sage, a magician, or a poet. . . . I was now Manfred on his glacier, and now [Shelley's] Prince Athanase with his solitary lamp, but I soon chose Alastor for my chief of men and longed to share his melancholy, and maybe at last to disappear from everybody's sight as he disappeared drifting in a boat along some slow-moving river among great trees." Since his father "exalted dramatic poetry above all other kinds," he experimented, he tells us, "in imitation of Shelley and of Spenser, play after play," and "invented fantastic and incoherent plots," partly derived from Shelley's narrative poems and lyrical dramas and partly from Spenser's *Faerie Queene*.[16]

Although Yeats's prose works frequently mention Shelley—Bornstein has located well over a hundred direct allusions—verbal echoes in the poems are relatively scarce. Yeats recreated whatever he read, reaching out beyond his "sources" for his own inimitable phrasing, and only a few Shelleyan expressions seem to have lodged deep enough in his memory to rise up unbidden for use at crucial imaginative moments. He was highly selective also in his use of Shelleyan imagery, though he paid it close attention in the years before 1900 and wrote of it extensively in the first of his two essays on Shelley.

When he thinks of Shelley, it is usually people or concepts or landscapes that bring his thoughts into focus. Certain Arcadian scenes in the early poetry suggest a Shelleyan origin. Concepts like that of Intellectual Beauty invariably engage Yeats's willing attention.* Some few of Shelley's heroic figures stand like well-lighted sculptures in the niches of his memory, as if he had taken to heart Shelley's view in *A Defence of*

---

* Yeats used the concept of Intellectual Beauty in *The Rose* volume of 1893, but with an important difference. He wrote: "The quality symbolized in The Rose differs from the Intellectual Beauty of Shelley and of Spenser in that I have imagined it as suffering with man and not as something pursued and seen from afar." (*VP*, 842.)

158

Poetry that the "great and lovely impersonations" of Homer or the tragedians of Periclean Athens embody "that ideal perfection and energy which every one finds to be the internal type of all that he loves, admires, and would become." Yeats's early Shelleyan "idols" exist on a level well below that of Shelley's own Homeric or Aeschylean models. But this fact did not prevent him from paying them due homage from his seventeenth year until his middle thirties.

The Poet who serves as protagonist in *Alastor* is a world wanderer, and Shelley's rather extravagant account of him centers on his search for a maiden whom he has seen in a vision and then lost.* This romantic quest consumes the short remainder of his life; his sufferings cause his hair to turn prematurely white; and he dies quietly in a green dell among the Caucasus Mountains without having effected a reunion with the visionary maid. A similar nympholeptic strain informs the fragment *Prince Athanase*, whose hero "seeks through the world the One he may love," only in the end to pine and die like the *Alastor* poet. The prince has a mentor, a white-haired Greek philosopher named Zonoras with whom he discusses Plato's *Symposium*. The romantic youth and the wise old man both appealed to young Yeats, as did the figure of Ahasuerus, the legendary Wandering Jew, who is summoned up by Queen Mab, Shelley's hierophant, to attack the vengeful God of Judaism and to relate the story of his mockery of Jesus Christ and his condemnation to eternal wandering. Ahasuerus reappears briefly in the lyrical drama, *Hellas*, to assure the Sultan Mahmud that thought is the only reality, all else being "motes of a sick eye, bubbles and dreams."†

Yeats wrote two formal essays on Shelley, one at the turn

---

* Yeats persistently and mistakenly supposed that the Poet of *Alastor* bore the same name as the poem itself.

† A. N. Jeffares (289) and T. R. Henn (321) both identify Ahasuerus with "Old Rocky Face" in Yeats's "The Gyres." George Bornstein notes that Shelley's account of Ahasuerus as knowing "The Present, and The Past, and the To-Come" seems related to "What is past, or passing, or to come" in "Sailing to Byzantium." (Bornstein, *Transformations of Romanticism*, 83.)

of the century and the other in 1932. The first, published in 1903, was "The Philosophy of Shelley's Poetry." It appeared in a collection that he called *Ideas of Good and Evil*, borrowing the title from the Rossetti Manuscript of William Blake. It was composed a little past the heyday of Shelley's influence on Yeats and at a time when he held strongly to the romantic conviction that "the imagination has some way of lighting on the truth that the reason has not, and that its commandments . . . are the most binding we can ever know."[17]

Having reread *Prometheus Unbound*, he thought that it unquestionably belonged "among the sacred books of the world." But when he asked a learned scholar about the "deep meanings" of Shelley's drama, the man disappointed him by saying that it was nothing but "Godwin's *Political Justice* put into rhyme, and that Shelley was a crude revolutionist" who "believed that the overturning of kings and priests would regenerate mankind."

Although for a time Yeats had mistaken Shelley for a "vague thinker" who mixed "occasional great poetry with a fantastic rhetoric," protracted study of his work soon revealed that a "system of belief" lay behind the poems, of which they were the imaginative projections. Shelley's ideal of political liberty, for example, was "one with Intellectual Beauty" rather than a mere emanation from the frigid rationalism of Godwin, for the "Spirit of Beauty" had "her throne of power" in every human heart, and Shelley had early resolved in his famous "Hymn" to make himself "a chief witness" for that power. These two points—that Shelley's poetry was associated with a half-hidden imaginative system, and that the central power in that system was Intellectual Beauty—were enough to contradict the opinions of the anonymous scholar—possibly Edward Dowden—whom Yeats had consulted. To a rising poet who thought of himself as "a voice" in a new and greater renaissance ("the revolt of the soul against the intellect"), Shelley seemed an ideal oracle.[18]

By 1900 Yeats's working knowledge of Shelley's poetry and prose was so extensive that he was able to compile a small anthology of quotations embodying the full range of Shelley's speculations upon Intellectual Beauty. He alludes seriatim to *A Defence of Poetry*, "The Witch of Atlas," "Laon and Cythna," the "Ode to Naples," "The Masque of Anarchy," *Queen Mab*, *Julian and Maddalo*, "Mont Blanc," "Rosalind and Helen," *Adonais*, "The Sensitive Plant," the "Hymn to Intellectual Beauty," *Prometheus Unbound*, and *The Triumph of Life* in such a fashion as to prove his easy familiarity with Shelley's central doctrines and poetical achievements. The second section of his essay, called "His Ruling Symbols," analyzes in some detail Shelley's use of water, rivers, and fountains, caverns, towers, and stars. Yeats points out there "there is hardly a poem of any length in which one does not find [the star] as a symbol of love, or liberty, or wisdom, or . . . that Intellectual Beauty which was to Shelley's mind the central power of the world." He praises Shelley's devotion to the "regeneration of the hearts of men." He connects Intellectual Beauty with "the Devas of the East and the Elemental Spirits of mediaeval Europe, and the Sidhe of ancient Ireland." He believes that Shelley was strongly fascinated by the traditions of magic and points to the Shelleyan conviction that "our little memories are but a part of some great Memory that renews the world and men's thoughts age after age."[19]

Shelley often reminded Yeats of William Blake in that both poets had developed complex cosmic visions. He says that Shelley understood "with Blake that the Holy Spirit is 'an intellectual fountain,' and that the kinds and degrees of beauty are the images of its authority" over the minds of men. He finds it significant, however, that Blake's dominant image is the sun whereas that of Shelley is the star:

In ancient times, it seems to me that Blake, who for all his protest was glad to be alive, and ever spoke of his gladness, would have worshipped in some chapel of the Sun, but that Shelley, who hated life because he sought 'more in life than any understood,' would have wandered, lost in a ceaseless reverie, in some chapel of the Star of infinite desire.

Yeats concludes his essay with a lofty rhetorical passage in which he attempts to reconstruct Shelley's vision:

> A vision of a boat drifting down a broad river between high hills where there were caves and towers, and following the light of one Star. . . . Voices would have told him how there is for every man some one scene, some one adventure, some one picture that is the image of his secret life, for wisdom first speaks in images, and that this one image, if he would brood over it his life long, would lead his soul, disentangled from unmeaning circumstances and the ebb and flow of the world, into that far household where the undying gods await all whose souls have become simple as a flame.[20]

But this secret life needed a "system of ordered images" to serve as its foundation. In his long essay called "Discoveries" (1906) in *The Cutting of an Agate*, Yeats said that "when imagination moves in a dim world like the country of sleep . . . we go to it for delight indeed but in our weariness." If, he continued,

> we are to sojourn there, that world must grow consistent with itself, emotion must be related to emotion by a system of ordered images. . . . It must grow to be symbolic, that is, for the soul can only achieve a distinct separated life where many related objects at once distinguish and arouse its energies in their fullness. All visionaries have entered into such a world in trances, and all ideal art has trance for warranty. Shelley seemed to Matthew Arnold to beat his ineffectual wings in the void, and I only made my pleasure in him contented pleasure by massing in my imagination his recurring images of towers and rivers, and caves with fountains in them, and that one Star of his, till his world had grown solid underfoot and consistent enough for the soul's habitation.[21]

In preparing his edition of Spenser's poems in October 1902, Yeats at once recognized their influence upon the work of Keats and Shelley. When Spenser wrote of the gardens of Phaedria and Acrasia, he showed his delight in "sensuous beauty" and "bodily happiness," a delight of which Keats was to become a chief romantic exponent. On the other hand, as evidenced by the *Fowre Hymnes*, Spenser had begun in English poetry, thought Yeats, "that worship of Intellectual Beauty which Shelley carried to a much greater subtlety and applied to the whole of life."[22]

The essayist might have added that this Neoplatonic aspect of Spenser's thought provided Shelley with a number of the images that would appear in *Adonais*. Among Spenser's *Hymnes* one discovers allusions to that "celestiall fyre / Which kindleth love"; "the mirrour of so heavenly light"; "doing away the drosse which dims the light / Of that faire beame"; "like as two mirrours by opposed reflexion"; "that fayrest starre / Which lights the world"; and "That eternal fount of love and grace." All of them have to do with purging away the corrupting forces of sensuality and worldliness.

When Yeats got round to writing his essay on Bishop Berkeley in 1931, he observed that the Romantic Movement seemed "related to the idealist philosophy," whereas the "naturalistic movement" of his own era was an outgrowth of "Locke's mechanical philosophy." Of this latter movement Stendhal's famous image of a "mirror dawdling down a lane" was a typical exemplum. The romantic mirror of the mind, on the other hand, faced upward toward the celestial fire of Spenser and Shelley, reflecting it for the benefit of a benighted mankind.[23]

Yeats's deliberations on the concept of *Anima Mundi* began taking shape in 1917, and his essay on the subject in *Per Amica* shows that he was about equally indebted to Spenser and Shelley. At one point he says: "I think of Anima Mundi as a great pool or garden." The garden in his mind was clearly that of Adonis in the third book of *The Faerie Queene*, for he quotes excerpts from two relevant stanzas. In the first one,

Spenser, that inveterate etymologizer, writes of the garden that it is "the first seminarie [that is, seed-bed] / Of all things that are borne to live and die / According to their kindes," The porter of the garden, "Old Genius," is constantly petitioned by "a thousand thousand naked babes" to give them "fleshly weeds" and to send them forth "to live in mortall state." In due course, after their experiences with "sinfull mire," they return to the garden of Adonis. Yeats's second excerpt indicated how they fare:

> After that they againe retourned beene,
> They in that garden planted be againe;
> And grow afresh, as they had never seene
> Fleshly corruption, nor mortall paine.

This pleasant fable of a garden of perpetual renewal for all those creatures who leave it, enter the realm of mortality, and at last return to it, anticipates to some degree the two Byzantium poems of 1926 and 1930.[24]

Side by side with it stands another concept, this time derived from Shelley's *Adonais*, which intersects the Spenserian account of the Garden of Adonis because Shelley was using the Venus-Adonis fable as the framework of his elegy. "If all our mental images," writes Yeats, "... are forms existing in the general vehicle of *Anima Mundi* and mirrored in our particular vehicle, many crooked things are made straight." This notion of an individual mirror, which reflects the forms that exist within *Anima Mundi*, is obviously borrowed from the fifty-fourth stanza of *Adonais*, where Shelley celebrates

> That light whose smile kindles the Universe,
> That Beauty in which all things work and move,
> That Benediction which the eclipsing Curse
> Of birth can quench not, that sustaining Love
> Which through the web of being blindly wove
> By man and beast and earth and air and sea,
> Burns bright or dim, as each are mirrors of
> The fire for which all thirst. . . .[25]

In his attempt to state the ineffable, Shelley enumerates the several aspects of the One or the World-Soul—light, beauty, benediction, love, and fire—as though no one of them would alone suffice. What he has in mind, however, is the vast reservoir of light and power to which the aspiring spirit can attain. All of nature, whether animate or inanimate, reflects this light, but it is the mind of man that succeeds best because his imagination is the clearest reflector. Yeats, who was well aware of the interlunations that occur between moments of vision, presently adds, "When I remember that Shelley calls our minds 'mirrors of the fire for which all thirst,' I cannot but ask the question all have asked, 'What or who has cracked the mirror?'" Yeats knew well enough the answer to his rhetorical question: Lockean empiricism, nineteenth-century science, materialism, utilitarianism, party politics, or any preoccupation with the merely mundane as over against the spiritual or the imaginative not only cracked but could also destroy the limpid surface of the mirror. Had he not shared with his father the tendency to disparage Wordsworth, he might have echoed the lines in the great ode about "the light of common day" supervening upon "the vision splendid." But in the *Anima Mundi* essay he did recall the ode and its author: "Our daily thought was certainly but the line of foam at the shallow edge of a vast luminous sea . . . Wordsworth's 'immortal sea which brought us hither' . . . and near whose edge children sport."[26]

Despite his long engrossment with Shelley, it is odd, as Bornstein notes, that Yeats did not mention him in his poetry until "The Phases of the Moon" (1918), where he grouped Milton's Il Penseroso and Shelley's Prince Athanase as disciples of Plato and solitary inhabitants of lonely towers like his own newly acquired "Thoor" in Ballylee, County Galway. In section three of "Nineteen Hundred and Nineteen," which Yeats composed in 1919-1922, Shelley reappears, again anonymously, but this time in notable conjunction with the mirror image that we have already traced to *Adonais*.

Some moralist or mythological poet
Compares the solitary soul to a swan;
I am satisfied with that,
Satisfied if a troubled mirror show it,
Before that brief gleam of its life be gone. . . .

The comparison of soul and swan appears in act two of Yeats's old favorite, *Prometheus Unbound*, where Asia sings that her "soul is an enchanted boat / Which, like a sleeping swan, doth float / Upon the silver waves." Not until 1927 was Shelley actually named, this time in "Blood and the Moon," again in connection with Yeats's own tower: "And Shelley had his towers, thought's crowned powers he called them once. . . ." The reference is to *Prometheus Unbound*, where the Chorus of Spirits in the "ecstatic" fourth act sing that they have come "from those skiey towers / Where Thought's crowned powers" sit watching the dance of the happy hours—happy because of the New Order, which has eliminated Jupiter and installed Divine Love in his place.[27]

Shelley appears at intervals in *A Vision*, where he is said to occupy Phase 17, along with Dante, Landor, and Yeats himself. Yeats writes of "a *Mask* of simplicity that is also intensity. This *Mask* may represent intellectual or sexual passion; seem some Ahasuerus or Athanase; be the gaunt Dante of the *Divine Comedy*; its corresponding Image may be Shelley's Venus Urania, Dante's Beatrice, or even the Great Yellow Rose of the *Paradiso*." When he is "out of phase," says Yeats, Shelley "dreams of converting the world, or of turning man of affairs and upsetting governments, and yet returns again and again to these two images of solitude," Athanase and Ahasuerus. At the same time, he is somewhat paranoid, never seeing "anything that opposes him as it really is." His compensation for his various losses lay in his "hopes for the future of mankind." Yet even the justice in *Prometheus Unbound* was only a "vague propagandist emotion," and the women who awaited its coming (Asia, Panthea) were "nothing but clouds." Shelley, in sum, "lacked the Vision of Evil, could not conceive of the

166

world as a continual conflict, so, though great poet he certainly was, he was not of the greatest kind."*

Yeats recapitulated these opinions when he wrote his rather surly essay on Shelley for publication in 1932. In his late sixties, he was prepared to recant many of his youthful admirations. "Shelley's art," he now said, "shows that he was an unconverted man though certainly a visionary, what people call 'psychic'; his landscapes are vaporised and generalized by his purpose, his spirits have not the separated existence even of those that in *Manfred* curse and yet have 'sweet and melancholy' voices. He was the tyrant of his own being. . . ." Moreover, "Shelley was not a mystic, his system of thought was constructed by his logical faculty to satisfy desire, not a symbolical revelation received after the suspension of all desire. He could neither say with Dante, 'His will is our peace,' nor with Finn in the Irish story, 'The best music is what happens.' "

In London in his early twenties, Yeats had felt far otherwise. Shelley had then seemed to share "our curiosities, our political problems, our conviction that, despite all experience to the contrary, love is enough; and unlike Blake, isolated by an arbitrary symbolism, he seemed to sum up all that was metaphysical in English poetry. When in middle life I looked back I found that he and not Blake, whom I had studied more and with more approval, had shaped my life."[28]

Yeats must have meant his spiritual life, since, in his imagination, he had for years fed on Shelley's poetry like manna. The implication of this late essay is that Shelley's influence had been on the whole deceptive. Yeats now says flatly (and

* *Vision*, 141, 143-44. One quatrain (c. 1926) in "Two songs from a Play" reads like a bitter parody of Shelley's hopeful lines in the final chorus of *Hellas*:
  A loftier Argo cleaves the main, / Fraught with a later prize, / Another Orpheus sings again, / And loves, and weeps, and dies. . . .
Yeats wrote:
  Another Troy must rise and set, / Another lineage feed the crow, / Another Argo's painted prow / Drive to a flashier bauble yet. (CP, 210)

falsely) that "Shelley the political revolutionary expected miracle, the Kingdom of God in the twinkling of an eye, like some Christian of the first century." He professes to wonder why Shelley was "terrified of the Last Day like a Victorian child." Blake had not shared in such terror; he was the one who had written: "For the cherub with the flaming sword is hereby commanded to leave his guard at the Tree of Life; and when he does the whole creation will be consumed and appear infinite and holy, whereas it now appears finite and corrupt."

In *Prometheus Unbound*, once revered as his "sacred book," Yeats had located a significant flaw: Shelley had never adequately explained the nature and function of Demogorgon, the mysterious power at the center of the earth into whose cavern Asia descends during the second act. Since Demogorgon's task is clearly "beneficent," why, Yeats wondered, does he "bear so terrible a shape," not only in the eyes of Jupiter, whom he is about to overthrow, but also in those of Asia, who represents Divine Love? In Yeats's judgment, the presence of Demogorgon made Shelley's plot incoherent and its interpretation impossible. He could only conclude that this mysterious persona was a nightmare image like that horrible apparition that Shelley saw on the stairs at the Villa Diodati: a woman who had eyes where the nipples of her breasts should have been. Yeats's comparison was erroneous. Had he ever pursued his early plan to explicate *Prometheus Unbound*, he would probably have discovered the real philosophical significance of Demogorgon, whose "mighty law" is that man must be regenerated if he has purged his heart and mind of hatred and superstition and thus prepared the way for the rebirth of universal love.

After the essay of 1932 Shelley never again resumed his former eminence in Yeats's mind. The main reason for this demotion is probably adumbrated in one of Yeats's letters to Olivia Shakespear of the preceding year. He recalled that in his youth he had "wanted to feel that any poet I cared for— Shelley let us say—saw more than he told of, had in some cases seen into the mystery." Accordingly, Yeats had "read more into certain poems than they contained" and was now prepared to admit the error of his youthful ways.[29]

Yeats was always in search of imaginative excitement, and he found it not only in the writings of Platonists and Neoplatonists like Spenser and Milton and Shelley* but also among the Gaelic storytellers and the votaries of the Dublin Hermetic Society and the wise words of Mohini Chatterjee who taught "by what seemed an invincible logic that those who die, in so far as they have imagined beauty or justice, are made part of that beauty or justice and move through the minds of living men, as Shelley believed." Yeats was here thinking of *Adonais*, stanzas forty-two and forty-three. The concept of a "timeless individuality" espoused by Shelley's spiritual ancestor, Plotinus, struck Yeats as offering a kind of imaginative release. "All about us," he wrote in "The Words upon the Window Pane," "there seems to start up a precise, inexplicable, teeming life, and earth becomes once more, not in rhetorical metaphor, but in reality, sacred." This teeming life, set within the framework of a sacramental universe, was the quality Yeats seized upon whenever he found it among his predecessors. It helps to explain two of his observations in his *Autobiography*: that "every passionate man" is "linked with another age, historical or imaginary, where alone he finds images that arouse his energy," and that "the distant in time and space" lives "only in the near and present."[30]

Yeats's last poem, "Under Ben Bulben," contains his final reference to Shelley:

---

* Among Yeats's classical nuclei were the *Enneads* of Plotinus, especially the fourth and fifth; *The Cave of the Nymphs* by Plotinus's pupil and biographer, Porphyry; and in the Renaissance a long essay on "The Immortality of the Soul" by Henry More, the Cambridge Platonist, which Yeats "toiled through" about 1917. More contended, as Shelley would do in *Adonais*, that "men and animals drew not only universals but particulars from a supersensual source."(*EI*, 407, 414.)

Swear by what the sages spoke
Round the Mareotic Lake*
That the Witch of Atlas knew,
Spoke and set the cocks a-crow.

Swear by those horsemen, by those women
Complexion and form prove superhuman
That pale, long-visaged company
That air in immortality
Completeness of their passions won;
Now they ride the wintry dawn
Where Ben Bulben sets the scene.

The horsemen and women whose pallor and form indicate
that they are superhuman and accordingly immortal had been
"sworn by" in Yeats's youthful poems. As early as 1900 he
had shown his close knowledge of Shelley's Witch and her
visions, "each in its thin sheath like a chrysalis," and noted
that "the Witch herself is a Naiad, and was born from one
of the Atlantides, who lay in 'a chamber of grey rock' until
she was changed by the sun's embrace into a cloud."[31]

But Yeats in the fall of 1938, aged seventy-three, had long
since said goodbye to all that. Shelley's otherworldliness had
attracted him and held him for years, but as he outgrew his
early idealism and was drawn ever more strongly to living
actualities, Shelley's star retreated farther into the "intense
inane." At forty-one Yeats had written, "There are two ways
before literature—upward into ever-growing subtlety . . . or
downward, taking the soul with us until all is simplified and
solidified again." In his *Autobiography* he had contrasted Shelley
with John Donne to Shelley's disadvantage: "Donne could be
as metaphysical as he pleased, and yet never seemed unhuman
and hysterical as Shelley often does, because he could be as
physical as he pleased." Simplicity, solidity, and humanity
were the qualities most sought after by the later Yeats. Shel-
ley's poetry, having taken the upward path into ever-growing

* Shelley spells the name of the lake Mareotid.

subtlety, like the song of his skylark, could no longer command Yeats's wholehearted support.[32]

    YEATS's first acquaintance with the poems of William Blake took place in the early 1880s when his father told him about Rossetti and Blake and gave him their poetry to read.[33] Within the same decade he met through his father a confirmed Blakean named Edwin John Ellis, an artist and poet seventeen years his senior. Around 1870 Ellis had discovered, as he believed, the key to Blake's Prophetic Books and was eager to prepare an edition in which his interpretation of the poems could be set forth at some length. Yeats at twenty-four, fresh from the publication of *The Wanderings of Oisin*, dedicated to Ellis, and *Crossways*, which used an epigraph from Blake, was already a veteran editor from his experience with *Fairy and Folk Tales of the Irish Peasantry* and *Poems and Ballads of Young Ireland*. He was now persuaded to collaborate on what became the most extensive piece of scholarship he ever undertook. Early in 1889 the two enthusiasts set to work.

In May Yeats told John O'Leary, his aged Fenian friend, that his own mysticism had enabled him to "make out Blake's prophetic books so well" that this century-old "riddle" would soon be solved. No one, said he, would ever call Blake mad again. By the end of the year, he and Ellis were at work on a "new long poem by Blake"—*The Four Zoas*—busily copying it out for printing in a text that Blake's twentieth-century editors were to find generally unreliable. But Yeats was far more interested in content than in textual accuracy. In 1890 he told Katherine Tynan, "You will like Blake's system of thought. It is profoundly Christian—though wrapped up in queer dress—and certainly amazingly poetical. It has done my own mind a great deal of good in liberating me from formulas and theories of several kinds. You will find it a difficult book, the Blake interpretation, but one that will open up for you, as it has for me, new kinds of poetic feeling and thought."[34]

Blake's system as such had nothing to do with the first

171

identifiable verbal echo of Blake in Yeats's youthful poetry. In Sligo as a teenager, about the time he first heard of Blake, he had listened to his father reading aloud from *Walden* and had begun to dream of "living in imitation of Thoreau on a little island" in Lough Gill. One day in 1890, having temporarily thrust aside his labors on the Blake edition, he took a walk over the grey pavements of Fleet Street in London, feeling "very homesick" for the joys of rural Ireland. Just at this point he heard "a little tinkle of water" from "a fountain in a shop window" and was reminded of the sound that lake water makes, lapping at a sandy shore on a calm day. The result of this experience was "The Lake Isle of Innisfree," which first appeared that December in *The National Observer* and afterwards in *The Rose* volume of 1893.[35]

The mixture of memories of *Walden* with the sound of the streetside fountain and his own romantic nostalgia was not the only impetus for this soon-to-be famous lyric. One of Blake's little poems in the Pickering Manuscript was named "The Smile," though it gave equal space to the frown, particularly the "frown of frowns" that "sticks in the heart's deep core." Ignoring the context in Blake, Yeats concluded his own poem:

> I will arise and go now, for always night and day
> I hear lake water lapping with low sounds by the shore;
> While I stand on the roadway, or on the pavements grey,
> I hear it in the deep heart's core.*

Through the fall of 1890 the collaborators made steady progress. On Friday, 3 October, Ellis gave an after-dinner speech during which he displayed a "huge chart" that Yeats had made, "representing Blake's symbolic scheme in a kind

---

* As George Bornstein reveals, the phrase had a future poetical history. Wallace Stevens twice echoed it, once in "Page from a Tale," which italicizes four excerpts from Yeats's "Innisfree," and again halfway through "In a Bad Time," when it was altered to "heart's strong core." So Blake's systolic image found its way into the vocabularies of two modern romantic poets. (Bornstein, *Transformations of Romanticism*, 252.)

of genealogical tree." The editors also prepared "a concordance of all Blake's mystical terms." Yeats sometimes complained of feeling imprisoned by his perpetual labors over "Blake-Blake-Blake." But Ellis's passion for the Prophetic Books and the illustrations—picked up, as Yeats said, in various Pre-Raphaelite studios—helped sustain the forward drive, keeping Ellis's mind "constantly on the edge of trance."[36]

Both men, as it happened, were also busy with other projects. A volume of Ellis's poems, *Fate in Arcadia*, appeared in London in 1892, and another, *Seen in These Days*, in 1895. Yeats was delighted by a story of Ellis's that told of Adam and Eve fleeing Paradise: "Adam asks Eve what she carries so carefully, and Eve replies that it is a little of the apple-core kept for the children."[37] Ellis also took time out to paint a frontispiece depicting Oisin, the hero, Niamh the heroine, and St. Patrick, the Christian interlocutor, for the limited second edition of *The Wanderings of Oisin*, also in 1892.* Yeats's accomplishments included *Representative Irish Tales* in 1891; *The Countess Kathleen, The Book of the Rhymer's Club,* and *Irish Fairy Tales* in 1892; and in 1893, when the Blake book was at last finished and published, *The Celtic Twilight* and *The Rose.*

The London publisher Bernard Quaritch had taken great pains with the Blake book, an elegant three-volume work bound in pale green and stamped in gold. Volume one, called *The System*, offered a long memoir, a summary of the so-called Literary Period, and a discussion of the chief symbols. Volume two, called *The Meaning*, gave some three hundred pages to paraphrase and interpretation of the poems and another hundred to Blake as artist. Volume three, called *The Books*, contained Blake's major works, partly in facsimile, partly in letterpress.

Yeats was by now a thorough convert to the work of Blake. In the summer of 1892 he had written his skeptical friend

---

* Ellis's verse-drama, *Sarcan the Bard* (1895), is related to Yeats's *The King's Threshold*.

O'Leary: "If I had not made magic my constant study I could not have written a single word of my Blake book. . . . The mystical life is the centre of all that I do and all that I think and all that I write. It holds to my work the same relation that the philosophy of Godwin held to the work of Shelley and I have always considered myself a voice of what I believe to be a greater renaissance—the revolt of the soul against the intellect—now beginning in the world."[38] In the essay called "Nationality and Literature" (1893) he said that behind human life and society lay "the causal universe itself." He agreed with "the words of my master William Blake" that this universe was "falling into division" but that its ultimate "resurrection into unity" could be foretold. Yeats was here quoting a line from "Night the First" of *The Four Zoas*, and it seems to have been his first specific echo of Blake's ideas in any of his critical writings outside the Ellis-Yeats volumes.

Throughout the 1890s Blake remained Yeats's recurrent companion. Soon after the Quaritch edition, he prepared a small volume of Blake's lyrics for publication in The Muses' Library series and in 1896 some articles for *The Savoy*. His prejudice against allegory as used in *The Faerie Queene* did not extend to the allegories of Blake, one of whose letters defined "the most sublime poetry" as "allegory addressed to the intellectual powers while it is altogether hidden from the corporeal understanding." Yeats's experience with Blake convinced him that "art and poetry, by constantly using symbolism, continually remind us that nature itself is a symbol. To remember this is to be redeemed from nature's death and destruction. This is Blake's message." In 1896 he wrote W. T. Horton: "I hold as Blake would have held also, that the intellect must do its utmost 'before inspiration is possible.' It claws the rubbish from the mouth of the sybil's cave but it is not the sybil." The sybil, evidently, was the imagination.[39]

In two essays published in 1897, "William Blake and the Imagination" and "Blake and His Illustrations to *The Divine Comedy*," he expatiated at length on Blake's thought. "There have been men," he wrote in the first of these, who loved the future like a mistress, and the future mixed her breath into their breath and shook her hair about them, and hid them from the understanding of their times. William Blake was one of these, and if he spoke confusedly and obscurely it was because he spoke of things for whose speaking he could find no models in the world he knew. . . . He was a symbolist who had to invent his symbols. . . . He was a man crying out for a mythology, and trying to make one because he could not find one to his hand.[40]

Already, though he did not make the point specifically, he seems to have been aware of certain resemblances between the teachings of Blake and those of Shelley. By the Reason, he said, Blake "meant deductions from the observations of the senses. . . . [This] binds us to mortality because it binds us to the senses, and divides us from each other by showing us our clashing interests; but the imagination divides us from mortality by the immortality of beauty"—a position, incidentally, that anticipated a central idea in the poetry of Wallace Stevens. Yeats may have been recalling Shelley's *Prometheus Unbound* when he said of Blake that "he cried again and again that everything that lives is holy, and that nothing is unholy except things that do not live—lethargies and cruelties, and timidities, and that denial of imagination which is the root they grew from in old times. Passions, because most living, are most holy . . . and man shall enter eternity borne upon their wings."[41]

In the essay on Blake's illustrations to the *Divine Comedy*, he returned to his favorite distinction between symbol and allegory: "The symbolic imagination, or, as Blake preferred to call it, *vision*, is not allegory, being a 'representation of what actually exists really and unchangeably.' A symbol is indeed the only possible expression of some invisible essence . . . while allegory is one of many possible representations of an embodied thing, or familiar principle, and belongs to the fancy and not to imagination: the one is a revelation, the other an amusement." This, along with the immediately ensuing passage, offers one of the rare hints in Yeats's writings that he was familiar with Coleridge's distinction between fancy and the secondary imagination. "Blake," he continued, "represented the shapes of beauty haunting our moments of inspiration. . . . It was of less importance to know men and nature than to distinguish the beings and substances of imagination from those of a more perishable kind, created by the fantasy, in uninspired moments, out of memory and whim." Such distinctions could best be achieved "by purifying one's mind, as with a flame, in study of the works of the great masters."[42]

Yeats also shared Blake's fierce devotion to particularization and minute discrimination. "All sublimity," Blake had asserted in his annotations to the works of Sir Joshua Reynolds, "is found on Minute Discrimination. . . . All knowledge is particular. . . . The Ancients were chiefly attentive to complicated and Minute Discrimination of character. It is the whole of art." Blake's "three primary commands," as Yeats calls them, "to seek a determinate outline, to avoid a generalised treatment, and to desire always abundance and exuberance, were insisted upon with vehement anger, and their opponents called again and again 'demons' and 'villains,' " owing to his "firm conviction that the things his opponents held white were indeed black, and the things they held black were white."[43]

Without following Blake in all of his Christological speculations, Yeats pointed out that "the historical Christ was indeed no more [at least for Blake] than the supreme symbol of the artistic imagination." He quoted *The Marriage of Heaven and Hell* where Blake's Devil says that "Jesus was all virtue, and acted from impulse, not from rules," and continued with a couplet—one of his special favorites—from *The Everlasting Gospel* in which Blake says that Jesus

> His seventy disciples sent
> Against religion and government.[44]

To act from impulse rather than from Mosaic rules and to place oneself in opposition to the powers of orthodoxy in law or religion struck Yeats as the essence of Blake's brand of romanticism. He himself half believed in what he called Blake's "strong persuasion that all [those who are] busy with government are men of darkness and 'something other than human life' " and pointed out that Shelley, his other early master, "was the next to take up the cry."*

Yeats would probably not have agreed with H.J.C. Grierson's characterization of Blake as "the sansculottist of the Romantic Revival," preferring to call him instead "the chanticleer of the new dawn."45 He quotes with sympathy three sentences from the aged Blake's letter to George Cumberland in which he described himself as "an old man feeble and tottering, but not in spirit & life, not in the real man the imagination which liveth for ever. In that I am stronger and stronger as this foolish body decays [a phenomenon that Yeats would later notice in himself]. . . . Flaxman is gone & we must all soon follow, every one to his own eternal house, leaving the delusive goddess Nature and her laws, to get into freedom from all law . . . into the mind in which every one is king and priest in his own house."46

Blake's "phrase about the king and priest," wrote Yeats, "is a memory of the crown and mitre set upon Dante's head before he entered Paradise. Our imaginations are but fragments of the universal imagination, portions of the universal body of God, and as we enlarge our imagination by imaginative sympathy, and transform with the beauty and peace of art the sorrows and joys of the world, we put off the limited mortal man more and more and put on the unlimited 'immortal man.' "47

The image of Blake as chanticleer appears in "Symbolism in Painting" (1898), where Yeats returns yet again to his earlier fixation upon the topic of symbolism. Keats, he now says,

* EI, 130. The phrase, "something other than human life," reappears in Yeats's footnote, dated 1914, to his poems "The Magi" and "The Dolls."

"is as much a symbolist as Blake" but "a fragmentary sym-
bolist" since "he does not set his symbols in the great proces-
sion as Blake would have him [do]" in an order suited to his
"imaginative energy." As of this date, a year or two before
the turn of the century, Yeats himself might also have been
called "a fragmentary symbolist—eager to "set his symbols
in the great procession" but as yet uncertain about the best
way to do it. Blake offered one important clue in plate 5 of
Milton, saying that "Mathematic Proportion was subdued by
Living Proportion." Yeats developed this idea in his essay,
"Discoveries" (1906): "Art bids us touch and taste and hear
and see the world, and shrink from what Blake calls mathe-
matic form, from every abstract thing, from all that is of the
brain only, from all that is not a fountain jetting from the
entire hopes, memories, and sensations of the Body." Twenty-
odd years later, in the midst of his work on *A Vision*, Yeats
retreated somewhat from this earlier position, saying that "the
mathematical structure, when taken up into the imagination,
is more than mathematical" and "that seemingly irrelevant
details fit together into a single theme."[48]

Discovering unity in the midst of multeity was one of the
values Yeats owed in part to Blake. When he put together a
selection of Blake's poems for publication in London in 1910,
he said that (like the Greek poets in Keats's "Ode to Maia")
Blake was "one of the great artificers of God who uttered
mysterious truths unto a little clan." Yeats might have been
writing of his own hopes in pointing out how Blake had man-
aged to unify his borrowings from multiple sources—"Swe-
denborg or Boehme . . . mystic or Kabalist"—turning them
"to his own purposes" and transferring them into "a new
system."[49]

As we have already noticed, Yeats at this time had not
wholly given up his interest in Shelley, another formulator of
a strong supporting intellectual-imaginative framework that
underlay the poems without unduly intruding upon them. In
November 1914, he set down the lines he called "A Medi-
tation in Time of War":

For one throb of the artery
While on that old grey stone I sat
Under the old wind-broken tree,
I knew that One is animate,
Mankind inanimate fantasy.

The indebtedness here, if indebtedness it is, seems about equally divided among Shelley's Ahasuerus in *Hellas*, who held that what we call reality is nothing but "bubbles and dreams," the "One" of Shelley's *Adonais*, that supernal power which remains "while the many change and pass," and finally the enigmatic remark in Blake's *Jerusalem:*

Every time less than the pulsation of an artery
Is equal in its period and value. . . .

That Blake's "pulsation of an artery" became Yeats's "throb of the artery" is easily attributable to the exigencies of meter, although it remains a question whether Yeats was in fact thinking of Blake rather than of his own natural heartbeat.

The only references to Blake in the *Anima Mundi* essay of May 1917 seem to have been chosen to emphasize his humanism and his broadly anthropocentric views. In *The Marriage of Heaven and Hell*, he had flatly said, "All deities reside in the human breast." Yeats quoted another apothegm from the source: "God only acts and is in existing beings or men." Some pages later he added another from Blake's lyric, "The Divine Image":

For mercy has a human heart
Pity a human face. . . .

Seven months afterward, Yeats completed the outline of the first part of *A Vision*. A dozen references give evidence of his continuing fraternal feeling for Blake, whom he places in Phase 16 of the Great Wheel, adjoining his own Phase 17. Blake's mythology, he says, discovers "symbolism to express the overflowing and bursting of the mind." Along with Rabelais, Aretino, and Paracelsus, other typical occupants of Phase 16, he

179

shows "an element of frenzy, and almost always a delight in certain glowing or shining images of concentrated force; in the smith's forge; in the heart; in the human form in its most vigorous development; in the solar disc; in some symbolical representation of the sexual organs; for the being must brag of its triumph over its own incoherence."[50]

Incoherence was a part of the problem. Although the example of Blake was evidently present to his mind as he formulated *A Vision*, it remained an example rather than a specific source book. He is straightforward in disposing of the notion that Blake was a direct influence.

> I had once known Blake as thoroughly as his unfinished confused Prophetic Books permitted, and I had read Swedenborg and Boehme, and my initiation into the 'Hermetic Students' had filled my head with Cabbalistic imagery, but there was nothing in Blake, Swedenborg and Boehme, or the Cabbala to help me now.*

In one important respect, however, he acknowledges a debt to Blake's thought: the *Weltanschauung* of the eternal conflict between contraries. "My mind had been full of Blake from boyhood up, and I saw the world as a conflict—Spectre and Emanation—and could distinguish between a contrary and a negation. 'Contraries are positive,' wrote Blake, 'a negation is not a contrary,' 'How great the gulph between simplicity and insipidity,' and again, 'There is a place at the bottom of the graves where contraries are equally true.' " These quotations, slightly inexact, are from the title engraving of Blake's *Milton* and from the second chapter of *Jerusalem*.[51] Yeats had impugned Shelley's inability to "conceive of the world as a continual conflict." His own inclinations in that direction drew him away from Shelley and toward Blake. As early as 1915, in "The Poet and The Actress," he had used the image of a

---

* *Vision*, 12. Morton Seiden has ably summarized resemblances and differences between the respective systems of Blake and Yeats, but Yeats's disavowal sounds final (Seiden, *William Butler Yeats*, esp. 18-30; cf. Harold Bloom in *Modern Poetry*, ed. John Hollander, N.Y., 1968, 513-17).

battle to express his views on the strategy of the artist. "Now the art I long for is also a battle, but it takes place in the depths of the soul, and one of the antagonists does not wear a shape known to the world or speak a mortal tongue. It is the struggle of the dream with the world. . . . There must be fable, mythology, that the dream and the reality may face one another in visible array. . . . The greater the contest the greater the art." Something like the same idea had been used to close his poem, "My House," in "Meditations in Time of Civil War" in 1921-1922, especially in the phrase, "Befitting emblems of adversity," which "exalt a lonely mind." How much of this he owed to Blake is, of course, a question, but there can be no doubt that seeing the world as a conflict was a concept of immense value to his poetry. By means of it, as Richard Ellmann says, he was able to see life "as a pitched battle fought by a whole cityful of faculties, gyres, phases, cycles, principles, spheres, spirits, and daimons, 'displaying the conflict in all its forms.' "[52]

He was thinking of Blake in another passage of *A Vision* when he characterized the poet of Phase 3 as one who "is content to permit his senses and his subconscious nature to dominate his intellect"—so that he exists "almost without intellect" in a state of bodily sanity. "His eyes and ears are open; one instinct balances another, and every season brings its delight." Yeats then slightly misquotes a quatrain from Blake's *Songs and Ballads*:

> He who bends to himself a joy*
> Does the winged life destroy,
> But he who kisses the joy as it flies
> Lives in eternity's sunrise.

Such a man as the second one in Blake's song "becomes an image where simplicity and intensity are united," a state of being in which Yeats himself could feel perfectly at home.[53]

Although Yeats's references to Blake, including direct quo-

* Blake wrote *binds*, not *bends*.

tations from the poetry and prose, are probably as numerous as those he makes to Shelley, actual verbal echoes are in both instances notably sparse. Apart from the "heart's deep core" in "The Lake Isle of Innisfree," the instances of conscious or unconscious lifting of phrases from Blake through the whole range of Yeats's poetry probably do not exceed a dozen. Three fairly typical instances may be cited from the period 1926-1931.

When Blake's brother Robert died in 1787, the poet saw the soul rising through the ceiling above the deathbed, "clapping its hands for joy." Several commentators have guessed that the second stanza of "Sailing to Byzantium" contains a passing allusion to this visionary phenomenon, though Robert Blake died young, and Yeats is writing of an aged man who is

> but a paltry thing,
> A tattered coat upon a stick, unless
> Soul clap its hands and sing, and louder sing
> For every tatter in its mortal dress. . . .[54]

The other two instances belong to 1931, the first in "Tom at Cruachan" (July), and the second in "Crazy Jane Talks with the Bishop," composed in November.

> On Cruachan's plain slept he
> That must sing in a rhyme
> That most would shake his soul:
> 'The stallion Eternity
> Mounted the mare of Time
> 'Gat the foal of the world.'

It is possible that Yeats's equine image could have grown out of the tenth proverb in The Marriage of Heaven and Hell, which says simply: "Eternity is in love with the productions of time."

In the second and deservedly far more famous poem, the bishop upbraids Jane for her sexual promiscuity, advising her to "live in a heavenly mansion, / Not in some foul sty." Her reply is defiant:

> A woman can be proud and stiff
> When on love intent;
> But Love has pitched his mansion in
> The place of excrement;
> For nothing can be sole or whole
> That has not been rent.

If this is related to Blake at all, it must be to the curious passage in *Jerusalem*, chapter four, where the Spectre, standing beside the forge of Los and "gratified" at the contention between Los and Enitharmon, utters these words:

> The Man who respects Woman shall be despised
> by Woman
> And deadly cunning & mean abjectness only, shall
> enjoy them
> For I will make their places of joy and love,
> excrementitious.

The "Last Poems" of 1936-1939 twice invoke the name of Blake, once in "An Acre of Grass," and again in "Under Ben Bulben." In the first occur these lines:

> Grant me an old man's frenzy,
> Myself must I remake
> Till I am Timon and Lear
> Or that William Blake
> Who beat upon the wall
> Till Truth obeyed his call. . . .

Blake's wall was that of Jerusalem:

> I give you the end of a golden string
> Only wind it into a ball.
> It will lead you in at Heaven's Gate
> Built into Jerusalem's wall.

183

Blake's golden thread was like that which Ariadne gave to Theseus, by which he was able to descend into the dark labyrinth and to return unharmed. Yeats had already used a comparable image in the second stanza of "Byzantium," where we are told that "Hades' bobbin bound in mummy-cloth / May unwind the winding path." Blake's quatrain could have struck Yeats simply because it suggested bobbins, mummy-cloths, and winding paths going upward—all of them associated with his favorite image of the gyre.

It is rather touching that Yeats's poetical loyalties should have led him to pay tribute to both Shelley and Blake in "Under Ben Bulben," the late poem that concludes with his own epitaph. We have already examined the reference to Shelley's "Witch of Atlas" in the opening section. Blake appears in the company of other artists in section 4, where Yeats begins with direct address to those poets, sculptors, and painters who have variously brought "the soul of man to God." "Measurement began our might," he writes, like the "forms a stark Egyptian thought." Among the Greeks he names Phidias, then turns to Michelangelo at work in the Sistine Chapel, and the men of the Quattrocento who painted dreamlike gardens where the soul could feel at ease under cloudless skies. Claude Lorrain in the seventeenth century carried on the great tradition, reopening upon canvas, as Samuel Palmer said, "the vistas of Eden." One of Claude's most gifted followers in the eighteenth century was the Welsh landscape artist, Richard Wilson. Yeats rounds out his list with two English painters who together bridged the gap between Blake's time and his own: Edward Calvert and Samuel Palmer, who had both known Blake in his final years and became his ardent disciples.

After the greater dream of the Quattrocento had gone, wrote Yeats,

> Calvert and Wilson, Blake and Claude,
> Prepared a rest for the people of God,
> Palmer's phrase, but after that
> Confusion fell upon our thought.

"Palmer's phrase," which Yeats slightly modifies, originated in his appraisal of Blake's woodcut illustrations to Ambrose Philips's "Imitation of Virgil's First *Eclogue*." As Palmer said, "They are like all that wonderful artist's works the drawing aside of the fleshly curtain, and the glimpse, which all the most holy, studious saints and sages have enjoyed, of the rest which remaineth to the people of God. The figures of Mr. Blake have that intense, soul-evidencing attitude and reaction, and that elastic nervous spring which belongs to uncaged immortal spirits."*

Palmer's reference to the "uncaged immortal spirits," of whom Blake was one, recalls Yeats's assertion of 1890 that Blake was for him a liberating force. Ten years later he had defined romanticism as "freedom of the spirit and imagination of man in literature," and called it "the movement most characteristic of the literature and art" in the whole nineteenth century.[55] The "elastic nervous spring" that Palmer praised in Blake ranks high among the qualities that Yeats, following his apprenticeship, managed to achieve in all his best poetry. Something like it had also been present in the work of those other English romantics whom Yeats chose as his early mentors. In 1910 he had put Blake chronologically at the head of the line, believing that his poetry marked "the first opening of the long-sealed well of romantic poetry." In 1931 he had placed himself among "the last romantics," as if with his departure and that of his like-minded companions, romanticism as a modern movement would finally die out. But others had risen up in England, Ireland, and America to carry on this immensely powerful tradition. After them would come many more in a "great procession," the end of which is not yet in sight as the twentieth century draws toward its close.

* Quoted in David Cecil, *Visionary and Dreamer*, Princeton: Princeton University Press, 1969, p. 39. As A. N. Jeffares points out, Yeats had given a part of Palmer's statement in his essay on Blake's illustrations to *The Divine Comedy* in 1924 (*EI*, 125; Jeffares, *Commentary*, 516-17).

Frost on the Pumpkin

Frost is an Emersonian Romantic who celebrates the minor incident, the eccentric attitude and the fleeting perception; he frequently does it with extraordinary beauty. —Yvor Winters, *Edwin Arlington Robinson*

THE NAME on the mailbox beside the blacktop highway between Ripton and Bread Loaf was Homer Noble. From there, turning north, the dirt road led gradually up a rise toward the Homer Noble Farm, in those years the summer seat of Robert Frost.

Along the sides of the road grew maples and alders, choke-cherry, now and again an elm, a few old apple trees, clumps of white birch, and most of the sturdy evergreens, self-seeded. Flowers nodded on the slanting roadbanks according to the season: daisies, buttercups, devil's paintbrush, sheepkill and heal-all and vetch, asters, milkweed, and steeplebush. Where the road pooled out into the green-and-brown farmyard, with the weathered stable door open to the afternoon sun and the handsome horses grazing in the north pasture, a path led through a break in the stone wall and up one further knoll. There, close to the top of the rise, with a westward sweep of distance toward the blue Adirondacks, stood the cabin.

Coming up the path that summer afternoon, one saw his old white head down beyond the field at the edge of the woods. Presently, punctually, knowing that he had agreed to conversation, he came up across the field with his rolling gait. The large, happy, old dog Gillie (Highland Scots for *male attendant*

186

on a chief) was at his heels. He shook hands briefly, with a quick twist of a smile, and said, "Come in." It was clear that he knew it was the title of one of his poems, and equally clear that he would not insist on anyone's making the connection.

The quiet cabin room on the south side was drenched with sunlight. It smelt pleasantly of pine lumber and of last evening's woodsmoke. The furniture was very simple. The rain of that morning had lingered on the underbrush in the woods, and his shoes and the wash pants were wet. Frost excused himself to change, disappearing into another room. Gillie exhaled dogwise, like the sigh we sigh, letting gravity flop him to the floor, chin on forepaws, eyes already contending with sleep. The fieldstone fireplace yawned beside the bookcase, which was populated with only a few books, lying at lazy angles. The highland chief returned quietly, shifted the poet's lapboard from the arms of the old chair, and sank into it as into the earned ease of warm water. But the old eyes were alight for fencing, the face alertly poised for talk. Frost was on his pumpkin.

When the frost is on the pumpkin, according to James Whitcomb Riley, and the morning sun greets the early riser, there's nothing like it to whet a man's euphoria. On summer afternoons like this one Frost always seemed to have his euphoria, too. He was relaxed and anecdotal, occupying his personal pumpkin with a kind of Thoreau-like balance and self-reliance. Anachronisms aside, it might have been this Frost of whom Thoreau was thinking when he said that he would rather sit on a pumpkin and have it all to himself than be crowded on a velvet cushion. On this summer pumpkin there was no crowding, except of ideas, events, remembered personalities.

One afternoon he began with the late Victorians and Edwardians, amongst whom he had sojourned in England before his own work was at all well known in his native land. One of these was William Ernest Henley, whose poems he admired, though he had not known him personally. Now he recited, half-satirically, the lines about being the captain of one's soul.

187

He recalled that Alfred Nutt had been Henley's publisher, bringing out his verse in the 1880s. The firm specialized in certain kinds of books, usually good books, with few but select authors in their stable. The dignity of their list and the connection with Henley had persuaded Frost to approach Nutt with his own poems. On being reminded of the Stevenson-Henley quarrel, Frost turned quickly to Stevenson, whose work he also liked. He was amused that women were attracted to the author of *Dr. Jekyll and Mr. Hyde* because they pitied him for his illnesses. But he disliked the Stevenson essay in which youthful stylists were urged to form their paragraphs by using other authors as models. Pursing up his mouth and looking firm and mighty, he scornfully repeated the phrase about "playing the sedulous ape." This idea, he said, had done great harm. It was "monkey business," no less, and he chuckled at his pun, once, low in throat, "huh-huh."

The mention of the young reminded his visitor of the country poem, "Out, Out—" about the death of a farm boy in an accident with a buzz saw. This poem, Frost said, was a reconstruction of an actual occurrence. It took place long ago on the road leading south from Bethel, New Hampshire, toward Franconia Notch. The boy's name was Fitzgerald. He belonged to a family that used to play baseball with Frost and included one who went on to become a minor leaguer with a New England team. After the accident the boy was rushed to the nearest hospital but died on the operating table of loss of blood and an overdose of ether. In the background of the poem is a mountain view of ranges rising. But the boy could not rise. Frost did not "think well" of this poem. He did not elaborate, although the inference was that it might be over-sentimental.[1]

He was not yet quite done with Stevenson. It was the writer's obligation to look at a thing, try to say it as it was, never to imitate the views of anybody else. Looking out of the west window toward the four o'clock sun, he hammered the point home. A writer had to "get up" his own way of saying things.

Queried on the very young, he answered "Even the young."
How young? "Even twelve or thirteen."

🍎 DURING HIS own youth, Frost had not felt so strongly
about the possibly damaging influence of other poets. In 1894,
aged twenty, he wrote Susan Hayes Ward, literary editor of
the New York *Independent*:

> When I am well I read a great deal and like a nearsighted
> person follow the text closely. I read novels in the hope
> of strengthening my executive faculties. Thomas Hardy
> has taught me the good use of a few words. . . . And as
> opposed to this man, Scott and Stevenson inspire me, by
> their prose, with the thought that we Scotchmen are bound
> to be romanticists—poets. Then as for poems my favor-
> ites are and have been these: Keats's "Hyperion," Shel-
> ley's "Prometheus," Tenneson's [*sic*] "Morte D'Arthur,"
> and Browning's "Saul,"—all of them about the giants.[2]

His Shelleyan period coincided with his courtship of his
fiancée, Elinor White, with whom he read aloud *The Revolt
of Islam, Prometheus Unbound*, most of the famous lyrics,
Epipsychidion, and even the early *Queen Mab*. In 1907 he
wrote an amusing verse letter parodying the style of Cole-
ridge's "The Rime of the Ancient Mariner." According to his
wife, Matthew Arnold and John Keats were the only poets
apart from E. A. Poe of whose works he had committed to
memory a substantial proportion. The only poem by Keats
that he did not like, she said, was *Endymion*.[3]

Wallace Stevens at about the same age was greatly attracted
to *Endymion* which he found so "intoxicating" that for ten
years or more he continued his reading in Keats, whose foot-
prints or soundprints were often visible or audible in his letters
and his poetry. In a recent essay on Stevens, Helen Vendler
offered a useful rubric for the always vexatious problem of
"influence" and "imitation." An artist, she wrote, can take
various paths in "commenting on a received aesthetic form."

189

He "may make certain implicit 'meanings' explicit; he may carry certain possibilities to further lengths; he may choose a detail, center down on it, and make it into an entire composition; he may alter the perspective from which the form is viewed; or he may view the phenomenon in a different moment of time."[4]

It is no adverse criticism of Frost's originality to say that a number of his poems are notable lyrical utterances on texts derived from others and long carried in his head like echoes of anterior times, places, and predicaments. "Acquainted With the Night," for example, appears to be his development of a line or two from the prophet Isaiah: "He was despised and rejected. . . . A man of sorrows, and acquainted with grief." Frost makes it *night* rather than *grief*, but the two are connected in many minds besides his own, including that of Keats in his sonnet, "To Sleep": "Then save me, or the passèd day will shine / Upon my pillow, breeding many woes. . . ." If *night* becomes Frost's word by eminent domain, Isaiah's *grief* is present like an undertone, a ghost in the cellarage, albeit supported by a hardbacked stoicism, and given a new locale in a nameless American city:

> I have been one acquainted with the night.
> I have walked out in rain—and back in rain.
> I have outwalked the furthest city light.
>
> I have looked down the saddest city lane.
> I have passed by the watchman on his beat.
> And dropped my eyes, unwilling to explain.
>
> I have stood still and stopped the sound of feet
> When far away an interrupted cry
> Came over houses from another street,
>
> But not to call me back or say good-by;
> And further still at an unearthly height,
> One luminary clock against the sky

Proclaimed the time was neither wrong nor right,
I have been one acquainted with the night.[5]

One finds here a note of defiance, a refusal to give in. The time is neither wrong nor right, but only time, ticking away like the clock against the sky, carrying with it, minute by minute, the burden of loneliness and sorrow that has to be borne, and if possible overcome.

Frost's practice with nearly all the forebears who gave him some of the ideas that appear in his poems was to frame up the "source" in such a way that it bore the stamp of his own character and experience. Although there is no way of proving it except to say that Emerson was his clear favorite among the American romantics, it is not difficult to believe that his poem, "After Apple-Picking," may owe something to a passage in Emerson's essay on "Intellect." Frost begins:

> My long two-pointed ladder's sticking through a tree
> Toward heaven still,
> And there's a barrel that I didn't fill
> Beside it, and there may be two or three
> Apples I didn't pick upon some bough.
> But I am done with apple-picking now.
> Essence of winter sleep is on the night,
> The scent of apples: I am drowsing off . . .
> Magnified apples appear and disappear,
> Stem end and blossom end,
> And every fleck of russet showing clear.
> My instep arch not only keeps the ache,
> It keeps the pressure of a ladder-round.[6]

"If you gather apples in sunshine," wrote Emerson, "or make hay, or hoe corn, and then retire indoors and shut your eyes and press them with your hand, you shall see apples hanging in the bright light with boughs and leaves thereto, or the tasselled grass, or the corn-flags, and this for five or six hours afterwards. . . . So lies the whole series of natural images with which your life has made you acquainted, in your memory, though you know it not; and a thrill of passion flashes light on their dark chamber, and the active power seizes instantly the fit image, as the word of its momentary thought."[7]

Frost's practice with his echoes of Keats, to return to Helen Vendler's list of poetic strategies, seems mainly to have involved choosing a detail, centering down on it, and then using it with a twist of his own as a consummate moment in a fresh composition. He had a nascent theory on the matter that he enunciated in 1914.

> Just so many sentence sounds belong to man as just so many vocal runs belong to one kind of bird. We come into the world with them and create none of them. What we feel as creation is only selection and grouping. We summon them from Heaven knows where under excitement with the audile [audial] imagination. And unless we are in an imaginative mood it is no use trying to make them, they will not rise. . . . We write of things we see and we write in accents we hear. Thus we gather both our material and our technique with the imagination from life; and our technique becomes as much material as material itself. . . . In poetry and under emotion every word is "moved" a little or much—moved from its old place, heightened, made, made new. See what Keats did to the word "alien" in the [Nightingale] ode. But as he made it special in that place he made it his—and his only in that place. He could never have used it again with just that turn. It takes the little one horse poets to do that. I am probably the only Am[erican] poet who haven't used it after him. . . . I want the unmade words to work with, not the familiar made ones that everybody exclaims Poetry! at. Of course the great fight of any poet is against the people who want him to write in a special language that has gradually separated from spoken language by this "making" process. His pleasure must always be to make his own words as he goes and never to depend for effect on words already made even if they be his own.[8]

By "words already made" Frost plainly is referring to the phenomenon that Wordsworth called "poetic diction." In his preface to *Lyrical Ballads* (1800), Wordsworth had said that readers would find little of it in the following volumes.

> I do not know how to give my Reader a more exact notion of the style in which it was my wish and intention to write, than by informing him that I have at all times endeavoured to look steadily at my subject; consequently there is, I hope, in these Poems little falsehood of description, and my ideas are expressed in language fitted to their respective importance. Something must have been gained by this practice . . . but it has necessarily cut me off from a large portion of phrases and figures of speech which from father to son have long been regarded as the common inheritance of Poets. I have also thought it expedient to restrict myself still further, having abstained from the use of many expressions, in themselves proper and beautiful, but which have been foolishly repeated by bad Poets, till such feelings of disgust are connected with them as it is scarcely possible by any art of association to overpower.

Frost, like Wordsworth, was willing and even eager to cut himself off from that "large portion of phrases and figures of speech which from father to son have long been regarded as the common inheritance of Poets." With the "unmade" words to work with, rather than "the familiar made ones that everybody exclaims Poetry! at," he could avoid the "special language that has become gradually separated from spoken language by the 'making' process." In 1915 Frost expatiated on this position.

> When Wordsworth said, "Write with your eyes on the object" . . . he really meant something more. That something carries out what I mean by writing with your ear to the voice. This is what Wordsworth did himself in all his best poetry, proving that there can be no creative

imagination unless there is a summoning up from experience, fresh from life, which has not hitherto been evoked. The power, however, to do this does not last very long in the life of a poet. After ten years Wordsworth had very nearly exhausted his, giving us only flashes of it now and then. As language really only exists in the mouths of men, here again Wordsworth was right in trying to reproduce in his poetry not only the words—and in their limited range, too, actually used in common speech—but their sound.[9]

Frost's wish to avoid the "special language that has become gradually separated from spoken language by the 'making' process" did not mean, however, that his visual or audial memory would not from time to time be flicked or touched or more deeply engaged by an adjective like *alien*, a verb like *spared*, a phrase like "acquainted with grief," or a picture like Emerson's of "apples hanging in the bright light with boughs and leaves thereto."

One such effect, borrowed from Keats, appeared in "Stopping by Woods on a Snowy Evening." Its distant origin was the opening quatrain of a sonnet already a century old:

> Keen fitful gusts are whisp'ring here and there
> Among the bushes half leafless, and dry;
> The stars look very cold about the sky,
> And I have many miles on foot to fare.

Frost's echo has since become so well known that it is pointed out in Bartlett's *Familiar Quotations*:

> The woods are lovely, dark and deep,
> But I have promises to keep,
> And miles to go before I sleep.[10]

It is winter in Frost, fall in Keats. Keats's narrator walks the streets of London, Frost's rides in a sleigh along a country road in New Hampshire. In Keats the air is cool and bleak,

194

in Frost it is filled with downy flakes of snow. But both travelers are far from home, with miles to go before they sleep, and this is the "made" concept that Frost has seized on.

"Mowing" shows that as a quondam farmer Frost knew by experience the sound of his "long scythe whispering to the ground," as well as something about "the earnest love that laid the swale in rows," letting a few "feeble-pointed spikes of flowers" fall by the way as too trivial to be saved. In another poem about mowing, "The Tuft of Flowers," he not only echoed his own line about the scythe whispering to ground but also one from Keats's "To Autumn." A butterfly leads the eye of Frost's farm worker to "a tall tuft of flowers beside a brook, / A leaping tongue of bloom the scythe had *spared*." The same verb had been used by Keats in his account of the figure of Autumn, who falls asleep after the labor of mowing, while her reaping hook, British for scythe, "*spares* the next swath and all its twinèd flowers."[11]

This might be called "imitation by agreement," where the verbal echo is exact and traceable. Another strategy could be called "imitation by contradiction," where the poet, fully aware of a position espoused by his source, chooses for various reasons *not* to agree, and forges a new poem in the very act of disagreement. Several of Frost's lyrics establish shadowy woodlands as regions of potential escape, but it is characteristic of him to reject the temptation to enter them. When the narrator stops by a patch of snow-filled forest in his sleigh, he calls the woodland "lovely, dark and deep." But then at once comes the realization that other interests and obligations restrain him: "I have promises to keep / And miles to go before I sleep."

Keats's most notable statement about the temptation to enter dark forestland comes in "Ode to a Nightingale":

O for a beaker full of the warm South . . .
That I might drink and leave the world unseen,
And with thee fade away into the forest dim. . . .

195

Such a prospect appeals to the poet as a way of leaving behind

> The weariness, the fever, and the fret
> Here, where men sit and hear each other groan . . .
> Where but to think is to be full of sorrow
> And leaden-eyed despairs. . . .

The temptation to follow the birdsong "through verdurous glooms" is strong enough to bring him nearly to the endstop of "easeful Death," with which he has long been "half in love." As in his sonnet to Sleep, he uses religious terms like *requiem* and *anthem* as part of the verbal environment. In the end the vision fades, the nightingale moves far ahead, almost out of earshot, and the narrator comes, as it were, back to ordinary earth, reassuming the familiar role of his "sole self" and half-convinced that he has been victimized by cheating fancy.

In Frost's "Come In," the speaker stands likewise at the edge of a forest listening to the song of a bird. It is dusk where he stands, dark inside.

> The last of the light of the sun
> That had died in the west
> Still lived for one song more
> In a thrush's breast.

Like Keats's nightingale, Frost's thrush is far off. The phrase "pillared dark," a brilliant image for nightfall among the boles of trees, faintly suggests the gloomy interior of a gothic cathedral, where requiems might be sung.

> Far in the pillared dark
> Thrush music went—
> Almost like a call to come in
> To the dark and lament.

To mourn over or bewail the maladies of the quotidian is different from the wish to escape them, as in Keats's vision. But this is not a temptation to which the narrator in Frost is willing to succumb. His rejection is abrupt and final, unlike the lingering conclusion to Keats's ode:

> But no, I was out for stars,
> I would not come in.
> I meant not even if asked
> And I hadn't been.

For a fleeting moment he has engaged a vision not unlike that of Keats, magnetized by the audial will-o'-the-wisp of birdsong. Yet the temptation to self-indulgence is also fleeting. No sooner has he taken note of it than he is ready to take leave of it. A man who is "out for stars" must stay clear of the forest.[12]

Although Frost might sometimes disagree with him on ethical or esthetic grounds, Keats was undoubtedly his favorite among the English romantic poets. Reginald L. Cook's valuable study, *Robert Frost: A Living Voice* (1974) records some of his off-the-cuff observations on Keats's achievement. He wryly regretted the confusion of Balboa and Cortez in the Chapman's *Homer* sonnet, yet admired the "wild surmise" of the penultimate line. The "cold finger" that the water nymph presses to her lips in *Hyperion* (I, 14) struck him strongly because of the naturalistic precision of the adjective. In his favorite of all the odes, he held that Keats ought to have inserted a hyphen in "winnowing wind" to show that he meant the wind in its role as winnower of the grain and only incidentally as the current of soft air that stirred the locks of Autumn personified.[13] The late poem, "Something like a Star," echoes Keats's "steadfast . . . Eremite" from the opening quatrain of the "Bright Star" sonnet.*

---

* CP, 575, Cook, *Robert Frost*, 285-86. Despite his early and enthusiastic reading of Shelley, Frost said little about him in his later years. Reginald Cook's volume contains only a few allusions, chiefly to such lesser lyrics as "A Lament," which may have contributed one word to "Come In," and "Stanzas Written in Dejection, Near Naples," which Frost appropriated as the title of his prophetic play-poem on the American moon-landings, an event he did not live to see.

Even when all such echoes and allusions have been gathered and evaluated, they do not, in sum, contradict Frost's contention that he leaned very little on books for the substance of his verse. In the old phrase, he knew many poems "by heart" and indeed took them to heart so well that a remembered line or phrase or image could sometimes stir him into launching a poem of his own. The closing line of "I Could Give All to Time" is relevant here: "And what I would not part with I have kept." So also is the sentence that concludes "At Woodward's Gardens": "It's knowing what to do with things that counts."[14]

A FAINTLY pejorative review of Frost's *Collected Poems* in 1949 concluded that he was a kind of triptych.[15] On one side stood the lecturer, in the center, the artist, on the third panel lurked the evader. The lecturer was the man everyone knew; the artist, though the quality of his work varied—a point well taken—had nevertheless achieved a memorable body of first-rate lyrics; the evader was the man nobody knew, and his habits in this respect had kept him from confronting the deepest problems that beset modern society. These views invite a brief reappraisal from the vantage point of 1983.

Frost as lecturer was very widely known. If Yeats could rightly call himself in "Among School Children" a "smiling public man," Frost could have fitted the epithet to himself at any age between forty and eighty. Large audiences came to hear him lecture and read every fall, winter, and spring: the wisecracking homilist, the witty master of the meaty monologue, the public man who seemed so much at ease but sometimes privately recalled with a grimace an early appearance in Boston. That horrific hour took him three months to prepare for but made him so "nervous" that he needed another three months to recover from it.

In his later years, if granted a running start, he could "get up" a lecture in two or three afternoons of comtemplation, although there were often periods of gloomy fretfulness in the

198

hours leading up to lecture time. He was something like an athlete, restive, needing to be by himself, resisting interruptions like a stranger, and conserving his energies for the race to come. But when the hour struck, he characteristically emerged into the crowded arena, rough-haired, tuxedoed, a book under his arm, alert behind the mask of sternness, catching the warmth of the crowd, taking his stance at the podium, stumbling a time or two, reaching out for the right stride, and at last moving off down the track in whatever direction he had pre-determined.

Beside the lecturer, his true *raison d'être*, was always the artist, whose work might be compared to a pointillist screen shot with highlights, never transparent but penetrable to the educated understanding. Each word glinted with its native fervors, like fireflies in a Vermont dusk, and part of the pleasure in reading him was to find the patterns they made on the blanket of the dark. He himself liked to use a different metaphor. Every poem was like a game of hint and seek, and he often said, "I like people that can take a hint—but won't take one when none's intended." As in the children's game from which the image was adapted, one roves for the clues, listens for the stir and rustle that betrays the quarry, and at last moves in to take possession. Frost's early lyric, "Revelation," is relevant:

> We make ourselves a place apart
> Behind light words that tease and flout,
> But oh, the agitated heart
> Till someone find us really out.
>
> 'Tis pity if the case require
> (Or so we say) that in the end
> We speak the literal to inspire
> The understanding of a friend.
>
> But so with all, from babes that play
> At hide-and-seek to God afar,
> So all who hide too well away
> Must speak and tell us where they are.[16]

The reviewer who emphasized Frost's evasiveness could not have looked often or warily enough into the hints that lurk behind the body of the poet's work—what Frost often called "my book," evidently thinking of it as a unit, as Whitman thought of *Leaves of Grass*. The mass of people were not invited into Frost's innermost sanctum, behind the curtain of reticence and reserve or the final wall of silence, New England style. This poet's romantic sympathies did not respond to anterior poets like the Byron of *Childe Harold* who made a pageant of his bleeding heart. Whoever, like Hamlet, had that within which passeth show ought to leave it, he felt, where it was. The ethical norm on bleeding hearts, whether personal or social, could be easily made over from one of Frost's lines: The stronger you are, the less you say.

Frost in his early sixties was firm against the idea of projecting one's personal sorrows outward to embrace an age.

You will often hear it said that the age of the world we live in is particularly bad. I am impatient of such talk. We have no way of knowing that this age is one of the worst in the world's history. Arnold claimed the honor for the age before this. Wordsworth claimed it for the last but one. And so on back through literature. I say they claimed the honor for their ages. They claimed it rather for themselves. It is immodest of a man to think of himself as going down before the worst forces ever mobilized by God. All ages of the world are bad—a great deal worse anyway than Heaven. . . . One can safely say after from six to thirty thousand years of experience that the evident design is a situation here in which it will always be about equally hard to save your soul . . . or if you dislike hearing your soul mentioned in open meeting, say your decency, your integrity. . . . The background is hugeness and confusion shading away from where we stand into black and utter chaos; and against the background any small man-made figure of order and concentration. What pleasanter than that this should be so? . . .

To me any little form I assert upon it is velvet, as the saying is, and to be considered for how much more it is than nothing.[17]

That Frost was among those who disliked hearing his soul discussed in open meeting should deceive no one into supposing that he slipped unscathed past the central fears and tortures of the age he lived through. Any objective appraisal of his work shows how fully and forcefully he wrestled with his angels both dark and light.

> They cannot scare me with their empty spaces
> Between stars—on stars where no human race is.
> I have it in me so much nearer home
> To scare himself with my own desert places.[18]

By the beginning of his eighth decade, Frost had accumulated as many scars as any other veteran. They remain visible deep in the grain of his poetry, as with the sawn cross-sections of great trees. Sometimes, watching the poet merrily at his work, balanced securely on his pumpkin, one could believe that they were not there. But they were there.

🍂 IT USED TO BE part of the game at these pumpkin sessions for his listeners to keep trying to push Frost toward intellectual commitments. He displayed delighted alacrity in seldom allowing himself to be backed against the ropes. As he bobbed and weaved, flicking his left into the face of an idea, holding his pile driver right in reserve for any lucky opening, one was sometimes reminded of a remark of Harvey Breit's, made on the occasion of the poet's eightieth birthday, "We have always wanted," wrote Breit, "to put an arm around him and protect him—and Mr. Frost needs protection about as much as Rocky Marciano."[19]

Frost was rarely found in a neutral corner, except perhaps momentarily, as if to catch his breath. He enjoyed taking the opposite side of any question, a habit that Emerson deplored in Thoreau. Call him a radical and he would presently start talking like a right-wing Republican. Praise Yeats's Byzantine nightingale and Frost would attack the idea of artificiality in verse.* Champion the vitalistic in poetry, and the smiling opponent would launch an attack on "mere life," quoting some very bad Whitman to bolster his position.

What sometimes resembled the evasiveness of a clever boxer could emerge as a complex exercise in argumentation. He liked to make what might be called noncommittal commitments. A commentator on his private theology would do well to use as an epigraph Frost's famous couplet: "We dance around in a ring and suppose / But the secret sits in the middle and knows."[20] It was not a boxing ring he had in mind, but the large circular periphery on which the human race is situated. During one session at the cabin he fixed an interlocutor with a fierce blue-eyed glance and said, "I have never had a religious experience." The impression was that he would not know what to do with one if he had ever had it. There was another year, sometime in the late 1940s, when he told his lecture audience that no one, not even a poet, "can *say* God." It was possible, of course, to talk "*about* God," drawing a circle in the air with his index finger to signify that by "about" he meant to mean "all around" the peripheries of Godhood whose center remained intact and uninvaded.

Yet the poetry is salted with ideas of God. "Sitting by a Bush in Broad Sunlight" offers a speculation on the double origin of the human species. An early poem on the "false god" of science is called "The Demiurge's Laugh." There is "The Strong Are Saying Nothing," with its temporal setting of springtime planting and its remarkably enigmatic conclusion:

> Wind goes from farm to farm in wave on wave,
> But carries no cry of what is hoped to be.
> There may be little or much beyond the grave,
> But the strong are saying nothing until they see.[21]

* Yeats's nightingale does, however, appear in *A Masque of Reason*, line 17.

If Frost was temperamentally inclined to shrug off the incubus-demon of the Absolute, he showed no disinclination to the pleasures of metaphysical speculation. *The Masque of Reason*, his ironic little redaction of the Book of Job, shows him at work with God and the Devil, Job and Job's Wife. Erie Volkert of Middlebury College gave it a memorable first production in the Little Theatre at the Bread Loaf School of English one summer evening in 1946. The faculty met beforehand at the house of the school's director, Reginald Cook, and Frost was present, though less than communicative. A black storm had arisen less than an hour before curtain time. Rain fell in torrents, roads ran rivers, lightning shattered trees in the surrounding forests, and thunder belched and boomed among the mountains. One of the company, trying to relieve Frost's evident tension with literary jocularity, reminded him of the world premiere of Milton's *Comus* three hundred and twelve years earlier. The man was going to make what he thought was a pertinent pun on the earl of Bridgewater in whose honor Milton's masque was presented at Ludlow Castle. But before he could establish the watery tie-up, Frost grunted, grinned, and went out to the porch for a look at the storm. When he came back he said that Milton was luckier. Luckier? How? "Milton didn't try to put God on the stage."*

Frost's worry was clearly not metaphysical but esthetic. Throughout the performance, heavy rain hammered on the roof of the theatre like a giant tympanum. The masque-God and masque-Devil were obliged to yell to make themselves heard. But there was nothing to suggest that evening that Frost took the noise as a sign of supernatural vengeance against his temerity. He knew very well that the Deity was busy with other matters. Drama, except in cosmic sense, was not His department.

In his speculations on the possible interrelations among Nature, Man, and God, Frost developed over the years what

* His sole poetical allusion to Blake comes in *A Masque of Reason*, when Job's wife recognizes God: "I'd know him by Blake's picture anywhere." See also one other brief allusion in ML, xix.

203

might be called an essentially antiromantic system: "keeping separates separate." If one tries to combine and interpret all he had to say on this topic, whether in the poems themselves, in public lectures, or in more or less private conversations, he is likely to conclude that in Frost's thought Nature, Man, and God remain as separate entities. Milton might seek in epic form to justify God's ways to man. Frost the inveterate lyricist, eschewing epical scope, would follow Milton's lead only part of the way. Romanticists like Wordsworth and Emerson might regard natural facts, properly interpreted, as signs or emblems of supernatural truths. Frost was not so sure. On or off the pumpkin he was willing to speculate ad libitum. Yet his "system"—so far as he ever formulated one—tended to relegate God, Man, and Nature to separate spheres of action. Keeping the distinction in mind, he seemed to say, would save us all a good deal of cloudy thinking.

Even though Frost often dealt in his poetry with natural objects, he was far from being what is ordinarily thought of as a "nature poet." In the poetic ritual, nature may sometimes *seem* to reflect and perhaps respond to certain human moods. Frost had read enough Ruskin to be aware of man's psychological temptation to project his own emotions or attitudes into lower forms of being. Yet he remained wary, like Ruskin, of falling into the sentimentalist's trap. "Beware," he quietly warned us, "of confusing *seems* and *is*. Nature has no human qualities. It is a distinct realm of being." This admonition of "bewareness" comes through in "The Need of Being Versed in Country Things." The poet is here so intent upon his point, and so crafty in its presentation, that he uses similes rather than metaphors, for even a metaphor, in a poem on this subject, would imply a greater degree of unity between the birds and the observer than Frost wishes us to infer. To accent the similes would be to emphasize essential discontinuity, to keep Nature and Man at arm's length from each other. To be "versed" in "country things" would be to know the essential difference between birdhood and manhood. Nature has this importance for the poet: it teaches him differentiation.[22]

It is also the unwitting catalyst in his poetic chemistry. Unless we are geologists, we must never imagine that there are sermons in stones. Yet this stone, that running brook, approached on a special day by a poet, a poet moreover with a full mind ready to react to a chance stimulus, *might* suddenly project him into a new motion, even a new vision. Such a catalytic phenomenon was no doubt what Wordsworth had in mind when he spoke of the "one impulse from a vernal wood" that might conceivably teach the open mind something not hitherto realized about moral evil and moral good. Since nature is unwitting, the wits must be ours. But to the ready wit, the prepared mind, all nature teems with prospective suggestions. Thoreau's story of the "strong and beautiful bug" that emerged from the table near the end of *Walden* gained its value from what Thoreau made of it. Frost's oven bird seems to ask, in all but words, what to make of a diminished thing.[23] The answer must be ours to make.

"Hyla Brook," a lovely small poem, builds to the affirmation, "We love the things we love for what they are," which is a human affirmation of the value we place on keeping nature natural and in its place. We catch the brook in June, songless, waterless, its bed sheeted with "dead leaves stuck together by the heat." But what it was in the other seasons we also know, and can love it equally for its aspect in frozen December or liquid May. The wit of Frost, catalyzed by the brook's appearance in June, can instantly evoke its likeness in earlier months. As in "The Need of Being Versed in Country Things," he employs a brilliant simile rather than a metaphor, and the first nine lines frame it off:

> By June our brook's run out of song and speed.
> Sought for much after that, it will be found
> Either to have gone groping underground
> (And taken with it all the Hyla breed
> That shouted in the mist a month ago,
> Like ghost of sleighbells in a ghost of snow)—
> Or flourished and come up in jewel-weed,

205

Weak foliage that is blown upon and bent
Even against the way its waters went.[24]

The peeper frogs of spring, shouting away in the mists of
May "like ghost of sleighbells in a ghost of snow" is as bril-
liant, as immediate, and as imaginative a compression of three
seasons into instantaneous perspective as we are likely to meet.
It matches the sharp etching of "bare ruined choirs, where
late the sweet birds sang," a place where Shakespeare is not,
strictly speaking, loving the things he loves for what they are,
but rather for what they have been and are no longer.

The essential brilliance of this poem is further enhanced not
only by the subtle music of alliteration but also by its hint,
carried in the title and in the fourth line, that we love the
things we love for what the poet can make of them. The
reference to the springtime frogs as members of "the Hyla
breed" throws into the seasonal perspective a good many
centuries more than this one where the poet is taking count
of a country book. It carries us back, indeed, to another spring-
time in the mists of classical antiquity when Hylas, page of
Herakles, went ashore for water on the Mysian coast, only
to be drawn into the spring by the nymphs of that locality
and to be lost to sight as rapidly, mysteriously, and completely
as the Hyla breed that vanished in the brook near Frost's old
home in Derry, New Hampshire. "The beautiful fables of the
Greeks," as Emerson said, "being proper creations of the
imagination and not of the fancy, are universal verities."[25]

In the work of Frost, nature is not sentient, does not "know."
It is only a kind of rough mechanism that operates and exists.
In what he says of it, considered for itself and not necessarily
for what the poet can make of it, two qualities stand out.
Nature lasts, endures; nature is either faintly or aggressively
sinister. It would of course be foolish to deny the pleasurable
stimuli that natural beauty offers to the senses and the wits.
The offering is various and abundant: rose pogonias, "blue-
berries as big as the end of your thumb," a tuft of flowers left

after mowing, the bloom of pear and cherry, a thrush's music receding into the depths of the woods, the perpetual stars in the night sky. Yet it is an offering whose essence is morally neutral, showing neither love nor hate—as in Frost's allusion to

> Those stars like some snow-white
> Minerva's snow-white marble eyes
> Without the gift of sight.[26]

It would be just as foolish to deny its durability, or its overwhelming power when that is unleashed, as in Frost's sonnet, "Once by the Pacific," or the early and excellent "Storm Fear," or that literally awesome "embodiment" of natural force that momentarily appears to the speaker in "The Most of It."

> He thought he kept the universe alone;
> For all the voice in answer he could wake
> Was but the mocking echo of his own
> From some tree-hidden cliff across the lake.
> Some morning from the boulder-broken beach
> He would cry out on life, that what it wants
> Is not its own love back in copy-speech,
> But counter-love, original response.
> And nothing ever came of what he cried
> Unless it was the embodiment that crashed
> In the cliff's talus on the other side,
> And then in the far distant water splashed,
> But after a time allowed for it to swim,
> Instead of proving human when it neared
> And someone else additional to him,
> As a great buck it powerfully appeared,
> Pushing the crumpled water up ahead,
> And landed pouring like a waterfall,
> And stumbled through the rocks with horny tread,
> And forced the underbrush—and that was all.[27]

Frost's liking for metaphysical speculation rises here to a memorable test. We think we keep our universe alone. Our cries yield no answers we can recognize as human, unless we count our own in "mocking echo," like the bounce of a sound-wave off the cold surface of the moon, mere "copyspeech" that throws our questions back into our faces, leaving us no wiser. Is love there? With what counter-love shall we answer it? Is hatred there? What original response can we make to its presence? No answer, unless we count that "embodiment" whose approach we may sometimes sense, a power half-sinister, forceful, not to be denied, coming over from "the other side," landing on the nearer shore, stumbling among the rocks "with horny tread." What was that stag? We may ask it in a paraphrase of another of Frost's lyrics: "Truth? The Devil himself? For once, then, something."

❦ TO KEEP SEPARATES separate is to underscore the essential otherness of Nature and of God in respect of Man's estate. To say that we are of Nature and God in that we exist beneath their respective sovereignties is not to say that they are of us. Frost is neither animistic enough to see God in Nature nor mystical enough to see Nature in God. Like the sculptured marble eyes of Minerva, the eye of Nature gives back no answering intellectual gleam. Nor does the Sphinx of Godhead respond in any verbal medium. God is not, to contradict Yeats's wonderfully imaginative phrase, slouching toward anywhere to be born, or born again, unless we count the birth within our imaginations of the concept of Godhood. Man is the measure, and the measurer. The "limitless trait in the hearts of men" is that they will accept no limits or bounds, nor will they stop asking questions. Still, no matter how long or industriously we may question, we will not find Nature through God, nor yet God through Nature. Frost has risen to this question often in his verse, though seldom more succinctly than in the closing stanza of "All Revelation."

Eyes meeting the response of eyes
Bring out the stars, bring out the flowers,
Thus concentrating earth and skies
So none need be afraid of size.
All revelation has been ours.[28]

Yet the view that "all revelation" has originated with us—
a humanistic affirmation—has not the tone of a boast. What
are we, for example, against the vast sweep of *natura natu-rans*? The word is "unnoticed."

You grasp the bark by a rugged pleat,
And look up small from the forest's feet.
The only leaf it drops goes wide,
Your name not written on either side.

You linger your little hour and are gone,
And still the woods sweep leafily on,
Not even missing the coral-root flower
You took as a trophy of the hour.[29]

The manner and degree of God's intercession in human
history is as enigmatic in Frost's thought as it commonly is
in our own personal experience. If God is the Secret at the
Center that does not reveal Itself, we have no certain way of
knowing how It is acting upon us. If God intercedes in human
affairs at all, it is in ways so inscrutable, by means so intricate
and complex, that we cannot expect to comprehend them.
The *how* or *how much* come bouncing back to us like the
sound of our voices from the cliff across the lake. One of
Frost's aphorisms says that "Heaven gives its glimpses only
to those not in position to look too close."[30] Or again, "On
Looking Up By Chance at the Constellations" he offers an
apt admonishment:

You'll wait a long, long time for anything much
To happen in heaven beyond the floats of cloud
And the Northern Lights that run like tingling nerves.
The sun and moon get crossed, but they never touch,

Nor strike out fire from each other, nor crash out loud.
The planets seem to interfere in their curves,
But nothing ever happens, no harm is done.
We may as well go patiently on with our life,
And look elsewhere than to stars and moon and sun
For the shocks and changes we need to keep us sane.
It is true the longest drouth will end in rain,
The longest peace in China will end in strife.
Still it wouldn't reward the watcher to stay awake
In hopes of seeing the calm of heaven break
On his particular time and personal sight.
That calm seems certainly safe to last tonight.[31]

The "limitless trait in the hearts of men" causes them, like
the swinger of birches, to climb the trunk "*toward* heaven,"
with italics supplied by Frost. When the tree can bear no more,
it dips its crown and sets men down again. But *toward* is not
to. Does man imagine, as in Arnold's "Buried Life," that he
thinks he knows "The hills where his life rose, / And the sea
where it goes?" Can he conjure up visions of the Insulae
Fortunatae out of the needs of his aspirational spirit? Frost's
reply rings with rueful laughter:

> But Islands of the Blessèd, bless you son,
> I never came upon a blessèd one.[32]

His mighty wrestlings with the angel of teleology are a nice
mixture of "touch-and-go" with "wait-and-see." The reflec-
tive lyric, "Our Hold on the Planet," begins with climatic
circumstance, moving on into a kind of affirmation:

> We asked for rain. It didn't flash and roar.
> It didn't lose its temper at our demand
> And blow a gale. It didn't misunderstand
> And give us more than our spokesman bargained for,
> And just because we owned to a wish for rain,
> Send us a flood and bid us be damned and drown.
> It gently threw us a glittering shower down.
> And when we had taken that into the roots of grain,

It threw us another and then another still
Till the spongy soil again was natal wet.
We may doubt the just proportion of good to ill.
There is much in nature against us. But we forget:
Take nature altogether since time began,
Including human nature, in peace and war,
And it must be a little more in favor of man,
Say a fraction of one percent at the very least
Or our number living wouldn't be steadily more,
Our hold on the planet wouldn't have so increased.[33]

If this poem is anything more than an implied answer to the doctrines of T. R. Malthus—and it is—it is a high-level affirmation that in the eternal war game between man and nature, including man's own nature, the score at approximately half-time is roughly 51-49 in man's favor. How the game will end we do not know: some say in fire, some say in ice, and perhaps, that far along, it does not matter anyhow. But for the time being the adversary shows no special fatigue. Many substitutes, some fearsome, wait on the sideline benches. That "glittering shower" was a chance *donnée*, a spot of luck. Like all such, it was welcome when it came out of the blue or the gray, but not to be counted on as more than one element in the world's weather, one meteor whisking through the total meteorological record. The poem mentions nature and human nature without presuming on God. If His hand is discernible, it is only in the grand pattern.

Frost could number the streaks on a pumpkin and feel reasonably secure. But he was also given sometimes to affirmation at the highest levels. Whoever tries to measure the height of his seat on the pumpkin with a spiritual altimeter would find that it approximated the height of Olympus. In certain moods he delighted to take the long view, not only of the distant blue Adirondacks but also of human affairs. In these moods, and they were not his only ones, the busy small alarums of men might be reduced to "considerable specks," but specks none-

211

theless, on the slow, majestic, perpetual belt of seasons and centuries.

This Olympian Frost was a limited pessimist. Whatever we may do, he once said, human society is always likely to be at sixes and sevens. It has never been otherwise, nor despite all our efforts will the sixes ever cease to be at odds with the sevens, for reasons deeply implicit in the mathematics of human relations. Still, this Olympian Frost was also a limited optimist. The record indicates that the human race has managed to hold its own. The optimist in Frost could therefore say that "it bids pretty fair." From his throne on the pumpkin he could employ a play-image to summarize his hunch:

> The play seems out for an almost infinite run.
> Don't mind a little thing like the actors fighting.
> The only thing I worry about is the sun.
> We'll be all right if nothing goes wrong with
>   the lighting.[34]

Pound's Prison Graffiti

THE PISAN CANTOS

> As a lone ant from a broken ant-hill from the
> wreckage of Europe, ego scriptor. —Canto 76

HE WAS OLD when we met him first, the grizzled veteran
of a thousand wars, literary and other, and standing on the
brink of his eightieth birthday. They said he would celebrate
the occasion quietly in Paris, taking the train from Mestre in
a day or two. This was thought to be fitting for several reasons,
not least that Paris was the place where he had established
himself forty years earlier as both catalyst and contributor to
modern literature—a bearded Caliban, in his own words, fiercely
intent upon casting out the Ariel of pretentious rhetoric.

The idea of meeting him had come up casually enough the
night before. We were dining on scampi and grilled tournedos
in Harry's Bar, enriched by small glasses of champagne in a
seemingly endless procession. Young Cipriani, the son of the
manager, hovered attentively. He was an old friend of our
host, Gianfranco Ivancich—handsome, brown-haired, brown-
eyed, forty-five, kindly, generous, brilliant, and articulate, a
Venetian by ancient lineage.

"Do you know Pound, Ezra Pound?" Gianfranco asked.

"No. Is he here?"

"In Venice, yes. Across the Canal." Gianfranco pointed over
his shoulder. "Have you met him?"

"No. Only an exchange of letters, not very satisfactory."

213

"Recently?"

"Six or seven years ago."

"You did not quarrel?"

"Not exactly."

"I am giving him lunch tomorrow. He will soon be eighty. He is leaving for Paris the day after. Will you come?"

"Yes," we said, and it was arranged.

Next morning Gianfranco appeared promptly at our hotel, still merry and full of bright talk. We crossed a corner of the Piazza San Marco and boarded the *traghetto*. The day was clear and cool, with a brisk breeze off the water. "Ideal October," said Gianfranco, gazing back at the Palace of the Doges. Waves were slapping the docks of the line of hotels. The far side was sunnier and warmer. Our feet echoed on the pavements and made small thunderlike sounds over the arches of the lesser bridges. Deep in the warren of dwellings and shops we crossed a final canal. Gianfranco pointed out the house of Cipriani. "It is where he stores the wines for Harry's Bar," he said, "and here is where Mr. Pound stores himself."

It was a narrow house fronting the sidewalk. The handsome white-haired lady who answered our knock was Olga Rudge, an Ohioan by birth, a former concert violinist, the mother of Pound's daughter Mary. She embraced Gianfranco, shook our hands. The ground floor room was square and rather sparsely furnished, with an open fireplace and a narrow stairway leading to the room above, the twin of this one. An American girl was there also, very pleasant and quick, with a short neat haircut. Last year she had done a portrait head of Pound, cast now in bronze. Neither the head nor the poet was yet visible.

He came deliberately down the stairs, a tall old man with square shoulders and thinning hair abundantly long and swept back from his forehead. Both beard and hair were gray, not white. His eyes were blue and he had a way of opening them wide and fixing his visitors with an intense stare, all the more disconcerting because the stare was not accompanied by speech. He was meticulously clean—hair, skin, the knobbly hands, the nails—and as gracious as one can be without words. The suit he wore was of gray flannel, with a blue shirt and a dark blue Italian tie. He shook his head vigorously when Olga Rudge insisted that he wear a topcoat, but in the end, as we walked out, he made a compromise, draping the camel's-hair coat like a cloak around his shoulders, and carrying a cane of yellow wood. "He must always have his stick," said Olga Rudge, smiling.

We had heard of his decrepitude, but it did not show. His carriage was erect, his gait deliberate and easy, there was neither shuffling nor any hesitation as he picked up his black shoes rhythmically and set them firmly down. When I walked ahead to snap his picture as he crossed a couple of bridges, he turned profile at the moment the shutter clicked. He was very slender, probably weighing no more than a hundred and twenty-five, and from the side his face was rather hawklike. His head was thrown back, he was enjoying the sun and the light breeze. A few Venetians greeted him as he passed, and he bowed back politely, with never a break in his stride. He might have been a lord.

This meeting, I thought, was like coming into a strange theater toward the end of the final act. We knew in a general way the drift the play had taken: the birth scene far off in Hailey, Idaho, in 1885; the bachelor and master of arts degrees in 1905-1906; expatriate on the grand tour in 1907. We had read the early book, *A Lume Spento*, and then those others that came in quick succession after he had settled in England, *Personae, Exultations, Canzoni, Ripostes*. The learned and multilingual young man established a reputation so rapidly that Robert Frost, meeting him in London in 1913, could write home to a friend, "I don't mind his calling me raw. He is reckoned raw himself and at the same time perhaps the most prominent of the younger poets here."[1] W. B. Yeats praised his "vigorous creative mind," adding that he was "certainly a creative personality of some sort," even though it was still too early to predict his future line of development. "His experiments are perhaps errors," wrote Yeats, "but I would always sooner give the laurel to vigorous errors than to any orthodoxy not inspired." Then later at Stone Cottage, Coleman's Hatch, in Sussex, while the war erupted and raged across the Channel: "Ezra Pound and his wife are staying with me, we have four rooms of a cottage on the edge of a heath and our back is to the woods."[2]

It was Yeats who had told Pound that Frost's *North of Boston* was the best thing that had come out of America for some time. Frost, rather bemusedly, called Pound "the stormy petrel" who had sent a "fierce article" to Harriet Monroe's *Poetry* magazine in Chicago, "denouncing a country that neglects fellows like me." Yet Frost, though happy enough at the public acclaim, could not help feeling that Pound was concerned with personal power. "All I asked," he wrote, in a free-verse poem addressed to Pound but wisely never sent, "was that you should hold to one thing: that you considered me a poet. That was why I clung to you as one clings to a group of insincere friends for fear they shall turn their thoughts against him the moment he is out of hearing. The truth is I was afraid of you."[3]

Others feared him, too, but turned to him for aid. Helping to launch and publicize the Imagist movement, guiding such little magazines as *The Egoist, Blast*, and *The Little Review*, he had hurled himself with restless energy into a program for the rehabilitation of modern poetry, backed by what Harriet Monroe called his "love of stirring up and leading forth other minds." In 1922 T. S. Eliot acknowledged his priceless editorial assistance with *The Waste Land* by dedicating the poem to him and lauding him in Dante's phrase as *"Il miglior fabbro,"* as, in manner of speaking, he had turned out to be—even contributing two words, *demobbed* and *demotic*, to the finished version. Ernest Hemingway, on first meeting him in Paris in 1922, had first written, like Frost before him, an attack on Pound that was never sent. But presently, as he told a friend, he discovered that Pound was really "a great guy and a wonderful editor" and volunteered to teach him how to box in return for lessons in how to write. In 1928 when Hemingway gashed his forehead in a domestic accident, Pound sent him from Rapallo a typical message: "Haow the hellsufferin tomcats did you git drunk enough to fall upwards thru the blithering skylight!!!!!" And Hemingway, four years after that, stated forthrightly that "any poet born in this century or in the last ten years of the preceding century who can honestly say that he has not been influenced by or learned greatly from the work of Ezra Pound deserves to be pitied rather than rebuked."[4]

So we came that noonday in Venice by a tortuous route to the door of the small *ristorante* where Gianfranco was known and received with obvious affection and a deluge of Italian and where Pound was treated with the deference due his age and reputation. He sat down at one end of the table and Gianfranco, flanked by Olga Rudge and the girl sculptress, at the other. Pound listened intently to all that was said, nodded and smiled in response to observations, widened his eyes once or twice in that special gesture of his, and said absolutely nothing.

Gianfranco had warned us of the "vow of silence" and thought that it was an act of contrition for having said too much over the airwaves of Rome Radio in the time of Mussolini. At home, of course, he talked with those closest to him, with his beautiful daughter, Mary, at Schloss Brunnenberg, with his adoring grandchildren. The taciturnity was reserved for public gatherings, and this counted as one of those. As befitted his years, he ate sparingly, declining soup and only lightly sampling the *malfatta*, a delicious kind of ravioli cut on the bias. After two mouthfuls he pushed his plate away, surprising my wife by saying to her the only two words he had yet uttered: "too heavy." At the next course he delicately made way with two small scallopini washed down with half a glass of dry white wine.

I mentioned the letter he had sent me from Rapallo in the spring of 1959, less than a year after his release from twelve years' imprisonment in St. Elizabeth's Hospital in Washington, D.C. It was a typically aggressive and humorous-serious document, poorly typed with blue ribbon on stationery of the Albergo Grande Italia & Lido and dated April seventh.

> Carlos Baker, Princeton, where Woodrow slopped. Yr/ bk/ on Hem, serious re/ literature and Paris, but you are ham ignorant of history. Whether any servant of Princeton dares combat the age-old falsification and READ any history, let alone adjusting his ideas to the 17 facts that the sons of hell and brain-washed adorers of F.D.R. spend billions to hide I do not know. There are faint signs that soon truth will trickle into the margins, but not into the main stream of u.s. university sewage. I see Chris Gauss [Dean of the College at Princeton who had died suddenly in November 1951] has passed on, but suppose Dex. White still rates above Andrew in Niebuhrian rhomboids.
>
> frankly yrs. Ez Pound.

At that date and remove, I could not recall enough of the letter to quote back to its author, but I did speak of Christian Gauss and of my liking for him, at which Pound nodded and smiled. I also wondered aloud at what he had meant by the phrase "Niebuhrian rhomboids," where the adjective did not seem to fit the noun. But Pound only grinned, folding his thin clean hands on the table before him.

The voluble conversation at the other end of the table now drew us in. We knew only vaguely of Pound's liaison of many years with Olga Rudge and of their child, Mary de Rachewiltz, now a beautiful woman of forty who lived with her half-Russian, half-Italian husband in a castle in the Tyrol. It was not in fact until six years later, with the publication of Mary's autobiography, that we learned the whole romantic story. Her book was called *Discretions*, doubtless as a kind of echo of her father's *Indiscretions*, published in 1923 only a couple of years before Mary was born at Bressanone. At the time of her birth, another woman in the maternity ward had lost her baby, and it was arranged that she should nurse the skinny little

218

Pound girl to blooming health, which she achieved in the farming community of Gais in the Tyrol as foster child to Johanna Marcher. The Marchers she called Mamme and Tatte. Pound and Olga Rudge were known to her as Mammile and Tattile, although later she began to call Pound by the name of "Babbo" and went often to Venice so that her real parents could smooth away the rougher edges of her peasant upbringing; here she learnt Italian and English as supplementary to the Tyrolese patois that she spoke during the rest of the year, swam at the Lido under Babbo's admiring supervision, and was hopefully given a violin by her gifted mother. Educated at a convent school with the musical name of Regio Instituto delle Nobili Signore Montalva alla Quiete, she first went to Rapallo just before the war, and fell in love with Casa 60, Sant' Ambrogio, a tall house of orange stucco whose Ionic columns were painted rather than real, and a green front door overgrown with honeysuckle. She was back in Gais when the news filtered through that Italy had surrendered, and she worked steadily through the rest of the war in hospitals in the north of Italy while Babbo kept quietly at his translations.

Then in 1945 a pair of partisans, ex-Fascist convicts eager for reward money, knocked with the butt of a gun on the door of Casa 60. Babbo was working on Confucius. "*Seguici, traditore,*" they said, and took him away. Olga Rudge and Mary saw him later at the Disciplinary Training Center near Pisa. He had aged noticeably; the army fatigues he was wearing did not fit his slender frame; he was writing the first batch of *Pisan Cantos* on a borrowed typewriter. When Mary next saw him in 1953, he had already languished for eight years in the Washington madhouse under indictment for treason. She must not bring her children there, he told her. "St. Elizabeth's is no fit place for the children to see their grandfather in. And there are rumors: granpaw might get sprung."

Finally one evening she heard the Italian newscast: *il poeta Americano* had been released. Through the combined efforts of Archibald MacLeish, Robert Frost, T. S. Eliot, and Ernest Hemingway, Pound was free to return to Italy after twelve

219

years in limbo. He made the trip on board the *Cristoforo Colombo*, a voyage of discovery in reverse. In Sirmione in 1957 Mary had said to MacLeish, who had labored so long to secure Pound's freedom, "He has a right to do whatever he likes, anything that makes him happy. . . . He makes his own laws and I accept them." MacLeish sent a generous check to be used to keep Pound warm, and there was another from Hemingway that Pound framed as a memento of an old friendship, which had included a walking tour of the Italian hill towns in 1923.[5]

If his remorse still held, it did not show as he sat happily in this small left-bank *ristorante*. Afterward we ambled back to the narrow little house beside the small canal, where a green bottle, some bits of straw, and a hemisphere of orange peel floated somnolently. Pound climbed the steps slowly to the skylighted room at the top of the house. He was not puffing and his color was good, though in that severe light his face looked drawn and the skin almost transparent. He drank a demitasse and took a sip or two of brandy. When a tape-recording of a recent canto was put on and played, he listened attentively to his own voice, reading the lines with a kind of gruff eloquence, and pronouncing the frequent foreign phrases with the easy skill of an old European hand. When we left, he stayed in his chair, watching the patterns of afternoon sunlight on the floor.

Two afternoons later in Paris, Pound and Olga Rudge were met by Dominique de Roux, who was then on the point of publishing the first French translation of the *Cantos*. "He is in a state of profound remorse," M. de Roux told reporters. The vow of silence was still in effect, though he relented occasionally. "I regret my past errors," he told de Roux, "but I hope to have done a little something for some artists."

On Friday the twenty-ninth, the day before his birthday, he sat on a sofa beside Miss Natalie Barney in the drawing room of her house where she had entertained the Parisian intellectuals of the 1920s and wordlessly received old admirers. He wore horn-rimmed glasses, a checked brown sports jacket, brown pants, and crepe-soled shoes. The long wings of his shirt collar were spread as of old across his lapels, and his hands rested on the grip of his yellow cane. Asked who were his favorite modern poets, he named Cummings and W. H. Auden. He also permitted himself a two-word judgment on the work of Allen Ginsberg. "He's vigorous," said Pound. It was the very adjective Yeats had used for Pound's own talent long ago in England.

By this date we were far away among the Austrian Alps, staying at the Hotel Taube in the market village of Schruns in the Vorarlberg. While Babbo sat beside Miss Barney on the Parisian sofa, we were walking out to the neighboring village of St. Gallenkirch. Some of the men of the town were laying sewer pipe along the bank of the stream, which was called the Litz, and others were raking autumn leaves. Bedding was being aired in the mountain-morning sunlight at the windows of the houses, and one or two of the women were sweeping their porches with rough brooms made of twigs. The lunch at the Taube was typical—four small trout apiece, cooked whole, with a homemade champignon soup, parsleyed pota- toes, and a salad of lettuce, red peppers, white beans, string beans, and cole slaw. For dessert there were rolled pancakes with a custard filling.

After one bite, my wife pushed her dessert plate toward me across the table.

"Don't you like them?"

"Yes, but after all the rest, they're too heavy."

"You're echoing Ezra Pound."

OTHER PRISONERS than Ezra Pound have left their graf- fiti on the walls of the world. Prisoners' poetry and prose are scattered across the literature of all countries. Cervantes apol- ogized for the sickly child—"like one begotten in a prison"— that became *Don Quixote*. Bunyan, serving time, wrote *Grace Abounding to the Chief of Sinners*. Richard Lovelace, thrown into Gatehouse Gaol for political reasons, wrote the song to

Althea, asserting for all time that iron bars do not necessarily make a cage. We should not forget Dostoevsky's *Notes from Underground*, or Wilde's *Ballad of Reading Gaol*, which evoked pity and terror in the 1890s, or Cummings's *The Enormous Room*, high-level concentration camp literature in the aftermath of the first World War. And in *Gulag III* Aleksandr Solzhenitsyn said flatly: "Prison released in me the ability to write."

Pound's *Pisan Cantos* belong to the same genre, for these eleven sequences grew directly out of the confinement in a military prison that preceded his much longer detention in St. Elizabeth's Hospital. It is commonly said—and indeed was repeatedly asserted when this group of cantos won the first Bollingen Prize—that Pound the man and Pound the poet were different people. Yet these strange poems, like those that preceded and followed them, show man and poet striving together in the same harness. In Cantos 74 to 84 we can watch the man making, out of the hellish experience he endured and the memories he called up as anodynes to his despair, a poem that might conceivably endure in another and grander sense. Walt Whitman, "exotic, still suspect," appears in passing in the eighty-second canto.[6] But Whitman's line from "Song of Myself"—"I am the man, I suffered, I was there"—which applies so exactly to Pound's prison predicament, is nowhere put to use.

Neither in *The Pisan Cantos* nor elsewhere did Pound find much occasion to celebrate the American romantic Whitman or the English romantics who had meant so much to Yeats.* In his *Guide to Kulchur* he remarked rather loftily that "the whole of the 18th century" was "a cliché which the Romantics broke up, in disorderly and amateur manner."[7] Although he had lauded Wordsworth's "imagisme" and his skill with nature-poetry, quoted his 1800 Preface in *Guide to Kulchur*, and used his name in "Homage to Sextus Propertius," he contin-

* See especially George Bornstein, *The Post-Romantic Consciousness of Ezra Pound*, ELS Monograph Series 8, University of Victoria, 1977, chap. 2.

ued to write of him as a "dull sheep" throughout the period 1917-1938.[8] He had evidently dipped into some of Coleridge's essays, praising him for having recognized "the miracle that might be wrought simply by one man's feeling a thing more clearly or more poignantly than anyone else had felt it before." His early poem, "In Durance," dated 1907, quoted four words from Coleridge's "On the Principles of Genial Criticism," that beauty is a "calling of the soul."[9]

Pound did not share Yeats's admiration for Blake. "To admire some of Blake's metric, you have to forget Lewis Carroll," he wrote in 1934, tossing aside "dippy William's" most famous lyric in a pipsqueak parody: "Tiger, Tiger, catch 'em quick! / All the little lambs are sick." Even Blake's engravings fell short of his artistic standards. He professed to find "more wisdom, perhaps more 'revolution' " in one of Whistler's portraits "than in all the Judaic drawings of the 'prophetic Blake.' " He repeated the point in *Guide to Kulchur* with a mention of Blake's "fanatic designs."[10] Canto 16 opened with a strange wild vision of Blake as a naked running form near a hell-mouth among mountains:

> Shouting, whirling his arms, the swift limbs,
> Howling against the evil,
> $\qquad$ his eyes rolling,
> Whirling like flaming cart-wheels,
> $\qquad$ and his head held backward to gaze on the evil
> As he ran from it. . . .

He came fairly close to Byron in "L'Homme Moyen Sensuel" of 1915, trying, not very successfully, to imitate the satiric couplets of *English Bards and Scotch Reviewers*. The hero was an American named Radway, who ended by joining the Baptist Broadway Temple. The epigraph came from *Don Juan*: "I hate a dumpy woman." Pound called it a "diversion," and in sending it to H. L. Mencken remarked that "the guts of all satire (*Don Juan*, for instance)" lay in skill with digressions. Yet he thought Byron a "rotten" technician and grouped him with Musset as a careless writer.[11]

With Keats he was kinder. His own sonnet, "Silet," dated from Verona in 1911, had opened with an echo of Keats's "When I have fears that I may cease to be," which in Pound became, "When I behold how black immortal ink / Drips from my pen." In 1914 he said that "Keats very probably made the last profitable rehash of Elizabethanism"—perhaps thinking of "The Eve of St. Agnes," though he did not say so. Four years later he observed that Keats had luckily "got so far as to see" that poetry "need not be the pack-mule of philosophy," which sounds like a distant echo of Goethe's opinion. Hugh Witemeyer has suggested that "a late Victorian passion for Keatsian romanticism" was apparent in the youthful Pound, whose later "rejection of the Romantics was in part a rejection of his earlier self." As for Shelley, he was lukewarm about the "Ode to the West Wind," and called "The Sensitive Plant" one of the "rottenest poems ever written." The only poem by Shelley that he seems to have admired was the last act of *The Cenci*, most of which takes place in a Roman prison.[12]

As he composed the Pisan sequence, Pound seems to have given no thought to romantic prison poetry. Apart from Shelley's *Julian and Maddalo*, *The Revolt of Islam* and *The Cenci*, Keats's sonnet to Leigh Hunt on the day of his release from gaol, and Coleridge's "This Limetree Bower My Prison," he could in any case have found little to sustain his latest effort. Byron's "The Prisoner of Chillon" perhaps comes spiritually closest, although Pound, unlike Bonnivard, never became a friend to his chains. His limited praise of the final act of *The Cenci*, where Beatrice goes quietly to her doom for having caused the murder of her psychotic father, can hardly be construed as an anticipation of his own predicament in 1945.

Unlike Shelley's heroine, Pound was not then certain of what his fate was going to be. His mailing address from 24 May to 16 November was MTOUSA DTC APO 782. Translated, this meant Mediterranean Theater of Operations, United States Army, Disciplinary Training Center. Translated further, it meant a large stockade surrounded by a tall barbed-wire fence, punctuated with no fewer than fourteen guard towers, and searingly lighted each night against the possibility of attempted escape by some of the desperadoes who were confined there. Near the center of the compound was a series of cages— "gorilla cages" Pound called them—with concrete floors and walls of heavy steel mesh, open to all weathers and to constant inspection by authorized personnel. These were the cells in which rapists and murderers were held before execution. Into one of them, which had been carefully reinforced beforehand with air-strip steel bands, was placed the poet Pound, an alleged traitor, for safer keeping. In the eighty-third canto he wrote:

Nor can who has passed a month in the death cells
    believe in capital punishment
No man who has passed a month in the death cells
    believes in cages for beasts . . . [13]

But it was in just such a cage, strong enough to hold a fighting bull, let alone a spindly sixty-year-old poet, that for nearly a month Pound rolled up in his blankets on the unyielding floor, as far as possible from the lavatory bucket in one corner, and caught such sleep as the glaring searchlights and the growl of passing trucks would allow. "When the morning sun lit up the shelves and battalions of the West, cloud over cloud," another June night was over. "Old Ez folded his blankets" and rose up to breakfast, handed in on a segmented Army food tray, and the unremitting sameness of yet one more day in solitary. He tried, as well as he could, to keep body and soul apart. To exercise his mind he was permitted a few books—Confucius and the Bible—and for his body's health he attempted shadowboxing, learned from Hemingway twenty-odd years earlier, and a simulated tennis game with neither net nor racquet nor ball, Pound versus Pound in a court six feet by four, the dimensions of a grave.

But the torture of his situation was more than body or mind could stand. After nearly a month, this "cultivated Barabbas," as one of his followers named him, lodged "amongst criminals

rather worse than thieves," collapsed at last in gibbering ter-
ror, overcome with claustrophobia and stricken with the bless-
ing of temporary amnesia. Fearing for his life, the Army doc-
tors transferred him out of his gorilla cage and into a tent
near the large prefabricated medical hut. Here, besides food
and medicine, he was given an army cot, as well as a bacon
box for use as a wardrobe, and later another packing case
and even a table, made for him by a kindly man named Ed-
wards:

> superb green and brown
> in Ward No. 4 a jacent benignity
> of the Baluba mask: "doan you tell no one
> I made you that table."[14]

Putting the table to use, Pound began to scribble down notes
for his work in progress:

> Pisa, in the 23rd year of the effort [Mussolini's]
> in sight of the tower
> And Till was hung yesterday
> for murder and rape with trimmings.

Or snatches of conversation by the other prisoners:

> Hey Snag wots in the bibl'?
> Wot are the books ov the bible?
> Name 'em, don't bullshit ME.[15]

Or the language of all common soldiers when they contem-
plate the sins of general officers: "All them g.d.m.f. Generals
c.s. all of 'em fascists."[16] Or the mild caninical musings of the
black turnkey Whiteside, once called "God's messenger":

> Ah certainly dew lak dawgs
> ah goin' tuh wash you

(No, not to the author, to the canine unwilling in question).

Or the lazy Abner who "this day lifted a shovel instead of
watchin' it to see if it would take action."[17]

The sprawling stockade stood outside Pisa on the road to

Viareggio where the poet Shelley's drowned body was washed ashore in the summer of 1822, a hundred years before Mussolini's march on Rome. Through the barbed wire Pound could see "a white ox on the road towards Pisa as if facing the tower" or, on wet days, "dark sheep in the drill field," or "beyond the eastern barbed wire" a "sow with nine boneen" who looked "matronly as any duchess at Claridge's." He watched passing butterflies and the hopping of "Lesbia's sparrows" and found a kind word for the "lion-coloured pup bringing fleas." He drove away the "prowling night-puss" that invaded the one-time bacon box now used as a wardrobe. "You can neither eat manuscript nor Confucius," he told her, "nor even hebrew scripture." On the eighth day of September he heard and recorded the birds singing the treble part in the eastern air:

f f

d

g

Sometimes at night he saw Arcturus through the smoke-hole of his tent, and by day "there was a smell of mint under the tent flaps, especially after the rain." He could see from his standpoint the stars and stripes rippling over the command post and thought of a name for it: "the bacon-rind banner," a term neither patriotic nor exact, since the poet of Arcturus chose, for the success of his image, to omit mention of four dozen other stars on a field of blue.[18]

Like the ubiquitous Kilroy, whose long-nosed image appeared on the walls of so many prisons, jakes, or bombed-out buildings, history now and then asserted itself among the poet's quotidian musings. The seventy-fourth canto which opens the historical sequence is not four lines old when we read of Manes, the name for the dead in the religion of ancient Rome, and of "Ben and Clara, *a Milano*, by the heels at Milano"—Pound's commemoration of the bloody fate of Mussolini and Clara Petacci, murdered on the shores of Lake Como that very

April and afterward hung upside down with other members of the *pro tem* "government" outside the Milanese filling station. Maggots are now at work upon "the dead bullock," but "the twice crucified," asks Pound, "where in history will you find it?"[19] Thereupon he sends a proxy message to "the Possum" (T. S. Eliot) that his "Hollow Men" were wrong in saying that the world ends with a whimper rather than a bang, for in Pound's recent experience the banging had preponderated. When the noise had ceased and the guns had fallen silent across the wreckage of Europe, Pound thought that the latrine, where he overheard the news, was perhaps the most "suitable place." And when Churchill, having led his nation through the war, was defeated in a Labour Party victory that July, Pound delightedly entered in Canto 80 a partial parody of Browning's "Home Thoughts from Abroad": "O to be in England now that Winston's out."[20] But graffiti like those do not necessarily command our strongest approbation.

🍎 ALTHOUGH he listened to the other prisoners as they passed his tent on the way to the dispensary and although he observed *natura naturans*—birds and butterflies, the maternal sow, the flea-bitten dog, the prowling cat, or the bright orange star in the Great Bear's tail—Pound's chief occupation as he slowly filled his notebooks was neither observing nor listening but remembering. *The Pisan Cantos* are as much as anything else an exercise in the disassociation of ideas in a kind of loose internal monologue, for the poet does not remember in chronological sequence. Instead he jumps from point to point over the map of Europe and refuses to worry over time, as we must do in attempting to follow him.

So with the onset of "a small rainstorm . . . out of cloud's mountain," which recalls

> the arrival of Joyce et fils
> at the haunt of Catullus
> with Jim's veneration of thunder and the
> Gardasee in magnificence,[21]

Pound's memory—here at any rate—is as exact as his po-
etical shorthand is enigmatic. The date was 8 June 1920 and
the place was Sirmione on the shores of Lago di Garda, where
Pound's favorite Catullus had owned a villa in Roman times.
Joyce, accompanied by his son Giorgio, then nearly fifteen,
had come to discuss with Pound the publication of *Ulysses*
and was soon persuaded that Sylvia Beach's bookshop in Paris
would be the ideal place, as in fact it turned out to be. A
month later Joyce wrote his patron Harriet Weaver about the
recent trip to Sirmione: "In spite of my dread of thunder-
storms and detestation of traveling, I went there bringing my
son with me to act as a lightning conductor."[22]

Figures out of the poet's past flicker across his mind like
replays of old films. Eliot is often Possum, the sobriquet he
had assumed only six years earlier as composer of *Old Pos-
sum's Book of Practical Cats,* the *jeu d'esprit* that warmed
the hearts of so many of his fellow cat-lovers and would
become a Broadway musical in the 1980s. In a free associa-
tion, Pound recalls the image of Grishkin in Eliot's early
"Whispers of Immortality"—

> Grishkin is nice: her Russian eye
> Is underlined for emphasis;
> Uncorseted, her friendly bust
> Gives promise of pneumatic bliss . . .
> The sleek Brazilian jaguar
> Does not in its arboreal gloom
> Distil so rank a feline smell
> As Grishkin in a drawing-room.

And so Pound, a quarter-century later:

> Or Grishkin's photo refound years after
> with the feeling that Mr. Eliot may have
> missed something, after all, in composing his vignette.[23]

The thought of his daughter Mary, who came with her
mother to see him in prison around the middle of October,

brings a complaint about the village in the Tyrol where she had been raised from infancy:

> Sold the school-house at Gais,
> Cut down the woods whose leaves served for
> bedding cattle
> So there was a lack of manure. . . .

And then again in the following canto a mere three words that Mary, who called her father Tatile, might have uttered to announce one of his infrequent visits to the Tyrol: "Tatile ist gekommen." Such a momentary verbal echo at first appears to be as inscrutable as the one in Joyce's *Ulysses*: "Bloom heard a jing, a little sound. He's off"—by which the alert reader is meant to understand that Bloom has suddenly heard the tinkle of the bell on Blazes Boylan's cart as he drives towards Eccles Street to keep an assignation with Bloom's wife Molly.[24]

Joyce is often in Pound's mind. So are "the Possum" and Ford Madox Ford and William Butler Yeats, three of these four having died in the past seven years, or, as Pound grandiloquently puts it, "Lordly men are to earth o'ergiven." He thinks of "Fordie that wrote of giants" (in his short fiction called "Riesenberg," 1911); "and William who dreamed of nobility" among the kings and warriors of the remote Irish past; "and Jim the comedian singing: Blarrney castle me darlin' you're nothing now but a StOWne."[25]

In the eighty-third canto he recalls "Stone Cottage in Sussex by the waste moor," which he had shared with Yeats far back in the midst of another war. Once, being upstairs, he heard what he took to be the sound of the wind soughing in the chimney. But it was "in reality Uncle William downstairs composing," and singing out the lines, having made, as Pound states it, "a great Peeeacock in the proide ov his oiye."* The poem, though Pound was under no obligation to say so, appeared in Yeats's *Responsibilities* volume of 1914:

* Pound added that Yeats had just then been reading "nearly all of Wordsworth for the sake of his conscience."

What's riches to him
That has made a great peacock
With the pride of his eye
The wind-beaten, stone-grey
And desolate Three Rock
Would nourish his whim.
Live he or die
Amid wet rocks and heather,
His ghost will be gay
Adding feather to feather
For the pride of his eye.[26]

Pound's reminiscence may have owed something to the fact that he had reviewed *Responsibilities* in Harriet Monroe's *Poetry* during May 1914. Up to that year, said he, no one had shown "any disposition to succeed [Yeats] as the best poet in England," adding that he was "so assuredly an immortal that there is no need for him to recast his style to suit our winds of doctrine." Pound could well have meant the winds of antiromantic doctrine, of which he was at this time the self-constituted Aeolus, blowing with all his considerable force against the decadent romanticism of the 1890s. "I've not a word against the glamour as it appears in Yeats's early poems," he continued, "but we have had so many other pseudo-glamours and glamourlets and mists and fogs since the nineties that one is about ready for hard light." This much-desired quality was visible, said Pound, in the first five lines of "The Magi":

Now as at all times I can see in the mind's eye,
In their stiff, painted clothes, the pale unsatisfied ones
Appear and disappear in the blue depth of the sky
With all their ancient faces like rain-beaten stones
And all their helms of silver hovering side by side. . . .

Of the two sorts of poetry that he most admired, one was like "music just forcing itself into articulate speech," and the other like sculpture or painting "just forced or forcing itself into

231

words." Such a poem as "The Magi" showed, he said, the vast difference between evocation and description, and the "unbridgeable" gap between genius and talent.

So he went on making his notes, scribbling and scrawling the words that summarized the events of a single day or the memories of forty or fifty years, intent upon the sequence that would grow to some 125 pages in print and would be published on 30 July 1948 to considerable, if not universal, approbation. "At night in September, October, and November," according to his biographer, Noel Stock,

> When the other patients had left the dispensary and he was free to go there and use the typewriter, he sometimes sat typing this new batch of verse from notes entered during the day into a series of Italian school exercise books. As he typed he hummed to himself in a high-pitched tone, swearing "well and profusely" . . . whenever he made a mistake. When he had finished a sizable amount, he would send the parcel to [his faithful wife] Dorothy Pound, who would pass it on to his daughter [Mary] for retyping. The fresh typescript would then be sent back to the camp.[27]

After the severe breakdown of the early summer, it was something of a wonder that he was able to keep his spirits up and to persuade himself to go on writing what might, after all, become the final section of the *Cantos*. In all probability he felt more moments of despair than ever got into the typescript, but a few appear, like the tips of icebergs, betokening the unutterable cold that stretched down under. "There is fatigue deep as the grave," he says once. Or again: "The loneliness of death came upon me (at 3 P.M. for an instant)." Or yet again, "Only shadows enter my tent as men pass between me and the sunset." And still further along:

> Down, Derry-down
> Oh let an old man rest.

232

The cold of November was already coming on when he concluded his eighty-fourth canto, the last of the prison sequence:

> If the hoar frost grip thy tent
> Thou wilt give thanks when night is spent.[28]

But his long night or nightmare was far from over. In the evening dark of Friday, 16 November, he was sitting in the dispensary reading *Mission to Moscow*, by Joseph E. Davies, when two young officers appeared. They told him that he was to be flown to Washington and must gather up his personal effects. Another young officer, an acquaintance of mine, happened to be present. His name was Robert Allen, and he had befriended the poet, helping him in such small ways as regulations permitted. When Pound reached the door of the pre-fab, Allen later wrote, he turned and, "with a half-smile, put both hands around his neck to form a noose and jerked up his chin." The prisoner named Till had been hanged for murder and rape, "with trimmings." The alleged traitor named Pound expected a similar fate.

He was taken by jeep to Rome, a matter of 250 kilometers along the coastal road, and put abroad a waiting aircraft. After dark on Sunday the eighteenth he disembarked at Bolling Field in Washington and was lodged temporarily in the District of Columbia jail. After a week of sporadic interviews, four psychiatrists at Gallinger Hosptial certified him to be of unsound mind, "suffering from a paranoid state" that rendered him "mentally unfit to advise properly with counsel or to participate intelligently and reasonably in his own defense." Four days before Christmas he was placed in a cell with barred windows in Howard Hall at St. Elizabeth's Federal Hospital for the Insane. The jury at his trail on 13 February 1946 took three minutes to confirm the diagnosis of the doctors. About the same time he was taken out of his cell and transferred to a hospital room of his own. There were no bars on these windows and he had a distant view of the Potomac across the wintry landscape. The imprisonment, which had begun with house arrest in Genoa in May, had already lasted for twenty-six weeks at the Pisan compound and five additional weeks in Washington. What no one knew at the time was that it would continue for twelve more years, until the indictment was finally dismissed on 18 April 1958 and the poet, aged seventy-two, was released at last in the custody of his wife.[29]

The reader of the prison cantos may justly regret the needless obscurities, the fractured syntax, the saltatory methodology, the absence of transitions, to say nothing of the prickly shards of anti-Semitism—all so different from the clean romantic fervor and the Odyssean flavor of Canto 1:

> And then went down to the ship,
> Set keel to breakers, forth on the godly sea, and
> We set up mast and sail on that swart ship.
> Bore sheep aboard her, and our bodies also
> Heavy with weeping, so winds from sternward
> Bore us onward with bellying canvas,
> Circe's this craft, the trim-coifed goddess.[30]

And yet, one wonders, how could this aging man, slowly recovering from a severe breakdown, tortured by fear and remorse, have so smoothed out and dominated the verses with that confidence and assertiveness that seem to have been among the vivid hallmarks of his character in the fortieth year of his age when the first sixteen cantos appeared and when his intellectual vigor and even his moral seriousness were still at his beck and call? The answer must be that he could not. *The Pisan Cantos* became an exercise in personal therapeutics, a way of limning, as Archibald MacLeish once said, "this poet's vision of hell" along with glimpses of the joys he had lost in the dark background and abysm of his times.[31]

Pound's exegetes have sought with minimal success to discover sustaining ideological or thematic structures in this sequence. D. S. Carne-Ross has rightly said that the poet "rejected coherent architectonics," which is perhaps another way of saying that the broken verses make more sense when we take them for what they essentially are, a gifted prisoner's graffiti, whether in Greek, Latin, French, German, Italian,

Spanish, or in Chinese ideographs—multinational linguistic fragments shored up against the poet's imminent ruin on the precise analogy of Eliot's *Waste Land* twenty-three years in the past.[32]

This is far from saying that Pound fails to reach certain conclusions, such as the famous and often quoted lyrics in the eighty-first canto that can be summed up respectively in one of Browning's lines in "Love Among the Ruins"—"Love is best"—and in the words of the *Book of Common Prayer*—"Trust not in wrong and robbery, give not yourselves unto vanity." Pound writes:

> What thou lov'st well remains,
>> the rest is dross
> What thou lov'st well shall not be reft from thee
> What thou lov'st well is thy true heritage. . . .
>
> Pull down thy vanity, it is not man
> Made courage, or made order, or made grace,
>> Pull down thy vanity, I say pull down.
> Learn of the green world what can be thy place
> In scaled invention or true artistry
> Pull down thy vanity. . . .
>
> Thou art a beaten dog beneath the hail,
> A swollen magpie in a fitful sun,
> Half black half white
> Nor knowst'ou wing from tail
> Pull down thy vanity
>> How mean thy hates
> Fostered in falsity,
>> Pull down thy vanity,
> Rathe to destroy, niggard in charity,
> Pull down thy vanity,
>> I say pull down.
> But to have done instead of not doing
>> this is not vanity
> To have, with decency, knocked

That a Blunt should open
        To have gathered from the air a live tradition
Or from a fine old eye the unconquered flame
This is not vanity.
Here error is all in the not done,
    all in the diffidence that faltered.[33]

One of Pound's most perspicuous commentators, George Dekker, has convincingly argued that "all that is essential" to the reader of such lines as these is "to know who Pound is, where he is, and when it is. For if the sequence holds together at all, it does so because it is fundamentally a dramatic monologue, because at last Odysseus-Pound has been trapped in the tragic plot of history, and because he has nothing but his own past and present to make poetry out of. This in itself is a formal advantage which he denies himself elsewhere in the poem except on rare occasions. Obscurity as such, if never a virtue, is much less crippling within a dramatic context."*

This seems to me an admirable statement of the strategy Pound adopted both in his poem and in his attitude toward the time he spent in the compound outside Pisa. Memory and imagination thrust back as well as they can against the harsh counterpressures of walls and fences and concrete floors, as if to assert with Richard Lovelace, a battered copy of whose poems Pound one day picked up in the latrine, that iron bars never make a cage for the roving mind that can transcend them.[34] Each of the quick-changing images and anecdotes is like a design drawn on the canvas of his tent, an imaginary ladder that will somehow get the old man over the fence and far away.

* Dekker, *Cantos of Ezra Pound*, 188-89. Dekker's point is supported by the passage on vanity quoted above. The single "obscure" reference—"To have, with decency, knocked / That a Blunt should open"—can be easily passed over. Pound may have had in mind the Wilfrid Scawen Blunt presentation recorded in *Poetry* for March 1914, p. 223.

T. S. Eliot

APOSTATE FROM ROMANTIC RULE

Every generation must make its own appraisal of the poetry of the past, in the light of the performance of its contemporaries and immediate predecessors. —Eliot, *The Use of Poetry and the Use of Criticism*

His criticism urged a program of the classical, the traditional, and the impersonal, while he was producing a poetry which is poignantly romantic, strikingly modernist, and intensely personal. —Leonard Unger, *T. S. Eliot: Moments and Patterns*

THE ATMOSPHERE of high seriousness and romantic gloom that pervades the bulk of T. S. Eliot's verse tends to obscure the fact that he began his long and distinguished career as a social satirist. Poems in this category are not very numerous, perhaps a dozen and a half in all, and totaling some eight hundred lines. Yet anyone with an eye for the importance of controlling stars must have noticed that Eliot was born in 1888, just two centuries after the birth of the satirist Alexander Pope, and a hundred years after that of the satirist Byron. Frost's Witch of Coös may have been on the right track when she asked, "Don't that make you suspicious / That there's something the dead are keeping back?"

The period of Eliot's social satire began in boyhood, continued through his undergraduate and graduate years at Harvard, the Sorbonne, and Merton College, Oxford, outlasted the Great War, and more or less ended with the satirical

237

sections of *The Waste Land* in 1922. An early, though not the earliest, example is "Spleen," one of his contributions to the *Harvard Advocate* (26 January 1910). The poem alerts us to his somewhat supercilious view of the urban bourgeoisie in the years immediately preceding the Great War, and even anticipates the caricature of J. Alfred Prufrock:

> Sunday: this satisfied procession
> Of definite Sunday faces;
> Bonnets, silk hats, and conscious graces
> In repetition that displaces
> Your mental self-possession
> By this unwarranted digression.
>
> Evening, lights, and tea!
> Children and cats in the alley;
> Dejection unable to rally
> Against this dull conspiracy.
>
> And life, a little bald and gray,
> Languid, fastidious, and bland,
> Punctilious of tie and suit
> (Somewhat impatient of delay)
> On the doorstep of the Absolute.[1]

Here, as a wise old Harvard senior, he is already beginning to write like a renegade from Victorian values. But he is certainly no anarchist and, indeed, to borrow Byron's phrase about Wordsworth, no more than a "mild apostate" from the cultural situation he is attacking. Already, too, he has placed himself as the incipient poet of urban life, conscious of class differentials, drawing a bead on all those self-satisfied "Sunday faces" that emerge from morning services, as well as the nocturnal gabble of "children and cats in the alley," ruffling the genteel social universe with their raucous subhuman lower-class cries. Easily visible among the stanzas of "Spleen" are some of the qualities that he would presently assail at length in Prufrock's interior monologue: men who are "a little bald and gray, languid, fastidious, and bland, punctilious of tie and suit." For Prufrock, too, displays a bald spot in the middle of his hair, though punctilious about his morning coat and the rich and modest necktie "asserted by a simple pin."

Whether or not we recognize the face of Eliot in the picture of Prufrock, the poet takes pleasure in a satirical self-portrait modeled on that of Edward Lear which begins:

> How pleasant to know Mr. Lear!
> Who has written such volumes of stuff!
> Some think him ill-tempered and queer,
> But a few think him pleasant enough. . . .
>
> His mind is concrete and fastidious,
> His nose is remarkably big;
> His visage is more or less hideous,
> His beard it resembles a wig. . . .
>
> He sits in a beautiful parlour,
> With hundreds of books on the wall;
> He drinks a great deal of Marsala,
> But never gets tipsy at all.

Eliot is self-critical to a far greater degree:

> How unpleasant to meet Mr. Eliot
> With his features of clerical cut,
> And his brow so grim
> And his mouth so prim
> And his conversation, so nicely
> Restricted to What Precisely
> And If and Perhaps and But. . . .[2]

Despite his somewhat clerical appearance, he had not yet in these years confronted the crucial episode of his spiritual life, his espousal of Anglo-Catholicism. When under Pound's guidance he read Gautier's *Emaux et Camées*, he discovered "L'Hippopotame," a curious little lyric on the poet's self-reliance. Eliot refashioned the original into an amusing commentary on the materialistic concerns of the True Church:

> The hippo's feeble steps may err
> In compassing material ends,
> While the True Church need never stir
> To gather in its dividends. . . .

> The hippopotamus's day
> Is passed in sleep; at night he hunts;
> God works in a mysterious way—
> The Church can sleep and feed at once. . . .

When the hippo is translated into heaven from the damp savannas of his nativity:

> He shall be washed as white as snow,
> By all the martyred virgins kist,
> While the True Church remains below
> Wrapt in the old miasmal mist.[3]

But Eliot's satirical targets are more often people than social institutions. While men like Prufrock and Bleistein, Mr. Eugenides, and Apeneck Sweeney may be pinned wriggling on the wall of his distaste, his strongest impulse appears to be misogynistic, as in the couplets that were deleted from *The Waste Land* at Pound's instigation. These last were a palpable imitation—Eliot as parodist again emergent—of Pope's charming portrait of Belinda awaking in *The Rape of the Lock*. But Eliot's Fresca, a down-to-earth maiden unattended by sylphs, exudes sounds and odors from which all charm has vanished, and the mood is far closer to that of Swift and his Celia than to that of Pope and his Belinda.

Eliot's publishers forbid quotation from his intentionally blowsy and ribald account of Fresca's matutinal activities— the imperious summoning of her hard-hoofed chambermaid, Amanda; the light breakfast; a quick visit to the stool, where she dips briefly into a novel by Richardson; a gossip-filled letter to a friend, presumably female; and at last a needful immersion in a perfumed bath.[4] The passage belongs roughly to the same order as the more economical portrait of the awakening of Sweeney's paramour in "Sweeney Erect," another notably misogynistic sequence.

If Pound was wise in urging the cancellation of such lines as these from a poem intent upon other and more serious matters, enough remains in the published poetry of these years to assert Eliot's antipathy toward the female of the species, as well as more than a suggestion of sexual disgust. In *The Pisan Cantos* Pound showed that he had long remembered the portrait of Grishkin emitting her feline fragrance in middle-class drawing rooms. At one end of the social scale is the garrulous lady of "Portrait," talking of Chopin's *Preludes* and twisting the stalks of lilacs in her fingers as she half-hints at her potential marriageability. Or the Princess Volupine, she of the "meagre, blue-nailed, phthisic hand" to whose questionable charm Burbank, laying aside his Baedeker, presently succumbs. Or the women in the salons whose arms "Are braceleted and white and bare / (But in the lamplight downed with light brown hair),"as they both tempt and reject the shy presumptions of Prufrock.

At the nether end of the same scale, the damp souls of housemaids despondently sprout at the servants' entrances to upper-class mansions, the London typist entertains the carbuncular young real estate agent, Lil's talkative Cockney friend in the pub narrates the sad tale of the marital problems of Lil and Albert, the Thames-maidens—maidens no more—register their complaints at fugitive seductions, Rachel Rabinovitch snatches hungrily at the pile of hothouse grapes, the lady boarders at Mrs. Turner's place are aghast at the caterwauling of Sweeney's latest sexual conquest, and the denizens of a thousand furnished rooms raise the dingy windowshades to the morning light and sit on the bed's edge clasping "the yellow soles of feet in the palms of both soiled hands."

In such poems as "The Love Song of J. Alfred Prufrock," Eliot would appear to be taking a cue from Baudelaire, "It is not merely in the use of the imagery of common life," he writes, "not merely in the use of imagery of the sordid life of a great metropolis, but in the elevation of such imagery to the *first intensity*—presenting it as it is, and yet making it represent something more than itself—that Baudelaire has created a mode of release and expression for other men."[5] The ironic "Love Song" goes beyond Baudelaire by setting up a curious imagistic triad to which Eliot returns in other poems of the same period. One leg of it is a clear and powerful representation of "the sordid life of a great metropolis"—a *sale* world of work-coarsened hands and "hard plebeian tread," an urban slum of narrow streets where smoke rises from "the pipes of lonely men in shirt sleeves, leaning out of windows," where one may spend "restless nights in one-night cheap hotels" or frequent "sawdust restaurants with oyster shells." This is the world of workaday mankind, dirty and damp, redolent of hot fat and stale beer, of unwashed bodies and clothing, of unsavoury odors, cheap lodgings, and rough characters like Sweeney—but also with a vitality from which Prufrock and his ilk instinctively recoil.

Over against this Baudelairean complex Eliot sets the *salon* world, through which men like Prufrock punctiliously sidestep, the world of carpeted and perfumed drawing rooms where intellectual women chatter of literature and art, a world of tea and cakes and ices and marmalade thinly spread. Here it is that Prufrock assumes the role of Polonius, attendant lord to the blue-stocking ladies, "deferential, glad to be of use / Politic, cautious, and meticulous, / Full of high sentence, but a bit obtuse," half ashamed of his pudency, dreaming of overwhelming questions which he dares not ask.

The third element of the triad is romantic and escapist, an imaginary saline world of pagan sea-sirens who might, Prufrock believes, sing to him as they once did to Ulysses and his crew, were it not for his stifling fears and his multiple indecisions. For this worldly Caspar Milquetoast, half-bored with the salon world, half revolted by the *sale* world, might have become, at least in his imagination, a kind of Supermerman, a Casanova of the chambers of the sea. But now it is too late. He grows old. He has lived so long out of the symbolic saline

242

element that he drowns in that thick emulsion of tea and ennui which makes up the salon world.

Interactions among these three tropes reappear in various permutations among several other poems of the period. The urbane ironist achieves his satiric effects by recording what happens when the salon world is invaded either by the vital vulgarians of Sweeney's persuasion or by the frank and easy paganism for which Prufrock's private image is the congress of amorous mermaids. A memorable example of the enfilade assault appears in "Aunt Helen."

> Miss Helen Slingsby was my maiden aunt
> And lived in a small house near a fashionable square
> Cared for by servants to the number of four.
> Now when she died there was silence in heaven
> And silence at her end of the street.
> The shutters were drawn and the undertaker
>   wiped his feet—
> He was aware that this sort of thing had occurred
>   before.
> The dogs were handsomely provided for,
> But shortly afterwards the parrot died too.
> The Dresden clock continued ticking on the
>   mantelpiece,
> And the footman sat upon the dining-table
> Holding the second housemaid on his knees—
> Who had always been so careful while her mistress
>   lived.[6]

This kind of situation, familiar enough to viewers of "Upstairs Downstairs" in some of its episodes, is Eliot's sardonic tribute to the force that makes the world go round, as Aunt Helen Slingsby, with her lap dogs and her caged parrot and polite tea parties for other aging spinsters like herself, could never afford to acknowledge. Even so slight an incident might have been raised at least to the second intensity by a headline in *The Boston Evening Transcript*: VULGAR VITALITY INVADES BACK BAY AND BEACON HILL. But the shutters were drawn and none but the footman and the house-maid took any notice.

As is well enough known, Eliot employs other satiric methods in these early poems, chiefly the reductive contrast between a banal present and a heroic past, a trick he confessed to having learnt from Joyce's *Ulysses*, though the dates of composition and Eliot's classical training suggest that he discovered it first for himself. The method is used effectively in "Sweeney Erect" and "Sweeney Among the Nightingales," both with puns in their titles and stings in their tails. It is evident also in "Dans Le Restaurant," one of his experiments with French *poésie*, where the slovenly old waiter disgusts a diner with an account of a juvenile sexual episode until the poem turns about-face to the sanative sea and the figure of the heroic Phlébas le Phénicien, drowned off the Cornish coast.

We are again reminded of Prufrock's triad in "Mr. Apollinax," where an aggressive foreign visitor invades and at least momentarily disturbs the polite academic world of Harvard and environs. When Bertrand Russell came to lecture at Cambridge in the spring of 1914, Eliot was studying philosophy, though the once-famous department had been cruelly decimated by the loss of William James, George Santayana, and Josiah Royce. Although Russell believed that Eliot had "the instincts of a philosopher," he found the young man "extraordinarily silent," and evidently lacking in the kind of animal force that he himself so insistently cultivated at this period of his early forties. In May he spent a pleasant bucolic weekend in the company of Eliot and another young philosophy instructor. The latter, as Russell sized him up, was an "Oxfordised Harvardian, cultivated, full of the classics, talking as like an Englishman" as he could, "but feeble—quite without the ferocity that is needed to redeem culture." Eliot he found to be "a very similar type, proficient in Plato, intimate in French literature from Villon to Vildrach," but also lacking "in the crude insistent passion that one must have in order to achieve anything." In the following year when Eliot married Vivien Haigh Wood, Russell treated the impoverished young pair with great kindness, put them up in his London flat, and even shared their quarters at Bosham in Sussex. The new Mrs. Eliot struck him as "a little vulgar, adventurous, full of life," while the twenty-seven-year-old husband was both "exquisite and listless." The bride said she had married Tom in order to "stimulate him" only to find that she could not do it. "Obviously," gossiped Russell, "he married in order to be stimulated." Quite as obviously it had not worked. A few months later Eliot was writing to Russell, "Vivien says you have been an angel to her. . . . I often wonder how things would have turned out but for you—I believe we shall owe her life to you, even."[7]

Much of this, but particularly Russell's springtime visit to Harvard, must have been in Eliot's mind when he composed "Mr. Apollinax." If he had lacked, as Russell supposed, the crude insistent passion and even ferocity necessary to the re-demption of culture, the young poet was perceptive enough to recognize the living embodiment of these qualities in Rus-sell. As Prufrock's mermaids represent for him the possibility of escape from tea-time ennui, Apollinax stands for a frontal assault upon the staid academic and social world of the dow-ager Mrs. Phlaccus and Professor Channing-Cheetah. Like Prufrock's dream girls, he is a vitalizing force who seems to have arisen from what Arnold called "the unplumbed salt estranging sea."

When Mr. Apollinax visited the United States
His laughter tinkled among the tea-cups . . .
In the palace of Mrs. Phlaccus, at Professor Channing-
        Cheetah's
He laughed like an irresponsible foetus.
His laughter was submarine and profound
Like the old man of the sea's
Hidden under coral islands
Where worried bodies of drowned men drift down

in the green silence,
Dropping from fingers of surf.
I looked for the head of Mr. Apollinax rolling under a
        chair.

Or grinning over a screen
With seaweed in its hair
I heard the beat of centaur's hoofs over the hard turf
As his dry and passionate talk devoured the afternoon.
"He is a charming man"—"But after all what did he
        mean?"—
"His pointed ears. . . . He must be unbalanced"—
"There was something he said that I might have
        challenged."
Of dowager Mrs. Phlaccus, and Professor and Mrs.
        Cheetah
I remember a slice of lemon, and a bitten macaroon.*

Although it is not among the best known of his early poems,
"Mr. Apollinax" may well be the best of Eliot's social satires—
a perfect embodiment of the manner in which an arrogant
and willful but also brilliant phenomenon like Russell (who,
incidentally, disliked President Lowell and had nothing but
scorn for the members of the philosophy department at Har-
vard) was able to shake and undermine the polite congruities
at something like Force Nine on the Richter Scale. The poet
who, according to Russell, lacked the necessary passion to
redeem the age, could at any rate recognize passion when it
appeared and praise it for its unsettling and no doubt welcome
intensity.

    After 1920-1922 Eliot's comic ironies dissolve in the direc-
tion of tragedy. The instincts of the philosopher that Russell

* CPP, 17. Some of the rhymes in "Mr. Apollinax" suggest without dupli-
cating Byron's often outrageous combinations in Don Juan. Examples would
include Channing-Cheetah's and foetus, unbalanced and challenged. George
Bornstein has noted the same phenomenon in "Prufrock" with such instances
as What is it and visit, ices and crisis (Bornstein, Transformations of Ro-
manticism, 130).

had noticed during his colloquies with his younger colleague in the Harvard Yard were presently to supersede those of the social satirist. When he returned to Cambridge in 1932-1933 to deliver the Charles Eliot Norton Lectures, he read the first of them in a low and scarcely audible voice, soberly and with great dignity, his eyes more often upon the typescript than upon his respectful audience. In the second lecture he permitted himself a glint of humor, beginning with a word of thanks to the anonymous donor who in the meantime had sent him a box of a then popular breakfast food called *Force*. Although he did not elaborate or apologize, or indeed much change the manner of his presentation, the hint does not seem to have fallen on stony ground. When Edmund Wilson heard him in a public reading later in the year, he was astonished to discover that Eliot "put on a better show" than George Bernard Shaw. His voice and manner projected "a kind of dramatic resonance" that Wilson could only admire.[8] If the old satirical cleverness and wit had now largely receded into the background, another set of qualities, not less admirable, had arisen to fill the temporary vacancy.*

❦ ACCORDING to F. O. Matthiessen, "the course of Eliot's development can be charted only by reckoning with such figures as Shelley and Swinburne and the Pre-Raphaelites, poets by whom he did not escape being influenced during the formative years of his adolescence."[9] The history of Eliot's engagement with romanticism, followed at intervals by sporadic disengagements, seems to have begun about 1902-1903 and to have resembled Yeats's encounters with Shelley and Blake in the early 1880s, an experience that the Irish poet described as a "sort of violent imaginative puberty." Eliot's first reading of FitzGerald's *Rubaiyat* at age fourteen was, as he said, "like a sudden conversion: the world appeared anew, painted with bright, delicious, and painful colours."[10] This adventure led

* I owe the *Force* anecdote to my friend and colleague, W. S. Howell.

him back in time to the work of Byron, Shelley, Keats, and the rest, an affair of the heart that lasted, by his estimate, until his Harvard years, *circa* 1909-1910, when a reversal set in.

The individual chiefly responsible for the change was Irving Babbitt, who "directed my interests, at a particular moment, in such a way that the marks of that direction"[11] lasted long, and whose influence, as Eliot asserted in 1961, was apparent in his own "recurrent theme of Classicism versus Romanticism."[12] Babbitt's imprint was especially evident in the extension lectures that Eliot delivered at Ilkley, Yorkshire, during the fall of 1916. He told his listeners that "contemporary intellectual movements in France" were largely a reaction from the nineteenth-century "romanticist" attitude, and he named as the chief romantic source Babbitt's old *bête noire*, Jean Jacques Rousseau. The definition of romanticism that he proposed in his opening lecture was "excess in any direction," a quick summary of Rousseau's doctrine.* He likewise held Rousseau responsible for (1) the exaltation of the personal and individual above the typical; (2) the emphasis on feeling rather than thought; (3) belief in the fundamental goodness of man; and (4) depreciation of form in art in favor of a glorification of spontaneity.[13] In *The Sacred Wood* essays, published four years later, Eliot was still under Babbitt's antiromantic spell when he affirmed that "what is permanent and good in romanticism is curiosity. . . . There may be a good deal to be said for Romanticism in life," but "there is no place for it in letters."[14]

The ideals of classicism, as Eliot set them forth in his Yorkshire lectures, were "form and restraint in art, discipline and authority in religion, and centralization in government." In 1928 he reformulated this early statement in the preface to *For Lancelot Andrewes*, declaring that he was himself "a classicist in literature, a royalist in politics, and an Anglo-Catholic

---

* Had he known of it in 1916, he would doubtless have turned up his nose at William Blake's Third Proverb of Hell: "The road of excess leads to the palace of wisdom."

248

in religion."* This fairly fits his definition of classicism in 1916: "essentially a belief in Original Sin and in the necessity of austere discipline," beliefs that were no doubt meant as counterforces to Rousseau's doctrine of man's "fundamental goodness" and to his preference for spontaneity over formal construction.

By the time of the Harvard lectures in 1932-1933, Eliot was far less interested in Babbitt's old dualism, saying, "I wish myself to avoid employing the terms Romanticism and Classicism, terms which inflame political passions, and tend to prejudice our conclusions."[15] In 1961 came his final statement on the matter in *To Criticize the Critic*, where the rugged old pair "have no longer the importance to me that they once had."[16]

Although in 1916 he had seemed to be predicting a revival of classicism, presumably under French leadership, he subsequently tried to give a proper hearing to the opposition. The word *change* often appears in his allusions to the Romantic Movement. One notable instance came in his famous essay on "Tradition and the Individual Talent" in *The Sacred Wood* of 1920:

> The poet ... must be aware that the mind of Europe— the mind of his own country ... is a mind which changes, and that this change is a development which abandons nothing *en route*, which does not superannuate either Shakespeare, or Homer, or the rock drawing of the Magdalenian draughtsmen.

And he added overleaf: "The poet must develop or produce the consciousness of the past ... throughout his career."[17]

In the Harvard lectures he continued to ring his changes on the word *change*. "Any radical change in poetic form," he

---

* In 1961 Eliot said that this sentence had followed him through life, as Shelley tells us his thought followed him: "And his own Thoughts, along that rugged way, / Pursued, like raging hounds, their father and their prey." This is the Actaeon image from *Adonais*, stanza 31. Eliot is implying that he is heartily sick of his early formulation.

wrote, "is likely to be the symptom of some very much deeper change in society and in the individual." Among the romantic pioneers in England, Wordsworth and Coleridge "illustrate the mind of an age of conscious change." Romanticism, moreover, is a term "which is constantly changing in different contexts. ... In its more comprehensive significance, 'Romanticism' comes to include nearly everything that distinguishes the last two hundred and fifty years ... from their predecessors."[18]

The stamp of romanticism is accordingly to be found throughout the period that runs from roughly 1683 to 1933. This is true both in criticism and in poetry. Eliot praised the romantic contribution to the criticism of Shakespeare and other Elizabethan dramatists, calling it "surprising, varied, and abundant," and citing the work of Coleridge, Lamb, Hazlitt, and De Quincey as having markedly altered earlier approaches to Shakespeare's plays.[19] As for changes brought about through poetry, he wisely remarked in his concluding lecture that poetry itself "may effect revolutions in sensibility such as are periodically needed; may help to break up the conventional modes of perception and valuation which are perpetually forming, and make people see the world afresh, or some new part of it."[20] To effect literary revolutions, break up conventional modes, and cause people to see the world afresh sounds very much like true romantic gospel. Although Eliot is generalizing and does not bring forward any examples, texts to support his contention could easily be located in the writings of all the major English romantics.

After the philosophic quatrains of Omar the Tentmaker,* Byron seems to have been the first to foment in Eliot's mind the mood of a maker of poetry. The inception of his satirical skills came in great part from his early enthusiasm for *Don Juan*. In the heyday of adolescence he composed the dozen

---

* In the Norton lectures Eliot confessed that he could "still enjoy FitzGerald's *Omar*," though he did not hold with that "rather smart and shallow view of life" (*UPUC*, 91).

ottava rima stanzas called "A Fable for Feasters." After a
Christmas dinner in a medieval monastery, the monks doze
contentedly:

> His feet upon the table superposed
> Each wisht he had not eaten so much goose.

At this point a ghost interrupts their post prandial slumbers:

> The Abbot sat as pasted to his chair.
> His eyes became the size of any dollar.
> The ghost then took him roughly by the hair
> And bade him come with him in accents hollow.

"Snatcht" by his unearthly captor, the Abbot vanishes up the
chimney; the church has no apparent choice but to canonize
him; and the chastened monks thereafter feast only on "milk
and breakfast food."[21]

The *dollar / hollow* rhyme is probably unworthy of Eliot's
model, and many of the lines are notably lacking in the true
Byronic polish. Twenty years later, without calling attention
to these minor lapses, Eliot said that his monkish *jeu d'esprit*
had been "tinged with that disillusion and cynicism only pos-
sible at the age of sixteen." Since neither of these qualities is
at all visible in the poem, Eliot's remark was probably made
tongue-in-cheek and not, as would at first appear, in humor-
less solemnity. But the essay in which it appears is plainly that
of a poet of forty-nine looking back with no great pleasure
on his "schoolboy infatuation" with the author of *Don Juan*.

His praise of Byron in the essay of 1937 was that he had
"the cardinal virtue of never being dull," that he was a verse-
narrator of "torrential fluency" (Eliot analyzed *The Giaour*
by way of proof), that he had "a genius for divagation," and
that his "continual banter and mockery" served as "an ad-
mirable antacid to the highfalutin which in the earlier ro-
mances" tended "to upset the reader's stomach."*

---

* In 1933 Eliot had classified Scott and Byron (in his more popular works)
as merely "society entertainment." *UPUC*, 87.

Byron's faults outweighed his virtues. He failed to conform to the ideal of concentration in poetry: had he distilled his verses, "there would have been nothing whatever left." His ambitious attempts to be "poetic" struck Eliot as a form of fakery. So also with his "peculiar diabolism" his "delight in posing as a damned creature," which he probably owed to his Calvinist upbringing. He seemed able to think of himself "both as an individual isolated and superior to other men because of his own crimes," and, at the same time, as a "naturally good and generous nature distorted by the crimes committed against it by others." While Byron shared in Shelley's Prometheanism and in his "Romantic passion for liberty," these qualities soon merged into Satanism, as in Milton's portrait of the fallen angel early in *Paradise Lost*, where pride seems to be a virtue rather than a cardinal sin. Apart from these matters, Byron's real failure as poet lay in his having "added nothing to the language," discovering "nothing in sounds . . . nothing in the meaning of individual words"— surely a questionable accusation. Finally, whenever he philosophized, what came out was platitudes, which sounds like a distant echo of Goethe's view.

For all Byron's faults, *Don Juan* remained, in Eliot's opinion, the greatest of his poems. The ottava rima stanza, he said, "was admirably suited to enhance" Byron's merits, "just as on a horse or in the water he was more at ease than on foot." Eliot shared in the still widespread notion of Juan as a passive character: in the love episodes, he was more acted upon than acting. "Even Haidée . . . that child of nature, appears rather as the seducer than the seduced." Eliot divides the poem into two main parts, Continental and English. Part one is picaresque, but part two (the last four cantos) is "the most substantial" because Byron's "acute animosity" against English society "sharpened his powers of observation," while the subject matter gave him an "adequate object" for a "genuine emotion" (a strong "hatred of hypocrisy"), so that his satire upon English society had no parallel in English literature.[22]

In short, the Byron essay seems to confirm Matthiessen's

assertion that Eliot, who followed Babbitt as an exponent of
the impersonal and nonautobiographical in poetry, could not
much admire "the impure artist who, like Rousseau or Byron,
exploits his idiosyncratic temperament at the expense of so-
ciety instead of finding its fulfilment in the impersonal struc-
ture of a work of art."[23] Yet despite certain reservations, and
along with his odd preference for cantos thirteen to sixteen
over one to twelve, Eliot did retain into maturity some of the
early enthusiasm for *Don Juan* that had eventuated in the
boyish yarn of "A Fable for Feasters."

William Blake was clearly not Eliot's man. The review essay
of 1920 shows that he had read little of the poet whom Yeats
had so enthusiastically explored and celebrated. About all that
Eliot finds to say of the *Songs of Innocence*, the *Songs of
Experience*, and the contents of the Rossetti Manuscript is
that they and their author are "very eighteenth-century" in
manner, that they show a "profound interest in and knowl-
edge of human emotions," and that they are presented in
"extremely simplified abstract form." Blake's virtues, as Eliot
sees them, include a considerable understanding of human
nature, an original sense of language and its music, and a "gift
of hallucinated vision," though not of the kind that Eliot was
to work into *The Family Reunion*. On the debit side, Blake
gave more importance to his "philosophy" than an artist should.
He would have been better off if his powers had been "con-
trolled by a respect for impersonal reason, for common sense,
for the objectivity of science." His "supernatural territories"
suggest "a certain meanness of culture," and "illustrate the
crankiness, the eccentricity, which frequently affects writers
outside of the Latin tradition." In sum, "What his genius
required, and what it sadly lacked, was a framework of ac-
cepted and traditional ideas which would have prevented him
from indulging in a philosophy of his own, and concentrated
his attention upon the problems of the poet."[24]
Seven years later Eliot returned to the subject in another
review essay, this time with a fierce frankness that runs oddly

parallel to Yeats's final appraisal of Shelley in 1932. Blake struck him now as "not even a first-rate visionary: his visions have a certain illiteracy about them." Philosophically he was an "autodidact amateur," and theologically "a heretic," both of these terms understandable responses from a serious and widely read poet who had recently joined the Church. Unlike Yeats, Eliot had apparently given little attention to the Prophetic Books. He was able to say only that they were "full of poetry, and fine poetry, too," but that they showed "very sadly" that "genius and inspiration" were "not enough for a poet." Blake needed "education . . . a kind of mental and moral discipline." Its absence vitiated his achievement.[25]

Eliot's brief further comment in one of the Norton lectures of 1933 offers no sign of retreat from the earlier position. "Blake," he says, "may have pretended, and with some claim, to have penetrated mysteries of heaven and hell, but no claim that Blake might make seems to descend upon the 'poet' in general." In a word, Blake "simply had the visions and made use of the poetry to set them forth." For Eliot he therefore remained an unique figure, a self-taught and ill-disciplined eccentric who stood far enough outside the great tradition not to be worthy of serious critical attention. Beulah and Golgonooza were not Eliot's chosen terrain.[26]

🍂 ELIOT ONCE wrote of his "daemonic possession" by one romantic poet at a time and dated his "intoxication" with Shelley from about 1903. By the time of the Harvard lectures in 1933, he was evidently troubled by the question of how far it was possible to enjoy Shelley's poetry "without sharing his views and sympathies."[27] Unlike Robert Frost, who had enthusiastically read it aloud to his girl during his courtship, Eliot confessed to being "thoroughly gravelled" by the notorious "free-love" passage in *Epipsychidion*:[28]

> True love in this differs from gold and clay
> That to divide is not to take away . . .

I never was attached to that great sect
Whose doctrine is, that each one should select
Out of the crowd a mistress or a friend
And all the rest, though fair and wise, commend
To cold oblivion. . . .*

Shelley the man struck him as "humourless, pedantic, self-centred, and almost a blackguard," in "astonishing contrast with the attractive Keats." But it was the ideology that bothered him most. As metaphysician and philosopher, said Eliot, Shelley was "very confused"—"able to be at once an eighteenth-century rationalist and a cloudy Platonist." The ideas he borrowed were often "shabby" and he "muddled them up with his own intuitions." Yet his finest long poems, "as well as some of his worst," were those "in which he took his ideas very seriously." Abstract thought always elicited from him a strong emotional response, blowing into incandescence the "fading coal" of the creative urge that he had discussed in *A Defence of Poetry*.[29]

Although Eliot would perhaps have been loath to admit it, his animadversions on Shelley the man differ very little from those of Matthew Arnold in the *Essays: Second Series*. For Arnold had likewise accused Shelley of "a want of humour and a self-delusion," adding that Shelley the man was "not entirely sane," nor was his poetry "entirely sane either." It is a curious fact, as Stephen Spender noticed, that Arnold's closing comment on Shelley—"in poetry, no less than in life, he is a beautiful and ineffectual angel, beating in the void his luminous wings in vain"—should have been distantly but distinctly echoed in Eliot's *Ash Wednesday*:

Because these wings are no longer wings to fly
But merely vans to beat the air
The air which is now thoroughly small and dry. . . .[30]

* Eliot intentionally transposes line 160-161 to precede 149-153 and misquotes line 160, writing "dross or clay" for Shelley's "gold and clay."

As Eliot said of his opinions about D. H. Lawrence, his remarks on Shelley "seem to form a tissue of praise and execration."[31] In November 1917, when he was still grouping Shelley with Swinburne, he said that "to write like Shelley, leaving blanks for the adjectives, or like Swinburne, whose adjectives are practically blanks" came to much the same thing.[32] In an early *Criterion* essay he included Shelley with Keats and Wordsworth as "poets of assured though modest merit." In November 1920, however, he quoted Shelley's lyric, "Music, when soft voices die," adding that it had what Swinburne lacked—"a beauty of music and a beauty of content. . . . It is clearly and simply expressed, with only two adjectives."[33]

He sometimes had a little fun at Shelley's expense on the question of appropriate imagery. The essay on Dryden in 1921 ridiculed the lines from *Hellas*: "The earth doth like a snake renew / Her winter weeds outworn" with the remark that "it is not so easy to see propriety in an image which divests a snake of 'winter weeds.' " Again, though the failure here is Eliot's own, since he had never apparently noticed how the stronger light of daybreak gradually blots out the morning star, he criticized as too vague the splendid lines in "To A Skylark" about "that silver sphere / Whose intense lamp narrows / In the white dawn clear."[34]

In turning to *Prometheus Unbound* in 1933, he made the point that "in poetry so fluent as Shelley's there is a good deal which is just bad jingling" and cited as an example the song of the First Spirit from the chorus of act one: "On a battle-trumpet's blast / I fled hither fast, fast, fast / 'Mid the darkness upward cast" and so on for five lines more. The jingle effect is there, certainly, though the songs of the other spirits, which likewise follow the drumbeat of trochaic tetrameter, move with greater dignity.* Eliot's point has some theoretical merit, that such "bad parts" tend to "contaminate" the whole, "so

---

* Northrop Frye amusingly refers to the "hideous but cheerful doggerel in which most of the fourth act is written" but does not suggest that the poem is thereby contaminated. See *A Study of English Romanticism*, New York, 1968, p. 120.

that when Shelley rises to the heights, at the end" of act four, in "lines to the content of which belief is neither given nor denied, we are unable to enjoy them fully. . . . Good lines amongst bad can never give more than a regretful pleasure."[35]

A similar reaction took place when he discovered (or perhaps rediscovered) in *Epipsychidion* such a "lovely image" as

> A vision like incarnate April, warning,
> With smiles and tears, Frost the Anatomy
> Into his summer grave.

He does not tell us that this admired and complex metaphor comes at the end of Shelley's paean of praise for Emilia Viviani, which, though somewhat extravagant, is all of a piece with what has gone before and stands as a notable specimen of the poet's hieratic style when writing of "sacred" subjects. Eliot can say only that he was "as much shocked at finding it in such indifferent company as pleased by finding it at all." He was perhaps too ready to impugn Shelley's poetic habits as well as those underlying ideas that he particularly disliked. "I can only regret," he wrote in summary, "that Shelley did not live to put his poetic gifts, which were certainly of the first order, at the service of more tenable beliefs."[36]

Eliot disappoints us by the scarcity of his references to Shelley's *A Defence of Poetry*, which he rates below Wordsworth's preface to the second edition of *Lyrical Ballads*. He expresses admiration for Shelley's image comparing "the mind in creation" to "a fading coal, which some invisible influence, like an inconstant wind, awakens to transitory brightness."* The only other reference to *A Defence* is an extract of four sentences from Shelley's long closing paragraph, with which Eliot takes issue, though he calls it "perhaps the first appearance [in critical literature] of the kinetic or revolutionary theory of poetry."[37]

Had he chosen to point out those aspects of Shelley's essay

---

* He notes that Joyce quotes this passage "somewhere in Ulysses." It occurs at page 192 of the Modern Library edition, New York, 1934. Shelley was one of Joyce's favorite poets.

with which he at least partly agreed, his service to his audience might have been greater. Shelley, for instance, said that "every great poet must inevitably innovate upon the example of his predecessors in the exact structure of his peculiar versification." Eliot in 1919 had held that "if we approach a poet without his prejudice we shall often find that not only the best, but the most individual parts of his work may be those in which the dead poets, his ancestors, assert their immortality most vigorously."

Again, Shelley alluded to "the episodes of that cyclic poem written by Time upon the memories of men. The Past, like an inspired rhapsodist, fills the theatre of everlasting generations with their harmony." In "Tradition and the Individual Talent," Eliot had said that "the historical sense involves a perception, not only of the pastness of the past, but of its presence; the historical sense compels a man to write not merely with his own generation in his bones, but with a feeling that the whole of the literature of Europe from Homer and within it the whole of the literature of his own country has a simultaneous existence and composes a simultaneous order." These paired opinions are not exact replicas of one another but it would have been valuable to have Eliot's views on both the similarities and the differences, for he knew and had eloquently said that no poet "has his complete meaning alone. . . . You cannot value him alone; you must set him, for contrast and comparison, among the dead." He had also made the arresting statement that "the past [is] altered by the present as much as the present is directed by the past."[38]

As a confirmed admirer of the *Divine Comedy*, Eliot is strangely silent about the references to Dante in *A Defence*. Yet Dante was a key figure in Shelley's pantheon of those poets who had "celebrated the dominion of love, planting as it were trophies in the human mind of that sublimest victory over sensuality and force." Dante "understood the secret things of love even more than Petrarch. His *Vita Nuova* is an inexhaustible fountain of purity of sentiment and language; it is

258

the idealized history of that period, and those intervals of his life which were dedicated to love. His apotheosis of Beatrice in Paradise, and the gradation of his own love and her love-liness, by which as by steps he feigns himself to have ascended to the throne of the Supreme Cause, is the most glorious imagination of modern poetry."* The *Paradiso* is accordingly "a perpetual hymn to everlasting love," and Dante's poetry is like a "bridge thrown over the stream of time, which unites the modern and ancient world." Modern mythology owes its systematic form to Dante and Milton. Without demoting Virgil, Shelley calls Dante the "second epic poet" after Homer, as well as "the first awakener of entranced Europe," who "created a language . . . out of a chaos of inharmonious barbarisms" and was likewise "the congregator of those great spirits who presided over the resurrection of learning; the Lucifer of that starry flock which in the thirteenth century shone forth from republican Italy, as from a heaven, into the darkness of the benighted world."

None of this got into Eliot's Harvard lecture. Yet as recently as 1929 he had stated that "Shelley, who knew Dante well, and who towards the end of his life was beginning to profit by it, [was] the one English poet of the nineteenth century who could even have begun to follow those footsteps."[39] What led him to this praise of the poet he would presently demean as "almost a blackguard" was Shelley's last poem, *The Triumph of Life* when he adapted Dantean terza rima to English metrics to fashion his tragic fable about the triumph of the worldly life over the idealist's vision. The lines in *The Triumph* that particularly struck Eliot at that time told of the nameless narrator's discovery of the distorted form of Rousseau beside the dusty highway where the *triumphus* was passing.

Eliot made up for his lapse of 1933 on Independence Day 1950 in the essay "What Dante Means to Me." Apropos of his own effort in *Little Gidding* to approximate the effect of

* Compare the passage on Beatrice in Yeats, "Ego Dominus Tuus."

Dante's terza rima in the "hallucinated scene after an air-raid," he pointed to Shelley once again as the foremost English poet to have responded strongly to the Dantean influence. Shelley had "a natural affinity with the poetic imagination of Dante," was saturated with the poetry, and wrote "some of the greatest and most Dantesque lines in English." Quoting ten stanzas of the passage on Rousseau, Eliot recalled that they had made an "indelible impression" upon him "over forty-five years ago." Now he was prepared to be generous to Shelley: "This," he says, "is better than I could do. But I quote it as one of the supreme tributes to Dante in English; for it testifies to what Dante has done, both for the style and for the soul, of a great English poet."

He finds a further example of Dantesque imagery in "Ode to the West Wind." Such a line as "Like stricken ghosts from an enchanter fleeing" would have been impossible without the *Inferno*, where the "various manifestations of *wind*, and the various sensations of *air*, are as important as are the aspects of *light* in the Paradiso."[40] Finally, he calls attention to the connections between *Epipsychidion* and the *Vita Nuova* as if he had not fully recognized them during his attack on Shelley's own *vita nuova* in 1933.*

In Eliot's recantation of his former animadversions on Shelley 1950 was a banner year. In the first act of *Prometheus Unbound*, shortly before the appearance of the Phantasm of Jupiter, the Earth, presented as a kind of Erdmutter-instructor, tells Prometheus that, before the fall of Babylon,

> The Magus Zoroaster, my dead child,
> Met his own image walking in the garden.
> That apparition, sole of men, he saw.
> For know there are two worlds of life and death:
> One that which thou beholdest; but the other

---

* Some commentators see the Rousseau passage as a source for the ugly account of the paramour on the bed in "Sweeney Erect." Careful comparison rapidly dissipates this notion. A better connection is probably with "The Hollow Men," who more nearly resemble the fallen and decayed Rousseau.

Is underneath the grave, where do inhabit
The shadows of all forms that think and live
Till death unite them and they part no more.

The Earth's revelation that each living form has its shadowy
counterpart "underneath the grave" and that only in death
are shadow and spiritual substance united evidently struck
Eliot as a way of dramatizing the mysterious prescience of Sir
Henry Harcourt-Reilly, the eminent London psychiatrist of
The Cocktail Party. Celia Coplestone, who vanished from
Mayfair society to become a nursing missionary on the Eastern
island of Kinkanja, was crucified near an anthill by the heathen
natives. Two years later Sir Henry asks his hostess: "Do you
mind if I quote poetry, Mrs. Chamberlayne?" He then recites
the passage from *Prometheus Unbound* to explain his re-
membrance that when he first met Celia, he "saw the image,
standing behind the chair / Of a Celia Coplestone whose face
showed the astonishment / Of the first few minutes after a
violent death."*

Eliot has very little to say about Keats, devoting only two
pages to him at the end of his Shelley-Keats lecture at Harvard,
and elsewhere recording only a few opinions about his poetry.
He told his audience that Keats was more attractive as a man
than Shelley, that he was "a singular figure in a varied and
remarkable period," and that he was "also a great poet."
Unlike Robert Frost, he could not find himself "happy about

---

* *CPP*, 384. Shelley scholars have not located a source for Shelley's anecdote
about Zoroaster. Jacques Duchesne-Guillemin, *The Western Response to
Zoroaster*, Oxford, 1958, p. 16, believes it Shelley's own invention. "He
appears to have freely combined the account of Zoroaster's visions with that
of the faithful soul's encounter with the Daena after Death. In order to convey
what he considered essential in the Zoroastrian message, namely a secret
correspondence and attraction between visible and spiritual realities, [Shelley]
fashioned a new Zoroaster." Philip R. Headings, *T. S. Eliot*, New York,
1964, p. 117, finds a resemblance between Shelley's Zoroaster passage and
the lines in *Little Gidding* where the narrator meets his own image after the
London air raid.

Hyperion": "It contains great lines, but I do not know whether it is a great poem." But the odes, especially the "Ode to Psyche," were "enough for his reputation." Without having "meditated deeply" on the matter, he thought that Keats's letters were "certainly the most notable and the most important ever written by any English poet." He quoted with admiration the passage on Men of Genius and Men of Power from the letter to Bailey of 22 November 1817, adding that this was "the sort of remark, which, when made by a man so young as was Keats," could "only be called the result of genius. There is hardly one statement of Keats about poetry, which, when considered carefully and with due allowance for the difficulties of communication, will not be found to be true; and what is more, true for greater and more mature poetry than anything that Keats ever wrote." Most of his remarks on poetry kept "pretty close to intuition," despite some evidence of a "shrewd and penetrating intellect."*

Eliot closed his lecture with certain generalizations which the romantic scholars in his audience regarded as hasty and ill-considered.†

> Wordsworth had a very delicate sensibility to social life and social changes. Wordsworth and Shelley both theorise. Keats has no theory, and to have formed one was irrelevant to his interests, and alien to his mind. If we take either Wordsworth or Shelley as representative of his age . . . we cannot so take Keats. But we cannot accuse

---

* Lionel Trilling's introduction to his *Selected Letters of John Keats*, New York, 1951, is very much more thorough and satisfactory than Eliot's somewhat impressionistic appreciation. Trilling observes that "the letters of great men naturally have an especial attraction; and among the letters of great men those of the great creative artists are likely to be the most intimate, the liveliest, and the fullest of wisdom. Yet even among the great artists Keats is perhaps the only one whose letters are of such kind as to have an interest which is virtually equal to that of their writer's canon of created work."

† For example, F. O. Matthiessen, who was there, later called the Norton lectures a "partial disappointment" because of Eliot's "rather commonplace statements." *Achievement*, p. 153.

Keats of any withdrawal, or refusal; he was merely about his business. He had no theories, yet in the sense appropriate to a poet, in the same sense, though to a lesser degree than Shakespeare, he had a 'philosophic' mind. He was occupied only with the highest use of poetry. . . .[41]

To say that Keats had "no theory" only two paragraphs after having quoted his highly theoretical letter on Men of Genius and Men of Power and to have ignored completely his theories on Negative Capability and the World as a Vale of Soul-making, to take only two examples, represented a considerable oversight on Eliot's part. Yet it is clear that he liked Keats the man (no blackguard he), found that his letters revealed "a charming personality," and believed that he might have gone on developing in devotion to his craft if death had not undone him at so young an age.

Although he reserves his praise chiefly for the odes, and especially "Psyche," which may seem to many Keatsian devotees a questionable choice, Eliot says next to nothing about their content, diction, themes, or form. The originator of "Sweeney Among the Nightingales" and the Philomel sequence in *The Waste Land* found in Keats's most famous ode "a number of feelings which have nothing particular to do with the nightingale, but which the nightingale, partly because of its attractive name, and partly because of its reputation, served to bring together." But this, as he well knew, is true of many synoptic images, and is certainly not peculiar to Keats. In 1929, commenting on the "Ode on a Grecian Urn," he said that the statement of equivalence in "Beauty is truth, truth beauty" meant nothing to him and that it must be seen as "a serious blemish on an otherwise beautiful poem."* Unhappily, neither of these observations adds anything to our understanding of the odes, and they display none of that critical acumen

---

* Eliot: "I suppose that Keats meant something by it, however remote his truth and his beauty may have been from these words in ordinary use." *Selected Essays*, p. 231n.

that Eliot could bring to a text when he was truly involved with it—as, for instance, in the case of Dante.[42]

Genuine echoes from Keats are accordingly rare in Eliot's poetry. Bornstein calls attention to a pair of examples from the very early verse: the Keats-like phrase, "spotless fanes of lucid purity," in Eliot's secondary school graduation poem of 1905, and the hint of romantic nympholepsy in the sonnet, "On a Portrait" (1909):

> Not like a tranquil goddess carved of stone
> But evanescent, as if one should meet
> A pensive lamia in some wood-retreat,
> An immaterial fancy of one's own.[43]

Citing the elaborate set piece that opens "A Game of Chess" in *The Waste Land*, Matthiessen cautiously remarked that "a comparison of this passage with Keats's description of perfume in 'Lamia' would not make Eliot's lines seem thin."[44] Grover Smith, Jr., isolated a kind of echo of the Grecian Urn ode in *Burnt Norton*, where the Chinese jar "moves perpetually in its stillness." If Keats's poem was indeed "the" source, it is the sole instance of a Keatsian echo in all the *Four Quartets*.[45]

What might have been an actual echo of the "Ode to a Nightingale" in *Little Gidding* was proposed by Eliot's friend John Hayward, who read with great care the various drafts of the poem. In Eliot's tentative line 120, "But as the passage now is brief and facile," Hayward suggested the substitution of "easeful" for "facile." But Eliot answered flatly: " 'Easeful' will never be any use until Keats's trademark has worn off."* The idea that Keats in his line, "I have been half in love with easeful Death," had trademarked the adjective ran curiously parallel to Robert Frost's observation in 1914 that Keats's use of "alien" when the Biblical Ruth "stood in tears amid the alien corn" had made it permanently his own: "As he made

---

* Helen Gardner, *The Composition of Four Quartets*, New York, 1978, p. 191.

it special in that place he made it his—and his only in that place."

Eliot's well-known habit of working into his poetry the words of other men and women—sometimes with due acknowledgment, sometimes not—makes the identification of his actual sources and analogues a matter of more importance than would be the case with a less eclectic "borrower." In a recent discussion of the making of *Four Quartets*, Walton Litz has raised two important questions: "How are we to distinguish the mere source, interesting but not crucial to the text, from the allusion which demands that we align Eliot's world with that of some past or present master? And what of the indeterminate ground between source and allusion, what we might call the 'umbra' of the poem, inhabited by ghosts that are intensely felt by the reader but scarcely visible in the text?" If we do attempt, as Litz suggests, "to discriminate between peripheral sources and the more profound literary presences," whether in *Four Quartets* or elsewhere in Eliot's work, it will usually but not always be found that the English romantic poets are not among the "profound literary presences," even though from time to time they do briefly emerge as "peripheral sources."[46]

❦ "THE NEAREST we get to pure literary criticism," wrote Eliot in 1961, "is the criticism of artists writing about their own art; and for this I turn to [Samuel] Johnson, and Wordsworth and Coleridge."[47] In preparing the fourth of his Norton lectures for 1932-1933, he presented Wordsworth and Coleridge as prophets and progenitors of an age of change. They were revolutionists rather than reformers: they were "not merely demolishing a debased tradition, but revolting against a whole social order," and "they began to make claims for poetry" that would reach "their highest point of exaggeration in Shelley's famous phrase, 'Poets are the unacknowledged legislators of the world.' " If Wordsworth thought that he was "simply occupied with reform of language, he was deceived; he was occupied with revolution of language, and his own language was as capable of artificiality, and no more capable of naturalness, than that of Pope—as Byron felt, and as Coleridge candidly pointed out."[48]

Eliot's concern in 1932 was not with the poetry of Wordsworth and Coleridge so much as with their respective places

> in the historical process of criticism. . . . What is best in [Coleridge's] criticism seems to come from his own delicacy and subtlety of insight as he reflected upon his own experience of writing poetry. Of the two poets as critics, it was Wordsworth who knew better what he was about: his critical insight [in the preface of 1800 and the supplementary essay of 1815] is enough to give him the highest place. . . . There is, in his poetry and his Preface, a profound spiritual revival. . . . Coleridge, with the authority due to his great reading, probably did much more than Wordsworth to bring attention to the profundity of the philosophic problems into which the study of poetry may take us.

Considered together, they "illustrate the mind of an age of conscious change. It is not merely that they were interested in a variety of speculative subjects . . . but that their interests were involved in each other. . . . We find not merely a variety of interests, even of passionate interests; it is all one passion expressed through them all: poetry was for them the expression of a totality of unified interests."[49] In this fashion, Eliot expresses his sense of the profound symbiotic relationship that existed between the two men.

Of Wordsworth's actual performance as poet, Eliot had little to say, choosing rather to center on his pronouncements about poetic language. Like Yeats, he admired "the bird of Wordsworth" in "The Solitary Reaper," though neither of them identified it as a cuckoo.[50] He called "Resolution and Independence" a "great poem" without further comment, although he must have been struck by the depressive melancholia of the fourth stanza, having himself known something

like it during the period when he was composing *The Waste
Land*:[51]

> As high as we have mounted in delight
> In our dejection do we sink as low;
> To me that morning did it happen so;
> And fears and fancies thick upon me came;
> Dim sadness—and blind thoughts, I knew
> not, nor could name.

Unlike Yeats, he does not appear to have tackled *The Prel-
ude* and *The Excursion*. Unlike Stevens, he ignored the son-
nets. He was apparently unmoved by the "Elegiac Stanzas"
on Peele Castle, and he passed by the immortality ode. Unlike
Coleridge, wrote Eliot, Wordsworth "had no ghastly shadows
at his back, no Eumenides to pursue him; or if he did, he gave
no sign and took no notice; and he went on droning on the
still sad music of infirmity to the verge of the grave" never
apparently troubled by the consciousness of having lost his
inspiration.[52]

This last assertion is manifestly untrue, as any reader of the
immortality ode must know; and Eliot the parodist, making
over the "still sad music of humanity" for the sake of a joke
on Wordsworth's decline, says nothing about the theme of
growth in Wordsworth's poetry, or of Dorothy's place in
"Tintern Abbey," even though in the same essay he praises
her as a "great woman," owing to her influence on her brother
and Coleridge.

Eliot now announced his decision to center his essay on
two major points: Coleridge's distinction between imagina-
tion and fancy, and Wordsworth's theory of poetic diction,
which he mistakenly believed that the two poets shared. His
comments on both topics were unhappily superficial, even
amateurish, though his reputation as critic and poet enabled
him to carry his assertions with a semblance of authority. In
saying, for example, that Wordsworth defined his purpose as
imitation and even adoption of "the very language of men,"
Eliot observed that this was only a restatement in different

words of what Dryden had said long before him—and Ezra Pound long after him.[53] The historical position was valid enough: poetic language must periodically be revivified with strong infusions of actuality.* But Eliot's bare phrase, "the very language of men," picked up from Coleridge, ignores Wordsworth's careful qualifications in defining his principal object: to relate or describe incidents and situations from common life, "as far as was possible, in a selection of language really used by men, and, at the same time, to throw over them a certain colouring of imagination." These qualifications made all the difference.

According to Eliot, the prevalent writing style in 1800 was "what any style of writing becomes when it falls into the hands of people who cannot even be called mediocre." Wordsworth's own version was probably better: "the gaudiness and inane phraseology of many modern writers," and "the triviality and meanness, both of thought and language, which some of my contemporaries have occasionally introduced into their metrical compositions." Eliot's further point was well taken— that Wordsworth "by no means worried himself to excess in observing his own principles." Coleridge's critique of Wordsworth in the *Biographia* might well have been quoted here: "I reflect with delight, how little a mere theory, though of his own workmanship, interferes with the processes of genuine imagination in a man of true poetic genius." And further, "were there excluded from Mr. Wordsworth's poetic compositions all, that a literal adherence to the theory of his preface *would* exclude, two-thirds at least of the marked beauties of his poetry must be erased."

---

* Eliot's best statement on this subject: "Every revolution in poetry is apt to be . . . a return to common speech. That is the revolution which Wordsworth announced in his preface, and he was right; but the same revolution had been carried out a century before by Oldham, Waller, Denham, and Dryden: and the same revolution was due again something over a century later. The followers of a revolution develop a new poetic idiom. . . . They polish or perfect it; meanwhile the spoken language goes on changing, and the poetic idiom goes out of date." *On Poetry and Poets*, New York, 1957, p. 23.

Having called Wordsworth a revolutionary in his introductory lecture, Eliot now retreated. Except on the points of "choosing incidents from common life" and presenting them in "the very language of men," he was "a most orthodox critic," and may possibly "have been no renegade but a man who thought, so far as he thought at all, for himself." Much of his poetry, like much of Coleridge's, was "just as turgid and artificial and elegant as any eighteenth century die-hard could wish."

Orthodox or not, Wordsworth was "deeply Aristotelian" on the matter of mimesis, advancing "a new version of imitation" that struck Eliot as "the best so far." He quoted the passage with evident relish: "Aristotle, I have been told, has said, that Poetry is the most philosophic of all writing; it is so; its object is truth, not individual and local, but general and operative." The phrase "it is so" seemed to Eliot "exhilarating." "Rather than be parrotted by a hundred generations," he wrote, "I had rather be neglected and have one man eventually come to my conclusions and say, 'This is an old author who found this out before I did.' " For the rest, Wordsworth's poetic program of instructing and edifying by invoking the pleasure principle plainly had "something in it." His revolutionary faith was evidently "vital to him" and could not be "disentangled from the nature of his poetry." Apart from his comments on mimesis, however, Eliot's remarks about the 1800 preface are neither better nor appreciably worse than those of a hundred other hasty paraphrasts.[54]

Much the same may be said of his critique on Coleridge's distinction between imagination and fancy. Like many others before and after him, he quoted the relevant passage from chapter thirteen of the *Biographia Litteraria* [*sic*]. He made a mock apology for possessing a mind "too heavy and concrete for any flight of abstruse reasoning." If, however, the difference between the two powers "amounts in practice to no more than the difference between good and bad poetry, have we done more than take a turn round Robin Hood's barn? It is only if fancy can be an ingredient in good poetry, and if you can show some good poetry which is the better for it; it is only if the distinction illuminates our immediate preference of one poet over another, that it can be of use to a practical mind like mine."[55]

His further insistence that memory operates in both imaginative and fanciful poetry is a point well taken. Yet this is all that he has to contribute. He prints two other quotations on the subject from chapters fourteen and fifteen of the *Biographia*, deriving his text from I. A. Richards's section on "The Imagination" in *Principles of Literary Criticism*. But these do not extend his discussion, except temporally, for his only comment on them is that they show "richness and depth" as well as "an awareness of complication . . . far out of the range of Dryden." His auditors, that winter's day in Cambridge, might have been justified in echoing Eliot's own previous words and wondering if he had done much more in discussing Coleridge than leading his hearers on yet another circuit of Robin Hood's barn.[56]

The weakness of his arguments was all the more surprising in that his professed admiration for Coleridge went back at least to 1920, when he began his essay on "The Perfect Critic" by saying that "Coleridge was perhaps the greatest of English critics, and in a sense the last." He did go on to point out that Coleridge's metaphysical interests sometimes caused him to "take leave of the data of criticism" with the result that he failed to "bring us back to the work of art with improved perception and intensified, because more conscious, enjoyment," which in Eliot's view remained the true and best function of the literary critic. It is unfortunate that he was unable to live up to this admirable dictum in what he told his Harvard audience about the 1800 preface and the imagination-fancy distinction.[57]

As for Coleridge the poet and Coleridge the "ruined man" who came near to making a vocation of his ruination, Eliot's feelings were evidently a good deal more intense. Both in 1932 and later, his attitude toward Coleridge seems to have been curiously fraternal. In 1955 he called him "rather a man of my own type, differing from myself chiefly in being immensely more learned, more industrious, and endowed with a more powerful and subtle mind." It would seem that the similarities were as important to Eliot as his modest rehearsal of the differences. Among the major English romantics, Coleridge was the one for whom he evidently felt the closest kinship.[58]

Of all the poems of Coleridge he seems to have been most struck by "Dejection: An Ode," calling it an instance of "passionate self-revelation" that rose "almost to the height of great poetry." Three minutes into his fourth Norton lecture, he quoted stanza six entire:

> There was a time when, though my path was rough,
> This joy within me dallied with distress,
> And all misfortunes were but as the stuff
> Whence Fancy made me dreams of happiness:
> For hope grew round me, like the twining vine,
> And fruits and foliage, not my own, seemed mine.
> But now afflictions bow me down to earth:
> Nor care I that they rob me of my mirth;
> But oh! each visitation
> Suspends what nature gave me at my birth,
> My shaping spirit of Imagination.
> For not to think of what I needs must feel,
> But to be still and patient, all I can;
> And haply by abstruse research to steal
> From my own nature all the natural man—
> This was my sole resource, my only plan:
> Till that which suits a part infects the whole,
> And now is almost grown the habit of my soul.*

These lines, wrote Eliot,

strike my ear as one of the saddest of confessions that I have ever read. When I spoke of Coleridge as drugging

---

* Eliot misquotes line 4, reading *dream*, a verb, in place of Coleridge's *dreams*, a noun. The sense is only slightly altered.

271

himself with metaphysics I was thinking seriously of these his own words: "haply by abstruse research to steal from my own nature all the natural man." Coleridge was one of those unhappy persons . . . of whom one might say, that if they had not been poets, they might have made something of their lives, might even have had a career. . . . It was better for Coleridge, as poet, to read books of travel and exploration than to read books of metaphysics and political economy. He did genuinely want to read books of metaphysics and political economy, for he had a certain talent for such subjects. But for a few years he had been visited by the Muse . . . and thenceforth was a haunted man; for anyone who has ever been visited by the Muse is thenceforth haunted. . . .

Coleridge, he continued, was subject to a "sudden, fitful and terrifying kind" of inspiration, with "ghastly shadows at his back" and Eumenides pursuing him. It is perhaps here, in the hauntedness, in the felt presence of pursuing Furies and ghastly shadows, that one aspect of Eliot's fraternal feeling for Coleridge emerges most stongly. Only six years later, in *The Family Reunion*, the protagonist, Harry, Lord Monchensey, is himself haunted by the Eumenides ("They were always there"), partly from a conviction that he has been responsible for the death of his wife, and partly also from his overwhelming sense of the loss of hope:

> You do not know what hope is, until you have lost it.
> You only know what it is not to hope:
> You do not know what it is to have hope taken from you,
> Or to fling it away, to join the legion of the hopeless. . . .

In such a passage as this, Lord Monchensey comes very close to being a "Coleridgean" character.[59]

Eliot returned to the problem of inspiration, specifically the buried life and its poetical manifestations, in a brief critique of "Kubla Khan" midway of his final Norton lecture. "The imagery of that fragment, certainly, whatever its origins in

272

Coleridge's reading, sank to the depths of Coleridge's feeling, was saturated, transformed there—'those are pearls that were his eyes'—and brought up into daylight again." Apart from the obvious echo of the song from *The Tempest*, which had been used so effectively in *The Waste Land*, Eliot was here harking back to his readings in *The Road to Xanadu*. In his fourth lecture he had said that

> Mr. Lowes has . . . demonstrated the importance of instinctive and unconscious, as well as deliberate selection. Coleridge's taste, at one period of life, led him first to read voraciously in a certain type of book, and then to select and store up certain kinds of imagery from those books. . . . The mind of any poet would be magnetised in its own way, to select automatically in his reading . . . the material—an image, a phrase, a word—which may be of use to him later. And this selection probably runs through the whole of his sensitive life."[60]

The relative scarcity of references to Coleridge's poetry in Eliot's essays makes it difficult to determine precisely when and to what degree his own mind was "magnetised" by Coleridgean phraseology. Yet he could hardly have failed to respond to one of the most arresting images in "The Rime of the Ancient Mariner":

> Like one, that on a lonesome road
> Doth walk in fear and dread,
> And having once turned round walks on,
> And turns no more his head;
> Because he knows, a frightful fiend
> Doth close behind him tread.

Coleridge's image seems suddenly to reappear, transformed, in "The Dry Salvages," the one among the *Four Quartets* devoted to the great waters, to rivers and the sea, exactly where a remembrance of "The Ancient Mariner" might most be expected to occur:

273

I have said before
That the past experience revived in the meaning
Is not the experience of one life only
But of many generations—not forgetting
Something that is probably quite ineffable:
The backward look behind the assurance
Of recorded history, the backward half-look
Over the shoulder, towards the primitive terror.[61]

One cannot, of course, be certain that Eliot was here making a conscious echo of the lines from Coleridge, but in the concluding lecture of the Norton series, he raised a relevant question:

Why, for all of us, out of all that we have heard, seen, felt, in a lifetime, do certain images recur, charged with emotion, rather than others? The song of one bird, the leap of one fish, at a particular place and time, the scent of one flower, an old woman on a German mountain path, six ruffians seen through an open window playing cards at night at a small French railway junction where there was a water-mill: such memories may have symbolic value, but of what we cannot tell, for they come to represent the depths of feeling into which we cannot peer.[62]

These remarks are significant. The romantic poet who was always present beneath Eliot's somewhat staid exterior, who had already written *Ash Wednesday* and the very moving Ariel poems, and was still to write *Four Quartets* and the plays, is completely accustomed to such "depths of feeling" somewhere below the upper levels of consciousness.* This is not the place to discuss at length the difficulties of Eliot's first marriage, which was in process of dissolution even as he wrote and delivered his Harvard lectures, or his long and unrequited friendship for Emily Hale—or the fact that these, taken to-

---

* In 1950 I. A. Richards acutely remarked that "something has at times hidden from Mr. Eliot even those purposes of some romantic poetry which most resembled his own." *Coleridge on Imagination*, p. 197.

gether, run very roughly parallel to Coleridge's own unfortunate experience of wedlock and his hopeless love for Sara Hutchinson, the "lady" addressed in "Dejection: An Ode" and the "Asra" ("woman beyond utterance dear") of the beautiful sonnet of 1801. We may recall that Bertrand Russell had early foreseen the possible deterioration of Eliot's marriage, characterizing Mrs. Eliot as one who lived "on a knife-edge," and prophesying that she would one day end either "as a criminal or a saint." In this last prediction Russell was wholly wrong. Yet there can be no doubt that Eliot's poetry between the wars, including *The Family Reunion*, bears here and there the visible stigmata of his unhappy union.*

Something of his predicament here at the bottom of the Great Depression was evidently in his mind as he ended his final Norton lecture. Poetry, as he told his audience,

> may make us from time to time a little more aware of the deeper un-named feelings which form the substratum of our being, to which we rarely penetrate; for our lives are mostly a constant evasion of ourselves, and an evasion of the visible and sensible world. But to say all this is only to say what you know already, if you have felt poetry and thought about your feelings. And I fear that I have already, throughout these lectures, trespassed beyond the bounds which a little self-knowledge tells me are my proper frontier. If, as James Thomson observed, 'lips only sing when they cannot kiss,' it may also be that poets only talk when they cannot sing. I am content to leave my theorising about poetry at this point. The sad ghost of Coleridge beckons to me from the shadows.[63]

If the old satirical cleverness and wit that marked the youthful Eliot had now largely receded into the background, another set of qualities, not less admirable, had arisen to fill the temporary vacancy of shuttles weaving the wind to no hortatory

---

* The best extant account of Eliot's first marriage and his long friendship with Emily Hale appears in T. S. Matthews, *Great Tom: Notes Towards the Definition of T. S. Eliot*, New York, 1974.

purpose. Although he calls the phantom by Coleridge's name, the romantic poet in Eliot must also have been thinking of that other sad ghost who beckoned to Prince Hamlet from the shadowy ramparts of Elsinore, far distant from the lecture hall where he closed his series to sustained applause.[64]

Wallace Stevens

LA VIE ANTÉRIEURE AND
LE BEL AUJOURD'HUI

Every man is like an actor's trunk, full of strange creatures, new and old. —Stevens, *Letters*

There is about every poet a vast world of other people from whom he derives himself and through himself his poetry. —Stevens, *Opus Posthumous*

IN 1934-1935 and again at mid-century, Wallace Stevens interested himself in the discrimination of romanticisms, both the quick and the dead. "When people speak of the romantic," he wrote in 1935, "they do so in what the French commonly call a *pejorative* sense. But poetry is essentially romantic, only the romantic poetry must be something constantly new and, therefore, just the opposite of what is spoken of as the romantic. Without this new romantic, one gets nowhere; with it, the most casual things take on transcendence, and the poet rushes brightly, and so on. What one is always doing is keeping the romantic pure, eliminating from it what people speak of as the romantic."*

---

* *LTRS*, 277. "Sailing After Lunch" is Stevens's poetical version of this passage from the letters. A defense of "the romantic," it opens with, "It is the word pejorative that hurts," and continues with the poet's prayer to "Mon Dieu" that the romantic should be here, there, and everywhere, yet must never "remain" or ever again "return." The poem concludes with the

Later in the same year he again characterized the romantic in its nonpejorative sense—"meaning always the living and at the same time the imaginative, the youthful, the delicate." This was "the vital element in poetry." It was accordingly "absurd to wince at being called a romantic poet. Unless one is that, one is not a poet at all. . . . It means, now-a-days, an uncommon intelligence. It means in a time like our own of violent feelings, equally violent feelings and the most skillful expression of the genuine."[1]

He had recently been reading Irving Babbitt, the famous humanist, who was just then reaching the end of his career at Harvard. Babbitt had maintained that "a thing is romantic when, as Aristotle would say, it is wonderful rather than probable. . . . A thing is romantic when it is strange, unexpected, intense, superlative, extreme, unique, etc." On these adjectival definitions Stevens elaborated:

> It must also be living. It must always be living. It is in the sense of living intensity, living singularity that it is the vital element in poetry. The most brilliant instance of the romantic in this sense is Mr. Eliot, who incessantly revives the past and creates the future. It is a process of cross-fertilization, an immense process, all arts considered, of hybridization. Mr. Eliot's "Prelude" with the smell of steaks in passageways, is an instance, in the sense that the smell of steak in the Parnassian air is a thing perfectly fulfilling Professor Babbitt's specification.[2]

Romanticism in the lesser sense, according to Stevens, connoted "obsolescence." He wished to attach this term "not to the romantic in general but to some phase of the romantic that has become stale. Just as there is always a romantic that is potent, so there is always a romantic that is impotent." One example of the romantic that had grown obsolescent, stale,

nautical wish "to be a pupil / Of the gorgeous wheel [the sun?] and so to give / That slight transcendence to the dirty sail, / By light, the way one feels, sharp white, / And then rush brightly through the summer air" (CP, 120-21).

and impotent, at least for Stevens, was the poetry of Sir Walter
Scott. He compared it to "the scenery of a play that has come
to an end . . . a scenery that has been trucked away and stood
somewhere on the horizon or just a little below. . . .* What
a modern poet desires, above everything else, is to be nothing
more than a poet of the present time. . . . He considers his
function to be this: to find, by means of his own thought and
feeling, what seems to him to be the poetry of his time and
differentiated from the poetry of Sir Walter Scott, or the poetry
of any other time."[3]

Stevens's position on the *now* as over against the *then* is an
almost exact replica of Emerson's in the essay called "Quo-
tation and Originality": "We cannot overstate our debt to the
Past but the moment has the supreme claim. The Past is for
us; but the sole terms on which it can become ours are its
subordination to the present."

Stevens's temporal independence, his insistence on discov-
ering, through his own thought and feeling, a poetry that
belonged to his own times, amounted almost to a benign
obsession. "If there are any literary relations between my things
and those of other writers," he said in 1935, "they are un-
conscious. Such a thing as adopting the method or the manner
of another writer is inconceivable. Granted the strong effect
of literature, it is an effect derived from the mass of things
that I have read in the past."[4] Nearly twenty years later he
was still convinced that "while . . . I come down from the
past, the past is my own and not something marked Coleridge,
Wordsworth, etc. . . . My reality-imagination complex is en-
tirely my own even though I see it in others."[5] Such statements
may remind us of William Blake's resolution: "I must create
a system or be enslav'd by another Man's." But Stevens de-
clined to call his own ideas systematic either in a philosophic
or an esthetic sense.

Many other leading modern poets share his views on literary

* Stevens employs dramatic imagery in "Of Modern Poetry"—scene, script,
theatre, speech, stage, audience, play, as Walton Litz has pointed out (*CP*,
239-40).

relations. Yeats, Frost, Eliot, and Auden all "come down from the past" but are commonly reluctant to submit to (or admit to) its dominance over their creative impulses. Each of them is aware of a particular past, his own in his lifetime, reasonably immediate, uniquely memorable, rather than a distant humming of ancestral voices "somewhere on the horizon or just a little below." Yet those voices are always there.

As his remarks on Eliot's *Preludes* show, Stevens was well acquainted with the phenomenon of cross-fertilization or hybridization as one element in the process of creativity. Lodged within the storehouse of the poet's memory are all the experiences, whether "literary" or otherwise "autobiographical," that have moved him in the past—"remembered habitations," as Stevens once called them, that may be subject to instant recollection if the proper conditions collaborate.

"Sometimes I am all memories," he wrote in 1909, and long afterwards he alluded to "the sounds that stick, inevitably modulating, in the blood."[6] Sounds and sights, together with the feelings that once accompanied them, may and often do meet and merge in new collocations and efflorescences, like fresh "flowers in last month's newspapers," to make the old words lively, to assure poetry's continuing vitality. Stevens knew very well that "poetry is a process of the personality of the poet. This is the element, the force, that keeps poetry a living thing, the modernizing and ever-modern influence."[7] One major corollary to this position was that the poet's "personality," which he sometimes called "temperament," contained whole congeries of memorials ready to take on "transcendence" as the poet rushed brightly among them.

❦ EXCEPT ON ONE or two occasions, Stevens habitually avoided the term *romanticism*, preferring to use "the romantic" because he saw in this concept a permanent element in human art and thought rather than a limited and measurable movement in the history of ideas. Up to the age of thirty-five his major romantic allegiance was to the poetry of John Keats, in which he had periodically immersed himself from 1899 to the time when many of the chief poems that would compose *Harmonium* emerged in a kind of bright rush fifteen years or so into the twentieth century.

The persuasive arguments of Helen Vendler seem now to have established the direct influence of the final stanza of Keats's ode, "To Autumn," upon the seven magnificent lines that conclude "Sunday Morning." This Vendler calls "the single most derivative moment in Stevens," suggesting "a deep engagement" on his part with the original poem. "Both poets," she writes, "use successive clauses of animal presence (gnats, lambs, crickets, redbreast, and swallows in Keats; deer, quail, and pigeons in Stevens); both poems close with birds in the sky (gathering swallows in Keats; flocks of pigeons in Stevens) and with the sense of sound (a whistling bird in each); and Keats' soft-dying day becomes Stevens' evening." There are likewise certain differences. "Whereas Keats rests in the polyphony of the creatures in their autumnal choir, Stevens (though his adoption of Keats' principal trope, enumeration, shows him to be not insensible to the plenitude around him in the scene) makes his landscape depend for its significance on what it can explicitly suggest about the truth of the human condition." Thus Stevens

> has adopted Keats' manner—the population of animals, the types of clauses, the diction, even the sunset landscape—without at all embracing Keats' essential stylistic argument against nostalgia. Nor has he imitated Keats' reticent diction and chaste rhetoric; instead, he writes with an increasing opulence of rhetorical music and imposes explicit metaphysical dimensions on the landscape. Nevertheless, the imitation, however inferior to its source, argues that Keats' ode had penetrated Stevens' consciousness and imagination absolutely and was already provoking him to see the world in its light, even if he found the world insufficient without attendant metaphysics.[8]

Although there is a good deal more to Helen Vendler's argument, the foregoing excerpts suggest the extent of Stevens's debt to Keats in one major instance, perhaps the most justly famous of all the poems in *Harmonium*. Here, for now, he had performed a poetical act that he would later call inconceivable: "adopting the method" as well as "the manner of another writer," even though the differences of aim and belief were wide, and even though the "imitation" was confined to the seven closing lines of a poem that ran to one hundred and twenty.

Still, it may not have been to Keats alone that Stevens was indebted for the conclusion to "Sunday Morning." In the summer of 1899 he had noted in his journal: "Birds sing at the edge of field at sunset. . . . Simple earthly happiness; singing for delight in beauty. A Full-hearted thoughtless lilt. Thought for Sonnet: Birds flying up from dark ground at evening: clover, deep grass, oats, etc. to circle + plunge beneath the golden clouds, in + about them, with golden spray on their wings like dew. Produce an imaginative flutter of color." Despite its obvious differences from the end of "Sunday Morning," this journal entry comes close to the spirit of the acceptance of the season's gifts (it was August in Pennsylvania) that prevails in "To Autumn." Keats would clearly have agreed with Stevens's offhand remark of 1951: "I like a world in which the passing of the season (or the passing of the seasons) is a matter of some importance."9

His first serious interest in Keats apparently dates from this same summer of 1899, probably in preparation for a course in romantic poetry that he was going to take that fall at Harvard. He was vacationing at Wily's, a boarding house or private hotel in Berkeley, Pennsylvania, and his journal entry for 18 July reads as follows:

> In the afternoon I sat in the piano room reading Keats' "Endymion," and listening to the occassional showers on the foliage outside. The fronds of a fern were dangling over my knees and I felt lazy and content. Once as I

looked up I saw a big, pure drop of rain slip from leaf to leaf of a clematis vine. The thought occurred to me that it was just such quick, unexpected, commonplace, specific things that poets and other observers jot down in their note-books. It was certainly a monstrous pleasure to be able to be specific about such a thing. . . .[10]

Stevens jotted it down in his journal that evening without the slightest notion that it would ever be of poetical use and yet, by that very act, fixed it in his memory. The gradual or quick and unexpected collocation and eventual miscibility of disparate ideas and images in the formation of a poem is impossible to explain. Still, as we know, it happens all the time, with mergers of the "real" and the "imaginative," the real and the real, the imaginative and the imaginative. In his various pronouncements on the way the poet operates, Stevens nearly always maintained that the most lasting fusions took place between what was real and what was imagined. It would seem farfetched indeed to suggest that his memories of a piano room, the sound of rain in the foliage outside, the sight of clear drops trickling down a vine, and Keats's forthright statement that "A thing of beauty is a joy forever," should have eventuated in certain images in "Peter Quince at the Clavier," first published in 1915. Was Quince at his keyboard a projected version of young Stevens in the piano room at Wily's? Was the refrain ("like a willow swept by rain") a distant echo of the rain in the trees that Stevens listened to in the intervals of his reading of *Endymion* that lazy July afternoon? The book that lay open on his knees began with the firm assertion that "A thing of beauty is a joy forever, / Its loveliness increases, it will never / Fade into nothingness." His reading in the following decade must have acquainted him with other Keatsian ideas: on the evanescence of earthly beauty ("She dwells with beauty, beauty that must die"), on the annual process of rebirth in the seasonal cycle ("Shed no tear! Oh, shed no tear! / The flower will bloom another year"), on beauty's perennial survival through works of art like the Grecian urn ("When old age shall this generation waste, / Thou shalt remain"). But neither Keats nor any of his known favorites among the French symbolist poets put the complex of death and rebirth quite as Stevens was to do in his enigmatic quatrain:

> Beauty is momentary in the mind—
> The fitful tracing of a portal;
> But in the flesh it is immortal.
> The body dies; the body's beauty lives. . . .

The immortality of beauty in the flesh is possible only in the human imagination. Bodily beauty can survive only through the "memorials" that art can offer. That such notions were already in Stevens's mind in the summer of 1899 is unlikely. But he still had fifteen years in which to meditate upon the intricate relations among beauty, immortality, and music that would emerge in "Peter Quince."

Meantime, his immersion in Keats's poetry sporadically continued. In 1907, writing to his girl, he showed that he knew "Keen Fitful Gusts." "How sweet and strange it seems— better than anything else—Spring's 'light green dress.' " The quoted phrase came from Keats's sonnet: "Of lovely Laura in her light green dress." It is a curious coincidence, as well as a tacit tribute to Keats, that Robert Frost echoed another line from the same sonnet, "I have many miles on foot to fare," in "Stopping by Woods on a Snowy Evening."

In the following year Stevens noted with some excitement that the manuscript of *Endymion* was to be found in J. P. Morgan's "celebrated collection," then on exhibition at Columbia University Library. He quoted with evident relish the now famous opening line: "A thing of beauty is a joy forever."[11]

Only a few months later he used the phrase "sensual ear," from the "Ode on a Grecian Urn." The lines he had in mind were from the second stanza:

Heard melodies are sweet, but those unheard
Are sweeter; therefore, ye soft pipes, play on;
Not to the sensual ear, but, more endear'd,
Pipe to the spirit ditties of no tone.

"Those long chords on the harp," wrote Stevens, "always so inexplicably sweet to me, vibrate on more than the 'sensual ear'—vibrate on the unknown. . . . And what one listens to at a concert, if one knew it, is not only the harmony of sounds, but the whispering of innumerable responsive spirits within one, momentarily revived."[12]

He had returned in this year of 1909 to the reading of *Endymion* as an antidote to the occasional boredom of living in New York. "I have two red bananas to eat and I am determined to read at least ten pages of Endymion. . . . It is such a bore to sit here when the weather is fine. But red bananas and Endymion are a partial solution. I begin: 'Increasing still in heart, and pleasant sense, / Upon his fairy journey on he hastes!'"[13]

Such echoes and excerpts were always meticulously placed inside quotation marks as if his Harvard training was still prominent in his mind. In sum they make clear his easy working familiarity with much of Keats's poetry. A small lyric composed in 1909 hints at the matter, though not the manner and form, of the sonnet, "On Sitting Down to Read *King Lear* Once Again." Stevens's pilgrim in the Country of Good Pleasance is made to say:

Under golden trees,
I might lose desire;
Rest, and never know
The mortal fire.
In that golden shade
I might soon forget;
Live, and not recall
The mortal debt.[14]

The speaker in Keats's sonnet bids farewell to "golden-tongued Romance," the "Queen of far away," bidding her to close her "olden pages" and be mute while once again he takes up *King Lear* to engage his imagination with the fierce dispute "betwixt damnation and impassion'd clay," until, having been "consumèd in the fire," he can develop "new Phoenix wings" to fly at his "desire." The iteration of "golden" in Stevens's lyric, the presence of the rhyme-words "fire" and "desire," and the explicit contrast between a golden romantic realm and one in which mortality prevails, hint strongly that among the innumerable responsive spirits that whispered in Stevens's memory at this date, Keats was undoubtedly one.

In the spring of 1910, Stevens was still reading and quoting Keats, this time from the "Epistle to John Hamilton Reynolds":

> It is a flaw
> In happiness, to see beyond our bourn—
> It forces us in summer skies to mourn,
> It spoils the singing of the Nightingale. . . .

If Stevens disagreed with Keats's rejection of metaphysical exploration, he gave no sign of it, simply quoting the passage without comment.[15]

Since Keats had been his bright familiar for the better part of ten years, it is no wonder that Stevens's poetry and letters should sometimes resound with Keatsian echoes and that the same should still be apparent in 1914-1915 when, in a veritable explosion of release, as Walton Litz has said, "the ideas and images of fifteen years tumbled forth in such a profusion of forms," ready to be gathered up in *Harmonium*.[16]

More than a little of Keats's appetitive gusto reappears in Stevens—in Crispin's love of "good fat guzzly fruit," in the musky muscadines, pineapples, and melons, the platter of pears, the dish of peaches.* The plums and pears of "Sunday Morn-

---

* This appetitive tendency seems not to have been taken into account by Helen Vendler when she wrote: "The lively things of this world—human, animal, vegetable—do not touch him as they did Keats or Wordsworth. . . .

ing" seem to have grown straight out of the Venus-Adonis episode in the second book of *Endymion*. The inventor of Porphyro's banquet in "The Eve of St. Agnes" could only have applauded Stevens's feast of delicacies as he stood hungrily before a Manhattan fruiterer's window in the fall of 1949: "Beauteous plums," he wrote, "peaches like Swedish blondes, pears that make you think of Rubens, and the first grapes pungent through the glass."[17]

Even in the 1950s he had not forgotten his early admiration for Keats, including the famous episode in "The Eve of St. Agnes" where the wintry moon, shining through the stained-glass casement in Madeline's chilly boudoir, throws "warm gules" of rose and amethyst over the praying girl. In a letter of 1953 Stevens explained his use of the term "pales" of red and green in the closing section of "Credences of Summer." There the "personae of summer" appear as characters in a play, wearing blue and yellow costumes (like the sky and the sun) that are "sashed and seamed" with "half pales of red, half pales of green"—"part of the mottled mood of summer's whole." Stevens explained that he had used *pales* in its heraldic sense, meaning perpendicular stripes in an escutcheon. This, he said, was the way Keats had used *gules* in describing "moonlight falling through a stained glass window." He slightly misquoted Keats's line ("And threw warm gules on Madeline's fair breast") remembering it as "And cast warm gules of red." But he did recall how a latter-day critic had pointed out that "moonlight passing through a window does not take on the color of the glass."[18] Thus at last Keats bowed awkwardly out of Stevens's memory, leaving the field to other influences.

❧ SINCE HIS DAYS as a special student at Harvard, Stevens had owned Richard Garnett's *Selected Poems of Shelley* (London, 1889). In 1906 he named Schiller and Shelley as poets

The natural cast of his eyes is upward, and the only phenomenon to which he is passionately attached is the weather" (Vendler, *On Extended Wings*, 47).

interested in "humanity," adding prophetically that "we do not pursue the ideal of the Universal Superman—at least not today. But we may the day after tomorrow." It is possible that he was thinking of Prometheus, the universal superman who, in Shelley's prophetic imagination, was to usher in a new era of cosmic love at some "all-nameless" and unpredictable hour.[19]

It was not, however, until the mid-1930s that he gave evidence of a continuing interest in Shelley. One example occurred in *Owl's Clover*, first published in 1936. Stevens evidently had in mind the gradual dissemination of poetical ideas—what Shelley had specifically prayed for in his petition to "the breath of Autumn's being," the wild west wind:

> Be thou, Spirit fierce,
> My spirit! Be thou me, impetuous one!
> Drive my dead thoughts over the universe
> Like withered leaves to quicken a new birth!
> And by the incantation of this verse,
> Scatter, as from an unextinguished hearth
> Ashes and sparks, my words among man-
>   kind!
> Be through my lips to unawakened earth
> The trumpet of a prophecy.

Stevens invoked the "celestial paramours"—elsewhere identified as "all the things in our nature that are celestial"—in another autumnal setting:

> Then, while the music makes you, make, yourselves,
> Long autumn sheens and pittering sounds like
>   sounds
> On pattering leaves and suddenly with lights,
> Astral and Shelleyan, diffuse new day. . . .

Stevens's somewhat enigmatic explication of this passage in a letter of 1940 says that the celestial paramours "are compelled by desire . . . to diffuse the new day," a view more or less consonant with Shelley's petition to the west wind, a notably celestial force.[20]

The passage continues:

Agree: the apple in the orchard, round
And red, will not be redder, rounder then
Than now. No: nor the ploughman in his bed
Be free to sleep there sounder, for the plough
And the dew and the ploughman still will best be one. . . .

Stevens's commentary on these lines is that "the astral and Shelleyan lights are not going to alter the structure of nature. Apples will always be apples, and whoever is a ploughman hereafter will be what the ploughman has always been. For all that, the astral and the Shelleyan will have transformed the world." Stevens is skeptical enough to insist that the apples in the orchards and the ploughman in his furrow or his bed are likely to remain unchanged by any action of the "celestial paramours." But at the level of those "things in our nature that are celestial" (the imaginative lights, "astral and Shelleyan"), some future transformation, while not certainly predictable, may well take place.[21]

The second apostrophe to the celestial paramours in *Owl's Clover* seems to demote Shelley from the astral level:

Mesdames, one might believe that Shelley lies
Less in the stars than in their earthy wake,
Since the radiant disclosures that you make
Are of an eternal vista, manqué and gold
And brown, an Italy of the mind, a place
Of fear before the disorder of the strange,
A time in which the poet's politics
Will rule in a poets' world. Yet that will be
A world impossible for poets, who
Complain and prophesy, in their complaints,
And are never of the world in which they live. . . .

Stevens did not explain this passage, which remains obscure. The "eternal vistas" of the celestial paramours seem to dissolve into a mundane "Italy of the mind" where fear, disorder, and poetical politics impede or inhibit the astral transformations. The closing lines, however, are at least tangential to the Shelley of the west wind ode, who *complains* ("I fall upon the thorns of life") and *prophesies* ("If winter comes, can spring be far behind?") as he seeks out a point of vantage in another and better world than that in which he lives. One of Stevens's criteria for the romantic poet was that he should spend his life "rejecting the accepted sense of things."* The definition precisely fits Shelley, whether astral or mundane.

These passages in *Owl's Clover* were not Stevens's first "echoes" of the "Ode to the West Wind." About a year earlier he had picked up the Shelleyan "Be thou" motif in a remarkable poem called "Mozart, 1935." It is built upon a dramatic contrast between order and chaos, and it begins and ends with a directive to the poet to be seated at the piano, like a later and less sentimental Peter Quince. All about him as he plays are threats of chaos, a siege against the order that the music represents. While he runs through his arpeggios, nameless and faceless alien forces cast stones upon the roof and carry a body in rags down the stairs. Snow falls. The streets are full of cries. It is, though Stevens never says so, the time of the Great Depression. But the poet must keep on playing. Mozart's music is "that lucid souvenir of the past . . . that airy dream of the future," as purely Shelleyan as the hortatory "Be thou," which is now taken up thematically:

> Be thou
> The voice of angry fear
> The voice of besieging pain
> Be thou that wintry sound as of a great wind howling,
> By which sorrow is released,
> Dismissed, abridged
> In a starry placating . . .
> Be seated, thou.

* Stevens applied this criterion to William Carlos Williams in a review of his *Collected Poems*, 1934, and categorized Dr. Williams as a modern romantic.

One of the major catalytic forces in Shelley's work from *Prometheus Unbound* to *The Triumph of Life* was his conviction about the necessity for spiritual change. He employed this theme in at least two of his most famous lyrics. "I change but I cannot die" is the central affirmation of "The Cloud." The speaker in the "Ode to the West Wind" welcomes the physical changes in earth, air, and sea that are brought about by the action of the "unseen presence" of the wind itself. Through the same agency, now to become (he hopes) a dominant force in his own mind, he foresees "a new birth," not physical but spiritual, throughout the (as yet) "unawakened earth."

These ideas strongly engaged Steven's imagination while he was writing *Notes Toward A Supreme Fiction* in the war year of 1942. He named his second canto "It Must Change," and in section ten clearly connected the west wind with the idea of change.

> The west wind was the music, the motion, the force
> To which the swans curveted, a will to change,
> A will to make iris frettings on the blank.
> There was a will to change. . . .

In section six of the same canto, he returned to the Shelleyan "Be thou" echo previously used in "Mozart, 1935." This time the musician is not a poet at the piano but a parliament of fowls in a summer garden. One of them is a sparrow (Stevens elsewhere calls him a "cat-bird") who insistently opposes the cacophonic "ké-ké" of the others with his melodious "be thous."

> Bethou me, said sparrow, to the crackled blade,
> And you, and you, bethou me as you blow,
> When in my coppice you behold me be.

The second *you* of the second line is obviously addressed to the wind, with which the sparrow is associated in his championship of change.

Stevens later explained that *coppice* was his family's private name for a stand of evergreens in their Hartford garden. The use of the word in the poem was meant to signal a change. "When the sparrow begins calling be-thou: *Bethou* me . . . he expresses one's own liking for the change; he invites attention from the summer grass; he mocks the wren, the jay, the robin. . . . In the face of death life asserts itself. Perhaps it makes an image out of the force with which it struggles to survive. Bethou is intended to be heard; it and ké-ké, which is inimical, are opposing sounds. Bethou is the spirit's own seduction."[22]

Despite the clear Shelleyan connections—the alliance between the west wind and the theme of change; the persistent echoes of "be thou" and "be thou me"; the reminder of Shelley's belief, as set forth in the ode, that "in the face of death life asserts itself"—Stevens has given his personal imprimatur to every image and idea derived from Shelley. It cannot justly be called a form of adaptation, it is rather a transformation behind which Shelley's own words seem "like ghosts from an enchanter fleeing." The whole comparison exactly illustrates what Stevens once called "the difference that we make in what we see / And our memorials of that difference."[23]

This phenomenon reappears in the use Stevens makes of "Ozymandias," the only good sonnet Shelley ever wrote. It is the report of "a traveller from an antique land," evidently Egypt. In the desert he has come upon "two vast and trunkless legs of stone." The rest of the statue has long since fallen, and lies half buried in the sands. Part of it is a "shattered visage" on which are still visible the "frown, / And wrinkled lip, and sneer of cold command," which suggest that the anonymous sculptor "well those passions read / Which yet survive, stamped on these lifeless things."

> And on the pedestal these words appear:
> 'My name is Ozymandias, king of kings:
> Look on my works, ye Mighty, and despair!'
> Nothing beside remains. Round the decay
> Of that colossal wreck, boundless and bare
> The lone and level sands stretch far away.

Shelley, who hated all despots, found in the traveler's tale an ironic commentary on the theme of *Sic Semper Tyrannus*. Stevens, with little interest in politics, seems to have been attracted most by the exotic name of the fallen ruler, who is usually identified with Ramses II. He called his poem, the eighth in the series of "It Must Change," an "illustration of illusion as value," as if illusion were a useful part of all our subliminal equipment, whether or not we want it or even know it. This is the poem that ends with one of the most beautiful (and philosophically truthful) lines in all of Stevens: "A fictive covering / Weaves always glistening from the heart and mind."

But the fictive covering that Stevens's poem weaves is sufficiently opaque to mask out any evidence of Shelleyan "influence" except for the name of Ozymandias and the visual setting of the sand on which Nanzia Nunzio places her discarded ornaments. At last, "stripped more nakedly / Than nakedness," she addresses Ozymandias:

> Speak to me that, which spoken, will array me
> In its own only precious ornament.
> Set on me the spirit's diamond coronal.
>
> Clothe me entire in the final filament,
> So that I tremble with such love so known
> And myself am precious for your perfecting.
>
> Then Ozymandias said the spouse, the bride
> Is never naked. A fictive covering
> Weaves always glistening from the heart and mind.

One other possible echo of the Ozymandias sonnet had earlier become audible in *Owl's Clover*. In part five, following the references to the "astral" Shelley in earlier sections, Stevens showed that his visual memory was haunted by images of broken statues like this of the Egyptian dynast. "A solemn voice," not unlike that of Shelley's returned traveler, describes a kind of waste land "at the end of the world." In that place the sun

Shines without fire on columns intercrossed,
White slapped on white, majestic marble heads,
Severed and tumbled into seedless grass,
Motionless, knowing neither dew nor frost . . .
And there are the white-maned horses' heads beyond
The help of any wind or any sky:
Parts of the immense detritus of a world
That is completely waste, that moves from waste
To waste, out of the hopeless waste of the past
Into a hopeful waste to come.

The sculptor who carved the statue of Shelley's Ozymandias seems to appear in the midst of this shambles of fallen objects, though lizards now inhabit the sockets of his eyes:

There lies the head of the sculptor in which the thought
Of lizards, in its eye, is more acute
Than the thought that once was native to the skull. . . .

Beside the desolate scene stands a "gigantic solitary urn, / A trash can at the end of the world," where "the dead / Give up dead things and the living turn away." Stevens himself turns away from the Shelleyan original with a closing image of two commingling lights, "immense reflections, whirling apart and wide away." Walton Litz has suggested that these are the lights of the past and future, which commingle at the astral level, as they seem to do here in the poet's imagination, to "diffuse new day." Once more, as in the instances previously examined, Stevens has begun with an apparent impetus from Shelley, from which he ultimately departs into his own highly original elaborations.

In "The Figure of the Youth as Virile Poet," one of the essays collected in *The Necessary Angel*, Stevens offers some reflections on Shelley's *Defence of Poetry*. Even though we lack a definition of poetry, he writes, "there are impressions, approximations. Shelley gives us an approximation when he gives us a definition in what he calls 'a general sense.' " (Shelley's words, in the second paragraph of *A Defence*, are: "Poetry, in a general sense, may be defined to be 'the expression of the imagination.' ") Stevens quotes with evident approval Shelley's further statements on poetry as "the very image of life expressed in its eternal truth"; as "at once the centre and circumference of knowledge . . . the record of the best and happiest moments of the happiest and best minds"; and as a power that "arrests the vanishing apparitions which haunt the interlunations of life."[24]

In "The Noble Rider and the Sound of Words," the essay immediately preceding "The Figure of the Youth," Stevens had implied his reservations about Shelley's "general definition" of poetry as "an expression of the imagination." Thinking of the figure of the charioteer and his winged horses in Plato's *Phaedrus*, Stevens said that "the imagination loses vitality as it ceases to adhere to what is real. When it adheres to the unreal and intensifies what is unreal, while its first effect may be extraordinary, that effect is the maximum effect that it will ever have." The problem with Plato (who was one of Shelley's gods, though Stevens does not say so), was that "his imagination does not adhere to what is real. On the contrary, having created something unreal, it adheres to it and intensifies its unreality."[25]

Stevens presently turns to consider the sculptor Verrocchio and his equestrian statue of Bartolommeo Colleoni in Venice—the "noble rider" of his title. "There, on the edge of the world in which we live today," Verrocchio "established a form of such nobility that it has never ceased to magnify us in our own eyes." Excellent as the sculptor's achievement is, however, "in this statue, the apposition between the imagination and reality is too favorable to the imagination," which is also the problem with Plato's charioteer.

In his emphasis on the exemplary nobility of the equestrian figure, Stevens appears to be paying homage to Shelley's belief "that men are powerfully impelled to achieve what their imaginations picture as the highest good." This sentence by George F. Whicher ably summarizes Shelley's opinion in *A Defence*

295

that Homer's embodiment of "the truth and beauty of friend-ship, patriotism, and the persevering devotion to an object" in figures like Achilles, Hector, and Ulysses must have "refined and enlarged the sentiments" of readers or auditors of the *Iliad* and the *Odyssey*. The process began with admiration of "such great and lovely impersonations" until "from admiring they imitated, and from imitation they identified themselves with the objects of their admiration." If Verrocchio's statue magnifies us in our own eyes, as Stevens says it does, it is clearly because it establishes, through an art form, an image of nobility to which we may all aspire. This is evidently, in Stevens's mind, one of the sanctions of art, and the line from Plato through Verrocchio to Shelley is in this sense strongly demarcated. Stevens's problem with all three was that "the apposition between the imagination and reality" was "too favorable to the imagination." We should probably remind ourselves of one of his *Adagia* which says simply, "Eventually an imaginary world is entirely without interest."[26]

❧ STEVENS entered a sturdy caveat against such procedures as we have been following. "I am not conscious of having been influenced by anybody," he told Richard Eberhart. ". . . But there is a kind of critic who spends his time dissecting what he reads for echoes, imitations, influences, as if no one was ever simply himself but is always compounded of a lot of other people."[27] His use of the poetry of Keats and Shelley was typical of his practice among ancestral voices. Despite a few clear echoes, he was never a slavish imitator. He did not want to seem to be "a second-hand poet." He might graze, or temporarily intersect with, a previous poetic formulation, but he remained his own man, even though the voice of mem-ory sometimes sang within his sensibility too insistently to be ignored. "The truth is," he wrote in 1948, "that a man's sense of the world dictates his subjects to him and that this sense is derived from his personality, his temperament, over which he has little control and possibly none, except superficially."

And again in the same essay: "It is often said of a man that his work is autobiographical in spite of every subterfuge. It cannot be otherwise."[28] Without being a scholar, he was a strongly appreciative and critical reader, and this background was a strong force in his poetic personality. If the background included the English romantic poets, as it demonstrably did, no one need be surprised to find occasional echoes, whether conscious or not.

"The romantic" in Stevens took many forms. One example was his espousal of romantic spontaneity. Of "The Emperor of Ice Cream" he remarked in 1933 that it was "an instance of letting myself go. Poems of this sort are the pleasantest on which to look back, because they seem to remain fresher than others. This represented what was in my mind at the moment, with the least possible manipulation." A couple of years later he proclaimed his enjoyment of "spontaneity and fluidity." In 1945 he said that "I almost always dislike anything that I do that doesn't fly in the window," and in 1954 asserted that "I have never felt that form matters enough to allow myself to be controlled by it."[29]

As a young man he had already made up his mind on a point in which he had been anticipated by many of the earlier romantics, including Blake and Wordsworth as well as Emerson: "I'm completely satisfied that behind every physical fact there is a divine force. Don't, therefore, look *at* facts, but *through* them."[30] He was equally explicit in 1946 when, under the stimulus provided by the philosopher H. D. Lewis, he declared that "an isolated fact, cut loose from the universe, has no significance for the poet."[31] That Wordsworth was a party to these beliefs is shown by Stevens's offhand remark that "one may find intimations of immortality in an object on the mantelpiece."[32] The familiar in Stevens commonly interacted with the strange. Shelley's *A Defence* had asserted that one function of the poet was to "make familiar objects be as if they were not familiar." Stevens said that the poetic imagination "always makes use of the familiar to produce the unfamiliar."[33]

297

The attraction he felt toward the unfamiliar was shown by a strong streak of exoticism in his nature. This, or something like it, appears among the second-generation romantics, Byron, Shelley, and Keats, and occasionally in Wordsworth (the dream of Araby in *Prelude* 5) and in Coleridge's "Kubla Khan." Stevens loved to envision distant lands to which he would never travel except in his imagination. Much of this emerges in the letters. "The impression of Greece," he wrote, "is one of the purest things in the world. It is not a thing, however, that you get from any book, but from fragments of poetry that have been preserved, and from statues and ruins, and a thousand things, all building up in the mind a noble conception of a pagan world of passion and love of beauty and life. It is a white world under a blue sky, still standing erect in remote sunshine."[34]

Liking fluidity and letting himself go, seizing upon any striking *donnée* that flew in at his window, shrugging off the constrictions of form in favor of vitality, looking through facts toward their larger connotations, using his imagination to present the familiar in the guise of the unfamiliar, and dreamily exploring exotic regions like Ceylon or the desert domain of Ozymandias—all these were among his romantic credos and his habits.

Yet another was his belief in the importance of feeling. In reviewing the selected poems of Marianne Moore, whom he called "a fresh romantic," he quoted with evident approval a sentence from A. E. Powell's *The Romantic Theory of Poetry*, which said that the romantic "seeks to reproduce for us the feeling as it lives within himself."[35] Stevens later enlarged upon this fugitive text, saying that "the inter-relation between things is what makes them fecund. . . . Les plus belles pages are those in which things do not stand alone but are operative as the result of interaction. . . . The inter-relation between reality and the imagination is the basis of the character of literature. The inter-relation between reality and the emotions is the basis of the vitality of literature. [The inter-relation] between reality and thought [is] the basis of [literature's] power."[36]

"Nature [is] my source of supply," he wrote in 1926, clearly reflecting a bias shared by all the English romantics except Blake.[37] One curious aspect of his natural imagery is an almost obsessive use of birds. All through the *Collected Poems* they sing, twitter, squawk, fly past in green light, coo, gabble, crow, and peck at the rinds of melons. In this respect he outdoes the English romantics, who are famous for their use of birds, whether actual or symbolic. Yet their thrushes and stockdoves, cuckoos and nightingales, skylarks and redbreasts are few in comparison to the occupants of Stevens's private aviary. All told he names at least three dozen, to say nothing of all those *innominati* whose wings are forever flashing in and out of his poems. A sentence from Joyce's *Finnegans Wake* seems applicable: "Nobirdy aviar soar anywing to eagle it."

Nature in Stevens was, however, nearly always amended and reformed to suit his poetic purposes. Like his romantic forebears, he characteristically made a highly individuated response to natural stimuli. This is why he could write of "the pictorializations of men . . . the objects of their passions, the objects before which they come and speak, with intense choosing, words that we remember and make our own. Their words have made a world that transcends the world and a life liveable in that transcendence."[38] Stevens's concept of transcendence should not be construed in Coleridgean or Kantian terms. He had in mind only a world and a life that extended above and beyond the naturalistic, and yet stopped short of the superhuman.

Byron and Coleridge are the only English romantics to whose poetry Stevens paid little attention. The sole allusion to Byron in the letters is sartorial, not poetical. On a hike from Van Cortlandt Park to Greenwich, Connecticut, the young Stevens turned back his shirt-collar "precisely like that corsair of hearts, le grand Byron." It has sometimes been maintained that Stevens was intentionally Byronic in his "mock-epic," "The Comedian as the Letter C." It is true that Crispin, whether hero or antihero, is making a sort of grand tour like Byron's Don Juan; and true also that both characters are partial projections of their respective creators. Byron was proud of having written an "epic" that held to the human plane without recourse to mythological manipulations. Stevens called "The Comedian" an "anti-mythological poem."[39] Like Byron, he alludes to Voltaire's Candide, as if that luckless young Frenchman were a totem figure for all comic writers, as in fact he is. Stevens accomplished his picaresque "verse-novel" in six cantos rather than sixteen, and in blank verse rather than ottava rima stanzas. But these resemblances appear to be mainly if not entirely adventitious.

Whether or not he was following Byron's practice, Stevens occasionally employed the satiric device of letting his readers down with a bump after a previous build-up in the opposite direction. One good example occurs in "On An Old Horn."

> If the stars that move together as one, disband,
> Flying like insects of fire in a cavern of night,
> Pipperoo, pippera, pipperum . . . The rest is rot.[40]

The sudden decline into pipperoos hints at Stevens's fear of having been overfanciful in his simile about fiery insects in a dark cavern. The Byron of Don Juan was well acquainted with such excesses and taught himself to counteract them with laughter, as Stevens does here.

One winter evening in 1909, Stevens tackled some of Coleridge's prose, reading on laboriously until midnight. "It is heavy work," he wrote, "reading things like that, that have so little in them that one feels to be contemporary, living."[41] More than thirty years later, he had decided, through his reading of I. A. Richards's Coleridge on Imagination, that "as poetry goes, as the imagination goes, as the approach to truth . . . or to being by way of the imagination goes, Coleridge is one of the great figures." Yet he was, on the other hand, "a man who may be said to have been defining poetry all his life in definitions that are valid enough but which no longer impress us primarily by their validity."[42] Stevens's only critical use of Coleridge was a brief account of the famous distinction between imagination and fancy, which he then applied satirically to Clark Mills's equestrian statue of General Andrew Jackson in Lafayette Square, Washington, which he had come to regard as a highly "fanciful" sculpture.[43]

When he asserted that his "reality-imagination complex" was his own rather than a mere redaction of theories by Coleridge and Wordsworth, he seems to have been entirely truthful. He did, however, share with Coleridge the conviction that the imagination is a power of the mind that takes impressions from the "real" world and by various acts of coadunation fuses them into new entities. Although he was aware, probably through his reading of Dr. Richards, of Coleridge's distinction between the primary and secondary imagination, he made nothing of it; and the distinction between imagination and fancy was employed only in the passage about the statue of Jackson.

Of all the books by the English romantics that survived in Stevens's library, the one with the greatest number of marginalia was Ernest Rhys's edition of Wordsworth's *Lyrical Poems* (1896), which he had probably marked up during the Harvard course in the fall of 1899. It is curious that apart from his offhand remark about "intimations of immortality," already cited, he had so little to say of the man usually thought of as the chief progenitor of English romanticism. It is true that late in life he quoted Wordsworth's 1800 preface to *Lyrical Ballads* as an example of the necessary revolt against eighteenth-century poetic diction. In preparing his essay on "The Relations Between Poetry and Painting," he was attracted by the chapter "On Reading Poetry and Seeing Pictures" in Leo Stein's *Appreciation* and quoted Stein's comment on the compositional value of a single line from Wordsworth's "Michael."[44]

What really seems to have seized his imagination was the sonnet, "Composed Upon Westminster Bridge," Wordsworth's matchless commentary on the sleeping city of London in the first light of dawn on 3 September 1802. While working on his "Noble Rider" essay, Stevens had turned to the British philosopher, C.E.M. Joad. One of Dr. Joad's favorite passages in Bergson's *Creative Evolution* dealt with the visual perception of motionless objects, and he addressed the question of how the world comes to look to us like "a collection of solid, static objects extended in space." Stevens answered Joad's question by saying that the subject matter of poetry is not to be found in such a "collection" but rather in "the life that is lived in the scene that it composes." If we happen to be thinking of Joad's philosophic observation, wrote Stevens, and then suddenly "hear a different and familiar description of the place," the experience can tell us a great deal about how poets "help people to live their lives."

Stevens illustrated his generalization by quoting five lines from Wordsworth's sonnet:

> This city now doth, like a garment, wear
> The beauty of the morning, silent, bare,
> Ships, towers, domes, theatres, and temples lie
> Open unto the fields, and to the sky;
> All bright and glittering in the smokeless air.

"What makes the poet the potent figure that he is, or was, or ought to be," wrote Stevens in summary, "is that he creates the world to which we turn incessantly and without knowing it and that he gives to life the supreme fictions without which we are unable to conceive of it."[45]

Just how often in his poetical life Stevens may have turned subconsciously back to Wordsworth's lines on London it is impossible to say. Yet he habitually made superb poems out of cityscapes, using his imagination to weave fictive coverings ("like a garment") over the stark realities of some of the "metropoles" that he knew from having lived in them. The most memorable of these would include "Academic Discourse at Havana," where the poet speaks from his balcony as if to awaken the slumberers in the city below; "A Postcard from the Volcano," where the poet, confronting the drab city of his birth, speaks as from the eminence of an aftertime; and "Of Hartford in a Purple Light," where the poet addresses the sun, "Master Soleil," as it casts "lights masculine" at noon and "lights feminine" at dusk over the distant river, the rail-road, and the cathedral of his adopted city.*

Arresting as these poems are, an even better one is the untitled seventh part of "It Must Be Abstract" in *Notes Toward A Supreme Fiction*. "Perhaps," said Stevens in one of the *Adagia*, "there is a degree of perception at which what is real and what is imagined are one: a state of clairvoyant observation, accessible ... to the poet or, say, the acutest poet."[46] Other pertinent passages appear in various letters between 1940 and 1952:

> As between reality and the imagination, we look forward to an era when there will exist the supreme balance between these two. .... Imagination has no source except in reality, and ceases to have any value when it departs from reality. Here is a fundamental principle about the imagination: It does not create except as it transforms. ... The various faculties of the mind co-exist and interact, and there is as much delight in this mere co-existence as a man and a woman find in each other's company. ... Sometimes I believe most in the imagination for a long time and then, without reasoning about it, turn to reality and believe in that and that alone. But both of these things project themselves endlessly and I want them to do just that. ... We live in a world of the imagination, in which reality and contact with it are the great blessings.[47]

The poem for which these remarks may serve as prologue begins in the known and friendly environs by the lake in Elizabeth Park near the poet's house in Hartford and then rises from this reality into imaginative abstraction:

> It feels good as it is without the giant,
> A thinker of the first idea. Perhaps
> The truth depends on a walk around a lake,

* In calling particular attention to these lyrics, I have omitted a relevant long poem, "An Ordinary Evening in New Haven," which has been extensively and brilliantly analyzed by Helen Vendler, *OEW*, 269-308.

A composing as the body tires, a stop
To see hepatica, a stop to watch
A definition growing certain and

A wait within that certainty, a rest
In the swags of pine-trees bordering the lake.
Perhaps there are times of inherent excellence,

As when the cock crows on the left and all
Is well, incalculable balances,
At which a kind of Swiss perfection comes

And a familiar music of the machine
Sets up its Schwärmerei, not balances
That we achieve but balances that happen,

As a man and woman meet and love forthwith.
Perhaps there are moments of awakening,
Extreme, fortuitous, personal, in which

We more than awaken, sit on the edge of sleep,
As on an elevation, and behold
The academies like structures in a mist.

In this magnificent poem, Stevens has accomplished some-
thing very close to that "supreme balance" between reality
and the imagination, that "state of clairvoyant observation"
which he thought to be accessible to "the acutest poet." One
need not connect the poem, or indeed any of Stevens's other
cityscapes, with Wordworth's sonnet on the view from West-
minster Bridge. As Stevens said, "the nature of poetry changes,
perhaps for no more significant reason than that poets come
and go." Still, as he also said, "a sense of reality keen enough
to be in excess of the normal sense of reality creates a reality
of its own." This is approximately what happens in both
poems, and that power which raises the normal sense of reality
into something in excess of itself must be the imagination of
the poet at his work.[48]

🐚 "WE LIVE," wrote Stevens in 1951, "in mental representations of the past."[49] Much of his best poetry is in effect an adjustment of the past to the present, a hybridization (as he said of Eliot) between the Parnassian air of distant climes and the quotidian aroma of steaks in passageways, between the anterior life stored up in the memory and the always living now.

His meditation on Baudelaire's lyric, "La Vie Antérieure," sets up one phase of the dualistic paradigm of past and present within the boundaries of which he lived and worked. He was struck by the opening line, "J'ai longtemps habité sous de vastes portiques." This idea of an earlier life, wrote Stevens, is

> part of one's inherited store of poetic subjects. Precisely, then, because it is traditional and because we understand its romantic nature and know what to expect from it, we are suddenly and profoundly touched when we hear it declaimed by a voice that says: "I lived, for long, under huge porticoes." It is as if we had stepped into a ruin and were startled by a flight of birds that rose as we entered. The familiar experience is made unfamiliar and from that time on, whenever we think of that particular scene, we remember how we held our breath and how the hungry doves of another world rose out of nothingness and whistled away. We stand looking at a remembered habitation. All old dwelling-places are subject to these transmogrifications and the experience of all of us includes a succession of old dwelling-places: abodes of the imagination, ancestral or memories of places that never existed.[50]

In Stevens's anterior life were many mansions, ancestral abodes of the imagination—some literary, as with Keats or Shelley or Wordsworth, and yet others, to use his own term, "transmogrifications" of actual locales. He said in 1935 that many of his poems had "actual backgrounds" even though "the real world seen by an imaginative man may very well seem like an imaginative construction."[51] One such actual

305

background was his birthplace, Reading, Pennsylvania. In the summer of 1945, John Harner sent him a batch of postcards with views of his native town. "It is curious," wrote Stevens in reply,

> that these postcards should so soon have become a part of antiquity, or at least of the antiquated. The one of the Mansion House is particularly interesting to me. Years after my parents had died [his father in 1911, his mother in 1912] and when I had no place to go to in Reading except to the Mansion House, I went there one night and was given a room at the foot of an air shaft. There wasn't a window in the room except one that opened on the shaft. There was no bathroom, just a basin and underneath the basin a few venomous cigarette butts. There I was, sentimentalizing over the fact that I was at home again, full of the milk and honey of such a state of mind, dumped into a hole in the wall with a couple of cigarette butts for company. This made me feel a certain satisfaction when the Mansion House was finally demolished. . . .*

Out of this experience seems to have come "A Postcard from the Volcano" (1935), which might have been called "An Epistle from Etna" or "A V-Letter from Vesuvius," though Stevens's own title is much the best. It is meant as a prophetic communication from the land of the dead to the land of the living. The living ought to know that some of the departed have left another and better testament than their bones.

> Children picking up our bones
> Will never know that these were once
> As quick as foxes on the hill;

* LTRS, 509. It is impossible to date this visit to the Mansion House, although he seems to have stayed overnight in Reading in June 1919 and stopped there again in May 1920, when he spent five minutes standing on the depot platform and gazing at the nearby houses, which were "dirty and shabby," while the whole city "looked like a dingy village" (LTRS, 213, 219).

And that in autumn, when the grapes
Made sharp air sharper by their smell
These had a being, breathing frost;

And least will guess that with our bones
We left much more, left what still is
The look of things, left what we felt

At what we saw. The spring clouds blow
Above the shuttered mansion-house
Beyond our gate, and the windy sky

Cries out a literate despair,
We knew for long the mansion's look
And what we said of it became

A part of what it is. . . . Children,
Still weaving budded aureoles,
Will speak our speech and never know,

Will say of the mansion that it seems
As if he that lived there left behind
A spirit storming in blank walls,

A dirty house in a gutted world,
A tatter of shadows peaked to white,
Smeared with the gold of the opulent sun.

Late in his life, Stevens described his poetry as "elegiac."[52]
The term exactly fits the tone and content of "A Postcard
from the Volcano" and many others among his most suc-
cessful lyrics. These are often, if not invariably, living records
of his imaginative encounters with *la vie antérieure* through
which he is able to touch us as profoundly as he was himself
touched by the line from Baudelaire.

Our consideration of this phase of the paradigm should not,
however, blind us to the second aspect, which is well sum-
marized in Stevens's commentary on a text from Mallarmé.
"There is," as he puts it, "a life apart from politics . . . a kind
of radiant and productive atmosphere. . . . The pleasure that

the poet has there is a pleasure of agreement with the radiant and productive world in which he lives. It is an agreement that Mallarmé found in the sound of *Le vierge, le vivace et le bel aujourd'hui.*"[53]

Although Stevens held firmly to his belief that "the world about us would be desolate except for the world within us,"[54] where all our anterior memories lie, and found with pleasure that "the interchange between these two worlds" could lead to "migratory passings to and fro, quickenings, Promethean liberations and discoveries," he had also begun to feel, in his search for a "new romanticism," that he had hitherto been standing "on the edge," that he wanted to "get to the center," that he had been somehow isolated, and wished to "share the common life . . . to achieve the normal, the central." The thing one ought to find, he said in another letter, "is normal life, insight into the commonplace, reconciliation with everyday reality" in order to make "studies of the general *joie de vivre* through the medium of a particular *joie de vivre.*"[55]

If *la vie antérieure* was always ready to be resurrected, there was always also the present, *le bel aujourd'hui*, the "radiant and productive atmosphere" of the "radiant and productive world" in which the poet lived. His striving for "reconciliation" with the present is visible in "Bouquet of Roses in Sunlight," where the flowers are "too much as they are to be changed by metaphor, / Too actual, things that in being real / Make any imaginings of them lesser things." In the long poem, "An Ordinary Evening in New Haven," he says that "we keep coming back and coming back / To the real," and that we seek "the poem of pure reality, untouched / By trope or deviation." Yet he also knew, and said in the same poem, how difficult it is "to say good-by to the past and to live and to be / In the present state of things."[56]

Among Stevens's most moving pronouncements on the modern poet's use of the past is "Recitation After Dinner." Midway of the poem he recalls Virgil's story of Aeneas carrying his father Anchises away from burning Troy: "the son who bears upon his back / The father that he loves, and bears him from / The ruins of the past." This son, he adds, "restores the father," and "the father keeps on living in the son." The conclusion of the poem summarizes its central theme with clarity and force:

> These survivals out of time and space
> Come to us every day. And yet they are
> Merely parts of the general fiction of the mind:
> Survivals of a good that we have loved,
> Made eminent in a reflected seeming-so.[57]

Stevens's recollections from the poetry of English romanticism represent a kind of father-son relationship in which the "fathers" continued to live on in the restorations provided by this brilliant modernist son. The spirit of Anchises thus survived in the spirit of Aeneas, made newly eminent through the poetry of a later time.

Et in Arcadia Ego

AUDEN AMONG THE
ROMANTICS

Parnassus has many mansions. —Auden, *The Dyer's Hand*

Most of the people you think about when you write are dead. You imagine people, poets in the past, people you admire very much; you imagine their ghosts looking over your shoulder. You ask them, "Well, do you think this will do?" —Auden, *Atlantic Monthly* 218 (August 1966)

Me alienated? Bosh! It's just / As a sworn citizen who must / Skirmish with it that I feel / Most at home with what is real. —Auden, *Epistle to a Godson*

AUDEN'S CASE against romanticism rests in great part upon his conviction that its proponents indulged in wishful thinking instead of facing up to the give and take of reality. This antiromantic prejudice arose early and remained late. It did not mean that he could find nothing in the romantic poets to admire. Of most of them, and particularly of Blake, Byron, and Wordsworth, he often wrote in terms of praise. It is clear that he had read all of them extensively and sometimes intensively. He not only quoted and echoed their verse and prose in his own but also made over in his own image ideas that were obviously derived from romantic texts. Yet the animadversions continued, mainly because of his belief that the romantics had invented and chosen to inhabit a dream world

310

against which he felt obliged to dissent on grounds of moral realism.

Even as early as his undergraduate days at Oxford, he accused his friend Stanley Fisher of "abysmal romanticism," and counted himself "an incurable classic." What he admired in contemporaneous romantic poets was their "classical" quality. Hardy, for example, was a romantic realist, and hence to that degree classical. A. E. Housman was a classic because he was "austere," a favorite adjective with the youthful Auden. He was even prepared to praise Walter de la Mare because of his technical skills, by which he was able to control his frequently romantic subject matter in the direction of "classical" form.[1]

The morally reprehensible dream of the *Insulae fortunatae* appears in his memorable sestina, "Paysage Moralisé" (1933), where the citizens of that country, which could be any country,

Each in his little bed conceived of islands
Where every day was dancing in the valleys . . .
Some waving pilgrims were describing islands,
"The gods," they promised, "visit us from islands,
Are stalking, head-up, lovely, through our cities;
Now is the time to leave your wretched valleys
And sail with them across the lime-green water,
Sitting at their white sides, forget your sorrow" . . .
It is our sorrow. Shall it melt? Ah, water
Would gush, flush, green these mountains and these valleys,
And we rebuild our cities, not dream of islands.[2]

Nearly a quarter-century later, as an epigraph to his essay on Robert Frost (1957), with whom he shared a stoic outlook, he quoted a couplet of Frost's from *A Witness Tree*: "But Islands of the Blessed, bless you, son, / I never came upon a blessed one."[3] In his *New Year Letter* of 1940, he summed up one phase of the romantic dream in the figure of the Unicorn:

O Unicorn among the cedars,
To whom no magic charm can lead us,
White childhood moving like a sigh
Through the green woods unharmed in thy
Sophisticated innocence. . . .[4]

And in *The Dyer's Hand* of 1962, that "compulsive classifier," who was always at work when Auden set himself to generalize, observed that "our dream pictures of the Happy Place where suffering and evil are unknown are of two kinds, the Edens and the New Jerusalems":

Every adult knows that he lives in a world where, though some are more fortunate than others, no one can escape physical and mental suffering, a world where everybody experiences some degree of contradiction between what he desires to do and what his conscience tells him he ought to do or others will allow him to do. Everybody wishes that this world were not like that, that he could live in a world where desires would conflict neither with each other nor with duties nor with the laws of nature, and a great number of us enjoy imagining what such a world would be like. . . .

Eden is a past world in which the contradictions of the present world have not yet arisen; New Jerusalem is a future world in which they have at last been resolved. Eden is a place where its inhabitants may do whatever they like to do; the motto over its gate is, "Do what thou wilt is here the Law." New Jerusalem is a place where its inhabitants like to do whatever they ought to do, and its motto is, "In His will is our peace." . . .[5]

If some of his own assertions seem to place him among the votaries of the New Jerusalem, he is eager to show that even in the vales of Arcady or the streets of the Just City, evils and dangers infiltrate the realms of gold and must be recognized as perennial threats. In "September 1, 1939," he wrote:

312

All I have is a voice
To undo the folded lie,
The romantic lie in the brain
Of the sensual man-in-the-street
And the lie of Authority
Whose buildings grope the sky. . . .[6]

Again, in the *New Year Letter*, dated 1 January 1940, he devoted a couple of hundred lines to Satan, saying:

All vague idealistic art
That coddles the uneasy heart
Is up his alley, and his pigeon
The woozier species of religion,
Even a novel, play or song,
If loud, lugubrious and long. (lines 590-595)[7]

His notes to this poem in *The Double Man* of 1941 offered two definitions: the classical artist was "one whose dementia is simply the occasion of release for his talent"; the romantic artist was "one whose dementia becomes his subject matter." In the verse letter, Auden had written with seeming scorn of the "moral asymmetric souls / The either-ors, the mongrel halves / Who find truth in a mirror." His note on these lines identifies this group as the "impatient romantics," and goes on: "The cause of romanticism is either laziness or impatience. The lazy romantic is too woolly-minded to recognize a paradox when he meets one. . . . The impatient romantic sees more clearly but sees only one side of the paradox. The other he ignores or defies."[8]

In *The Age of Anxiety* (1947) the romantic point of view is represented in the poem chiefly through Rosetta, the only woman among the four protagonists. She has dreamed in adolescence of owning a house on a headland overlooking the sea, with a sun-filled sequestered cove under the cliffs. Later she is made to say:

How tempting to trespass in these Italian gardens
With their smirk ouches and sweetsmelling borders,

> To lean on the low
> Parapet of some pursive fountain
> And drowse through the unctuous day. . . .*

This passage follows at an interval a statement by Malin, the critical classicist, who recognizes the dangers of wishful thinking:

> These old-world hamlets and haphazard lanes
> Are perilous places: how plausible here
> All arcadian cults of carnal perfection,
> How intoxicating the platonic myth.

At least equally perilous was the advent of the Second World War. Elaborating on the old saw that "if wishes were horses, beggars would ride," Auden summed up in a neat couplet his view of 1940:

> But wishes are not horses, this
> *Annus* is not *mirabilis.* . . .[9]

This was the year in which, among many other woes, the legions of Hitler were abroad, France had fallen, London was being systematically bombed, and the Blitzkrieg was laying waste dozens if not hundreds of old world cities and hamlets. Images of invasion were not new to Auden. In 1932 had appeared "The Quarry," one of the most fearsome dramatizations of assault-from-without upon a placid rural setting; and in 1938 came the silently threatening "Gare du Midi" where the agent who will destroy the Just City arrives at the station and vanishes amongst the hurrying crowds.

Even in Arcadia peril must lurk, like James's beast in the jungle. Late in his life (1965) Auden achieved one of his most memorable explorations of the subject, "Et in Arcadia Ego." The title suggests a classical source like the Sicilian Theocritus

---

* Auden's love of rare vocables is evident here. *Smirk ouches* evidently means "neat settings" as for precious stones; a *pursive* fountain is one that exhales water in recurrent gasps: *unctuous* indicates something soft or adhesive.

or Roman Virgil. In fact, as one of Erwin Panofsky's brilliant essays makes clear, the term did not appear until the seventeenth century in Italy when the painter Giovanni Guercino did a picture in which the Latin legend can be read.* It means "Even in Arcadia, there am I," and it is spoken by Death. Well known in painting, it was the subject of two canvases by Poussin. Goethe quoted it in *Faust*, and it appears in Evelyn Waugh's *Brideshead Revisited* where an Oxford undergraduate who might have been Auden decorates his room with a skull from the medical school, nesting it in a bed of roses.

Auden's poem begins with a portrait of civilized woman, turns to another of civilized man, shows the dark ferocity that lies behind each modern figure, and concludes with a suggestion of the horrors of the Holocaust through the godless arrogance of the Autobahn cutting through the countryside and the gelding knife concealed in the stables.

> Who, now, seeing Her so
> Happily married,
> Housewife, helpmate to Man,
>
> Can imagine the screeching
> Virago, the Amazon,
> Earth Mother was?
>
> Her jungle growths
> Are abated,
> Her exorbitant monsters abashed,
>
> Her soil mumbled,
> Where crops, aligned precisely,
> Will soon be orient:
>
> A church clock subdivides the day,
> Up the lane at sundown
> Geese podge home.

* Erwin Panofsky, *Meaning in the Visual Arts*, New York, 1957, pp. 295-320.

As for Him:
What has happened to the Brute
Epics and nightmares tell of?

No bishops pursue
Their archdeacons with axes,
In the crumbling lair

Of a robber baron
Sightseers picnic
Who carry no daggers.

I well might think myself
A humanist,
Could I manage not to see

How the autobahn
Thwarts the landscape
In godless Roman arrogance,

The farmer's children
Tiptoe past the shed
Where the gelding-knife is kept. (SP, 250-251)

A similar theme is variously engaged in romantic poetry—
in Wordsworth's "Nutting," for example, where the poet rue-
fully contemplates the "mutilated bower," for which his own
greed is responsible; or the "Elegiac Stanzas" on Peele Castle,
which warns against false dreams of bliss; or the superb sonnet
that begins "Surprised by joy." It forms the substance of Cole-
ridge's "Fears in Solitude" and appears by implication in "Kubla
Khan." It is visible in Shelley's "The Sensitive Plant" and "The
Mask of Anarchy." It surfaces in Keats's "Ode to a Night-
ingale," "Ode on a Grecian Urn," and in the concluding stanza
of the "Ode on Melancholy." Blake used a version of it in
"The Garden of Love," in "I saw a chapel all of gold," and
in the "Argument" to Auden's favorite *The Marriage of Heaven
and Hell*. Byron repeatedly plays upon it in the course of
Childe Harold's Pilgrimage. None of these was Auden's source
for "Et in Arcadia Ego." He needed no other stimulus than

316

the events of the "low dishonest decade" that ostensibly closed in September 1939 yet in sundry forms had always been a part of human history. There are few places in modern literature where the spectre that invades the green Arcadian sanctum has been more awefully dramatized.

Auden's most extended treatments of romanticism both appeared in 1950: three essays grouped under the title of *The Enchafèd Flood, or The Romantic Iconography of the Sea,* and another to serve as introduction for volume four of *Poets of the English Language* in the Viking Portable series. The so-called iconographic essays were a tour de force of literary allusion. The opening lecture quoted Wordsworth, Coleridge, Byron, Melville, and Poe and emphasized the maritime theme with selections from *Genesis* and *Revelation*; Homer, Euripides, Pindar, Horace, and Dante; the Anglo-Saxon *Wanderer* and *Seafarer*, and Sebastian Brant's *Narrenschiff*. Melville's *White Jacket* appeared alongside *Othello, The Winter's Tale,* and *The Tempest*, and there were quotations from Nietzsche and Kierkegaard, Baudelaire and Mallarmé, Tennyson, Hopkins, and Edward Lear, as well as *Twenty Thousand Leagues Under the Sea* and *The Hunting of the Snark*, the last two having been among his boyhood passions. This referential pastiche was Auden's attempt to syncretize the materials of his argument on the place of the sea in Western literature.*

His expository method was loose enough to accommodate whatever aperçus entered his head, as many did; the organization consisted of short essays with systematic subtitles; transitions were quick and often slippery. The presentation of so many different points of view made diversity paramount and unity impossible. Sometimes he offered patches of solid ground, like the long analysis of *Moby-Dick* in the third lecture. But the saltatory method generally prevailed.

---

* *The Enchafèd Flood* had been given as lectures at the University of Virginia in March 1949. At Swarthmore College in 1943 Auden offered a seminar, "Romanticism from Rousseau to Hitler," in which he examined a "heterogeneous collection" of writers including Kierkegaard, Kafka, Rilke, Pascal, and Melville, perhaps the germ of what became the *Enchafèd Flood* lectures.

His initial text was an extended quotation from book five of Wordsworth's *Prelude*. This was the visionary passage in which the nameless narrator, musing over *Don Quixote* in a cave by the sea, falls asleep and dreams of an encounter with a mysterious Bedouin in the Arabian desert. The Arab carries a stone and a shell, which presently take the form of two books, Euclid's *Elements* and a poetical ode prophesying a second deluge. The first weds man to man "by purest bond / Of nature, undisturbed by space and time." The other has "voices more than all the winds," and is "a joy, a consolation, and a hope." The Arab rides away, "with the fleet waters of the drowning world / In chase of him," and the dreamer awakens in terror.

Auden interprets the stone and the shell as geometric and poetic truth and quickly connects them with the desert and the sea. Both are regions of freedom but also of loneliness, and the romantic heroes who traverse them are typical Isolatoes. In Shakespeare, for example, the sea is often a place of purgatorial suffering, and so dangerous that to cross it "betrays a rashness bordering on hubris." Yet the sea voyage represents the "true condition of man." Life ashore is trivial; the sea is the locale of decisive events. The desert may also become a place of punishment or purgation. It is "the Omega of temporal existence." The sea is the Alpha, "symbolic of potentiality." Freely associating ideas of sea and sand, Auden says that the concepts of the happy prelapsarian island and the oasis in the desert betoken "enclosed places of safety" and that a hopeless nostalgia for such environing protection is common among romantic writers. He seems to invoke his own continuing prejudice against the dream of "an earthly paradise where there is no conflict between natural desire and moral duty" and also to find in Wordsworth's image of the rising deluge a confirmation of his own persistent nightmare of the Just City or the peaceful place invaded by destructive forces.[10]

The introduction to the Viking Portable volume covering English and American poetry from Blake to Poe was as straightforward as the *Flood* essays were complex and involuted. The argument here was that the Romantic Movement markedly changed the style and subject matter of poetry as well as the poet's conception of his function. "The divine element in man" was now seen to be his capacity for "self-consciousness." The hero whom the romantic poet celebrated was himself, since "the only consciousness accessible to him" was his own. Romantic assertions about the supreme value of art were based upon the belief that "consciousness is the noblest human quality." This explained why the subtitle of *The Prelude*, which Auden called "the greatest long poem of the period," was "The Growth of a Poet's Mind." In a poetry whose subject is consciousness, the primary materials are symbols, which are charged "with more affect [i.e., passion] than a rational inspection can account for."[11]

Neither this essay nor those that make up *The Enchafèd Flood* could rightly be called a major contribution to the interpretation of romanticism. Both were too perfunctory to stand as dependable analyses of the vast social and esthetic phenomenon that Auden was addressing. Yet both are of interest for what they reveal about Auden's resolute attempt to understand the historical movement against which he was in partial rebellion.

Late in *The Dyer's Hand*, he wrote of the tendency among critics and historians to invent watchwords or shibboleths:

All the various battle cries, Classicism, Romanticism, Naturalism, Surrealism, The-language-really-used-by-men, The music-of-the-future, etc., are of interest to art historians because of the practical help which, however absurd they may seem as theories, they have been to artists in discovering how to create the kind of works which were proper to their powers. . . . Every encounter with a work of art is a personal encounter; what it *says* is not information but a revelation of itself which is simultaneously a revelation of ourselves. We may dislike any particular work we encounter or prefer another to it, but, to the degree that our dislike or our preference is genuine, we admit its genuineness as a work of art. The only real negative judgment is indifference. As Rossini put it: "All kinds of music are good except the boring kind."[12]

Such statements as this suggest that there was ample room in Auden's literary bookbag for Romantics as well as Classics. He closed his essay on D. H. Lawrence with the judicious statement that "Parnassus has many mansions."[13] More than most of his contemporaries, he had occupied a considerable number of them, and one of them was called romanticism.

❦ IN THE WINTER of 1926-1927 Nevill Coghill of Exeter College, Oxford, was serving as Wystan Auden's tutor. One day Auden "blew in" from Christ Church for his tutorial hour. As Coghill long afterward remembered their opening conversation, Auden said, "I have torn up all my poems." Coghill: "Indeed! Why?" Auden: "Because they were no good. Based on Wordsworth. No good nowadays. . . . You ought to read Eliot. I've been reading Eliot. I now see the way I want to write. I've written two new poems this week. Listen!"[14]

This was a remarkable turnabout. The influence of Wordsworth had apparently lasted four or five years. According to Auden's biographer, Humphrey Carpenter, his first poem was a sonnet about a tarn near the Auden family cottage in the Lake District, written about 1922 when the fledgling poet was fifteen. Another lyric of the same period (called "California" after a village near Birmingham) contained echoes of "The Solitary Reaper." Wordsworth's lines

> I listened, motionless and still;
> And, as I mounted up the hill,
> The music in my heart I bore. . . .

became in Auden's poem:

> For this I stopped and stood quite still,
> Then turned with quick steps down that hill.

If this was a fair sample of Wordsworth's influence upon the early Auden, it was perhaps as well that he had now turned at age twenty to modernist verse under the aegis of Eliot.[15]

Evidence that he continued to think about his early mentor appears in a passage from the journal that he kept in 1929 when he had gone down from Oxford and was living in Berlin. By this date, if not earlier, he had classified Wordsworth as a nature poet, much of whose career had been devoted to a typical romantic dream, a retreat into fantasy. "Along with the growing self-consciousness of man during the last 150 years," he wrote, "has developed Wordsworthian nature-worship, the nostalgia for the womb of Nature which cannot be re-entered by a consciousness increasingly independent but afraid."[16]

In two essays of the early 1960s he elaborated upon this notion. "Natural mystical experiences, visions that is to say, concerned with created beings, not with a creator God, and without overt religious content, are of two kinds, which one might call the Vision of Dame Kind and the Vision of Eros." The latter is "concerned with a single person, who is revealed to the subject as being of infinite sacred importance." But the "classic descriptions" of the Vision of Dame Kind "are to be found . . . in certain of Wordsworth's poems, like *The Prelude*, the Immortality Ode, Tintern Abbey, and The Ruined Cottage." "The objects of this vision may be inorganic—mountains, rivers, seas—or organic—trees, flowers, beasts—but they are all non-human, though human artifacts like buildings may be included. Occasionally human figures are involved, but if so, they are invariably . . . strangers to the subject, people working in the fields, passers-by, beggars, or the like," with whom the visionary "has no personal relation." The basic experience "is an overwhelming conviction that the objects confronting him have a numinous significance and importance, that the existence of everything he is aware of is holy.* And the basic emotion is one of innocent joy, though this joy

* This last phrase is Blakean: "Everything that lives is holy." See below.

can include, of course, a reverent dread. . . . So long as the vision lasts the self is 'noughted,' for its attention is completely absorbed in what it contemplates. . . . In some cases, the subject speaks of this sense of communion as if he were himself *in* every object, and they in him. Thus Wordsworth in *The Ruined Cottage*:

> . . . sensation, soul and form
> All melted in him. They swallowed up
> His animal being; in them did he live
> And by them he did live."

Although Auden was no great lover of Nature in the Wordsworthian sense and found no dependable evidence of divinity in the workings of *natura naturans*,* or more than fugitive comfort in the contemplation of natural scenery, he seems to echo Wordsworth's Great Ode (where Nature is described as "the homely Nurse" who does "all she can / To make her Foster-child, her Inmate Man, / Forget the glories he hath known") when he calls Nature "our placid and suburban nurse." But this may be only another instance of the "nanny-image" that he so often employs in various contexts. It is of interest that in an essay of 1944 he remarked that "If Wordsworth is the great English poet of Nature, then Tennyson is the great English poet of the Nursery," citing a passage from *In Memoriam* to support his contention.[17]

"Dame Kind" is Auden's customary name for the goddess Nature, known in medieval literature as the *mater generationis* or the *mundanae regionis regina* who presides over the sublunary world. Auden adopts the old term *Kind* to refer to Nature in general, and calls her *Dame Kind* after the fashion

---

* Auden's poetry contains some evidence of his agreement with Schopenhauer's view: nature reveals to us that "the life and death of the individual is of absolutely no consequence." (*Sämtliche Werke*, ed. A. Hübscher, 3rd ed., Wiesbaden, 1972, 3:541-42). See, for one example, the closing line of "Voltaire at Ferney."

of Chaucer, who named various abstractions Dame Idelnesse, Dame Resoun, or Dame Fortuna.*

Among the medieval word-portraits, Natura was commonly depicted as beautiful. But Auden, emphasizing her *mater generationis* aspect, makes his own Dame Kind considerably more uncouth than Wordsworth's "homely nurse." In his poem, "Dame Kind," of 1960 he writes,

> Steatopygous, sow-dugged
> > and owl-headed,
> To Whom—Whom else?—the first innocent blood
> > was formally shed
> By a chinned mammal that hard times
> > had turned carnivore. . . .

But he ends the passage on a note of Audenesque jocularity:

> She mayn't be all She might be but
> > She *is* our Mum.[18]

Nature appears rarely among the cityscapes of *The Age of Anxiety* and is in fact condemned in part four for "her unending stream of irrelevant events without composition or center, her reckless waste of value, her alternate looks of idiotic inertia and insane ferocity."[19]

Detailed examination of natural objects has little place in Auden's poetry. Like Dr. Johnson's Imlac he favors the panoramic vista and seldom stoops to number the streaks on the tulip, or, in Wordsworth's phrase, to "peep and botanize," close to the lowly herbage. Once in a great while we come upon a phrase like "goat-faced grasshoppers" (AA, 83). This might be only another of his Bosch-like inventions with surrealistic overtones, yet it happens to be a very exact descriptive term: this *is* the shape of the grasshopper face, and the adjective suggests that despite his admitted and almost Tenny-

---

* For background see George D. Economou, *The Goddess Natura in Medieval Literature*, Cambridge, Mass., 1972.

sonian myopia, he may at times have taken more notice of the minutiae of nature than he gave himself credit for.*

For all his animadversions on *natura naturans*, he nevertheless sometimes surprises us with a sidelong glance of approbation, as in the memorable "Woods" among his *Bucolics* (1952):

> Old sounds re-educate an ear grown coarse,
> As Pan's green father suddenly raps out
> A burst of undecipherable Morse. . . .

This was the same poet who asserted in 1962 that "every set of verses, whatever their subject matter may be, are by their formal nature a hymn to Natural Law and a gesture of astonishment at the greatest of all mysteries, the order of the universe."[20] And in 1972, as if to round out two decades of almost worshipful awareness, he said flatly that "I have always felt that to be walking this earth is a miracle I must do my best to deserve."[21] None of these statements would have astonished Wordsworth, even though he would have phrased them differently.

Always a brilliant practitioner of the thumbnail biographical sketch—as for example in "Voltaire at Ferney," or the poems on Forster, Arnold, Edward Lear, Pascal, Montaigne, Rimbaud, Melville, Luther, and Freud—Auden brings up Wordsworth's career for comment in *New Year Letter*. The passage occurs in the midst of his commentary on the devil, one of whose favorite strategies is "The False Association." This consists of inducing men "to associate truth with a lie," then demonstrating the lie in such a way that they will "treat babe and bath-water the same," throwing out both. Wordsworth's French experience offered an example:

> Thus Wordsworth fell into temptation
> In France during a long vacation,

---

* In the late poem, "A Shock," Auden calls himself the "gunshy myopic grandchild of Anglican clergymen."

324

Saw in the fall of the Bastille
The Parousia of Liberty,*
And weaving a platonic dream
Round a provisional regime
That sloganised the Rights of Man,
A liberal fellow-traveler ran
With Sans-culotte and Jacobin,
Nor guessed what circles he was in,
But ended as the Devil knew
An earnest Englishman would do,
Left by Napoleon in the lurch,
Supporting the Established Church,
The Congress of Vienna and
The Squire's paternalistic hand.²²

Thomas McFarland has written of Wordsworth's "early visions of general societal apocalypse" and compared them to "the Jacobin mania of our own era," as embodied in the Marxist ordering of the USSR.²³ Auden anticipated him in these judgments, following up his account of Wordsworth by saying:

Like his, our lives have been coeval
With a political upheaval,
Like him, we had the luck to see
A rare discontinuity,
Old Russia suddenly mutate
Into a proletarian state. . . .

Yet his chief interest was in Wordsworth's poetry. In his essay on Walter de la Mare, he says that "in every poet there dwells an Ariel, who sings, and a Prospero, who comprehends, but in any particular poem, sometimes in the whole work of a particular poet, one of the partners plays a greater role than the other. . . . Thus Campion . . . is an example of an Ariel-dominated poet. . . . In Wordsworth's *Prelude* . . . Prospero dominates and Ariel contributes very little; it might *almost*

---

* *Parousia*: adapted from theology, meaning The Second Coming.

have been written in prose."²⁴ This confirms what he had already written in *The Dyer's Hand*, that "of all the English poets" Wordsworth was "the one with the least element of Ariel that is compatible with being a poet at all."²⁵ Yet there were Ariel-like lyrics in Wordsworth. Auden recalls "To the Cuckoo," but typically makes a joke of it, citing an old set of verses from *Punch*, where two middle-aged academic examiners are taking a rural stroll at the vernal equinox:

> FIRST EXAMINER: O Cuckoo! shall I call thee Bird,
>   Or but a wandering voice?
> SECOND EXAMINER: State the alternatives preferred
>   With reasons for your choice.²⁶

In his sixties, however, he himself wrote a "Short Ode to the Cuckoo," which concludes:

> Hence, in my diary,
> Where I normally enter nothing but social
> engagements and, lately, the death of friends, I
> scribble year after year when I first hear you,
> of a holy moment.²⁷

Despite his avowed preference for the real over the imagined, Auden thought that "too much fuss" had been made over Wordsworth's doctrine of the "real language of men" as the best language for poetry. Like many other critics before and since, he believed that Wordsworth wrote better verse when he ignored his own theory than when he followed it. Thus, says Auden, the image of the cuckoo "breaking the silence of the seas / Among the farthest Hebrides," or the final lines of the great ode: "To me the meanest flower that blows can give / Thoughts that do often lie too deep for tears," both showed that Wordsworth had been wise to forget his theories and give his muse free rein. "To find, 'natural speech' in the verse of the early nineteenth century," said Auden, "one must go to the least 'romantic' and most Popean in spirit of the poets—to the Byron of *Don Juan* and the Tom Moore of *The Fudge Family in Paris.*"²⁸

His longest disquisition on the subject came in his introduction to the *Oxford Book of Light Verse* in 1938.

> The case of Wordsworth, the greatest of the Romantic poets, is instructive. While stating that he intended to write in the language really used by men, in particular by Westmorland farmers, whenever he tries to do so he is not completely successful, while in his best work, the Odes and *The Prelude*, his diction is poetic, and far removed from the spoken word.

He finds the subtitle of *The Prelude* illuminating in this respect:

> Wordsworth was a person who early in life had an intense experience or series of experiences about inanimate nature, which he spent the rest of his poetical life trying to describe. He was not really interested in farm labourers or anyone else for themselves, but only in so far as they helped to explain this vision, and his own relation to it. When he objects to eighteenth-century diction as "artificial" what he really means is artificial for his particular purpose. . . .
>
> Wordsworth's case is paralleled by the history of most of the romantic poets, both of his day and of the century following. Isolated in an amorphous society with no real communal ties, bewildered by its complexity, horrified by its ugliness and power, and uncertain of an audience, they turned away from the life of their time to the comtemplation of their own emotions and the creation of imaginary worlds, Wordsworth to Nature, Keats and Mallarmé to the world of pure poetry, Shelley to a future Golden Age. . . . Instead of the poet regarding himself as an entertainer, he becomes a prophet, "the unacknowledged legislator of the world." . . . This is not, of course, to condemn the Romantic poets, but to explain why they

327

wrote the kind of poetry they did, why their best work is personal, intense, often difficult, and generally rather gloomy.

The release from social pressure was, at first, extremely stimulating. The private world was a previously unexplored field, and the technical discoveries made were as great as those being made in industry. But the feeling of excitement was followed by a feeling of loss. For if it is true that the closer bound the artist is to his community the harder it is for him to see with a detached vision, it is also true that when he is too isolated, though he may see clearly enough what he does see, that dwindles in quantity and importance. . . . For the private world is fascinating, but it is exhaustible. . . . The poet finds it difficult to grow beyond a certain point.[29]

AUDEN'S enchantment with Byron reached a sort of climax of 1936, when he carried a copy of the complete poems in his haversack on his voyage to Iceland and read *Don Juan* entire for the first time. Soon after his arrival he wrote his wife, Erika Mann, about a "bright idea" that his reading had engendered: "I suddenly thought I might write [Byron] a chatty letter in light verse about anything I could think of, Europe, literature, myself. He's the right person, I think, because he was a townee, a European, and disliked Wordsworth and that kind of approach to nature, and I find that very sympathetic. This letter in itself will have very little to do with Iceland, but will be rather a description of an effect of travelling in distant places which is to make one reflect on one's past and one's culture from the outside. . . . I hope my idea will work for at the moment I am rather pleased with it."[30]

With astonishing speed the "bright idea" evolved into the *Letter to Lord Byron*, which, at 1300 lines, stands among Auden's longest poems, and certainly among the most lighthearted. He uses direct address:

So if ostensibly I write to you
To chat about your poetry and mine,
There're many other reasons; though it's true
That I have, at the age of twenty-nine
Just read Don Juan and I found it fine.
I read it on the boat to Reykjavik
Except when eating or asleep or sick.

In place of Byron's ottava rima stanzas (rhyming ABA-BABCC) he chose rhyme-royal (ABABBCC), the same that Chaucer had used in *Troilus and Criseyde* and elsewhere. Auden writes:

Ottava Rima would, I know, be proper,
The proper instrument on which to pay
My compliments, but I should come a cropper;
Rhyme-royal's difficult enough to play.
But if no classics as in Chaucer's day,
At least my modern pieces shall be cheery
Like English bishops on the Quantum Theory.

The result is cheery and witty enough to have pleased both Chaucer and the Addressee. At one point Auden plays with Wordsworth's sonnet to Milton:

Byron, thou should'st be living at this hour!
What would you do, I wonder, if you were?
Britannia's lost prestige and cash and power,
Her middle classes show some wear and tear,
We've learned to bomb each other from the air;
I can't imagine what the Duke of Wellington
Would say about the music of Duke Ellington . . .

You've had your packet from the critics, though:
They grant you warmth of heart, but at your head
Their moral and aesthetic brickbats throw.
A "vulgar genius" so George Eliot said,
Which doesn't matter as George Eliot's dead,
But T. S. Eliot, I am sad to find,
Damns you with: "an uninteresting mind."

Like Byron before him, Auden allows himself some gibes at Wordsworth:

> I'm also glad to find I've your authority
> For finding Wordsworth a most bleak old bore,
> Though I'm afraid we're in a sad minority
> For every year his followers get more,
> Their number must have doubled since the war.
> They come in train-loads to the Lakes, and swarms
> Of pupil-teachers study him in *Storm's*.*

And in the autobiographical fourth section of his letter, he recollects his adolescent enthusiasms:

> We all grow up the same way, more or less;
> Life is not known to give away her presents;
> She only swops. The unself-consciousness
> That children share with animals and peasants
> Sinks in the "stürm und drang" of Adolescence.
> Like other boys I lost my taste for sweets,
> Discovered sunsets, passion, God, and Keats.

Near the end of part five he imagines a kind of British Valhalla where past poetic greats are amusing themselves:

> Are Poets saved? Well, let's suppose they are,
> And take a peep. I don't see any books.
> Shakespeare is lounging grandly at the bar,
> Milton is dozing, judging by his looks,
> Shelley is playing poker with two crooks,
> Blake's adding pince-nez to an ad. for players,
> Chaucer is buried in the latest Sayers.
>
> Lord Alfred rags with Arthur on the floor,
> Housman, all scholarship forgot at last,
> Sips up the stolen waters through a straw,
> Browning's complaining that Keats bowls too fast,

---

* A literary outline series much used in England at this time.

And you have been composing as they passed
A clerihew on Wordsworth and his tie,
A rather dirty limerick on Pye.

I hope this reaches you in your abode,
This letter that's already far too long,
Just like the Prelude or the Great North Road;
But here I end my conversational song.
I hope you don't think mail from strangers wrong.
As to its length, I tell myself you'll need it.
You've all eternity in which to read it.

As a light versifier who was a confirmed admirer of light versification by others, Auden was seldom more at ease than in this verse-letter, a triumph of its kind. Byron could not have heard of the clerihew, a form of comic poetry invented by Edmund Clerihew Bentley (1875-1956), of which Auden availed himself in his *Academic Graffiti* to poke further fun at his two favorite romantics:

> William Blake
> Found Newton hard to take,
> And was not enormously taken
> With Francis Bacon.

> Lord Byron
> Once succumbed to a Siren:
> His flesh was weak,
> Hers Greek.*

"Light verse can be serious," wrote Auden in his introduction to the *Oxford Book of Light Verse* (1938). "It has only come to mean *vers de société*, triolets, smoke-room limericks,

* These clerihews do not appear in *Letters from Iceland*, although Auden was already aware of the form and gave his Icelandic friends one of his earliest examples:
  Jonathan Swift / Never went up in a lift, / Neither did Robinson Crusoe / Do so.

because, under the social conditions which produced the Romantic Revival, and which have persisted, more or less, ever since, it has been only in trivial matters that poets have felt in sufficient intimacy with their audience to be able to forget themselves and their singing-robes." Apart, therefore, from ballads, nonsense verse, and nursery rhymes, he wished to concentrate on poetry that dealt with the social life of any given period, as in Chaucer, Pope, and Byron. From Chaucer he chose "The Miller's Tale" and "The Wife of Bath's Prologue"; from Pope a selection from "The Rape of the Lock," "To a Lady," and the "Epistle to Dr. Arbuthnot"; and from Byron some extracts from "The Vision of Judgment" and *Don Juan*. The other romantic poets received little attention, Blake being represented by "Auguries of Innocence" and seven verse-epigrams (none of them very good), Coleridge by a silly *jeu d'esprit* called "The Devil's Thoughts," and Wordsworth (questionably) by "The Reverie of Poor Susan." Keats and Shelley do not appear at all, though each wrote enough light verse to merit consideration. But Byron, said Auden, was "the first writer of Light Verse in the modern sense. His success lasts as long as he takes nothing very seriously; the moment he tries to be profound and 'poetic' he fails."

After this, there is a twenty-year hiatus in Auden's public pronouncements on Byron. What seems to have reawakened his interest was Leslie A. Marchand's masterly three-volume biography, which appeared in 1958 and was the subject of a long review by Auden in *The New Yorker* for 26 April. He drew heavily on this review for his Oxford lecture, "Don Juan," in the following month, and this in turn was revised and printed in *The Dyer's Hand* of 1962.*

In the Ancestral Voices chapter on Byron (*supra*) we have already considered at some length Auden's views on *Don Juan*

---

* His swan song on Byron was a yet further revision of previous materials that appeared in *The New York Review of Books* on 18 August 1966 and then became the introduction to an anthology of Byron's poetry and prose published later in the year by New American Library.

as set forth in *The Dyer's Hand*. There, as also in earlier and later versions, he rejected the great body of Byron's verse except for *Beppo, The Vision of Judgment,* and *Don Juan*. For the rest he liked only a few of the lyrics and the "charming" occasional pieces, half a dozen stanzas from *Childe Harold*, and as many lines from *Cain*. The one "serious" poem that he singled out for praise was "Darkness," composed at the Villa Diodati in the summer of 1816. This he called "a fine piece of blank verse marred by some false sentiment."

It was a curious choice, although we may notice that, like the passage on the stone and the shell in Wordsworth's *Prelude*, on which Auden expatiated in *The Enchafèd Flood*, "Darkness" purports to be a dream vision of the end of the world. "I had a dream, which was not all a dream," it begins:

> The bright sun was extinguished, and the stars
> Did wander darkling in the eternal space,
> Rayless and pathless, and the icy earth
> Swung blind and blackening in the moonless air. . . .

In the end, all life has perished, the human race and the animal kingdom have both been blotted out, and all the waters of the earth lie still:

> Ships sailorless lay rotting on the sea,
> And their masts fell down piecemeal: as they dropp'd
> They slept on the abyss without a surge—
> The waves were dead; the tides were in their grave,
> The moon, their mistress, had expired before;
> The winds were wither'd in the stagnant air,
> And the clouds perish'd; Darkness had no need
> Of aid from them—She was the Universe.

Precisely why he liked "Darkness" is not clear. Possibly this brief but powerful exposure to an imagination of eschatological doom struck some deep chord in Auden's complex internal wiring. As many of his own serious lyrics show, he shared a taste for the apocalyptic. Yet it is clear enough that Byron's chief attraction for Auden was his comic spirit and its corollary, his determination to stay with the world as he knew it, hoping to persuade his readers to accept with good humor and even good grace the basic recalcitrances in human affairs "as facts of life against which it is useless to rebel."[31]

"So long as Byron tried to write Poetry with a capital P," said Auden, "to express deep emotions and profound thoughts, his work deserved that epithet he most dreaded, *una seccatura*." His chief defect as a serious poet was not, however, a drying out so much as a "lack of reverence for words." But this same defect became a virtue for Byron as comic poet. "Few, if any, English poets have rivaled Byron's ability to put words through the hoops." This skill, "like that of the lion tamer," required "hard work to perfect." Even though he wrote "with facility, he took a great deal more pains than he pretended." This alone could account for Auden's fraternal admiration for his ablest romantic predecessor in the comic mode.[32]

His final summing up occurs in the essay of 1966. "If a romantic poet is one who believes . . . that Imagination is a power of vision which enables man to perceive the sacred truth behind sensory phenomena and, therefore, the noblest of all the mental faculties, then Byron was . . . one of the least romantic poets who ever lived." Always an admirer of Dryden and Pope because they were "realists" who "instead of creating imaginary characters and landscapes, described living people and existing things," he shared with them a kind of worldliness in which the "primary poetic concern was neither with non-human nature nor with their own personal emotions, but with man as a social-political animal." Despite his frequent bouts with melancholia, says Auden, Byron's journals and letters show that his customary riposte was "to make a joke of them." Nietzsche defined a joke as "an epitaph on an emotion," and this was one of Byron's most characteristic attitudes.

Byron's comic genius represented his real self, and "his poetic history is a quest . . . to discover the true verse vehicle for a comic poet in his time." This he found in the ottava

334

rima stanza. Sometimes he used it for satiric purposes, but his orientation was mainly comic. "Satire," wrote Auden, "is angry and optimistic—it believes that the evil it attacks can be abolished; comedy is good-tempered and pessimistic—it believes that, however much we may wish we could, we cannot change human nature, and must make the best of a bad job." Auden reiterated this position so often that one comes in the end to believe that he shared it with Byron. It is probably as clear a statement of one aspect of his own antiromantic posture as he ever made.[33]

During and after his Oxford years, Auden sporadically dipped into the poetry and prose of William Blake, particularly *The Marriage of Heaven and Hell*, the proverbs, and the "Auguries of Innocence." Although he never became a confirmed Blakean, he made more use of these shorter pieces than any of his major contemporaries except Yeats; saw Blake as a predecessor of the rebel D. H. Lawrence; and connected him in his own thought with the synoptic writings of Marx, Freud, and Groddeck.

All their various "kerygmas" (i.e., proclamations), as he wrote from the vantage point of 1956, could be classified as Christian heresies. One could not imagine their "coming into existence except in a civilization which claimed to be based, religiously, on the belief that the Word was made flesh and dwelt among us, and that in consequence, matter, the natural order, is real and redeemable, not a shadowy appearance or the cause of evil, and historical time is real and significant, not meaningless or an endless series of cycles." Like most heretics, Blake and the others had arisen in order to make "a doctrinal protest against what one might call a heresy of behavior exhibited by the orthodox of their day," finding in that behavior certain actions and attitudes of which, as heretics, they disapproved, and hence promulgating doctrines that were "equally one-sided in the opposite direction."

If, as Auden maintained, "the basic human problem is man's

anxiety in time," this problem was manifest in the Freudian formulation as "man's present anxiety over himself in relation to his past and his parents." In Marxian theory, it appeared as man's "present anxiety over himself in relation to his future and his neighbors." Although such statements, like many of Auden's paradigmatic constructs, may strike us as a little too pat and a shade too clever, the ideas they embody were useful to him as a shorthand summary of his own intellectual progression through the forests of *Angst*, from about 1927, when he turned twenty, until 1939-1940, when he left his native England for the United States.[34]

During much of this period he showed a gradually growing interest in Blake, if only because of Blake's opposition to repression and his visions of helping to found the New Jerusalem. Auden's study of Freud and Groddeck suggested to him one possible approach to the sickness of a repressed society, imprisoned in a mental waste land of its own invention. His exploration of Marxism represented another side of the question, whether political revolution might conceivably lead to a new and acceptable order for the long future, in its "romantic promise that with the triumph of Communism the State shall wither away."[35] Richard Hoggart has summarized Blake's gifts to Auden: "opposition to frustration and fear, the call for liberation and energy, and the insistence that the springs of feeling must not be allowed to run dry."[36]

One of Auden's earliest allusions to Blake confirms Hoggart's generalization. The poems of 1930 included "Get there if you can and see the land you once were proud to own."[37] Blake, Lawrence, and Homer Lane appear as exemplars:

> When we asked the way to Heaven, these directed
> us ahead
> To the padded room, the clinic, and the hangman's
> little shed . . .
> Lawrence, Blake and Homer Lane, once healers in our
> English land;

These are dead as iron for ever; these can never
    hold our hand.
Lawrence was brought down by smut-hounds, Blake
    went dotty as he sang,
Homer Lane was killed in action by the Twickenham
    Baptist gang. . . .*

Two other poems in the same volume echo Blake directly. In "1929" (part 4) Auden seized on a Blakean concept to which he would return ten years later: "This is the dragon's day, the devourer's. . . ." "The Questioner Who Sits So Sly" is a borrowing from the "Auguries of Innocence." Blake wrote:

> The Questioner who sits so sly
> Shall never know how to Reply
> He who replies to words of Doubt
> Doth put the Light of Knowledge out.

Auden's poem, one of his most difficult, only appropriates Blake's title. The couplets that follow neither echo nor imitate Blake.[38]

Another tag from Blake served as epigraph for his essay, "Psychology and Art Today" (1935): "Mutual forgiveness of each vice / Such are the gates of paradise. . . ." These are the lines of Blake's "For the Sexes: The Gates of Paradise." Auden's preference for such gnomic utterances over the sprawling lines and obscure symbolism of the Prophetic Books is further evidenced in his introduction to *The Oxford Book of Light Verse* (1938), where he classifies Blake's "proverbial manner" as one kind of light verse that should be taken seriously. It may well be, as Monroe Spears has observed, that he learned from Blake the technique of "charging an innocent form with a violently contrasting content."[39]

The references to Blake become far more numerous during

---

* Lane, an American psychologist who taught that "all instinctive behavior is not just biologically 'good' but *morally* desirable too" was a "healer" who could not heal himself. He died of typhoid in France in 1925. Carpenter, *W. H. Auden: A Biography*, Boston, 1981, pp. 86ff.

the period 1939-1941. Through the spring and summer of 1939, Auden wrote a lengthy essay called "The Prolific and the Devourer," his own version of a text from *The Marriage of Heaven and Hell*. According to Blake,

> The giants who formed this world into its sensual existence and now seem to live in it in chains, are in truth the causes of its life & the source of all activity, but the chains are the cunning of the weak and tame minds, which have power to resist energy. . . . Thus one portion of being is the Prolific, the other, the Devouring: to the devourer it seems as if the producer was in his chains, but it is not so, he only takes portions of existence and fancies that the whole. But the Prolific would cease to be Prolific unless the Devourer as a sea recieved [*sic*] the excess of his delights. . . . These two classes of men are always upon earth, & they should be enemies; whoever tries to reconcile them seeks to destroy existence. Religion is an endeavour to reconcile the two.

To one like Auden who delighted in breaking down all concepts into twos and threes, Blake's fable had its attractions. "It is just a new Marriage of Heaven and Hell that I am doing," he told a friend in May. Loosely following the method of Pascal's *Pensées*, he evolved a four-part essay in which he adapted Blake's terms to his own purposes, choosing to interpret the Prolifics as artists and poets, and the Devourers as politicians. Humphrey Carpenter calls the result "a kind of catechism of his beliefs" as of 1939, providing "a remarkable picture of his mind at a period when his attitudes were beginning to undergo a very great change."[40]

He was now coming to share the view enunciated by Blake at the end of *The Marriage of Heaven and Hell*: "Every thing that lives is holy." In part two of "The Prolific and the Devourer" he says that "there are not 'good' and 'evil' existences. . . . Everything that is is holy. . . . Evil is not an existence, but a state of disharmony between existences." In an essay contributed to Clifton Fadiman's collection under the title *I Be-*

lieve (1939) he used Blake's line about the holiness of all living things as an epigraph. The same phrase, slightly altered, recurs in the poem "Pascal," completed in August 1939. One autumn night, wrote Auden, "the cold burst into flames; creation was on fire," and Pascal "had place like Abraham and Jacob. . . . For isolation had been utterly consumed, / and everything that could exist was holy."

Auden emphasized the enormous gap between Prolifics and Devourers and concluded that the Devourers had always won. "The political history of the world," he wrote, "would have been the same if not a poem had been written, not a picture painted nor a bar of music composed." He restated this sorrowful conviction in his elegy for Yeats who had died in this same year of 1939: "Poetry makes nothing happen: it survives / In the valley of its saying where executives / Would never want to tamper." And in his next major effort, *New Year Letter* (1940-1941), referring to the European conflagration, he said flatly: "No words men write can stop the war."[41]

Even as he began this long poem, he paused to elaborate on a Blakean text from the "Songs and Ballads,"

> What is it men in women do require
> The lineaments of Gratified Desire
> What is it women do in men require
> The lineaments of Gratified Desire?

Auden's lyric, "The Riddle," first published in July 1939, modifies Blake's lines to suit the exigencies of his own metrics:

> Lovers running each to each . . .
> Learn what love alone can teach:
> Happy on a tousled bed
> Praise Blake's acumen who said:
> "One thing only we require
> Of each other; we must see
> In another's lineaments
> Gratified desire." . . .[42]

Blake figures frequently in *New Year Letter*, Auden's often brilliant commentary on the state of the world as of 1 January 1940, with many flashbacks into anterior times. Part one describes a "summary tribunal" sitting in "perpetual session," with Dante at the center of the bench and with Blake on his right hand. Much as he had done in the thumbnail sketch of Wordsworth, already noticed above, he offered a "biography" of Blake, the "choleric enthusiast":

> Self-educated William Blake
> Who threw his spectre in the lake,
> Broke off relations in a curse
> With the Newtonian Universe,
> But even as a child would pet
> The tigers Voltaire never met,
> Took walks with them through Lambeth, and
> Spoke to Isaiah in the Strand,
> And heard inside each mortal thing
> Its holy emanation sing.[43]

Auden calls Blake the "English forerunner" of Nietzsche, adding that both men spent their lives "storming" against their adversaries.[44] Blake's anger over the stupidity of his coevals is once more empahsized in part three:

> Blake shouted insults, Rousseau wept,
> Ironic Kierkegaard stared long
> And muttered "All are in the wrong,"
> While Baudelaire went mad protesting
> That progress is not interesting. . . .[45]

The extensive "notes" in prose and verse that served as running commentary for the *New Year Letter* when it first appeared in *The Double Man* (1941) contain nine allusions to Blake, including *The Marriage of Heaven and Hell*, *Jerusalem*, and the sets of annotations to Lavater's *Aphorisms on Man* and to Spurzheim's *Observations on Insanity*. Far from indicating a profound knowledge of Blake's "system," these quotations are of the sort that Auden might have picked up by leafing through a volume of Blake's verse and prose in search of interesting apothegms and anecdotes. He records Blake's opinions roughly as follows: that some forms of dualistic thought grow out of worldly political experience; that evil, if active, may be preferable to a merely passive good; that seeming contrarieties may be equally true; that the world is divided between the Prolifics and the Devourers; that William Cowper was probably wise in wishing to be as mad as Blake; and that Blake was right in opposing Rousseau's doctrine of the General Will. Diverse as they are, when taken together, they suggest that in Auden's eyes Blake's iconoclasms were essentially healthy, that his rage against "mind-forg'd manacles" was justified, and that his vision of England's green and pleasant land as it might become was still worth contemplation in the cruelly beleaguered twentieth century.[46]

The spirit of Blake is visible in part three of *New Year Letter* when Auden says that

> Three quarters of these people know
> Instinctively what ought to be
> The nature of society
> And how they'd live there if they could . . .
> How readily would we become
> The seamless live continuum
> Of supple and coherent stuff
> Whose form is truth, whose content love . . .
> How grandly would our virtues bloom
> In a more conscionable dust
> Where Freedom dwells because it must,
> Necessity because it can,
> And men confederate in Man.[47]

But Auden remains at least partly skeptical. His next couplet reiterates his moral realism, and his characteristic determination not to lose himself in wistful romantic dreams: "But wishes are not horses, this / *Annus* is not *mirabilis*." Such an attitude may help to explain why Blake's name was so rarely invoked during the period 1941-1961. A passage in *The Dyer's*

341

Hand (1962) proved, however, that he had not been forgotten. Auden called attention to Blake's "loss of belief in the significance and reality of sensory phenomena," citing the famous anecdote in which the sun appeared to the ordinary materialistic multitude as a "round golden disc the size of a guinea," whereas to Blake's visionary eye it suggested "a host crying holy, holy, holy." This meant, said Auden, that Blake, "like the Newtonians he hated," was willing to accept "a division between the physical and the spiritual," but unlike them, regarded "the material universe as the abode of Satan" and accordingly attached no value to the testimony provided by his physical eyes.[48]

This went farther than Auden wished to go. Yet he seems to have shared Blake's views on the true identity of "The Enemy." After a decade of rampant unbelief, *circa* 1927-1937, he had gradually drifted back into a kind of emotional consociation with Christianity. Having become a regular churchgoer during his American years, he continued the practice when he bought his house in Austria in 1957. At morning mass in the village church of Kirchstetten one Whitsunday, the clangor of the bells in the tower brought back into his memory the satiric portrait of Nobodaddy, Blake's name for the false and jealous Jehovah:

In the onion-tower overhead
bells clash at the Elevation, calling
on Austria to change. . . . Rejoice, the bells
cry to me. Blake's Old Nobodaddy
in his astronomic telescopic heaven,
the Big White Christian upstairs, is dead
and won't come hazing us no more, nor bless our bombs.[49]

One last Blake allusion appears in a free-verse statement of 1972, which Auden called, simply, "Contra Blake." It reads like the Voice of Experience, Bunyanizing the Proverb of Hell, which said that "The Road of Excess leads to the Palace of Wisdom." At sixty-five, Auden knew better:

The Road of Excess
leads, more often than not, to
the Slough of Despond.[50]

❧ THE ADORER of dichotomies that dwelt within Auden's
critical intellect took over Coleridge's distinction between the
Primary and Secondary functions of the Imagination and came
up with another, which used the terms but markedly changed
the concepts. Although Auden maintained that he and Cole-
ridge were "both trying to describe the same phenomena,"
the differences between chapter thirteen of the *Biographia
Literaria* and part two of *The Dyer's Hand* are considerable.
Auden departed even further from his source than he had
done with his reinterpretations of two other pairs, the stone
and shell passage from Wordsworth's *Prelude* and Blake's
observations on Prolifics and Devourers in *The Marriage of
Heaven and Hell*.

Where Coleridge called the Primary Imagination "the living
Power and prime Agent of all human Perception," and "a
repetition in the finite mind of the eternal act of creation in
the infinite I AM," Auden transmuted his own version into a
passive power solely concerned with "sacred beings and events."
The Primary Imagination must respond to these experiences
of sacredness, and its response was always a sense of awe,
which might range anywhere along the scale of emotions from
"joyous wonder to panic dread." Many of us, said Auden,
"have sacred landscapes," which are partly unique to our-
selves—his own appears to have been the limestone region of
the Pennines, dotted with derelict mining machinery, and me-
morialized through "In Praise of Limestone" (1948). Yet "some
sacred beings are sacred to all imaginations at all times," such
as the moon, fire, and snakes, or "those four important beings
which can only be defined in terms of non-being: Darkness,
Silence, Nothing, Death."*

* Keats's "Belle Dame," wrote Auden in 1962, "is no less a sacred figure
than [Dante's] Beatrice." In "Today's Poet," *Mademoiselle*, April 1962.

343

His Secondary Imagination operates on a different mental level. "It is active, not passive, and its categories are . . . the beautiful and ugly," pertaining to Form rather than to Being. Beautiful forms produce pleasure and a sense of the absence of conflict. Seeing the ugly leads to conflict in the mind but simultaneously arouses a desire to correct the ugliness in the direction of the beautiful. The Secondary Imagination is "bourgeois" (the term is not pejorative) in that it approves of "regularity, of spatial symmetry and temporal repetition, of law and order: it disapproves of loose ends, irrelevance and mess."

> Both kinds of imagination are essential to the health of the mind. Without the inspiration of sacred awe, its beautiful forms would soon become banal, its rhythms mechanical; without the activity of the Secondary Imagination the passivity of the Primary would be the mind's undoing; sooner or later its sacred beings would possess it, it would come to think of itself as sacred, exclude the outer world as profane and so go mad.[51]

Although Auden does not say so, it is possible that he was thinking of Blake as an example of one so possessed by his sacred beings that he excluded the outer world as profane, and so went mad. But this is beside the present point: that Auden modified Coleridge's original terms into consonance with his own esthetic theories.*

It is probable that his readings in Coleridge's poetry were fairly extensive, but none of them struck his critical fancy except "The Ancient Mariner" and "Kubla Khan," the first because of its mythological and symbolic aspects, and the other because it was a "trance poem." He makes only a passing reference to "Dejection: An Ode," the autobiographical verses that had so deeply impressed Eliot in 1932. Auden had an excellent ear, and some of Coleridge's rhythms and man-

---

* Another version of Auden's view of "the sacred" appears in "Today's Poet," *Mademoiselle*, April, 1962.

nerisms lodged in his capacious memory. Reviewing a life of Oscar Wilde in 1963, he quoted from *The Ballad of Reading Gaol* to show how closely Wilde had followed the Coleridgean prosody, with its internal rhymes:

> They glided past, they glided fast,
> Like travellers through a mist:
> They mocked the moon in a rigadoon
> Of delicate turn and twist,
> And with formal pace and loathsome grace
> The phantoms kept their tryst.[52]

But his familiarity with Coleridge had begun much earlier. In Egypt in 1938 on his way to China with Isherwood, he recalled two lines from "The Ancient Mariner."

> The Sun's rim dips; the stars rush out,
> At one stride comes the dark. . . .

"Coleridge was wrong," he wrote in a letter. "The stars do *not* rush out in the tropics."[53]

Composing *The Enchafèd Flood* in 1949-1950, Auden discussed the "protestant variety of individual myths" of which "The Ancient Mariner" was one. He linked the poem with Melville's *Moby-Dick* and Rimbaud's *Bateau Ivre*, and laid stress on the notion of the ship as a metaphor for human society and on the recurrent images of loneliness in these and other romantic classics.

His inaugural lecture as Professor of Poetry at Oxford in 1956 named "Kubla Khan" as the "only documented case of a trance poem which we possess." Despite its "extraordinary poetic merits," the existing "fragment," as he called it, struck him as "disjointed," and he took notice of Coleridge's half-apologetic introduction, which described the tale of Kubla as "a psychological curiosity" rather than a finished work.* By

---

* Thomas McFarland notices Coleridge's anxious attempt to "deflect judgment by saying that ["Kubla Khan"] was incomplete—though it seems in fact about as fully terminated as any poem in the language." *Romanticism and the Forms of Ruin*, Princeton, 1981, p. 225.

1962, when he wrote the prologue to *The Dyer's Hand*, Auden had changed his mind but not his judgment on the worth of the poem, having learned in the interim that Coleridge's yarn about the origin of "Kubla Khan" had in fact been a "fib," invented to account for his sense of the failure of the poem. His realistic conclusion was that "if poems could be created in a trance without the conscious participation of the poet, the writing of poetry would be so boring or even unpleasant an operation that only a substantial reward in money or social prestige could induce a man to be a poet."[54] Although he had made use of the stone and shell passage from Wordsworth's *Prelude*, it may have been his lifelong prejudice against "dream-poetry" and romantic complaints over the loss of visionary paradises that kept him from grappling with the more profound psychological implications of "Kubla Khan." Apart from "The Ancient Mariner," which he had apparently read in his youth and kept ready in the portmanteau of his memory, his interest in Coleridge as critic and poet would appear to have been marginal.

It was quite otherwise with Keats, on whom Auden's most extensive commentary was a reveiw of Lionel Trilling's edition of the *Selected Letters* in 1951. He called Trilling's introduction "one of the best essays on Keats that I have read. Against certain of the Romantic writers, the charges of moral wooliness and self-idolatry brought by Irving Babbitt and others are, I believe, legitimate, but I fully share Professor Trilling's conviction that Keats is not among them."

Keats was "a man with a vocation, whose life was consciously dedicated to poetry. . . . Dedicated artists are liable to suffer from two complaints, a humorless over-earnest attitude toward art, and a lack of ordinary social responsibility. . . . From both of these defects Keats is completely and refreshingly free. As convinced as any writer of the seriousness and value of art, he never sounds like an abbé of the esthetic, and . . . never forgets the reality of the situation." Except for Shakespeare, Keats's references to other poets are, says Auden, infrequent. "He admired Wordsworth while thinking that he was a freak genius, an 'egotistical sublime' whose didacticism had to be accepted, but not as an example to be imitated; while he was not malicious about either, it is clear that he did not think much of the Byron and Shelley he had read."

Shelley's *Adonais*, Auden continued, was largely responsible for the "fantastic distortion" that Keats was killed by a bad review—a position, incidentally, that Byron humorously upheld in *Don Juan*. He suggests that Shelley may have been subconsciously jealous of Keats's superior gifts. Hence the portrait of Keats in *Adonais* as a "lovable weakling, a sort of male and literary *Dame aux Camélias*," and "a sensitive plant without an idea in his head." In fact, says Auden, Keats showed "a rare combination of witty and original intelligence with common sense." Even the two sentences for which Keats was so often attacked, the concluding lines of the Grecian Urn ode, and the exclamation, "O for a life of sensations rather than thoughts," when read in their respective contexts, clearly "do not mean what their hostile critics say they mean."[55]

Auden develops this last point in *The Dyer's Hand*. "If asked who said *Beauty is Truth, Truth Beauty*, a great many readers would answer 'Keats.' But Keats said nothing of the sort. It is what he said the Grecian Urn said, his description and criticism of a certain kind of work of art, the kind from which the evils and problems of this life, the 'heart high-sorrowful and cloyed,' are deliberately excluded. The Urn, for example, depicts, among other beautiful sights, the citadel of a hill town; it does not depict warfare, the evil which makes the citadel necessary."[56]

The passage here recalled reads as follows:

> To what green altar, O mysterious priest,
> Lead'st thou that heifer lowing at the skies
> And all her silken flanks with garlands drest?
> What little town by river or sea shore,
> Or mountain-built with peaceful citadel,
> Is emptied of its folk this pious morn?

In the year after his review of Trilling, Auden brought out
The Shield of Achilles. Stanza four of the title poem contains
references to

> ritual pieties
> White flower-garlanded heifers,
> Libation and sacrifice . . .

where Keats's *pious* becomes Auden's *pieties*, and where Keats's
garlanded heifer is pluralized as Auden's verses move the vic-
tims toward the "libation and sacrifice" at the altar.

Writing in his Trilling review of the marked differences
between Keats's epistolary manner and his serious poetry,
Auden said that "no one who has read the Odes, so calm and
majestic in pace, so skillfully and tightly organized, could
possibly foresee the helter-skelter rush of the letters in which
the thoughts tumble over each other, defying the laws of gram-
mar, spelling and punctuation." Except for the Grecian Urn,
however, he had little to say of any other odes except the
"Nightingale," which he was inclined to disparage. In his
preface to volume four of *Poets of the English Language*, he
mentioned the variations in the roles of bird and poet through-
out the Nightingale ode. Sometimes the bird appears as "the
unconscious creature contrasted with the conscious man";
again the birdsong is not distinct from the poet but a part of
his experience and a symbol of himself as poet; or again the
poet sings of the bird, thereby doing what a bird cannot do,
"immortalizing the immediate moment." In romantic poetry,
said Auden, the "real novelty" consisted in such structural
change-abouts, quite unlike the "syllogistic construction" of
Marvell's "To His Coy Mistress," roughly a hundred and forty
years earlier. But it was a novelty to which Auden himself did
not feel strongly drawn.

In *The Dyer's Hand* he agreed with D. H. Lawrence's view
that Keats (or his *alter ego* in the ode) is "so preoccupied with
his own feelings that he cannot really listen to the nightingale."
Such a phrase as "thy plaintive anthem" was therefore a fal-
sification: according to Lawrence, the actual birdsong was

much more like "Caruso at his jauntiest." This observation proved, said Auden, that unlike the romantic Keats, Lawrence never confused the feelings that some animal or flower aroused in him with what he saw and heard and knew about them.[57] On the other hand, Auden had earlier praised Keats for his assertion in the letters that the poet is the least poetical thing in existence because he has no identity. "He is saying," wrote Auden, "that the man of power who has this identity is less human, more like the sun or the birds of nature, which can only be themselves."[58]

Auden's observations on Keats do not mention *Endymion* or *Hyperion*, the odes to Psyche, Melancholy, and Autumn, or any of the sonnets, or even "Isabella," which ought to have appealed to a poet of Auden's sometimes operatic tastes. Yet his summary statement on Keats's career was generally sympathetic. "On the evidence of his letters," he wrote in 1951, "Keats was the rare and tragic exception" to the rule that "artists have not died before completing their work." His death intervened "before he had found a style and form in which he could incarnate all sides of his sensibility." If he had by some miracle survived the onslaught of tuberculosis, what would have become of him? In Auden's opinion, such poems as "The Eve of St. Agnes," even "though beautiful in their descriptive details, suffer from a lack of narrative and character interest; the actors and their actions are too stock." Yet if Keats had lived on into his thirties, "he might well have learned how to use all the psychological insight, wit, and irony which his letters show him to have possessed, in writing tales which would have made him the equal of and only successor to Chaucer." Despite its necessarily provisional quality, this is higher praise than Auden lavished on any other major English romantic poet.[59]

"I cannot read Shelley with pleasure," wrote Auden in 1936. "I find . . . the Weltanschauung of Prometheus more to my taste than that of Coriolanus, but I would much rather read the latter." In what might have been an echo of Eliot's Harvard

lecture on Shelley (1933), Auden said that Shelley "never looked
at or listened to anything, except ideas." In fact, he continued,
"the very nature of Shelley's intellectual interests demanded
a far wider range of experiences than most poets require . . .
and his inability to have and record them makes, for me, the
bulk of his work, with the exception of a few short pieces,
empty and unsympathetic."[60] He called Shelley a neurotic with
"a just grievance" and in another essay of 1948 exclaimed:
"How glad I am that the silliest remark ever made about poets,
'the unacknowledged legislators of the world,' was made by
a poet whose work I detest." The Auden who made this judg-
ment was the Auden who sincerely believed that "poetry makes
nothing happen," and was accordingly critical of the Shelley
of *A Defence* who had posited an intellectual-artistic elite that
had guided the imaginations of men since Homer's time like
greatly gifted "generals of the armies of the mind."[61]

One of Shelley's "short pieces," "To A Skylark," had spo-
ken of such poets as these, lying "hidden in the light of thought,"
singing their hymns unbidden until the world was wrought
"to sympathy with hopes and fears" that might otherwise
have gone unheeded. In 1935 Auden had stated firmly that
"poetry is not concerned with telling people what to do, but
with extending our knowledge of good and evil . . . leading
us to the point where it is possible for us to make a rational
and moral choice."[62] With this position the mature Shelley of
1818-1822 would certainly have agreed, and he would also
have applauded Auden's lines in the threnody for Yeats:

> Follow, poet, follow right
> To the bottom of the night,
> With your unconstraining voice
> Still persuade us to rejoice. . . .
>
> In the deserts of the heart
> Let the healing fountain start,
> In the prison of his days
> Teach the free man how to praise.

Few modern poets have more exactly summarized the *Welt-anschauung* of *Prometheus Unbound*, even though Auden's idiom is markedly different from that of Shelley.

It is possible that Auden was here distantly recollecting the song of the Echoes:

> O, follow, follow,
> As our voice recedeth
> Through the caverns hollow

which anticipates and urges the descent of Asia to the "mighty darkness" of the Cave of Demogorgon in *Prometheus Unbound*, act two, for it is here that the crucial episode occurs, with Demogorgon rising up to dethrone Jupiter and thus to release both Prometheus and all mankind from the prison of their days.*

For all his professed dislike of Shelley's poems, Auden had read some of them with enough attention to leave other echoes in his memory. In "1929," for example, he wrote of the "vanishing music of isolated larks" and in *The Age of Anxiety* referred to the song of the lark "swallowed up in the blazing blue."[63] In another and even better poem, the early "Something is Bound to Happen," his image of "gradual ruin spreading like a stain" is a palpable borrowing of "the contagion of the world's slow stain" from *Adonais*.[64] His "Epitaph on a Tyrant" (1939) says of the protagonist, "When he cried little children died in the streets," evidently a reminiscence of the more elaborate passage in *The Mask of Anarchy* about Lord Eldon, the tyrannical judge known in his day for weeping on the bench:

> His big tears, for he wept well,
> Turned to millstones as they fell;
> And the little children who
> Round his feet played to and fro,

---

* Auden makes a single passing reference to "Demagorgan" [*sic*] in "Depravity: A Sermon" in a listing that includes Gabriel and Michael, Abdiel and Azazael. He offers no identification.

351

Thinking every tear a gem
Had their brains knocked out by them.[65]

In the same year Auden thought of Shelley once again in his sonnet sequence on China, "In Time of War":

Fear builds enormous ranges casting shadows
Heavy, bird-silencing, upon the outer world,
Hills that our grief sighs over like a Shelley, parting
All that we feel from all that we perceive. . . .[66]

Finally, it may be that Auden, ᴏ whom eschatological subjects were notably attractive, echoed, though with a difference, the closing chorus of Shelley's *Hellas*. This is the poem that Yeats sardonically parodied and Eliot criticized for its snakeskin image. It opens:

The world's great age begins anew,
The golden years return,
The earth doth like a snake renew
Her winter weeds outworn:
Heaven smiles, and faiths and empires gleam
Like wrecks of a dissolving dream.

Shelley was imaginatively celebrating the arrival of a new epoch. Auden's *New Year Letter* (lines 1706-1708) anticipates a time when

love illuminates again
The city and the lion's den,
The world's great rage, the travel of young men. . . .

From Shelley's "the world's great age begins anew" to Auden's "love illuminates again . . . the world's great rage" is ostensibly a long leap. Yet Auden was in his way as strong a proponent of the reparative powers of love, construed as Agape, as Shelley had been, and hailed it as chief healer in many poetical contexts.

References

INTRODUCTION

EDITIONS CITED

EP, *LE*: Ezra Pound, *Literary Essays*, N.Y., 1964
EP, *SP*: Ezra Pound, *Selected Prose, 1909-1965*, ed. William Cookson, N.Y., 1973
RF, *CP*: Robert Frost, *Complete Poems*, N.Y., 1949
RF, *LTRS*: Robert Frost, *Selected Letters*, ed. Lawrance Thompson, N.Y., 1964
TSE, *CP*: T. S. Eliot, *Complete Poems and Plays*, N.Y., 1952
TSE, *OPP*: T. S. Eliot, *On Poetry and Poets*, N.Y., 1957
TSE, *SE*: T. S. Eliot, *Selected Essays*, N.Y., 1964
TSE, *SW*: T. S. Eliot, *The Sacred Wood*, London, 1920
TSE, *TCC*: T. S. Eliot, *To Criticize the Critic*, N.Y., 1965
TSE, *UPUC*: T. S. Eliot, *The Use of Poetry and the Use of Criticism*, London, 1933
WBY, *AUTO*: W. B. Yeats, *Autobiography*, N.Y., 1953
WBY, *CP*: W. B. Yeats, *Collected Poems*, N.Y., 1956
WBY, *EI*: W. B. Yeats, *Essays and Introductions*, N.Y., 1961
WBY, *Explorations*: W. B. Yeats, *Explorations*, London, 1969
WBY, *LTRS*: W. B. Yeats, *Letters*, ed. Allan Wade, London, 1954
WBY, *Vision*: W. B. Yeats, *A Vision*, N.Y., 1961
WHA, *CP*: W. H. Auden, *Collected Poems*, N.Y., 1945
WHA, *EA*: W. H. Auden, *The English Auden, 1927-1939*, ed. Edward Mendelson, N.Y., 1977
WHA, *DH*: W. H. Auden, *The Dyer's Hand*, N.Y., 1962
WHA, *PAW*: W. H. Auden in *Poets at Work*, ed. Charles D. Abbott, N.Y., 1948
WS, *CP*: Wallace Stevens, *Collected Poems*, N.Y., 1955
WS, *LTRS*: Wallace Stevens, *Letters*, ed. Holly Stevens, N.Y., 1966
WS, *NA*: Wallace Stevens, *The Necessary Angel*, N.Y., 1951

Bloom, *Anxiety*: Harold Bloom, *The Anxiety of Influence*, N.Y., 1973

REFERENCES

Bloom, *Stevens*: Harold Bloom, *Wallace Stevens*, Ithaca, N.Y., 1977

Bornstein: George Bornstein, *Transformations of Romanticism in Yeats, Eliot, and Stevens*, Chicago, 1976

Carpenter: Humphrey Carpenter, *W. H. Auden, A Biography*, Boston, 1981

Cook: Reginald L. Cook, *The Dimensions of Robert Frost*, N.Y., 1958

Donoghue: Denis Donoghue, *The Third Voice*, Princeton, 1959

Emerson: R. W. Emerson, *The Complete Writings*, N.Y., 1929

Frye: Northrop Frye, *The Anatomy of Criticism*, Princeton, 1957

Gardner: Helen Gardner, *The Making of Four Quartets*, N.Y., 1978

Hines: Thomas J. Hines, *The Later Stevens*, Lewisburg, Pa., 1976

Kenner: Hugh Kenner, *The Pound Era*, N.Y., 1971

L & T: *Robert Frost: Poetry and Prose*, ed. Edward C. Lathem and Lawrance Thompson, N.Y., 1972

McFarland: Thomas McFarland, *Romanticism and the Forms of Ruin*, Princeton, 1981

Thompson 1: Lawrance Thompson, *Robert Frost, The Early Years*, N.Y., 1966

Thompson 2: Lawrance Thompson, *Robert Frost, The Years of Triumph*, N.Y., 1970

Vendler: Helen Vendler in *Wallace Stevens: A Celebration*, Princeton, 1980

NOTES

1. Frye, 97; WS, *LTRS*, 722
2. Emerson, 789
3. TSE, *SW*, 48-50
4. WBY, *AUTO*, 267; WBY, *EI*, 352
5. McFarland, 276-77
6. Kenner, 80; EP, *LE*, 12
7. Donoghue, 18
8. Cook, 50
9. TSE, *UPUC*, 78
10. Ibid., 148
11. WS, *CP*, 407
12. Bloom, *Anxiety*, 71, 30, 94, 5
13. Ibid., 26, 88, 117, 140
14. WHA, *CP*, 268-69
15. Kenner, 164
16. RF, *CP*, 451
17. EP, *LE*, 7, 72, 277, 373
18. WBY, *AUTO*, 298, 188, 285, 143; WBY, *EI*, 351

19. TSE, *UPUC*, 72-75; TSE, *SW*, 148
20. Thompson 1:70, 136, 190, 428; Thompson 2:602; L & T, 261-62
21. WS, *NA*, 13-14, 32, 58, 117; WS, *CP*, 397
22. WS, *LTRS*, 247; WS, *NA*, 41, 31, 75, 162
23. WHA, *DH*, 341; WHA, *CP*, 284-85
24. WBY, *Explorations*, 304
25. TSE, *UPUC*, 67-69
26. Bornstein, 83
27. Thompson 1:180
28. TSE, *SW*, 1
29. TSE, *UPUC*, 67-69, 76-77
30. WS, *LTRS*, 121
31. WS, *NA*, 41
32. WS, *LTRS*, 792

33. WHA, *DH*, 54-57
34. WHA, *DH*, 16, 33
35. Cook, 50
36. WS, *LTRS*, 82
37. Hines, 44
38. Bornstein, 6; WS, *CP*, 239
39. WBY, *Explorations*, 299
40. WBY, *AUTO*, 263
41. TSE, *UPUC*, 146; TSE, *TCC*, 138; TSE, *OPP*, 119-20
42. TSE, *UPUC*, 67
43. WBY, *Explorations*, 299
44. WBY, *EI*, 150; WBY, *Poems of William Blake*, London, 1910, xxiii, xxxi
45. WBY, *EI*, 116; WBY, *LTRS*, 211, 227, 262
46. WBY, *LTRS*, 873; WBY, *EI*, 78, 91-95
47. WBY, *Vision*, 12, 137; WBY, *LTRS*, 158
48. WBY, *Vision*, 72; WBY, *AUTO*, 329
49. RF, *CP*, 588. A prose allusion is in "The Constant Symbol," *Poems of Robert Frost*, Modern Library (1946), xix
50. EP, *LE*, 27; EP, *SP*, 418
51. WS, *LTRS*, 177; WS, *NA*, 160
52. Kenner, 415
53. TSE, *UPUC*, 87; TSE, *SE*, 275-80; TSE, *Nation and Athenaeum* 41 (17 Sept. 1927)
54. Carpenter, 267-74
55. Frye, 298; WHA, *CP*, 270
56. WHA, *DH*, 394
57. WBY, *LTRS*, 467
58. Cook, 50
59. WS, *LTRS*, 177
60. TSE, *OPP*, 223-39
61. RF, *LTRS*, 141; Gardner, 191

62. TSE, *UPUC*, 100-102
63. EP, *LE*, 292
64. WHA, *Partisan Review* 18 (Nov.-Dec. 1951), 701-706
65. Ibid.; TSE, *UPUC*, 100
66. TSE, *SE*, 9
67. WHA, *Partisan Review* 18 (Nov.-Dec. 1951), 701-706
68. TSE, *SE*, 231n
69. WHA, *DH*, 337
70. WBY, *LTRS*, 406, 354, 608; WBY, *AUTO*, 298; WBY, *EI*, 370; WBY, *CP*, 159
71. WBY, *AUTO*, 103; WBY, *CP*, 91-92
72. WBY, *LTRS*, 583, 653
73. WS, *CP*, 56
74. WS, *LTRS*, 97, 119, 136, 167; Vendler, 171-95; WS, *CP*, 369
75. WS, *LTRS*, 781
76. WS, *LTRS*, 89
77. WS, *NA*, 44, 6
78. Bloom, *Stevens*, 208, 287; WS, *CP*, 433
79. WS, *CP*, 440-41
80. WBY, *AUTO*, 53, 119; WBY, *EI*, 65
81. WBY, *AUTO*, 39-40
82. WBY, *EI*, 294, 89
83. WBY, *Vision*, 141, 144
84. WBY, *EI*, 421, 424; cf. *Vision*, 144
85. TSE, *UPUC*, 88-99
86. TSE, *TCC*, 130-32
87. RF, *LTRS*, 20; RF, *CP*, 16, 247-55, 483
88. WHA, *New Verse* (April-May 1936), 23-24
89. WHA, *PAW*, 177; WHA, *EA*, 329
90. WHA, *CP*, 351, 267, 111, 59

REFERENCES

W. B. YEATS

EDITIONS CITED

Amica: Per Amica Silentia Lunae, London, 1918
Auto: Autobiography of W. B. Yeats, N.Y., 1953
Blake Poems: Poems of William Blake, ed. W. B. Yeats, London, 1910
CP: Collected Poems, N.Y., 1966
EI: Essays and Introductions, N.Y., 1961
JBY, *LTRS: J. B. Yeats, letters to his son . . . and others*, N.Y. 1946
WBY, *LTRS: Letters of William Butler Yeats*, ed. Allan Wade, London, 1954
Spenser Poems: Selected Poems of Edmund Spenser, ed. W. B. Yeats, London, 1906
UP: Uncollected Prose of W. B. Yeats, ed. J. P. Frayne, N.Y., 1970
VP: Variorum Edition of the Poems of W. B. Yeats, ed. Peter Allt and Russell K. Alspach, N.Y., 1957
Vision: A Vision, N.Y., 1956
WWP: Words Upon the Window Pane, Dublin, 1934

OTHER REFERENCES

Blake, *LTRS: The Letters of William Blake*, ed. Geoffrey Keynes, London, 1956
Bornstein: George Bornstein, *Transformations of Romanticism in Yeats, Eliot, and Stevens*, Chicago, 1976
Ellmann: Richard Ellmann, *Yeats: The Man and the Masks*, N.Y., 1948
Henn: T. R. Henn, *The Lonely Tower*, 2nd ed., London, 1965
Jeffares: A. Norman Jeffares, *W. B. Yeats, Man and Poet*, New Haven, 1949
Jeffares, *Commentary*: A. Norman Jeffares, *A Commentary on the Collected Poems of W. B. Yeats*, Stanford, 1968
Seiden: Morton Irving Seiden, *William Butler Yeats: The Poet as Mythmaker*, East Lansing, Mich., 1962

NOTES

1. *EI*, 346, 328; *AUTO*, 39-40
2. JBY, *LTRS*, 215, 205-206, 221; *AUTO*, 54
3. *EI*, 154, 347-48
4. WBY, *LTRS*, 590; *AUTO*, 143; *Vision*, 134
5. *Amica*, 28, 43; *EI*, 351
6. WBY, *LTRS*, 710
7. Ibid., 709-710; Byron, *Don Juan* 2:185; *Vision*, 148
8. WBY's high-style use of ottava rima noted by WHA in *DH*, 397
9. WBY, *LTRS*, 406, 583
10. Ibid., 608
11. Bornstein, 252; *Spenser Poems*, intro., xlvi
12. *Amica*, "Anima Hominis," section 3
13. *Vision*, 134

14. *EI*, 362; *AUTO*, 165; *EI*, 378, 382; *Spenser Poems*, xlv
15. *EI*, 314, 352-53
16. *AUTO*, 39-40
17. *EI*, 65-66
18. *EI*, 65-67; WBY, *LTRS*, 211
19. *EI*, 74-79, 88-89
20. Ibid., 94-95
21. Ibid., 293-94
22. Ibid., 383, 366
23. Ibid., 405-405
24. *Amica*, 63, 83; Spenser, *Faerie Queene* 3:vi, 30-33
25. *Amica*, 63
26. Ibid., 51, 85-86
27. Bornstein, 50; *CP*, 161, 206, 233
28. *EI*, 421-24
29. WBY, *LTRS*, 781
30. Quoted Jeffares, 32; *WWP*, 32-33; *AUTO*, 93, 267
31. *EI*, 84-85
32. Ibid., 266-67; *AUTO*, 196
33. *AUTO*, 70
34. WBY, *LTRS*, 145, 152-53
35. *AUTO*, 43, 94
36. WBY, *LTRS*, 157-58; *AUTO*, 99-100
37. *AUTO*, 98
38. WBY, *LTRS*, 211
39. Ibid., 227, 262; Blake, *LTRS* 88 (6 July 1803)
40. *EI*, 111, 114
41. Ibid., 111-13
42. Ibid., 116-17
43. Ibid., 123
44. Ibid., 137
45. Ibid., 150
46. Blake, *LTRS*, 202 (12 April 1827)
47. *EI*, 138
48. Ibid., 149-50, 292-93; *Vision*, 134
49. *Blake Poems*, intro., xxxi-xxxv
50. *Vision*, 138-39
51. Ibid., 72
52. Ellmann, 236
53. *Vision*, 108
54. Mentioned by WBY in intro. to *Blake Poems*, xxx
55. *UP* 1:183

FROST ON THE PUMPKIN

EDITIONS CITED

CP: *Complete Poems of Robert Frost*, N.Y., 1949
L & T: *Robert Frost: Poetry and Prose*, ed. Edward C. Lathem and Lawrance Thompson, N.Y., 1972
ML: *The Poetry of Robert Frost*, Modern Library, N.Y., 1946
LTRS: *Selected Letters of Robert Frost*, ed. Lawrance Thompson, N.Y., 1964

OTHER REFERENCES

Bacon: Helen H. Bacon, "The Contemporary Reader and Robert Frost," *St. Johns Review* (Summer 1981)
Breit: Harvey Breit, *New York Times Book Review* (11 April 1954)
Cook: Reginald L. Cook, *Robert Frost: The Living Voice*, Amherst, 1974
Emerson: *The Complete Writings of Ralph Waldo Emerson*, N.Y., 1929

Humphries: Rolfe Humphries, *Nation* (23 July 1949)
Thompson: Lawrance Thompson, *Robert Frost: The Early Years*, N.Y., 1966
Vendler: Helen Vendler, in *Wallace Stevens: A Celebration*, Princeton, 1980

NOTES

1. *CP*, 171
2. *LTRS*, 20
3. Ibid, 20; Thompson, 136-37, 337-38, 500, 560
4. Vendler, 172
5. *CP*, 324
6. Ibid., 88
7. Emerson, 225
8. *LTRS*, 140-41; cf. 83-84
9. L & T, 262
10. *CP*, 275
11. Ibid., 25, 31
12. Ibid., 446
13. Cook, 69, 111, 68, 244, 51, 61. Frost labeled as "claptrap" the Beauty-Truth equation in "Grecian Urn" (*LTRS*, 141)
14. *CP*, 447, 379
15. Humphries, 92
16. *CP*, 27
17. L & T, 343-44
18. *CP*, 386
19. Breit, 8
20. *CP*, 495
21. *CP*, 391
22. *CP*, 300
23. Ibid., 150
24. Ibid., 149
25. Emerson, 133. Frost used another classical model in "One More Brevity" (1953). Bacon, 3-10. This time it was *Aeneid* 8
26. *CP*, 12
27. Ibid., 451
28. Ibid., 444
29. Ibid., 309
30. Ibid., 311
31. Ibid., 346
32. Ibid., 499
33. Ibid., 469
34. Ibid., 555

POUND'S PRISON GRAFFITI

EDITIONS CITED

Cantos: The Cantos of Ezra Pound, N.Y., 1964
GK: Ezra Pound, *Guide to Kulchur*, N.Y., 1952
LE: Ezra Pound, *Literary Essays*, N.Y., 1954
EP, LTRS: Letters of Ezra Pound, ed. D. D. Paige, N.Y., 1950
Personae: Ezra Pound, *Personae*, N.Y., 1955
SP: Ezra Pound, *Selected Prose*, ed. William Cookson, N.Y., 1973

OTHER REFERENCES

Baker: Carlos Baker, *Ernest Hemingway: A Life Story*, N.Y., 1969
Davie 1: Donald Davie, *Ezra Pound: Poet as Sculptor*, N.Y., 1968
Davie 2: Donald Davie, *Ezra Pound*, N.Y., 1975
Dekker: George Dekker, *The Cantos of Ezra Pound*, N.Y., 1963

EH, *LTRS: Selected Letters of Ernest Hemingway*, ed. Carlos Baker, N.Y., 1981

Ford: *The Cantos of Ezra Pound: Some Testimonies*, ed. Ford Madox Ford, N.Y., 1933

JJ, *LTRS: Selected Letters of James Joyce*, ed. Richard Ellmann, N.Y., 1975

MacLeish: Archibald MacLeish, *Poetry and Opinion*, Urbana, Ill., 1950

Rachewiltz: Mary de Rachewiltz, *Discretions*, Boston, 1971

RF, *LTRS: Selected Letters of Robert Frost*, ed. Lawrance Thompson, N.Y., 1964

Schneidau: Herbert N. Schneidau, "Pound and Wordsworth on Poetry and Prose," in *Romantic and Modern*, ed. George Bornstein, Pittsburgh, 1977

Stock: Noel Stock, *The Life of Ezra Pound*, N.Y., 1970

Torrey: E. Fuller Torrey, M.D., "The Protection of Ezra Pound," *Psychology Today* (November 1981)

TSE, *CPP*: T. S. Eliot, *Complete Poems and Plays*, N.Y., 1958

WBY, *CP*: W. B. Yeats, *Collected Poems*, N.Y., 1956

WBY, *LTRS: Letters of W. B. Yeats*, ed. Allan Wade, London, 1954

Witemeyer: Hugh Witemeyer, "Walter Savage Landor and Ezra Pound," in *Romantic and Modern*, ed. George Bornstein, Pittsburgh, 1977

NOTES

1. RF, *LTRS*, 74
2. WBY, *LTRS*, 585, 590
3. RF, *LTRS*, 70-74, 84-86
4. EH, *LTRS*, 62-65; Pound to EH, 11 March 1928, quoted in Baker, 190. Ford, contains EH to Ford, 21 November 1932
5. Rachewiltz, 30, 45-67, 96-103, 149-61, 194-98, 236-58, 287-307; Baker, 107
6. *Cantos*, 561
7. EP, *GK*, 181
8. EP, *LE*, 277; EP, *GK*, 284, 288; EP, *LTRS*, 90. See also Schneidau, 133-35
9. EP, *LE*, 277; Witemeyer, 160; *Personae*, 20; Davie 2:14
10. EP, *LE*, 72; EP, *SP*, 418; EP, *GK*, 181
11. *Personae*, 238-46; EP, *LTRS*, 58, 90, 134

12. Davie 1:33; EP, *LE*, 216, 292, 305; Witemeyer, 147
13. *Cantos*, 565
14. Ibid., 461, 521, 554
15. Ibid., 456, 503
16. Ibid., 463
17. Ibid., 517, 493
18. Ibid., 454-55, 550, 531-32, 560, 494, 454, 518
19. Ibid., 451
20. Ibid., 549
21. Ibid., 484
22. JJ, *LTRS*, 265
23. TSE, *CPP*, 33; *Cantos*, 495
24. *Cantos*, 500, 509
25. Ibid., 459; Hugh Kenner, *New York Times Book Review* (14 Nov. 1982)
26. *Cantos*, 569-70; WBY, *CP*, 119
27. Stock, 406-14

28. *Cantos*, 569, 562, 550, 571, 576
29. Stock, 415-50; Torrey, 57-66
30. *Cantos*, 7
31. MacLeish, 52

32. See "Mr. Saturday" in Mac-Leish, 3-4
33. *Cantos*, 556-57
34. *Cantos*, 547

T. S. ELIOT

EDITIONS CITED

CPP: T. S. Eliot, *Complete Poems and Plays, 1909-1950*, N.Y., 1958
OPP: T. S. Eliot, *On Poetry and Poets*, N.Y., 1957
PWEY: T. S. Eliot, *Poems Written in Early Youth*, London, 1967
SE: T. S. Eliot, *Selected Essays*, N.Y., 1950
SW: T. S. Eliot, *The Sacred Wood*, London, 1920
TCC: T. S. Eliot, *To Criticize the Critic*, N.Y., 1965
UPUC: T. S. Eliot, *The Use of Poetry and the Use of Criticism*, London, 1933
WLFT: *The Waste Land: A Facsimile and Transcript*, ed. Valerie Eliot, N.Y., 1970

OTHER REFERENCES

Bornstein: George Bornstein, *Transformations of Romanticism in Yeats, Eliot, and Stevens*, Chicago, 1976
Gardner: Helen Gardner, *The Composition of Four Quartets*, N.Y., 1978
Litz: A. Walton Litz, "From *Burnt Norton* to *Little Gidding*," Review 2 (1980)
Matthews: T. S. Matthews, *Great Tom: Notes Towards the Definition of T. S. Eliot*, N.Y., 1974
Matthiessen: F. O. Matthiessen, *The Achievement of T. S. Eliot*, N.Y., 1947
Russell: Bertrand Russell, *Autobiography*, vols. 1 and 2, Boston, 1967, 1968
Schuchard: Ronald Schuchard, "T. S. Eliot as an Extension Lecturer, 1916-1919," *Review of English Studies* 25 (May 1974)
Smidt: Kristian Smidt, *Poetry and Belief in the World of T. S. Eliot*, Oslo, 1949
Smith: Grover Smith, *T. S. Eliot's Poetry and Plays*, Chicago, 1952
Spender: Stephen Spender, *T. S. Eliot*, N.Y., 1975
Thompson: Lawrance Thompson, *Robert Frost: The Early Years*, N.Y., 1966
Wilson: Edmund Wilson, *Letters on Literature and Politics, 1912-1972*, ed. Elena Wilson, N.Y., 1977

NOTES

1. *PWEY*, 26
2. *CPP*, 93

3. Ibid., 30-31
4. *WLFT*, passim

5. *SE*, 377
6. *CPP*, 17
7. Russell 1:325-27; 2:9-10, 29, 61, 64
8. Wilson, 230
9. Matthiessen, 23
10. *UPUC*, 33
11. Smidt, 29
12. *TCC*, 17
13. Schuchard, 163-73
14. *SW*, 31-32
15. *UPUC*, 129
16. *TCC*, 15
17. *SW*, 51-52
18. *UPUC*, 75, 81, 128
19. Ibid., 109-10
20. Ibid., 155
21. *PWEY*, 13-16
22. *OPP*, 223-39
23. Matthiessen, 145
24. *SW*, 151-58. First published, *Athenaeum* 4685 (13 February 1920)
25. *Nation and Athenaeum* 41 (17 September 1927)
26. *UPUC*, 87
27. Ibid., 95
28. Thompson 1:136-37; *UPUC*, 92
29. *UPUC*, 89-90, 93, 99. TSE dismisses "The Witch of Atlas" as "a trifle."
30. Spender, 75
31. *TCC*, 24
32. Ibid., 169
33. *SW*, 147
34. *SE*, 265; Spender, 125-26
35. *UPUC*, 91-92
36. Ibid., 93, 97
37. Ibid., 93-94
38. *SW*, 49-50
39. *SE*, 225
40. *TCC*, 130-32
41. *UPUC*, 100-102
42. *SE*, 231n
43. Bornstein, 98-99
44. Matthiessen, 85
45. Smith, 250
46. Litz, 7-8
47. *TCC*, 26
48. *UPUC*, 25-26
49. Ibid., 80-81
50. *SW*, 148
51. *UPUC*, 73
52. Ibid., 69
53. Ibid., 71-72
54. Ibid., 25-26, 71-74
55. Ibid., 76-77. See also *SE*, 256-57
56. *UPUC*, 79-80
57. *SW*, 1, 13
58. *UPUC*, 69; *TCC*, 138
59. *CPP*, 232, 249
60. *UPUC*, 146, 78
61. *CPP*, 133
62. *UPUC*, 148
63. Ibid., 156
64. See *SW*, 95, where TSE mentions "Coleridge, who made a Hamlet of Coleridge."

WALLACE STEVENS

EDITIONS CITED

CP: Wallace Stevens, *Collected Poems*, N.Y., 1955
LTRS: *Letters of Wallace Stevens*, ed. Holly Stevens, N.Y., 1966
NA: Wallace Stevens, *The Necessary Angel*, N.Y., 1951

REFERENCES

OP: Wallace Stevens, *Opus Posthumous*, ed. Samuel French Morse, N.Y., 1957

OTHER REFERENCES

Litz: A. Walton Litz, *Introspective Voyager: The Poetic Development of Wallace Stevens*, N.Y., 1972
Vendler, *Celebration*: Helen Vendler, in *Wallace Stevens: A Celebration*, Princeton, 1980
Vendler, *OEW*: Helen Vendler, *On Extended Wings: Wallace Stevens' Longer Poems*, Cambridge, Mass., 1969

NOTES

1. *OP*, 251-52
2. Ibid., 252-53
3. Ibid., 251, 180, 244
4. *LTRS*, 290
5. Ibid., 792
6. Ibid., 131; *CP*, 407
7. *NA*, 45
8. Vendler, *Celebration*, 171-95
9. *LTRS*, 32, 721
10. Ibid, 28-29
11. Ibid., 110
12. Ibid., 136
13. Ibid., 148
14. Ibid., 119
15. Ibid., 167
16. Litz, 21
17. *LTRS*, 647
18. *LTRS*, 781
19. Ibid., 89
20. Ibid., 367
21. Ibid., 367
22. Ibid., 438
23. *CP*, 344
24. *NA*, 44
25. Ibid., 6
26. *OP*, 175
27. *LTRS* , 813
28. *NA*, 121-22
29. *LTRS*, 264, 276, 505, 817
30. Ibid., 32
31. *OP*, 235
32. *NA*, 75
33. Ibid., 165
34. *LTRS*, 101
35. Ibid., 279; *OP*, 251
36. *OP*, 293-94
37. *LTRS*, 247
38. *NA*, 129-30
39. *LTRS*, 177, 778
40. *CP*, 230
41. *LTRS*, 121
42. *NA*, 41
43. Ibid., 10-11
44. Ibid., 13-14, 162-63
45. Ibid., 25, 31
46. *OP*, 166
47. *LTRS*, 363-64, 368, 747, 753
48. *NA*, 40, 79
49. *LTRS*, 722
50. *OP*, 203-04
51. *LTRS*, 289
52. Ibid., 729
53. *NA*, 57
54. Ibid., 169
55. *LTRS*, 352, 643, 404
56. *CP*, 430, 471, 478
57. *OP*, 87-88; cf. *NA*, 52-53

AUDEN AMONG THE ROMANTICS

EDITIONS CITED

AA: *The Age of Anxiety*, N.Y., 1947
AG: *Academic Graffiti*, London, 1971
AH: *About the House*, N.Y., 1965
CP: *Collected Poems*, N.Y., 1945
DH: *The Dyer's Hand*, N.Y., 1962
DM: *The Double Man*, N.Y., 1941
EA: *The English Auden, 1927-1939*, ed. Edward Mendelson, N.Y., 1977
EF: *The Enchaféd Flood*, N.Y., 1950
EG: *Epistle to a Godson*, N.Y., 1972
FA: *Forewords and Afterwords*, N.Y., 1973
HC: *Homage to Clio*, N.Y., 1960
LI: *Letters from Iceland*, 2nd ed., N.Y., 1967
NYL: "New Year Letter" in *Collected Poems*, N.Y., 1945
SP: W. H. Auden, *Selected Poems*, N.Y., 1979

OTHER REFERENCES

Abbott: Charles D. Abbott, *Poets at Work*, N.Y., 1948
Carpenter: Humphrey Carpenter, *W. H. Auden: A Biography*, Boston, 1981
Hoggart: Richard Hoggart, *Auden: An Introductory Essay*, New Haven, 1951
McFarland: Thomas McFarland, *Romanticism and the Forms of Ruin*, Princeton, 1981
Mendelson: Edward Mendelson, *Early Auden*, N.Y., 1981
Spears: Monroe K. Spears, *The Poetry of W. H. Auden*, N.Y., 1963

NOTES

1. Carpenter, 44-45
2. CP, 47-48
3. DH, 337
4. NYL, 315
5. DH, 409-10
6. EA, 245
7. CP, 282-83
8. DM, 115
9. AA, 85-87; NYL, 313
10. EF, Lecture 1
11. *Poets of the English Language* 4:xiii-xviii
12. DH, 482
13. Ibid., 295
14. N. Coghill, "Sweeney Agonistes," in *T. S. Eliot: A Symposium*, London, 1948, p. 82
15. Carpenter, 29; Mendelson, 27
16. EA, 298; Mendelson, 66
17. FA, 58-59, 100-101, 228
18. HC, 53
19. AA, 103
20. "Today's Poet," *Mademoiselle* (April 1962)
21. Carpenter, 317
22. CP, 284-85

23. McFarland, 214
24. *FA*, 385
25. *DH*, 341
26. Ibid., 32
27. *EG*, 56
28. *FA*, 119
29. *EA*, 365-66
30. *LI*, 141
31. *DH*, 388
32. Ibid., 395, 399-400
33. *N. Y. Review of Books* (18 August 1966), 12, 14
34. Spears, 174-78
35. Carpenter, 152
36. Hoggart, 119-20
37. *EA*, 48-49
38. *CP*, 67, 177-79
39. Spears, 112
40. Carpenter, 267-69
41. *CP*, 273
42. Ibid., 150
43. Ibid., 270
44. *DM*, 91
45. *CP*, 303
46. *DM*, 105, 108, 110, 133, 139

47. *CP*, 312-13
48. *DH*, 79
49. *AH*, 82
50. *EG*, 65
51. *DH*, 54-57
52. *FA*, 321-22
53. Carpenter, 234
54. *DH*, 16, 33
55. *Partisan Review* 18 (Nov.-Dec. 1951), 701-706
56. *DH*, 337
57. Ibid., 290
58. *Poets of the English Language* 4:xv
59. *Partisan Review* 18 (Nov.-Dec. 1951), 701-706
60. *New Verse* (April-May 1936), 22-24
61. Abbott, 177
62. *EA*, 329
63. *CP*, 64; *AA*, 78
64. *CP*, 34-35
65. Ibid., 99
66. Ibid., 341

Index

Library of Congress Cataloging in Publication Data

Baker, Carlos Heard, 1909-
The echoing green.

Bibliography: p.
Includes index.
1. American poetry—20th century—History and criticism.
2. Romanticism. 3. Modernism (Literature) 4. Influence
(Literary, artistic, etc.) 5. English poetry—History
and criticism. I. Title.

PS310.R66B34 1984   811'.52'09   83-43058
ISBN 0-691-06595-0